THE

INSTITUTES OF JUSTINIAN

TRANSLATED INTO ENGLISH

WITH AN INDEX

BY

J. B. MOYLE, D.C.L.

OF LINCOLN'S INN, BARRISTER-AT-LAW
FELLOW AND LATE TUTOR OF NEW COLLEGE, OXFORD

FOURTH EDITION

OXFORD

AT THE CLARENDON PRESS

LONDON, NEW YORK AND TORONTO: HENRY FROWDE

ALSO SOLD BY

STEVENS & SONS, LIMITED, 119 & 120 CHANCERY LANE, LONDON

1906

LONDON

HENRY FROWDE, M.A.

PUBLISHER TO THE UNIVERSITY OF OXFORD

AND

STEVENS & SONS, LIMITED

PREFACE

IN writing this translation I have derived much assistance from Mr. Poste's translation of the Institutes of Gaius. Where, as is often the case, the words of the latter are transcribed literally or in substance by Justinian, I have frequently adopted Mr. Poste's rendering with very little if any alteration, and I must acknowledge once for all my debt to him. I have also consulted the translation of Mr. Sandars, and that by Mr. J. A. Cross embodied in Dr. Hunter's 'Roman Law', and have found Schrader's Commentary of great service in assisting me to bring out the full meaning of the more difficult parts of the text.

In the rendering of technical terms my usual plan has been to discover, if possible, some English equivalent which will fairly represent them: thus 'tutor' has been uniformly translated 'guardian', 'fideicommissum' 'fiduciary or trust bequest', &c. Where I have found this out of my power, I have not unfrequently adopted an English form of the original Latin word, where this (though probably not to be found in any English dictionary) has won an air of familiarity for itself by the usage of writers on Roman Law: e.g. 'adrogation', 'agnation'. Lastly, where I could do neither of these things, the original Latin term has been retained; as, for instance, in the names of many of the servitudes in Book II. 3, and in the Title on 'bonorum possessio' in Book III: and this has been done even in cases where (though a tolerable equivalent was at hand, as with the names of coins) the employment of an English word might appear somewhat grotesque.

J. B. M.

OXFORD, *January*, 1883.

NOTE TO THE FOURTH EDITION

As I said in a note to the Second Edition of this translation, but few changes have been made in it since it was
first published in 1883 as a portion of an edition of the
Institutes. A few phrases have been altered, and one
or two errors and omissions which have been pointed out
to me have been corrected. But those who were good
enough to review it in the Press as a rule found it
both accurate and readable, and while most of the changes
have been due to their criticisms, I have thought it best
to accept their judgement, and reissue it substantially as
it was when it first appeared.

J. B. M.

Oxford, *December*, 1905.

CONTENTS

PROOEMIVM

IN the name of Our Lord Jesus Christ.

The Emperor Caesar Flavius Justinian, conqueror of the Alamanni, the Goths, the Franks, the Germans, the Antes, the Alani, the Vandals, the Africans, pious, prosperous, renowned, victorious, and triumphant, ever august,

To the youth desirous of studying the law :

The imperial majesty should be armed with laws as well as glorified with arms, that there may be good government in times both of war and of peace, and the ruler of Rome may not only be victorious over his enemies, but may show himself as scrupulously regardful of justice as triumphant over his conquered foes.

With deepest application and forethought, and by the 1 blessing of God, we have attained both of these objects. The barbarian nations which we have subjugated know our valour, Africa and other provinces without number being once more, after so long an interval, reduced beneath the sway of Rome by victories granted by Heaven, and themselves bearing witness to our dominion. All peoples too are ruled by laws which we have either enacted or arranged. Having removed 2 every inconsistency from the sacred constitutions, hitherto inharmonious and confused, we extended our care to the immense volumes of the older jurisprudence; and, like sailors crossing the mid-ocean, by the favour of Heaven have now completed a work of which we once despaired. When this, 3 with God's blessing, had been done, we called together that distinguished man Tribonian, master and ex-quaestor of our sacred palace, and the illustrious Theophilus and Dorotheus, professors of law, of whose ability, legal knowledge, and trusty observance of our orders we have received many and genuine proofs, and specially commissioned them to compose by our authority and advice a book of Institutes, whereby you may be enabled to learn your first lessons in law no longer from ancient fables, but to grasp them by the brilliant light of imperial learning, and that your ears and minds may receive nothing useless or incorrect, but only what holds good in actual fact. And thus whereas in past time even the foremost of you were unable to read the imperial constitutions until after four years, you, who have been so honoured and fortunate as to receive both the beginning and the end of your legal teaching from the mouth of the Emperor, can

4 now enter on the study of them without delay. After the completion therefore of the fifty books of the Digest or Pandects, in which all the earlier law has been collected by the aid of the said distinguished Tribonian and other illustrious and most able men, we directed the division of these same Institutes into four books, comprising the first

5 elements of the whole science of law. In these the law previously obtaining has been briefly stated, as well as that which after becoming disused has been again brought to light

6 by our imperial aid. Compiled from all the Institutes of the ancient jurists, and in particular from the commentaries of our Gaius on both the Institutes and the common cases, and from many other legal works, these Institutes were submitted to us by the three learned men aforesaid, and after reading and examining them we have given them the fullest force of our constitutions.

7 Receive then these laws with your best powers and with the eagerness of study, and show yourselves so learned as to be encouraged to hope that when you have compassed the whole field of law you may have ability to govern such portion of the state as may be entrusted to you.

Given at Constantinople the 21st day of November, in the third consulate of the Emperor Justinian, Father of his Country, ever august.

BOOK I

Title I

OF JUSTICE AND LAW

JUSTICE is the set and constant purpose which gives to every man his due. Jurisprudence is the knowledge of things 1 divine and human, the science of the just and the unjust.

Having laid down these general definitions, and our object 2 being the exposition of the law of the Roman people, we think that the most advantageous plan will be to commence with an easy and simple path, and then to proceed to details with a most careful and scrupulous exactness of interpretation. Otherwise, if we begin by burdening the student's memory, as yet weak and untrained, with a multitude and variety of matters, one of two things will happen : either we shall cause him wholly to desert the study of law, or else we shall bring him at last, after great labour, and often, too, distrustful of his own powers (the commonest cause, among the young, of ill-success), to a point which he might have reached earlier, without such labour and confident in himself, had he been led along a smoother path.

The precepts of the law are these : to live honestly, to 3 injure no one, and to give every man his due. The study 4 of law consists of two branches, law public, and law private. The former relates to the welfare of the Roman State ; the latter to the advantage of the individual citizen. Of private law then we may say that it is of threefold origin, being collected from the precepts of nature, from those of the law of nations, or from those of the civil law of Rome.

Title II

OF THE LAW OF NATURE, THE LAW OF NATIONS, AND THE CIVIL LAW

The law of nature is that which she has taught all animals ; a law not peculiar to the human race, but shared by all living creatures, whether denizens of the air, the dry land, or the

sea. Hence comes the union of male and female, which we
call marriage; hence the procreation and rearing of children,
for this is a law by the knowledge of which we see even the
1 lower animals are distinguished. The civil law of Rome, and
the law of all nations, differ from each other thus. The laws
of every people governed by statutes and customs are partly
peculiar to itself, partly common to all mankind. Those
rules which a state enacts for its own members are peculiar
to itself, and are called civil law: those rules prescribed by
natural reason for all men are observed by all peoples alike,
and are called the law of nations. Thus the laws of the
Roman people are partly peculiar to itself, partly common
to all nations; a distinction of which we shall take notice
2 as occasion offers. Civil law takes its name from the state
wherein it binds; for instance, the civil law of Athens, it
being quite correct to speak thus of the enactments of Solon
or Draco. So too we call the law observed by the Roman
people the civil law of the Romans, or the law of the Quirites;
the law, that is to say, which they observe, the Romans being
called Quirites after Quirinus. Whenever we speak, however,
of civil law, without any qualification, we mean our own;
exactly as, when 'the poet' is spoken of, without addition or
qualification, the Greeks understand the great Homer, and we
understand Vergil. But the law of nations is common to the
whole human race; for nations have settled certain things
for themselves as occasion and the necessities of human life
required. For instance, wars arose, and then followed captivity
and slavery, which are contrary to the law of nature; for by
the law of nature all men from the beginning were born free.
The law of nations again is the source of almost all contracts;
for instance, sale, hire, partnership, deposit, loan for consumption, and very many others.
3 Our law is partly written, partly unwritten, as among the
Greeks. The written law consists of statutes, plebiscites,
senatusconsults, enactments of the Emperors, edicts of the
magistrates, and answers of those learned in the law.
4 A statute is an enactment of the Roman people, which it
used to make on the motion of a senatorial magistrate, as
for instance a consul. A plebiscite is an enactment of the

commonalty, such as was made on the motion of one of their own magistrates, as a tribune. The commonalty differs from the people as a species from its genus; for 'the people' includes the whole aggregate of citizens, among them patricians and senators, while the term 'commonalty' embraces only such citizens as are not patricians or senators. After the passing, however, of the statute called the lex Hortensia, plebiscites acquired for the first time the force of statutes. A senatusconsult is a command and ordinance of 5 the senate, for when the Roman people had been so increased that it was difficult to assemble it together for the purpose of enacting statutes, it seemed right that the senate should be consulted instead of the people. Again, what the Emperor 6 determines has the force of a statute, the people having conferred on him all their authority and power by the *lex regia*, which was passed concerning his office and authority. Consequently, whatever the Emperor settles by rescript, or decides in his judicial capacity, or ordains by edicts, is clearly a statute : and these are what are called constitutions. Some of these of course are personal, and not to be followed as precedents, since this is not the Emperor's will ; for a favour bestowed on individual merit, or a penalty inflicted for individual wrongdoing, or relief given without a precedent, do not go beyond the particular person : though others are general, and bind all beyond a doubt. The edicts of the 7 praetors too have no small legal authority, and these we are used to call the *ius honorarium*, because those who occupy posts of honour in the state, in other words the magistrates, have given authority to this branch of law. The curule aediles also used to issue an edict relating to certain matters, which forms part of the *ius honorarium*. The answers of 8 those learned in the law are the opinions and views of persons authorized to determine and expound the law; for it was of old provided that certain persons should publicly interpret the laws, who were called jurisconsults, and whom the Emperor privileged to give formal answers. If they were unanimous the judge was forbidden by imperial constitution to depart from their opinion, so great was its authority. The unwritten 9 law is that which usage has approved : for ancient customs,

when approved by consent of those who follow them, are like
10 statute. And this division of the civil law into two kinds
seems not inappropriate, for it appears to have originated in
the institutions of two states, namely Athens and Lace-
daemon ; it having been usual in the latter to commit to
memory what was observed as law, while the Athenians
observed only what they had made permanent in written
statutes.

11 But the laws of nature, which are observed by all nations
alike, are established, as it were, by divine providence, and
remain ever fixed and immutable : but the municipal laws of
each individual state are subject to frequent change, either
by the tacit consent of the people, or by the subsequent
enactment of another statute.

12 The whole of the law which we observe relates either to
persons, or to things, or to actions. And first let us speak of
persons : for it is useless to know the law without knowing
the persons for whose sake it was established.

Title III

OF THE LAW OF PERSONS

In the law of persons, then, the first division is into free
1 men and slaves. Freedom, from which men are called free,
is a man's natural power of doing what he pleases, so far as
2 he is not prevented by force or law : slavery is an institution
of the law of nations, against nature subjecting one man to
3 the dominion of another. The name 'slave' is derived from
the practice of generals to order the preservation and sale of
captives, instead of killing them ; hence they are also called
mancipia, because they are taken from the enemy by the
4 strong hand. Slaves are either born so, their mothers being
slaves themselves ; or they become so, and this either by the
law of nations, that is to say by capture in war, or by the
civil law, as when a free man, over twenty years of age,
collusively allows himself to be sold in order that he may
5 share the purchase money. The condition of all slaves is one
and the same : in the conditions of free men there are many
distinctions ; to begin with, they are either free born, or made
free.

TITLE IV

OF MEN FREE BORN

A freeborn man is one free from his birth, being the off-spring of parents united in wedlock, whether both be free born or both made free, or one made free and the other free born. He is also free born if his mother be free, even though his father be a slave, and so also is he whose paternity is uncertain, being the offspring of promiscuous intercourse, but whose mother is free. It is enough if the mother be free at the moment of birth, though a slave at that of conception: and conversely if she be free at the time of conception, and then becomes a slave before the birth of the child, the latter is held to be free born, on the ground that an unborn child ought not to be prejudiced by the mother's misfortune. Hence arose the question whether the child of a woman is born free, or a slave, who, while pregnant, is manumitted, and then becomes a slave again before delivery. Marcellus thinks he is born free, for it is enough if the mother of an unborn infant is free at any moment between conception and delivery: and this view is right. The status of a man born free is not prejudiced by his being placed in the position of a slave and then being manumitted: for it has been decided that manumission cannot stand in the way of rights acquired by birth.

TITLE V

OF FREEDMEN

Those are freedmen, or made free, who have been manumitted from legal slavery. Manumission is the giving of freedom; for while a man is in slavery he is subject to the power once known as *manus*; and from that power he is set free by manumission. All this originated in the law of nations; for by natural law all men were born free—slavery, and by consequence manumission, being unknown. But afterwards slavery came in by the law of nations, and was followed by the boon of manumission; so that though we are all known by the common name of 'man', three classes of men came into existence with the law of nations, namely men

free born, slaves, and thirdly freedmen who had ceased to be
1 slaves.   Manumission may take place in various ways; either
in the holy church, according to the sacred constitutions, or
by default in a fictitious vindication, or before friends, or
by letter, or by testament or any other expression of a man's
last will: and indeed there are many other modes in which
freedom may be acquired, introduced by the constitutions of
2 earlier emperors as well as by our own.   It is usual for slaves
to be manumitted by their masters at any time, even when
the magistrate is merely passing by, as for instance while the
praetor or proconsul or governor of a province is going to the
baths or the theatre.

3   Of freedmen there were formerly three grades; for those
who were manumitted sometimes obtained a higher freedom
fully recognized by the laws, and became Roman citizens;
sometimes a lower form, becoming by the lex Iunia Norbana
Latins; and sometimes finally a liberty still more circum-
scribed, being placed by the lex Aelia Sentia on the footing
of enemies surrendered at discretion.   This last and lowest
class, however, has long ceased to exist, and the title of Latin
also had become rare: and so in our goodness, which desires
to raise and improve in every matter, we have amended this
in two constitutions, and reintroduced the earlier usage; for
in the earliest infancy of Rome there was but one simple type
of liberty, namely that possessed by the manumitter, the only
distinction possible being that the latter was free born, while
the manumitted slave became a freedman.   We have abolished
the class of *dediticii*, or enemies surrendered at discretion, by
our constitution, published among those our decisions, by
which, at the suggestion of the eminent Tribonian, our
quaestor, we have set at rest the disputes of the older law.
By another constitution, which shines brightly among the
imperial enactments, and suggested by the same quaestor, we
have altered the position of the *Latini Iuniani,* and dispensed with all the rules relating to their condition; and
have endowed with the citizenship of Rome all freedmen
alike, without regard to the age of the person manumitted,
the nature of the master's ownership, or the mode of manumission, in accordance with the earlier usage; with the

addition of many new modes in which freedom coupled with the Roman citizenship, the only kind of freedom now known, may be bestowed on slaves.

TITLE VI

OF PERSONS UNABLE TO MANUMIT, AND THE CAUSES OF THEIR INCAPACITY

In some cases, however, manumission is not permitted ; for an owner who would defraud his creditors by an intended manumission attempts in vain to manumit, the act being made of no effect by the lex Aelia Sentia. A master, however, 1 who is insolvent may institute one of his slaves heir in his will, conferring freedom on him at the same time, so that he may become free and his sole and necessary heir, provided no one else takes as heir under the will, either because no one else was instituted at all, or because the person instituted for some reason or other does not take the inheritance. And this was a judicious provision of the lex Aelia Sentia, for it was most desirable that persons in embarrassed circumstances, who could get no other heir, should have a slave as necessary heir to satisfy their creditors' claims, or that at least (if he did not do this) the creditors might sell the estate in the slave's name, so as to save the memory of the deceased from disrepute. The law is the same if a slave be instituted heir without 2 liberty being expressly given him, this being enacted by our constitution in all cases, and not merely where the master is insolvent; so that in accordance with the modern spirit of humanity, institution will be equivalent to a gift of liberty ; for it is unlikely, in spite of the omission of the grant of freedom, that one should have wished the person whom one has chosen as one's heir to remain a slave, so that one should have no heir at all. If a person is insolvent at the time of 3 manumission, or becomes so by the manumission itself, this is manumission in fraud of creditors. It is, however, now settled law, that the gift of liberty is not avoided unless the intention of the manumitter was fraudulent, even though his property is in fact insufficient to meet his creditors' claims ; for men often hope and believe that they are better off than they really are. Consequently, we understand a gift of liberty to be avoided only when the creditors are defrauded both by the intention of the manumitter, and in fact: that is to say, by his property being insufficient to meet their claims.

4   The same lex Aelia Sentia makes it unlawful for a master under twenty years of age to manumit, except in the mode of fictitious vindication, preceded by proof of some legitimate
5 motive before the council. It is a legitimate motive of manumission if the slave to be manumitted be, for instance, the father or mother of the manumitter, or his son or daughter, or his natural brother or sister, or governor or nurse or teacher, or foster-son or foster-daughter or foster-brother, or a slave whom he wishes to make his agent, or a female slave whom he intends to marry; provided he marry her within six months, and provided that the slave intended as an agent is not less than seventeen years of age at the time of manu-
6 mission. When a motive for manumission, whether true or false, has once been proved, the council cannot withdraw its sanction.

7   Thus the lex Aelia Sentia having prescribed a certain mode of manumission for owners under twenty, it followed that though a person fourteen years of age could make a will, and therein institute an heir and leave legacies, yet he could not confer liberty on a slave until he had completed his twentieth year. But it seemed an intolerable hardship that a man who had the power of disposing freely of all his property by will should not be allowed to give his freedom to a single slave : wherefore we allow him to deal in his last will as he pleases with his slaves as with the rest of his property, and even to give them their liberty if he will. But liberty being a boon beyond price, for which very reason the power of manumission was denied by the older law to owners under twenty years of age, we have as it were selected a middle course, and permitted persons under twenty years of age to manumit their slaves by will, but not until they have completed their seventeenth and entered on their eighteenth year. For when ancient custom allowed persons of this age to plead on behalf of others, why should not their judgement be deemed sound enough to enable them to use discretion in giving freedom to their own slaves?

TITLE VII

OF THE REPEAL OF THE LEX FUFIA CANINIA

Moreover, by the lex Fufia Caninia a limit was placed on the number of slaves who could be manumitted by their master's testament: but this law we have thought fit to repeal, as an obstacle to freedom and to some extent invidious, for it was certainly inhuman to take away from a man on his deathbed the right of liberating the whole of his slaves, which he could have exercised at any moment during his lifetime, unless there were some other obstacle to the act of manumission.

TITLE VIII

OF PERSONS INDEPENDENT OR DEPENDENT

Another division of the law relating to persons classifies them as either independent or dependent. Those again who are dependent are in the power either of parents or of masters. Let us first then consider those who are dependent, for by learning who these are we shall at the same time learn who are independent. And first let us look at those who are in the power of masters.

Now slaves are in the power of masters, a power recognized 1 by the law of all nations, for all nations present the spectacle of masters invested with power of life and death over slaves; and to whatever is acquired through a slave his owner is entitled. But in the present day no one under our sway 2 is permitted to indulge in excessive harshness towards his slaves, without some reason recognized by law; for, by a constitution of the Emperor Antoninus Pius, a man is made as liable to punishment for killing his own slave as for killing the slave of another person; and extreme severity on the part of masters is checked by another constitution whereby the same Emperor, in answer to inquiries from presidents of provinces concerning slaves who take refuge at churches or statues of the Emperor, commanded that on proof of intolerable cruelty a master should be compelled to sell his slaves on fair terms, so as to receive their value. And both of these are reasonable enactments, for the public interest requires that no one should make an evil use of his own property.

The terms of the rescript of Antoninus to Aelius Marcianus are as follow:—'The powers of masters over their slaves ought to continue undiminished, nor ought any man to be deprived of his lawful rights; but it is the master's own interest that relief justly sought against cruelty, insufficient sustenance, or intolerable wrong, should not be denied. I enjoin you then to look into the complaints of the slaves of Iulius Sabinus, who have fled for protection to the statue of the Emperor, and if you find them treated with undue harshness or other ignominious wrong, order them to be sold, so that they may not again fall under the power of their master; and the latter will find that if he attempts to evade this my enactment, I shall visit his offence with severe punishment.'

TITLE IX

OF PATERNAL POWER

Our children whom we have begotten in lawful wedlock are
1 in our power. Wedlock or matrimony is the union of male and female, involving the habitual intercourse of daily life.
2 The power which we have over our children is peculiar to
3 Roman citizens, and is found in no other nation. The offspring then of you and your wife is in your power, and so too is that of your son and his wife, that is to say, your grandson and granddaughter, and so on. But the offspring of your daughter is not in your power, but in that of its own father.

TITLE X

OF MARRIAGE

Roman citizens are joined together in lawful wedlock when they are united according to law, the man having reached years of puberty, and the woman being of a marriageable age, whether they be independent or dependent: provided that, in the latter case, they must have the consent of the parents in whose power they respectively are, the necessity of which, and even of its being given before the marriage takes place, is recognized no less by natural reason than by law. Hence the question has arisen, can the daughter or son of a lunatic lawfully contract marriage? and as the doubt still remained with regard to the son, we decided that, like the daughter, the son of a lunatic might marry even without the intervention of his father, according to the mode prescribed by our constitution.

It is not every woman that can be taken to wife: for marriage 1 with certain classes of persons is forbidden. Thus, persons related as ascendant and descendant are incapable of lawfully intermarrying; for instance, father and daughter, grandfather and granddaughter, mother and son, grandmother and grandson, and so on *ad infinitum*; and the union of such persons is called criminal and incestuous. And so absolute is the rule, that persons related as ascendant and descendant merely by adoption are so utterly prohibited from intermarriage that dissolution of the adoption does not dissolve the prohibition: so that an adoptive daughter or granddaughter cannot be taken to wife even after emancipation.

Collateral relations also are subject to similar prohibitions, 2 but not so stringent. Brother and sister indeed are prohibited from intermarriage, whether they are both of the same father and mother, or have only one parent in common: but though an adoptive sister cannot, during the subsistence of the adoption, become a man's wife, yet if the adoption is dissolved by her emancipation, or if the man is emancipated, there is no impediment to their intermarriage. Consequently, if a man wished to adopt his son-in-law, he ought first to emancipate his daughter: and if he wished to adopt his daughter-in-law, he ought first to emancipate his son. A man may not marry 3 his brother's or his sister's daughter, or even his or her granddaughter, though she is in the fourth degree; for when we may not marry a person's daughter, we may not marry the granddaughter either. But there seems to be no obstacle to a man's marrying the daughter of a woman whom his father has adopted, for she is no relation of his by either natural or civil law. The children of two brothers or sisters, or of 4 a brother and sister, may lawfully intermarry. Again, a man 5 may not marry his father's sister, even though the tie be merely adoptive, or his mother's sister: for they are considered to stand in the relation of ascendants. For the same reason too a man may not marry his great-aunt either paternal or maternal. Certain marriages again are prohibited on the 6

ground of affinity, or the tie between a man or his wife and
the kin of the other respectively. For instance, a man may
not marry his wife's daughter or his son's wife, for both are to
him in the position of daughters. By wife's daughter or son's
wife we must be understood to mean persons who have been
thus related to us; for if a woman is still your daughter-in-
law, that is, is still married to your son, you cannot marry
her for another reason, namely, because she cannot be the
wife of two persons at once. So too if a woman is still your
stepdaughter, that is, if her mother is still married to you,
you cannot marry her for the same reason, namely, because
7 a man cannot have two wives at the same time. Again, it is
forbidden for a man to marry his wife's mother or his father's
wife, because to him they are in the position of a mother,
though in this case too our statement applies only after the
relationship has finally terminated ; otherwise, if a woman is
still your stepmother, that is, is married to your father, the
common rule of law prevents her from marrying you, because
a woman cannot have two husbands at the same time: and if
she is still your wife's mother, that is, if her daughter is still
married to you, you cannot marry her because you cannot
8 have two wives at the same time. But a son of the husband
by another wife, and a daughter of the wife by another
husband, and vice versa, can lawfully intermarry, even though
9 they have a brother or sister born of the second marriage. If
a woman who has been divorced from you has a daughter by
a second husband, she is not your stepdaughter, but Iulian
is of opinion that you ought not to marry her, on the ground
that though your son's betrothed is not your daughter-in-law,
nor your father's betrothed your stepmother, yet it is more
decent and more in accordance with what is right to abstain
10 from intermarrying with them. It is certain that the rules
relating to the prohibited degrees of marriage apply to slaves:
supposing, for instance, that a father and daughter, or a brother
11 and sister, acquired freedom by manumission. There are also
other persons who for various reasons are forbidden to intermarry, a list of whom we have permitted to be inserted in the
books of the Digest or Pandects collected from the older law.
12   Alliances which infringe the rules here stated do not confer

the status of husband and wife, nor is there in such case either wedlock or marriage or dowry. Consequently children born of such a connexion are not in their father's power, but as regards the latter are in the position of children born of promiscuous intercourse, who, their paternity being uncertain, are deemed to have no father at all, and who are called bastards, either from the Greek word denoting illicit intercourse, or because they are fatherless. Consequently, on the dissolution of such a connexion there can be no claim for return of dowry. Persons who contract prohibited marriages are subjected to penalties set forth in our sacred constitutions.

Sometimes it happens that children who are not born in 13 their father's power are subsequently brought under it. Such for instance is the case of a natural son made subject to his father's power by being inscribed a member of the curia ; and so too is that of a child of a free woman with whom his father cohabited, though he could have lawfully married her, who is subjected to the power of his father by the subsequent execution of a dowry deed according to the terms of our constitution : and the same boon is in effect bestowed by that enactment on children subsequently born of the same marriage.

TITLE XI

OF ADOPTIONS

Not only natural children are subject, as we said, to paternal power, but also adoptive children. Adoption is of two forms, 1 being effected either by rescript of the Emperor, or by the judicial authority of a magistrate. The first is the mode in which we adopt independent persons, and this form of adoption is called adrogation : the second is the mode in which we adopt a person subject to the power of an ascendant, whether a descendant in the first degree, as a son or daughter, or in a remoter degree, as a grandson, granddaughter, great-grandson, or great-granddaughter. But by 2 the law, as now settled by our constitution, when a child in power is given in adoption to a stranger by his natural father, the power of the latter is not extinguished : no right passes to the adoptive father, nor is the person adopted in his power,

though we have given a right of succession in case of the
adoptive father dying intestate. But if the person to whom
the child is given in adoption by its natural father is not
a stranger, but the child's own maternal grandfather, or,
supposing the father to have been emancipated, its paternal
grandfather, or its great-grandfather paternal or maternal,
in this case, because the rights given by nature and those
given by adoption are vested in one and the same person,
the old power of the adoptive father is left unimpaired, the
strength of the natural bond of blood being augmented by
the civil one of adoption, so that the child is in the family
and power of an adoptive father, between whom and himself
3 there existed antecedently the relationship described. When
a child under the age of puberty is adopted by rescript of the
Emperor, the adrogation is only permitted after cause shown,
the goodness of the motive and the expediency of the step
for the pupil being inquired into. The adrogation is also
made under certain conditions; that is to say, the adrogator
has to give security to a public agent or attorney of the
people, that if the pupil should die within the age of puberty,
he will return his property to the persons who would have
succeeded him had no adoption taken place. The adoptive
father again may not emancipate them unless upon inquiry
they are found deserving of emancipation, or without restoring
them their property. Finally, if he disinherits him at death,
or emancipates him in his lifetime without just cause, he is
obliged to leave him a fourth of his own property, besides
that which he brought him when adopted, or by subsequent
4 acquisition. It is settled that a man cannot adopt another
person older than himself, for adoption imitates nature, and
it would be unnatural for a son to be older than his father.
Consequently a man who desires either to adopt or to adrogate
a son ought to be older than the latter by the full term of
5 puberty, or eighteen years. A man may adopt a person as
grandson or granddaughter, or as great-grandson or great-
granddaughter, and so on, without having a son at all him-
6 self; and similarly he may adopt another man's son as
7 grandson, or another man's grandson as son. If he wishes
to adopt some one as grandson, whether as the son of an

adoptive son of his own, or of a natural son who is in his power, the consent of this son ought to be obtained, lest a family heir be thrust upon him against his will: but on the other hand, if a grandfather wishes to give a grandson by a son in adoption to some one else, the son's consent is not requisite. An adoptive child is in most respects in the 8 same position, as regards the father, as a natural child born in lawful wedlock. Consequently a man can give in adoption to another a person whom he has adopted by imperial rescript, or before the praetor or governor of a province, provided that in this latter case he was not a stranger (i. e. was a natural descendant) before he adopted him himself. Both forms of 9 adoption agree in this point, that persons incapable of procreation by natural impotence are permitted to adopt, whereas castrated persons are not allowed to do so. Again, women 10 cannot adopt, for even their natural children are not subject to their power; but by the imperial clemency they are enabled to adopt, to comfort them for the loss of children who have been taken from them. It is peculiar to adoption 11 by imperial rescript, that children in the power of the person adrogated, as well as their father, fall under the power of the adrogator, assuming the position of grandchildren. Thus Augustus did not adopt Tiberius until Tiberius had adopted Germanicus, in order that the latter might become his own grandson directly the second adoption was made. The old 12 writers record a judicious opinion contained in the writings of Cato, that the adoption of a slave by his master is equivalent to manumission. In accordance with this we have in our wisdom ruled by a constitution that a slave to whom his master gives the title of son by the solemn form of a record is thereby made free, although this is not sufficient to confer on him the rights of a son.

TITLE XII

OF THE MODES IN WHICH PATERNAL POWER IS EXTINGUISHED

Let us now examine the modes in which persons dependent on a superior become independent. How slaves are freed from the power of their masters can be gathered from what has already been said respecting their manumission. Children under paternal power become independent at the parent's death, subject, however, to the following distinction. The death of a father always releases his sons and daughters from dependence ; the death of a grandfather releases his grandchildren from dependence only provided that it does not subject them to the power of their father. Thus, if at the death of the grandfather the father is alive and in his power, the grandchildren, after the grandfather's death, are in the power of the father; but if at the time of the grandfather's death the father is dead, or not subject to the grandfather, the grandchildren will not fall under his power, but become independent.

1 As deportation to an island for some penal offence entails loss of citizenship, such removal of a man from the list of Roman citizens has, like his death, the effect of liberating his children from his power ; and conversely, the deportation of a person subject to paternal power terminates the power of the parent. In either case, however, if the condemned person is pardoned by the grace of the Emperor, he recovers all his former rights. 2 Relegation to an island does not extinguish paternal power, whether it is the parent or the child who is relegated. 3 Again, a father's power is extinguished by his becoming a 'slave of punishment', for instance, by being condemned 4 to the mines or exposed to wild beasts. A person in paternal power does not become independent by entering the army or becoming a senator, for military service or consular dignity does not set a son free from the power of his father. But by our constitution the supreme dignity of the patriciate frees a son from power immediately on the receipt of the imperial patent ; for who would allow anything so unreasonable as that, while a father is able by emancipation to release his son from the tie of his power, the imperial majesty should be unable to release from dependence on another the man whom it has selected as a father of the 5 State? Again, capture of the father by the enemy makes him a slave of the latter ; but the status of his children is suspended by his right of subsequent restoration by postliminium ; for on escape from captivity a man recovers all his former rights, and among them the right of paternal power

over his children, the law of postliminium resting on a fiction
that the captive has never been absent from the state. But
if he dies in captivity the son is reckoned to have been independent from the moment of his father's capture. So too,
if a son or a grandson is captured by the enemy, the power
of his ascendant is provisionally suspended, though he may
again be subjected to it by postliminium. This term is
derived from *limen* and *post*, which explains why we say that
a person who has been captured by the enemy and has come
back into our territories has returned by postliminium : for
just as the threshold forms the boundary of a house, so the
ancients represented the boundaries of the empire as a
threshold ; and this is also the origin of the term *limes*, signifying a kind of end and limit. Thus postliminium means
that the captive returns by the same threshold at which he
was lost. A captive who is recovered after a victory over the
enemy is deemed to have returned by postliminium. Eman- 6
cipation also liberates children from the power of the parent.
Formerly it was effected either by the observance of an old
form prescribed by statute by which the son was fictitiously
sold and then manumitted, or by imperial rescript. Our
forethought, however, has amended this by a constitution, which
has abolished the old fictitious form, and enabled parents to
go directly to a competent judge or magistrate, and in his
presence release their sons or daughters, grandsons or granddaughters, and so on, from their power. After this, the father
has by the praetor's edict the same rights over the property
of the emancipated child as a patron has over the property of
his freedman : and if at the time of emancipation the child,
whether son or daughter, or in some remoter degree of relationship, is beneath the age of puberty, the father becomes by
the emancipation his or her guardian. It is to be noted, 7
however, that a grandfather who has both a son, and by that
son a grandson or granddaughter, in his power, may either
release the son from his power and retain the grandson or
granddaughter, or retain the son and release the grandson or
granddaughter, or emancipate both together ; and a great-
grandfather has the same latitude of choice. Again, if a father 8
gives a son whom he has in his power in adoption to the son's

natural grandfather or great-grandfather, in accordance with our constitution on this subject, that is to say, by declaring his intention, before a judge with jurisdiction in the matter, in the official records, and in the presence and with the consent of the person adopted, the natural father's power is thereby extinguished, and passes to the adoptive father, adoption by whom under these circumstances retains, as we said, all its 9 old legal consequences. It is to be noted, that if your daughter-in-law conceives by your son, and you emancipate or give the latter in adoption during her pregnancy, the child when born will be in your power ; but if the child is conceived after its father's emancipation or adoption, it is in the power of its natural father or its adoptive grandfather, as the case 10 may be. Children, whether natural or adoptive, are only very rarely able to compel their parent to release them from his power.

Title XIII

OF GUARDIANSHIPS

Let us now pass on to another classification of persons. Persons not subject to power may still be subject either to guardians or to curators, or may be exempt from both forms of control. We will first examine what persons are subject to guardians and curators, and thus we shall know who are exempt from both kinds of control. And first of persons 1 subject to guardianship or tutelage. Guardianship, as defined by Servius, is authority and control over a free person, given and allowed by the civil law, in order to protect 2 one too young to defend himself: and guardians are those persons who possess this authority and control, their name being derived from their very functions ; for they are called guardians as being protectors and defenders, just as those entrusted with the care of sacred buildings are called *aeditui*. 3 The law allows a parent to appoint guardians in his will for those children in his power who have not attained the age of puberty, without distinction between sons and daughters ; but a grandson or granddaughter can receive a testamentary guardian only provided that the death of the testator does not bring them under the power of their own father. Thus, if your son is in your power at the time of your death, your grandchildren by him cannot have a guardian given them by your will, although they are in your power, because your death leaves them in the power of their father. And as 4 in many other matters afterborn children are treated on the footing of children born before the execution of the will, so it is ruled that afterborn children, as well as children born before the will was made, may have guardians therein appointed to them, provided that if born in the testator's lifetime they would be family heirs and in his power. If 5 a testamentary guardian be given by a father to his emancipated son, he must be approved by the governor in all cases, though inquiry into the case is unnecessary.

TITLE XIV

WHO CAN BE APPOINTED GUARDIANS BY WILL

Persons who are in the power of others may be appointed testamentary guardians no less than those who are independent ; and a man can also validly appoint one of his 1 own slaves as testamentary guardian, giving him at the same time his liberty ; and even in the absence of express manumission his freedom is to be presumed to have been tacitly conferred on him, whereby his appointment becomes a valid act, although of course it is otherwise if the testator appointed him guardian in the erroneous belief that he was free. The appointment of another man's slave as guardian, without any addition or qualification, is void, though valid if the words 'when he shall be free' are added : but this latter form is ineffectual if the slave is the testator's own, the appointment being void from the beginning. If a lunatic or minor is 2 appointed testamentary guardian, he cannot act until, if a lunatic, he recovers his faculties, and, if a minor, he attains the age of twenty-five years.

There is no doubt that a guardian may be appointed for 3 and from a certain time, or conditionally, or before the institution of the heir. A guardian cannot, however, be appointed for a particular matter or business, because his duties 4 relate to the person, and not merely to a particular business or matter.

5 If a man appoints guardians to his sons or daughters, he is held to have intended them also for such as may be after-born, for the latter are included in the terms son and daughter. In the case of grandsons, a question may arise whether they are implicitly included in an appointment of guardians to sons; to which we reply, that they are included in an appointment of guardians if the term used is 'children', but not if it is 'sons': for the words son and grandson have quite different meanings. Of course an appointment to after-born children includes all children, and not sons only.

Title XV

OF THE STATUTORY GUARDIANSHIP OF AGNATES

In default of a testamentary guardian, the statute of the Twelve Tables assigns the guardianship to the nearest agnates,

1 who are hence called statutory guardians. Agnates are persons related to one another by males, that is, through their male ascendants; for instance, a brother by the same father, a brother's son, or such son's son, a father's brother, his son or son's son. But persons related only by blood through females are not agnates, but merely cognates. Thus the son of your father's sister is no agnate of yours, but merely your cognate, and vice versa; for children are members of their

2 father's family, and not of their mother's. It was said that the statute confers the guardianship, in case of intestacy, on the nearest agnates; but by intestacy must here be understood not only complete intestacy of a person having power to appoint a testamentary guardian, but also the mere omission to make such appointment, and also the case of a person appointed testamentary guardian dying in the testator's life-

3 time. Loss of status of any kind ordinarily extinguishes rights by agnation, for agnation is a title of civil law. Not every kind of loss of status, however, affects rights by cogna-tion; because civil changes cannot affect rights annexed to a natural title to the same extent that they can affect those annexed to a civil one.

TITLE XVI

OF LOSS OF STATUS

Loss of status, or change in one's previous civil rights, is of three orders, greatest, minor or intermediate, and least. The greatest loss of status is the simultaneous loss of citizen- 1 ship and freedom, exemplified in those persons who by a terrible sentence are made 'slaves of punishment', in freed-men condemned for ingratitude to their patrons, and in those who allow themselves to be sold in order to share the purchase-money when paid. Minor or intermediate loss of 2 status is loss of citizenship unaccompanied by loss of liberty, and is incident to interdiction of fire and water and to deportation to an island. The least loss of status occurs when 3 citizenship and freedom are retained, but a man's domestic position is altered, and is exemplified by adrogation and emancipation. A slave does not suffer loss of status by 4 being manumitted, for while a slave he had no civil rights: and where the change is one of dignity, rather than of civil 5 rights, there is no loss of status ; thus it is no loss of status to be removed from the senate.

When it was said that rights by cognation are not affected 6 by loss of status, only the least loss of status was meant ; by the greatest loss of status they are destroyed—for instance, by a cognate's becoming a slave—and are not recovered even by subsequent manumission. Again, deportation to an island, which entails minor or intermediate loss of status, destroys rights by cognation. When agnates are entitled to be 7 guardians, it is not all who are so entitled, but only those of the nearest degree, though if all are in the same degree, all are entitled.

TITLE XVII

OF THE STATUTORY GUARDIANSHIP OF PATRONS

The same statute of the Twelve Tables assigns the guardian-ship of freedmen and freedwomen to the patron and his children, and this guardianship, like that of agnates, is called statutory guardianship ; not that it is anywhere expressly enacted in that statute, but because its interpretation by the jurists has procured for it as much reception as it could have obtained from express enactment: the fact that the inheritance of a freedman or freedwoman, when they die intestate, was given by the statute to the patron and his children, being deemed a proof that they were intended to have the guardianship also, partly because in dealing with agnates the statute coupled guardianship with succession, and partly on the principle that where the advantage of the succession is, there, as a rule, ought too to be the burden of the guardianship. We say 'as a rule', because if a slave below the age of puberty is manumitted by a woman, though she is entitled, as patroness, to the succession, another person is guardian.

TITLE XVIII

OF THE STATUTORY GUARDIANSHIP OF PARENTS

The analogy of the patron guardian led to another kind of so-called statutory guardianship, namely that of a parent over a son or daughter, or a grandson or granddaughter by a son, or any other descendant through males, whom he emancipates below the age of puberty: in which case he will be statutory guardian.

TITLE XIX

OF FIDUCIARY GUARDIANSHIP

There is another kind of guardianship known as fiduciary guardianship, which arises in the following manner. If a parent emancipates a son or daughter, a grandson or grand-daughter, or other descendant while under the age of puberty, he becomes their statutory guardian: but if at his death he leaves male children, they become fiduciary guardians of their own sons, or brothers and sisters, or other relatives who had been thus emancipated. But on the decease of a patron who is statutory guardian his children become statutory guardians also; for a son of a deceased person, supposing him not to have been emancipated during his father's lifetime, becomes independent at the latter's death, and does not fall under the power of his brothers, nor, consequently, under their guardianship; whereas a freedman, had he remained a slave, would at his master's death have become the slave of the latter's children. The guardianship, however, is not cast on these persons unless they are of full age, which indeed has been made a general rule in guardianship and curatorship of every kind by our constitution.

TITLE XX

OF ATILIAN GUARDIANS, AND THOSE APPOINTED UNDER THE LEX IULIA ET TITIA

Failing every other kind of guardian, at Rome one used to be appointed under the lex Atilia by the praetor of the city and the majority of the tribunes of the people ; in the provinces one was appointed under the lex Iulia et Titia by the president of the province. Again, on the appointment of 1 a testamentary guardian subject to a condition, or on an appointment limited to take effect after a certain time, a substitute could be appointed under these statutes during the pendency of the condition, or until the expiration of the term : and even if no condition was attached to the appointment of a testamentary guardian, a temporary guardian could be obtained under these statutes until the succession had vested. In all these cases the office of the guardian so appointed determined as soon as the condition was fulfilled, or the term expired, or the succession vested in the heir. On 2 the capture of a guardian by the enemy, the same statutes regulated the appointment of a substitute, who continued in office until the return of the captive ; for if he returned, he recovered the guardianship by the law of postliminium. But 3 guardians have now ceased to be appointed under these statutes, the place of the magistrates directed by them to appoint being taken, first, by the consuls, who began to appoint guardians to pupils of either sex after inquiry into the case, and then by the praetors, who were substituted for the consuls by imperial constitutions ; for these statutes contained no provisions as to security to be taken from guardians for the safety of their pupils' property, or compelling them to accept the office in case of disinclination. Under the present 4 law, guardians are appointed at Rome by the prefect of the city, and by the praetor when the case falls within his juris-

diction; in the provinces they are appointed, after inquiry, by the governor, or by inferior magistrates at the latter's
5 behest if the pupil's property is of no great value. By our constitution, however, we have done away with all difficulties of this kind relating to the appointing person, and dispensed with the necessity of waiting for an order from the governor, by enacting that if the property of the pupil or adult does not exceed five hundred *solidi*, guardians or curators shall be appointed by the officers known as defenders of the city, along with the holy bishop of the place, or in the presence of other public persons, or by the magistrates, or by the judge of the city of Alexandria; security being given in the amounts required by the constitution, and those who take it being responsible if it be insufficient.

6 The wardship of children below the age of puberty is in accordance with the law of nature, which prescribes that persons of immature years shall be under another's guidance
7 and control. As guardians have the management of their pupils' business, they are liable to be sued on account of their administration as soon as the pupil attains the age of puberty.

TITLE XXI

OF THE AUTHORITY OF GUARDIANS

In some cases a pupil cannot lawfully act without the authority of his guardian, in others he can. Such authority, for instance, is not necessary when a pupil stipulates for the delivery of property, though it is otherwise where he is the promisor; for it is an established rule that the guardian's authority is not necessary for any act by which the pupil simply improves his own position, though it cannot be dispensed with where he proposes to make it worse. Consequently, unless the guardian authorizes all transactions generating bilateral obligations, such as sale, hire, agency, and deposit, the pupil is not bound, though he can compel the other contracting party to discharge his own obligation.
1 Pupils, however, require their guardian's authority before they can enter on an inheritance, demand the possession of goods, or accept an inheritance by way of trust, even though such

act be advantageous to them, and involves no chance of loss.
If the guardian thinks the transaction will be beneficial to 2
his pupil, his authority should be given presently and on the
spot. Subsequent ratification, or authority given by letter,
has no effect. In case of a suit between guardian and pupil, 3
as the former cannot lawfully authorize an act in which he
is personally concerned or interested, a curator is now appointed, in lieu of the old praetorian guardian, with whose
co-operation the suit is carried on, his office determining as
soon as it is decided.

Title XXII

OF THE MODES IN WHICH GUARDIANSHIP IS TERMINATED

Pupils of either sex are freed from guardianship when they
reach the age of puberty, which the ancients were inclined to
determine, in the case of males, not only by age, but also by
reference to the physical development of individuals. Our
majesty, however, has deemed it not unworthy of the purity
of our times to apply in the case of males also the moral
considerations which, even among the ancients, forbade in
the case of females as indecent the inspection of the person.
Consequently by the promulgation of our sacred constitution
we have enacted that puberty in males shall be considered
to commence immediately on the completion of the fourteenth year, leaving unaltered the rule judiciously laid down
by the ancients as to females, according to which they are
held fit for marriage after completing their twelfth year.
Again, tutelage is terminated by adrogation or deportation 1
of the pupil before he attains the age of puberty, or by his
being reduced to slavery or taken captive by the enemy.
So too if a testamentary guardian be appointed to hold office 2
until the occurrence of a condition, on this occurrence his
office determines. Similarly tutelage is terminated by the 3
death either of pupil or of guardian. If a guardian suffers 4
such a loss of status as entails loss of either liberty or
citizenship, his office thereby completely determines. It is,
however, only the statutory kind of guardianship which is
destroyed by a guardian's undergoing the least loss of status,
for instance, by his giving himself in adoption. Tutelage is

in every case put an end to by the pupil's suffering loss of
5 status, even of the lowest order. Testamentary guardians
appointed to serve until a certain time lay down their office
6 when that time arrives. Finally, persons cease to be
guardians who are removed from their office on suspicion,
or who are enabled to lay down the burden of the tutelage
by a reasonable ground of excuse, according to rules to be
presently stated.

Title XXIII

OF CURATORS

Males, even after puberty, and females after reaching
marriageable years, receive curators until completing their
twenty-fifth year, because, though past the age fixed by
law as the time of puberty, they are not yet old enough
1 to administer their own affairs. Curators are appointed
by the same magistrates who appoint guardians. They
cannot legally be appointed by will, though such appointment, if made, is usually confirmed by an order of the
2 praetor or governor of the province. A person who has
reached the age of puberty cannot be compelled to have
a curator, except for the purpose of conducting a suit : for
curators, unlike guardians, can be appointed for a particular
3 matter. Lunatics and prodigals, even though more than
twenty-five years of age, are by the statute of the Twelve
Tables placed under their agnates as curators ; but now, as
a rule, curators are appointed for them at Rome by the
prefect of the city or praetor, and in the provinces by the
4 governor, after inquiry into the case. Curators should also
be given to persons of weak mind, to the deaf, the dumb,
and those suffering from chronic disease, because they are
5 not competent to manage their own affairs. Sometimes
even pupils have curators, as, for instance, when a statutory
guardian is unfit for his office : for if a pupil already has
one guardian, he cannot have another given him. Again, if
a testamentary guardian, or one appointed by the praetor or
governor, is not a good man of business, though perfectly
honest in his management of the pupil's affairs, it is usual for
a curator to be appointed to act with him. Again, curators

are usually appointed in the room of guardians temporarily excused from the duties of their office.

If a guardian is prevented from managing his pupil's affairs 6 by ill-health or other unavoidable cause, and the pupil is absent or an infant, the praetor or governor of the province will, at the guardian's risk, appoint by decree a person selected by the latter to act as agent of the pupil.

Title XXIV

OF THE SECURITY TO BE GIVEN BY GUARDIANS AND CURATORS

To prevent the property of pupils and of persons under curators from being wasted or diminished by their curators or guardians the praetor provides for security being given by the latter against maladministration. This rule, however, is not without exceptions, for testamentary guardians are not obliged to give security, the testator having had full opportunities of personally testing their fidelity and carefulness, and guardians and curators appointed upon inquiry are similarly exempted, because they have been expressly chosen as the best men for the place. If two or more are appointed by testament, or 1 by a magistrate upon inquiry, any one of them may offer security for indemnifying the pupil or person to whom he is curator against loss, and be preferred to his colleague, in order that he may either obtain the sole administration, or else induce his colleague to offer larger security than himself, and so become sole administrator by preference. Thus he cannot directly call upon his colleague to give security; he ought to offer it himself, and so give his colleague the option of receiving security on the one hand, or of giving it on the other. If none of them offer security, and the testator left directions as to which was to administer the property, this person must undertake it : in default of this, the office is cast by the praetor's edict on the person whom the majority of guardians or curators shall choose. If they cannot agree, the praetor must interpose. The same rule, authorizing a majority to elect one to administer the property, is to be applied where several are appointed after inquiry by a magistrate. It is 2 to be noted that, besides the liability of guardians and

curators to their pupils, or the persons for whom they act,
for the management of their property, there is a subsidiary
action against the magistrate accepting the security, which
may be resorted to where all other remedies prove inadequate,
and which lies against those magistrates who have either
altogether omitted to take security from guardians or curators,
or taken it to an insufficient amount. According to the
doctrines stated by the jurists, as well as by imperial constitutions, this action may be brought against the magistrate's
3 heirs as well as against him personally; and these same constitutions ordain that guardians or curators who make default
in giving security may be compelled to do so by legal dis-
4 traint of their goods. This action, however, will not lie against
the prefect of the city, the praetor, or the governor of a
province, or any other magistrate authorized to appoint
guardians, but only against those to whose usual duties the
taking of security belongs.

TITLE XXV

OF GUARDIANS' AND CURATORS' GROUNDS OF EXEMPTION

There are various grounds on which persons are exempted
from serving the office of guardian or curator, of which the
most common is their having a certain number of children,
whether in power or emancipated. If, that is to say, a man
has, in Rome, three children living, in Italy four, or in the
provinces five, he may claim exemption from these, as from
other public offices; for it is settled that the office of a
guardian or curator is a public one. Adopted children cannot
be reckoned for this purpose, though natural children given
in adoption to others may: similarly grandchildren by a son
may be reckoned, so as to represent their father, while those
by a daughter may not. It is, however, only living children
who avail to excuse their fathers from serving as guardian
or curator; such as have died are of no account, though the
question has arisen whether this rule does not admit of an
exception where they have died in war; and it is agreed that
this is so, but only where they have fallen on the field of
battle: for these, because they have died for their country,
1 are deemed to live eternally in fame. The Emperor Marcus,

too, replied by rescript, as is recorded in his Semestria, that employment in the service of the Treasury is a valid excuse from serving as guardian or curator so long as that employment lasts. Again, those are excused from these offices who 2 are absent in the service of the state ; and a person already guardian or curator who has to absent himself on public business is excused from acting in either of these capacities during such absence, a curator being appointed to act temporarily in his stead. On his return, he has to resume the burden of the tutelage, without being entitled to claim a year's exemption, as has been settled since the opinion of Papinian was delivered in the fifth book of his replies ; for the year's exemption or vacation belongs only to such as are called to a new tutelage. By a rescript of the Emperor 3 Marcus persons holding any magistracy may plead this as a ground of exemption, though it will not enable them to resign an office of this kind already entered upon. No guardian or 4 curator can excuse himself on the ground of an action pending between himself and his ward, unless it relates to the latter's whole estate or to an inheritance. Again, a man who is 5 already guardian or curator to three persons without having sought after the office is entitled to exemption from further burdens of the kind so long as he is actually engaged with these, provided that the joint guardianship of several pupils, or administration of an undivided estate, as where the wards are brothers, is reckoned as one only. If a man can prove 6 that through poverty he is unequal to the burden of the office, this, according to rescripts of the imperial brothers and of the Emperor Marcus, is a valid ground of excuse. Ill- 7 health again is a sufficient excuse if it be such as to prevent a man from attending to even his own affairs : and the Em- 8 peror Pius decided by a rescript that persons unable to read ought to be excused, though even these are not incapable of transacting business. A man too is at once excused if he 9 can show that a father has appointed him testamentary guardian out of enmity, while conversely no one can in any case claim exemption who promised the ward's father that he would act as guardian to them: and it was settled by a rescript 10 of M. Aurelius and L. Verus that the allegation that one

was unacquainted with the pupil's father cannot be admitted
11 as a ground of excuse. Enmity against the ward's father, if
extremely bitter, and if there was no reconciliation, is usually
accepted as a reason for exemption from the office of guardian;
12 and similarly a person can claim to be excused whose status
or civil rights have been disputed by the father of the ward
13 in an action. Again, a person over seventy years of age can
claim to be excused from acting as guardian or curator, and
by the older law persons less than twenty-five were similarly
exempted. But our constitution, having forbidden the latter
to aspire to these functions, has made excuses unnecessary.
The effect of this enactment is that no pupil or person under
twenty-five years of age is to be called to a statutory
guardianship; for it was most incongruous to place persons
under the guardianship or administration of those who are
known themselves to need assistance in the management of
their own affairs, and are themselves governed by others.
14 The same rule is to be observed with soldiers, who, even
though they desire it, may not be admitted to the office of
15 guardian: and finally grammarians, rhetoricians, and physicians
at Rome, and those who follow these callings in their own
country and are within the number fixed by law, are exempted
from being guardians or curators.

16 If a person who has several grounds of excuse wishes to
obtain exemption, and some of them are not allowed, he is
not prohibited from alleging others, provided he does this
within the time prescribed. Those desirous of excusing themselves do not appeal, but ought to allege their grounds of
excuse within fifty days next after they hear of their appointment, whatever the form of the latter, and whatever kind of
guardians they may be, if they are within a hundred miles of
the place where they were appointed : if they live at a distance
of more than a hundred miles, they are allowed a day for
every twenty miles, and thirty days in addition, but this time,
as Scaevola has said, must never be so reckoned as to amount
17 to less than fifty days. A person appointed guardian is
18 deemed to be appointed to the whole patrimony ; and after he
has once acted as guardian he cannot be compelled against
his will to become the same person's curator—not even if the

father who appointed him testamentary guardian added in the will that he made him curator too, as soon as the ward reached fourteen years of age—this having been decided by a rescript of the Emperors Severus and Antoninus. Another 19 rescript of the same emperors settled that a man is entitled to be excused from becoming his own wife's curator, even after intermeddling with her affairs. No man is discharged from 20 the burden of guardianship who has procured exemption by false allegations.

Title XXVI

OF GUARDIANS OR CURATORS WHO ARE SUSPECTED

The accusation of guardians or curators on suspicion originated in the statute of the Twelve Tables; the removal 1 of those who are accused on suspicion is part of the jurisdiction, at Rome, of the praetor, and in the provinces of their governors and of the proconsul's legate. Having shown what 2 magistrates can take cognizance of this subject, let us see what persons are liable to be accused on suspicion. All guardians are liable, whether appointed by testament or otherwise; consequently even a statutory guardian may be made the object of such an accusation. But what is to be said of a patron guardian? Even here we must reply that he too is liable; though we must remember that his reputation must be spared in the event of his removal on suspicion. The 3 next point is to see what persons may bring this accusation; and it is to be observed that the action partakes of a public character, that is to say, is open to all. Indeed, by a rescript of Severus and Antoninus even women are made competent to bring it, but only those who can allege a close tie of affection as their motive; for instance, a mother, nurse, grandmother, or sister. And the praetor will allow any woman to prefer the accusation in whom he finds an affection real enough to induce her to save a pupil from suffering harm, without seeming to be more forward than becomes her sex. Persons below the 4 age of puberty cannot accuse their guardians on suspicion; but by a rescript of Severus and Antoninus it has been permitted to those who have reached that age to deal thus with their curators, after taking the advice of their nearest

5 relations. A guardian is 'suspected' who does not faithfully discharge his tutorial functions, though he may be perfectly solvent, as was the opinion also of Julian. Indeed, Julian writes that a guardian may be removed on suspicion before he commences his administration, and a constitution has been 6 issued in accordance with this view. A person removed from office on suspicion incurs infamy if his offence was fraud, 7 but not if it was merely negligence. As Papinian held, on a person being accused on suspicion he is suspended from the 8 administration until the action is decided. If a guardian or curator who is accused on suspicion dies after the commencement of the action, but before it has been decided, the action 9 is thereby extinguished ; and if a guardian fails to appear to a summons of which the object is to fix by judicial order a certain rate of maintenance for the pupil, the rescript of the Emperors Severus and Antoninus provides that the pupil may be put in possession of the guardian's property, and orders the sale of the perishable portions thereof after appointment of a curator. Consequently, a guardian may be removed as suspected who does not provide his pupil with sufficient maintenance. If, on the other hand, the guardian appears, and alleges that the pupil's property is too inconsiderable to admit of maintenance being decreed, and it is shown that the allegation is false, the proper course is for him to be sent for punishment to the prefect of the city, like those 11 who purchase a guardianship by bribery. So too a freedman, convicted of having acted fraudulently as guardian of the sons or grandsons of his patron, should be sent to the prefect of the 12 city for punishment. Finally, it is to be noted, that guardians or curators who are guilty of fraud in their administration must be removed from their office even though they offer to give security, for giving security does not change the evil intent of the guardian, but only gives him a larger space of time 13 wherein he may injure the pupil's property : for a man's mere character or conduct may be such as to justify one's deeming him 'suspected'. No guardian or curator, however, may be removed on suspicion merely because he is poor, provided he is also faithful and diligent.

BOOK II

OF THE DIFFERENT KINDS OF THINGS

IN the preceding book we have expounded the law of Persons : now let us proceed to the law of Things. Of these, some admit of private ownership, while others, it is held, cannot belong to individuals : for some things are by natural law common to all, some are public, some belong to a society or corporation, and some belong to no one. But most things belong to individuals, being acquired by various titles, as will appear from what follows.

Thus, the following things are by natural law common 1 to all—the air, running water, the sea, and consequently the sea-shore. No one therefore is forbidden access to the sea-shore, provided he abstains from injury to houses, monuments, and buildings generally ; for these are not, like the sea itself, subject to the law of nations. On the other 2 hand, all rivers and harbours are public, so that all persons have a right to fish therein. The sea-shore extends to 3 the limit of the highest tide in time of storm or winter. Again, the public use of the banks of a river, as of the river 4 itself, is part of the law of nations ; consequently every one is entitled to bring his vessel to the bank, and fasten cables to the trees growing there, and use it as a resting-place for the cargo, as freely as he may navigate the river itself. But the ownership of the bank is in the owner of the adjoining land, and consequently so too is the ownership of the trees which grow upon it. Again, the public use of the sea-shore, as of 5 the sea itself, is part of the law of nations ; consequently every one is free to build a cottage upon it for purposes of retreat, as well as to dry his nets and haul them up from the sea. But they cannot be said to belong to any one as private property, but rather are subject to the same law as the sea itself, with the soil or sand which lies beneath it. As 6 examples of things belonging to a society or corporation, and not to individuals, may be cited buildings in cities—theatres, racecourses, and such other similar things as belong to cities in their corporate capacity.

7 Things which are sacred, devoted to superstitious uses, or sanctioned, belong to no one, for what is subject to divine law 8 is no one's property. Those things are sacred which have been duly consecrated to God by His ministers, such as churches and votive offerings which have been properly dedicated to His service; and these we have by our constitution forbidden to be alienated or pledged, except to redeem captives from bondage. If any one attempts to consecrate a thing for himself and by his own authority, its character is unaltered, and it does not become sacred. The ground on which a sacred building is erected remains sacred even after the destruction of the building, as was declared also 9 by Papinian. Any one can devote a place to superstitious uses of his own free will, that is to say, by burying a dead body in his own land. It is not lawful, however, to bury in land which one owns jointly with some one else, and which has not hitherto been used for this purpose, without the other's consent, though one may lawfully bury in a common sepulchre even without such consent. Again, the owner may not devote a place to superstitious uses in which another has a usufruct, without the consent of the latter. It is lawful to bury in another man's ground, if he gives permission, and the ground thereby becomes religious even though he should not give his consent to the interment till after it has 10 taken place. Sanctioned things too, such as city walls and gates, are, in a sense, subject to divine law, and therefore are not owned by any individual. Such walls are said to be 'sanctioned', because any offence against them is visited with capital punishment; for which reason those parts of the laws in which we establish a penalty for their transgressors are called sanctions.

11 Things become the private property of individuals in many ways; for the titles by which we acquire ownership in them are some of them titles of natural law, which, as we said, is called the law of nations, while some of them are titles of

civil law. It will thus be most convenient to take the older law first: and natural law is clearly the older, having been instituted by nature at the first origin of mankind, whereas civil laws first came into existence when states began to be founded, magistrates to be created, and laws to be written.

Wild animals, birds, and fish, that is to say all the creatures 12 which the land, the sea, and the sky produce, as soon as they are caught by any one become at once the property of their captor by the law of nations; for natural reason admits the title of the first occupant to that which previously had no owner. So far as the occupant's title is concerned, it is immaterial whether it is on his own land or on that of another that he catches wild animals or birds, though it is clear that if he goes on another man's land for the sake of hunting or fowling, the latter may forbid him entry if aware of his purpose. An animal thus caught by you is deemed your property so long as it is completely under your control; but so soon as it has escaped from your control, and recovered its natural liberty, it ceases to be yours, and belongs to the first person who subsequently catches it. It is deemed to have recovered its natural liberty when you have lost sight of it, or when, though it is still in your sight, it would be difficult to pursue it. It has been doubted whether a wild 13 animal becomes your property immediately you have wounded it so severely as to be able to catch it. Some have thought that it becomes yours at once, and remains so as long as you pursue it, though it ceases to be yours when you cease the pursuit, and becomes again the property of any one who catches it: others have been of opinion that it does not belong to you till you have actually caught it. And we confirm this latter view, for it may happen in many ways that you will not capture it. Bees again are naturally wild; 14 hence if a swarm settles on your tree, it is no more considered yours, until you have hived it, than the birds which build their nests there, and consequently if it is hived by some one else, it becomes his property. So too any one may take the honey-combs which bees may chance to have made, though, of course, if you see some one coming on your land for this purpose, you have a right to forbid him entry before that

purpose is effected. A swarm which has flown from your hive is considered to remain yours so long as it is in your sight and easy of pursuit: otherwise it belongs to the first
15 person who catches it. Peafowl too and pigeons are naturally wild, and it is no valid objection that they are used to return to the same spots from which they fly away, for bees do this, and it is admitted that bees are wild by nature; and some people have deer so tame that they will go into the woods and yet habitually come back again, and still no one denies that they are naturally wild. With regard, however, to animals which have this habit of going away and coming back again, the rule has been established that they are deemed yours so long as they have the intent to return: for if they cease to have this intention they cease to be yours, and belong to the first person who takes them; and when they lose the habit they seem also to have lost the
16 intention of returning. Fowls and geese are not naturally wild, as is shown by the fact that there are some kinds of fowls and geese which we call wild kinds. Hence if your geese or fowls are frightened and fly away, they are considered to continue yours wherever they may be, even though you have lost sight of them; and any one who keeps them intending thereby to make a profit is held guilty of theft.
17 Things again which we capture from the enemy at once become ours by the law of nations, so that by this rule even free men become our slaves, though, if they escape from our power and return to their own people, they recover their
18 previous condition. Precious stones too, and gems, and all other things found on the sea-shore, become immediately by
19 natural law the property of the finder: and by the same law the young of animals of which you are the owner become your property also.
20 Moreover, soil which a river has added to your land by alluvion becomes yours by the law of nations. Alluvion is an imperceptible addition; and that which is added so gradually that you cannot perceive the exact increase from
21 one moment of time to another is added by alluvion. If, however, the violence of the stream sweeps away a parcel of your land and carries it down to the land of your neighbour

it clearly remains yours; though of course if in process of time it becomes firmly attached to your neighbour's land, and the trees which it carried with it strike root in the latter, they are deemed from that time to have become part and parcel thereof. When an island rises in the sea, though this 22 rarely happens, it belongs to the first occupant; for, until occupied, it is held to belong to no one. If, however (as often occurs), an island rises in a river, and it lies in the middle of the stream, it belongs in common to the landowners on either bank, in proportion to the extent of their riparian interest; but if it lies nearer to one bank than to the other, it belongs to the landowners on that bank only. If a river divides into two channels, and by uniting again these channels transform a man's land into an island, the ownership of that land is in no way altered: but if a river entirely leaves 23 its old channel, and begins to run in a new one, the old channel belongs to the landowners on either side of it in proportion to the extent of their riparian interest, while the new one acquires the same legal character as the river itself, and becomes public. But if after a while the river returns to its old channel, the new channel again becomes the property of those who possess the land along its banks. It is otherwise if 24 one's land is wholly flooded, for a flood does not permanently alter the nature of the land, and consequently if the water goes back the soil clearly belongs to its previous owner.

When a man makes a new object out of materials belonging 25 to another, the question usually arises, to which of them, by natural reason, does this new object belong—to the man who made it, or to the owner of the materials? For instance, one man may make wine, or oil, or corn, out of another man's grapes, olives, or sheaves; or a vessel out of his gold, silver, or bronze; or mead of his wine and honey; or a plaster or eyesalve out of his drugs; or cloth out of his wool; or a ship, a chest, or a chair out of his timber. After many controversies between the Sabinians and Proculians, the law has now been settled as follows, in accordance with the view of those who followed a middle course between the opinions of the two schools. If the new object can be reduced to the materials of which it was made, it belongs to the owner of the materials;

if not, it belongs to the person who made it. For instance, a vessel can be melted down, and so reduced to the rude material—bronze, silver, or gold—of which it is made: but it is impossible to reconvert wine into grapes, oil into olives, or corn into sheaves, or even mead into the wine and honey of which it was compounded. But if a man makes a new object out of materials which belong partly to him and partly to another—for instance, mead of his own wine and another's honey, or a plaster or eyesalve of drugs which are not all his own, or cloth of wool which belongs only in part to him— in this case there can be no doubt that the new object belongs to its creator, for he has contributed not only part

26 of the material, but the labour by which it was made. If, however, a man weaves into his own cloth another man's purple, the latter, though the more valuable, becomes part of the cloth by accession; but its former owner can maintain an action of theft against the purloiner, and also a condiction, or action for reparative damages, whether it was he who made the cloth, or some one else; for although the destruction of property is a bar to a real action for its recovery, it is no bar to a condiction against the thief and certain other

27 possessors. If materials belonging to two persons are mixed by consent—for instance, if they mix their wines, or melt together their gold or their silver—the result of the mixture belongs to them in common. And the law is the same if the materials are of different kinds, and their mixture conse-quently results in a new object, as where mead is made by mixing wine and honey, or electrum by mixing gold and silver; for even here it is not doubted that the new object belongs in common to the owners of the materials. And if it is by accident, and not by the intention of the owners, that materials have become mixed, the law is the same, whether

28 they were of the same or of different kinds. But if the corn of Titius has become mixed with yours, and this by mutual consent, the whole will belong to you in common, because the separate bodies or grains, which before belonged to one or the other of you in severalty, have by consent on both sides been made your joint property. If, however, the mixture was accidental, or if Titius mixed the two parcels of corn without

your consent, they do not belong to you in common, because
the separate grains remain distinct, and their substance is
unaltered; and in such cases the corn no more becomes
common property than does a flock formed by the accidental
mixture of Titius's sheep with yours. But if either of you keeps
the whole of the mixed corn, the other can bring a real action
for the recovery of such part of it as belongs to him, it being
part of the province of the judge to determine the quality
of the wheat which belonged to each. If a man builds upon 29
his own ground with another's materials, the building is
deemed to be his property, for buildings become a part of
the ground on which they stand. And yet he who was
owner of the materials does not cease to own them, but he
cannot bring a real action for their recovery, or sue for their
production, by reason of a clause in the Twelve Tables
providing that no one shall be compelled to take out of
his house materials (*tignum*), even though they belong to
another, which have once been built into it, but that double
their value may be recovered by the action called *de tigno
iniuncto*. The term *tignum* includes every kind of material
employed in building, and the object of this provision is to
avoid the necessity of having buildings pulled down; but if
through some cause or other they should be destroyed, the
owner of the materials, unless he has already sued for double
value, may bring a real action for recovery, or a personal
action for production. On the other hand, if one man builds 30
a house on another's land with his own materials, the house
belongs to the owner of the land. In this case, however, the
right of the previous owner in the materials is extinguished,
because he is deemed to have voluntarily parted with them,
though only, of course, if he was aware that the land on which
he was building belonged to another man. Consequently,
though the house should be destroyed, he cannot claim the
materials by real action. Of course, if the builder of the
house has possession of the land, and the owner of the latter
claims the house by real action, but refuses to pay for the
materials and the workmen's wages, he can be defeated by
the plea of fraud, provided the builder's possession is in good
faith: for if he knew that the land belonged to some one else

it may be urged against him that he was to blame for rashly
building on land owned to his knowledge by another man.
31 If Titius plants another man's shrub in land belonging to
himself, the shrub will become his; and, conversely, if he
plants his own shrub in the land of Maevius, it will belong
to Maevius.   In neither case, however, will the ownership be
transferred until the shrub has taken root: for, until it has
done this, it continues to belong to its original owner.   So
strict indeed is the rule that the ownership of the shrub is
transferred from the moment it has taken root, that if
a neighbour's tree grows so close to the land of Titius that
the soil of the latter presses round it, whereby it drives its
roots entirely into the same, we say the tree becomes the
property of Titius, on the ground that it would be unreasonable to allow the owner of a tree to be a different person from
the owner of the land in which it is rooted.   Consequently,
if a tree which grows on the boundaries of two estates drives
its roots even partially into the neighbour's soil, it becomes
32 the common property of the two landowners.   On the same
principle corn is reckoned to become a part of the soil in
which it is sown.   But exactly as (according to what we said)
a man who builds on another's land can defend himself by the
plea of fraud when sued for the building by the owner of the
land, so here too one who has in good faith and at his own
expense put crops into another man's soil can shelter himself
behind the same plea, if refused compensation for labour and
33 outlay.   Writing again, even though it be in letters of gold,
becomes a part of the paper or parchment, exactly as
buildings and sown crops become part of the soil, and consequently if Titius writes a poem, or a history, or a speech
on your paper or parchment, the whole will be held to belong
to you, and not to Titius.   But if you sue Titius to recover
your books or parchments, and refuse to pay the value of the
writing, he will be able to defend himself by the plea of fraud,
provided that he obtained possession of the paper or parch-
34 ment in good faith.   Where, on the other hand, one man
paints a picture on another's board, some think that the
board belongs, by accession, to the painter, others, that the
painting, however great its excellence, becomes part of

the board. The former appears to us the better opinion,
for it is absurd that a painting by Apelles or Parrhasius
should be an accessory of a board which, in itself, is
thoroughly worthless. Hence, if the owner of the board
has possession of the picture, and is sued for it by the
painter, who nevertheless refuses to pay the cost of the board,
he will be able to repel him by the plea of fraud. If, on
the other hand, the painter has possession, it follows from
what has been said that the former owner of the board, [if he
is to be able to sue at all], must claim it by a modified and
not by a direct action ; and in this case, if he refuses to pay
the cost of the picture, he can be repelled by the plea of
fraud, provided that the possession of the painter be in good
faith ; for it is clear, that if the board was stolen by the
painter, or some one else, from its former owner, the latter can
bring the action of theft.

If a man in good faith buys land from another who is not 35
its owner, though he believed he was, or acquires it in good
faith by gift or some other lawful title, natural reason directs
that the fruits which he has gathered shall be his, in consideration of his care and cultivation: consequently if the
owner subsequently appears and claims the land by real
action, he cannot sue for fruits which the possessor has consumed. This, however, is not allowed to one who takes possession of land which to his knowledge belongs to another
person, and therefore he is obliged not only to restore the
land, but to make compensation for fruits even though they
have been consumed. A person who has a usufruct in land 36
does not become owner of the fruits which grow thereon
until he has himself gathered them ; consequently fruits
which, at the moment of his decease, though ripe, are yet un-
gathered, do not belong to his heir, but to the owner of the
land. What has been said applies also in the main to the
lessee of land. The term 'fruits', when used of animals, com- 37
prises their young, as well as milk, hair, and wool ; thus
lambs, kids, calves, and foals, belong at once, by the natural
law of ownership, to the fructuary. But the term does not
include the offspring of a female slave, which consequently
belongs to her master ; for it seemed absurd to reckon human

beings as fruits, when it is for their sake that all other fruits
38 have been provided by nature. The usufructuary of a flock,
as Julian held, ought to replace any of the animals which die
from the young of the rest, and, if his usufruct be of land, to
replace dead vines or trees; for it is his duty to cultivate
according to law and use them like a careful head of a family.
39 If a man found a treasure in his own land, the Emperor
Hadrian, following natural equity, adjudged to him the
ownership of it, as he also did to a man who found one by
accident in soil which was sacred or religious. If he found
it in another man's land by accident, and without specially
searching for it, he gave half to the finder, half to the owner
of the soil; and upon this principle, if a treasure were found
in land belonging to the Emperor, he decided that half should
belong to the latter, and half to the finder; and consistently
with this, if a man finds one in land which belongs to the
imperial treasury or the people, half belongs to him, and half
to the treasury or the State.
40 Delivery again is a mode in which we acquire things by
natural law; for it is most agreeable to natural equity that
where a man wishes to transfer his property to another person
his wish should be confirmed. Consequently corporeal things,
whatever be their nature, admit of delivery, and delivery by
their owner makes them the property of the alienee; this,
for instance, is the mode of alienating stipendiary and tri-
butary estates, that is to say, estates lying in provincial soil;
between which, however, and estates in Italy there now exists,
41 according to our constitution, no difference. And ownership
is transferred whether the motive of the delivery be the desire
to make a gift, to confer a dowry, or any other motive whatsoever. When, however, a thing is sold and delivered, it does
not become the purchaser's property until he has paid the
price to the vendor, or satisfied him in some other way, as
by getting some one else to accept liability for him, or by
pledge. And this rule, though laid down also in the statute
of the Twelve Tables, is rightly said to be a dictate of the
law of all nations, that is, of natural law. But if the vendor
gives the purchaser credit, the goods sold belong to the latter
42 at once. It is immaterial whether the person who makes

delivery is the owner himself, or some one else acting with his consent. Consequently, if any one is entrusted by an 43 owner with the management of his business at his own free discretion, and in the execution of his commission sells and delivers any article, he makes the receiver its owner. In 44 some cases even the owner's bare will is sufficient, without delivery, to transfer ownership. For instance, if a man sells or makes you a present of a thing which he has previously lent or let to you or placed in your custody, though it was not from that motive he originally delivered it to you, yet by the very fact that he suffers it to be yours you at once become its owner as fully as if it had been originally delivered for the purpose of passing the property. So too if a man sells 45 goods lying in a warehouse, he transfers the ownership of them to the purchaser immediately he has delivered to the latter the keys of the warehouse. Nay, in some cases the will of 46 the owner, though directed only towards an uncertain person, transfers the ownership of the thing, as for instance when praetors and consuls throw money to a crowd : here they know not which specific coin each person will get, yet they make the unknown recipient immediate owner, because it is their will that each shall have what he gets. Accordingly, 47 it is true that if a man takes possession of property abandoned by its previous owner, he at once becomes its owner himself : and a thing is said to be abandoned which its owner throws away with the deliberate intention that it shall no longer be part of his property, and of which, consequently, he immediately ceases to be owner. It is otherwise with things 48 which are thrown overboard during a storm, in order to lighten the ship ; in the ownership of these things there is no change, because the reason for which they are thrown overboard is obviously not that the owner does not care to own them any longer, but that he and the ship besides may be more likely to escape the perils of the sea. Consequently any one who carries them off after they are washed on shore, or who picks them up at sea and keeps them, intending to make a profit thereby, commits a theft ; for such things seem to be in much the same position as those which fall out of a carriage in motion unknown to their owners.

TITLE II

OF INCORPOREAL THINGS

Some things again are corporeal, and others incorporeal.
1 Those are corporeal which in their own nature are tangible, such as land, slaves, clothing, gold, silver, and others innumer-
2 able. Things incorporeal are such as are intangible: rights, for instance, such as inheritance, usufruct, and obligations, however acquired. And it is no objection to this definition that an inheritance comprises things which are corporeal; for the fruits of land enjoyed by a usufructuary are corporeal too, and obligations generally relate to the conveyance of something corporeal, such as land, slaves, or money, and yet the right of succession, the right of usufruct, and the right existing
3 in every obligation, are incorporeal. So too the rights appurtenant to land, whether in town or country, which are usually called servitudes, are incorporeal things.

TITLE III

OF SERVITUDES

The following are rights appurtenant to country estates: *iter*, the right of passage at will for a man only, not of driving beast or vehicles; *actus*, the right of driving beasts or vehicles (of which two the latter contains the former, though the former does not contain the latter, so that a man who has *iter* has not necessarily *actus*, while if he has *actus* he has also *iter*, and consequently can pass himself even though unaccompanied by cattle); *via*, which is the right of going, of driving any thing whatsoever, and of walking, and which thus contains both *iter* and *actus*; and fourthly, *aquaeductus*, the right of
1 conducting water over another man's land. Servitudes appurtenant to town estates are rights which are attached to buildings; and they are said to appertain to town estates because all buildings are called 'town estates', even though they are actually in the country. The following are servitudes of this kind—the obligation of a man to support the weight of his neighbour's house, to allow a beam to be let into his wall, or to receive the rain from his neighbour's roof on to

his own either in drops or from a shoot, or from a gutter into his yard ; the converse right of exemption from any of these obligations ; and the right of preventing a neighbour from raising his buildings, lest thereby one's ancient lights be obstructed. Some think that among servitudes appurtenant to 2 country estates ought properly to be reckoned the rights of drawing water, of watering cattle, of pasture, of burning lime, and of digging sand.

These servitudes are called rights attached to estates, 3 because without estates they cannot come into existence ; for no one can acquire or own a servitude attached to a town or country estate unless he has an estate for it to be attached to. When a landowner wishes to create any of these rights in 4 favour of his neighbour, the proper mode of creation is agreement followed by stipulation. By testament too one can impose on one's heir an obligation not to raise the height of his house so as to obstruct his neighbour's ancient lights, or bind him to allow a neighbour to let a beam into his wall, to receive the rain water from a neighbour's pipe, or allow a neighbour a right of way, of driving cattle or vehicles over his land, or conducting water over it.

TITLE IV

OF USUFRUCT

Usufruct is the right of using and taking the fruits of property not one's own, without impairing the substance of that property ; for being a right over a corporeal thing, it is necessarily extinguished itself along with the extinction of the latter. Usufruct is thus a right detached from the aggregate 1 of rights involved in ownership, and this separation can be effected in very many ways : for instance, if one man gives another a usufruct by legacy, the legatee has the usufruct, while the heir has merely the bare ownership ; and, conversely, if a man gives a legacy of an estate, reserving the usufruct, the usufruct belongs to the heir, while only the bare ownership is vested in the legatee. Similarly, he can give to one man a legacy of the usufruct, to another one of the estate, subject to the other's usufruct. If it is wished to create a usufruct in favour of another person otherwise than by testament, the proper mode is agreement followed by stipulation. However, lest ownership should be entirely value-less through the permanent separation from it of the usufruct, certain modes have been approved in which usufruct may be 2 extinguished, and thereby revert to the owner. A usufruct may be created not only in land or buildings, but also in slaves, cattle, and other objects generally, except such as are actually consumed by being used, of which a genuine usufruct is impossible by both natural and civil law. Among them are wine, oil, grain, clothing, and perhaps we may also say coined money ; for a sum of money is in a sense extinguished by changing hands, as it constantly does in simply being used. For convenience sake, however, the senate enacted that a usu-fruct could be created in such things, provided that due security be given to the heir. Thus if a usufruct of money be given by legacy, that money, on being delivered to the legatee, becomes his property, though he has to give security to the heir that he will repay an equivalent sum on his dying or undergoing a loss of status. And all things of this class, when delivered to the legatee, become his property, though they are first appraised, and the legatee then gives security that if he dies or undergoes a loss of status he will pay the value which was put upon them. Thus in point of fact the senate did not introduce a usufruct of such things, for that was beyond its power, but established a right analogous to 3 usufruct by requiring security. Usufruct determines by the death of the usufructuary, by his undergoing either of the greater kinds of loss of status, by its improper exercise, and by its non-exercise during the time fixed by law ; all of which points are settled by our constitution. It is also extinguished when surrendered to the owner by the usu-fructuary (though transfer to a third person is inoperative); and again, conversely, by the fructuary becoming owner of the thing, this being called consolidation. Obviously, a usufruct of a house is extinguished by the house being burnt down, or falling through an earthquake or faulty construc-tion ; and in such a case a usufruct of the site cannot be 4 claimed. When a usufruct determines, it reverts to and is reunited with the ownership; and from that moment he who before was but bare owner of the thing begins to have full power over it.

TITLE V

OF USE AND HABITATION

A bare use, or right of using a thing, is created in the same mode as a usufruct, and the modes in which it may determine are the same as those just described. A use is 1 a less right than a usufruct; for if a man has a bare use of an estate, he is deemed entitled to use the vegetables, fruit, flowers, hay, straw, and wood upon it only so far as his daily needs require: he may remain on the land only so long as he does not inconvenience its owner, or impede those who are engaged in its cultivation; but he cannot let or sell or give away his right to a third person, whereas a usufructuary may. Again, a man who has the use of a house is deemed entitled 2 only to live in it himself; he cannot transfer his right to a third person, and it scarcely seems to be agreed that he may take in a guest; but besides himself he may lodge there his wife, children, and freedmen, and other free persons who form as regular a part of his establishment as his slaves. Similarly, if a woman has the use of a house, her husband may dwell there with her. When a man has the use of 3 a slave, he has only the right of personally using his labour and services; in no way is he allowed to transfer his right to a third person, and the same applies to the use of beasts of burden. If a legacy be given of the use of a herd or of 4 a flock of sheep, the usuary may not use the milk, lambs, or wool, for these are fruits; but of course he may use the animals for the purpose of manuring his land.

If a right of habitation be given to a man by legacy or in 5 some other mode, this seems to be neither a use nor a usufruct, but a distinct and as it were independent right; and by a constitution which we have published in accordance with the opinion of Marcellus, and in the interests of utility, we have permitted persons possessed of this right not only to live in the building themselves, but also to let it out to others.

What we have here said concerning servitudes, and the 6

rights of usufruct, use, and habitation, will be sufficient; of inheritance and obligations we will treat in their proper places respectively. And having now briefly expounded the modes in which we acquire things by the law of nations, let us turn and see in what modes they are acquired by statute or by civil law.

TITLE VI

OF USUCAPION AND LONG POSSESSION

It was a rule of the civil law that if a man in good faith bought a thing, or received it by way of gift, or on any other lawful ground, from a person who was not its owner, but whom he believed to be such, he should acquire it by usucapion—if a movable, by one year's possession, and by two years' possession if an immovable, though in this case only if it were in Italian soil;—the reason of the rule being the inexpediency of allowing ownership to be long unascertained. The ancients thus considered that the periods mentioned were sufficient to enable owners to look after their property; but we have arrived at a better opinion, in order to save people from being over-quickly defrauded of their own, and to prevent the benefit of this institution from being confined to only a certain part of the empire. We have consequently published a constitution on the subject, enacting that the period of usucapion for movables shall be three years, and that ownership of immovables shall be acquired by long possession—possession, that is to say, for ten years, if both parties dwell in the same province, and for twenty years if in different provinces; and things may in these modes be acquired in full ownership, provided the possession commences on a lawful ground, not only in Italy but in every land subject to our sway.

1 Some things, however, notwithstanding the good faith of the possessor, and the duration of his possession, cannot be acquired by usucapion; as is the case, for instance, if one possesses a free man, a thing sacred or religious, or a runaway
2 slave. Things again of which the owner lost possession by theft, or possession of which was gained by violence, cannot be acquired by usucapion, even by a person who has possessed

them in good faith for the specified period : for stolen things are declared incapable of usucapion by the statute of the Twelve Tables and by the lex Atinia, and things taken with violence by the lex Iulia et Plautia. The statement that 3 things stolen or violently possessed cannot, by statute, be acquired by usucapion, means, not that the thief or violent dispossessor is incapable of usucapion—for these are barred by another reason, namely the fact that their possession is not in good faith ; but that even a person who has purchased the thing from them in good faith, or received it on some other lawful ground, is incapable of acquiring by usucapion. Consequently, in things movable even a person who possesses in good faith can seldom acquire ownership by usucapion, for he who sells, or on some other ground delivers possession of a thing belonging to another, commits a theft. However, 4 this admits of exception ; for if an heir, who believes a thing lent or let to, or deposited with, the person whom he succeeds, to be a portion of the inheritance, sells or gives it by way of dowry to another who receives it in good faith, there is no doubt that the latter can acquire the ownership of it by usucapion ; for the thing is here not tainted with the flaw attaching to stolen property, because an heir does not commit a theft who in good faith conveys a thing away believing it to be his own. Again, the usufructuary of a female slave, who 5 believes her offspring to be his property, and sells or gives it away, does not commit a theft : for theft implies unlawful intention. There are also other ways in which one man can 6 transfer to another property which is not his own, without committing a theft, and thereby enable the receiver to acquire by usucapion. Usucapion of property classed among things 7 immovable is an easier matter ; for it may easily happen that a man may, without violence, obtain possession of land which, owing to the absence or negligence of its owner, or to his having died and left no successor, is presently possessed by no one. Now this man himself does not possess in good faith, because he knows the land on which he has seized is certainly not his own : but if he delivers it to another who receives it in good faith, the latter can acquire it by long possession, because it has neither been stolen nor violently possessed ; for the idea held by some of the ancients, that a piece of land or a place can be stolen, has now been exploded, and imperial constitutions have been enacted in the interests of persons possessing immovables, to the effect that no one ought to be deprived of a thing of which he has 8 had long and unquestioned possession. Sometimes indeed even things which have been stolen or violently possessed can be acquired by usucapion, as for instance after they have again come under the power of their real owner : for by this they are relieved from the taint which had attached to them, 9 and so become capable of usucapion. Things belonging to our treasury cannot be acquired by usucapion. But there is on record an opinion of Papinian, supported by rescripts of the Emperors Pius, Severus, and Antoninus, that if, before the property of a deceased person who has left no heir is reported to the exchequer, some one has bought or received some 10 part thereof, he can acquire it by usucapion. Finally, it is to be observed that things are incapable of being acquired through usucapion by a purchaser in good faith, or by one who possesses on some other lawful ground, unless they are free from all flaws which vitiate the usucapion.

11 If there be a mistake as to the ground on which possession is acquired, and which it is wrongly supposed will support usucapion, usucapion cannot take place. Thus a man's possession may be founded on a supposed sale or gift, whereas in point of fact there has been no sale or gift at all.

12 Long possession which has begun to run in favour of a deceased person continues to run on in favour of his heir or praetorian successor, even though he knows that the land belongs to another person. But if the deceased's possession had not a lawful inception, it is not available to the heir or praetorian successor, although ignorant of this. Our constitution has enacted that in usucapion too a similar rule shall be observed, and that the benefit of the possession shall 13 continue in favour of the successor. The Emperors Severus and Antoninus have decided by a rescript that a purchaser too may reckon as his own the time during which his vendor has possessed the thing.

14 Finally, it is provided by an edict of the Emperor Marcus

that after an interval of five years a purchaser from the
treasury of property belonging to a third person may repel
the owner, if sued by him, by an exception. But a constitution issued by Zeno of sacred memory has protected
persons who acquire things from the treasury by purchase,
gift, or other title, affording them complete security from the
moment of the transfer, and guaranteeing their success in
any action relating thereto, whether they be plaintiffs or
defendants ; while it allows those who claim any action
in respect of such property as owners or pledgees to sue
the imperial treasury at any time within four years from the
transaction. A divine constitution which we ourselves have
lately issued has extended the operation of Zeno's enactment,
respecting conveyances by the treasury, to persons who have
acquired anything from our palace or that of the Empress.

TITLE VII

OF GIFTS

Another mode in which property is acquired is gift. Gifts
are of two kinds ; those made in contemplation of death, and
those not so made. Gifts of the first kind are those made in 1
view of approaching death, the intention of the giver being
that in the event of his decease the thing given should belong
to the donee, but that if he should survive or should desire to
revoke the gift, or if the donee should die first, the thing
should be restored to him. These gifts in contemplation of
death now stand on exactly the same footing as legacies ;
for as in some respects they were more like ordinary gifts,
in others more like legacies, the jurists doubted under which
of these two classes they should be placed, some being for
gift, others for legacy : and consequently we have enacted by
constitution that in nearly every respect they shall be treated
like legacies, and shall be governed by the rules laid down
respecting them in our constitution. In a word, a gift in
contemplation of death is where the donor would rather have
the thing himself than that the donee should have it, and
that the latter should rather have it than his own heir. An
illustration may be found in Homer, where Telemachus makes
a gift to Piraeus.

2　Gifts which are made without contemplation of death, which we call gifts between the living, are of another kind, and have nothing in common with legacies. If the transaction be complete, they cannot be revoked at pleasure; and it is complete when the donor has manifested his intention, whether in writing or not. Our constitution has settled that such a manifestation of intention binds the donor to deliver, exactly as in the case of sale; so that even before delivery gifts are completely effectual, and the donor is under a legal obligation to deliver the object. Enactments of earlier emperors required that such gifts, if in excess of two hundred *solidi*, should be officially registered; but our constitution has raised this maximum to five hundred *solidi*, and dispensed with the necessity of registering gifts of this or of a less amount; indeed it has even specified some gifts which are completely valid, and require no registration, irrespective of their amount. We have devised many other regulations in order to facilitate and secure gifts, all of which may be gathered from the constitutions which we have issued on this topic. It is to be observed, however, that even where gifts have been completely executed we have by our constitution under certain circumstances enabled donors to revoke them, but only on proof of ingratitude on the part of the recipient of the bounty; the aim of this reservation being to protect persons, who have given their property to others, from suffering at the hands of these latter injury or loss in any of the modes detailed in our

3　constitution. There is another specific kind of gift between the living, with which the earlier jurists were quite unacquainted, and which owed its later introduction to more recent emperors. It was called gift before marriage, and was subject to the implied condition that it should not be binding until the marriage had taken place; its name being due to the fact that it was always made before the union of the parties, and could never take place after the marriage had once been celebrated. The first change in this matter was made by our imperial father Justin, who, as it had been allowed to increase dowries even after marriage, issued a constitution authorizing the increase of gifts before marriage during the continuance of the marriage tie in cases where an increase had been made to the dowry. The name 'gift before marriage' was, however, still retained, though now inappropriate, because the increase was made to it after the marriage. We, however, in our desire to perfect the law, and to make names suit the things which they are used to denote, have by a constitution permitted such gifts to be first made, and not merely increased, after the celebration of the marriage, and have directed that they shall be called gifts 'on account of' (and not 'before') marriage, thereby assimilating them to dowries; for as dowries are not only increased, but actually constituted, during marriage, so now gifts on account of marriage may be not only made before the union of the parties, but may be first made as well as increased during the continuance of that union.

There was formerly too another civil mode of acquisition, 4 namely, by accrual, which operated in the following way: if a person who owned a slave jointly with Titius gave him his liberty himself alone by vindication or by testament, his share in the slave was lost, and went to the other joint owner by accrual. But as this rule was very bad as a precedent—for both the slave was cheated of his liberty, and the kinder masters suffered all the loss while the harsher ones reaped all the gain—we have deemed it necessary to suppress a usage which seemed so odious, and have by our constitution provided a merciful remedy, by discovering a means by which the manumitter, the other joint owner, and the liberated slave, may all alike be benefited. Freedom, in whose behalf even the ancient legislators clearly established many rules at variance with the general principles of law, will be actually acquired by the slave; the manumitter will have the pleasure of seeing the benefit of his kindness undisturbed; while the other joint owner, by receiving a money equivalent proportionate to his interest, and on the scale which we have fixed, will be indemnified against all loss.

TITLE VIII

OF PERSONS WHO MAY, AND WHO MAY NOT ALIENATE

It sometimes happens that an owner cannot alienate, and that a non-owner can. Thus the alienation of dowry land by the husband, without the consent of the wife, is prohibited by the lex Iulia, although, since it has been given to him as dowry, he is its owner. We, however, have amended the lex Iulia, and thus introduced an improvement; for that statute applied only to land in Italy, and though it prohibited a mortgage of the land even with the wife's consent, it forbade it to be alienated only without her concurrence. To correct these two defects we have forbidden mortgages as well as alienations of dowry land even when it is situated in the provinces, so that such land can now be dealt with in neither of these ways, even if the wife concurs, lest the weakness of the female sex should be used as a means to the wasting

1 of their property. Conversely a pledgee, in pursuance of his agreement, may alienate the pledge, though not its owner; this, however, may seem to rest on the assent of the pledgor given at the inception of the contract, in which it was agreed that the pledgee should have a power of sale in default of repayment. But in order that creditors may not be hindered from pursuing their lawful rights, or debtors be deemed to be overlightly deprived of their property, provisions have been inserted in our constitution and a definite procedure established for the sale of pledges, by which the interests of both creditors

2 and debtors have been abundantly guarded. We must next observe that no pupil of either sex can alienate anything without his or her guardian's authority. Consequently, if a pupil attempts to lend money without such authority, no property passes, and he does not impose a contractual obligation; hence the money, if it exists, can be recovered by real action. If the money which he attempted to lend has been spent in good faith by the would-be borrower, it can be sued for by the personal action called condiction; if it has been fraudulently spent, the pupil can sue by personal action for its production. On the other hand, things can be validly conveyed to pupils of either sex without the guardian's authority; accordingly, if a debtor wishes to pay a pupil, he must obtain the sanction of the guardian to the transaction, else he will not be released. In a constitution which we issued to the advocates of Caesarea at the instance of the distinguished Tribonian, quaestor of our most sacred palace, it has with the

clearest reason been enacted, that the debtor of a pupil may safely pay a guardian or curator by having first obtained permission by the order of a judge, for which no fee is to be payable: and if the judge makes the order, and the debtor in pursuance thereof makes payment, he is completely protected by this form of discharge. Supposing, however, that the form of payment be other than that which we have fixed, and that the pupil, though he still has the money in his possession, or has been otherwise enriched by it, attempts to recover the debt by action, he can be repelled by the plea of fraud. If on the other hand he has squandered the money or had it stolen from him, the plea of fraud will not avail the debtor, who will be condemned to pay again, as a penalty for having carelessly paid without the guardian's authority, and not in accordance with our regulation. Pupils of either sex cannot validly satisfy a debt without their guardian's authority, because the money paid does not become the creditor's property ; the principle being that no pupil is capable of alienation without his guardian's sanction.

TITLE IX

OF PERSONS THROUGH WHOM WE ACQUIRE

We acquire property not only by our own acts, but also by the acts of persons in our power, of slaves in whom we have a usufruct, and of freemen and slaves belonging to another but whom we possess in good faith. Let us now examine these cases in detail. Formerly, whatever was received by 1 a child in power of either sex, with the exception of military peculium, was acquired for the parent without any distinction ; and the parent was entitled to give away or sell to one child, or to a stranger, what had been acquired through another, or dispose of it in any other way that he pleased. This, however, seemed to us to be a cruel rule, and consequently by a general constitution which we have issued we have improved the children's position, and yet reserved to parents all that was their due. This enacts that whatever a child gains by and through property, of which his father allows him the control, is acquired, according to the old practice, for the father alone ; for what unfairness is there in property derived

from the father returning to him? But of anything which the
child derives from any source other than his father, though
his father will have a usufruct therein, the ownership is to
belong to the child, that he may not have the mortification of
seeing the gains which he has made by his own toil or good
2 fortune transferred to another. We have also made a new
rule relating to the right which a father had under earlier
constitutions, when he emancipated a child, of retaining
absolutely, if he pleased, a third part of such property of
the child as he himself had no ownership in, as a kind
of consideration for emancipating him. The harsh result of
this was that a son was by emancipation deprived of the
ownership of a third of his property; and thus the honour
which he got by being emancipated and made independent
was balanced by the diminution in his fortune. We have
therefore enacted that the parent, in such a case, shall no
longer retain the ownership of a third of the child's property,
but, in lieu thereof, the usufruct of one half; and thus the son
will remain absolute owner of the whole of his fortune, while
the father will reap a greater benefit than before, by being
3 entitled to the enjoyment of a half instead of a third. Again,
all rights which your slaves acquire by tradition, stipulation,
or any other title, are acquired for you, even though the
acquisition be without your knowledge, or even against your
will; for a slave, who is in the power of another person, can
have nothing of his own. Consequently, if he is instituted
heir, he must, in order to be able to accept the inheritance,
have the command of his master; and if he has that command, and accepts the inheritance, it is acquired for his
master exactly as if the latter had himself been instituted
heir; and it is precisely the same with a legacy. And not
only is ownership acquired for you by those in your power,
but also possession; for you are deemed to possess everything
of which they have obtained detention, and thus they are to
you instruments through whom ownership may be acquired
4 by usucapion or long possession. Respecting slaves in whom
a person has only a usufruct, the rule is, that what they
acquire by means of the property of the usufructuary, or by
their own work, is acquired for him; but what they acquire

by any other means belongs to their owner, to whom they belong themselves. Accordingly, if such a slave is instituted heir, or made legatee or donee, the succession, legacy, or gift is acquired, not for the usufructuary, but for the owner. And a man who in good faith possesses a free man or a slave belonging to another person has the same rights as a usufructuary; what they acquire by any other mode than the two we have mentioned belongs in the one case to the free man, in the other to the slave's real master. After a possessor in good faith has acquired the ownership of a slave by usucapion, everything which the slave acquires belongs to him without distinction; but a fructuary cannot acquire ownership of a slave in this way, because in the first place he does not possess the slave at all, but has merely a right of usufruct in him, and because in the second place he is aware of the existence of another owner. Moreover, you can acquire possession as well as ownership through slaves in whom you have a usufruct or whom you possess in good faith, and through free persons whom in good faith you believe to be your slaves, though as regards all these classes we must be understood to speak with strict reference to the distinction drawn above, and to mean only detention which they have obtained by means of your property or their own work. From this it appears that free men not subject to your power, 5 or whom you do not possess in good faith, and other persons' slaves, of whom you are neither usufructuaries nor just possessors, cannot under any circumstances acquire for you; and this is the meaning of the maxim that a man cannot be the means of acquiring anything for one who is a stranger in relation to him. To this maxim there is but one exception— namely, that, as is ruled in a constitution of the Emperor Severus, a free person, such as a general agent, can acquire possession for you, and that not only when you know, but even when you do not know of the fact of acquisition: and through this possession ownership can be immediately acquired also, if it was the owner who delivered the thing; and if it was not, it can be acquired ultimately by usucapion or by the plea of long possession.

So much at present concerning the modes of acquiring 6

rights over single things : for direct and fiduciary bequests, which are also among such modes, will find a more suitable place in a later portion of our treatise. We proceed therefore to the titles whereby an aggregate of rights is acquired. If you become the successors, civil or praetorian, of a person deceased, or adopt an independent person by adrogation, or become assignees of a deceased's estate in order to secure their liberty to slaves manumitted by his will, the whole estate of those persons is transferred to you in an aggregate mass. Let us begin with inheritances, whose mode of devolution is twofold, according as a person dies testate or intestate; and of these two modes we will first treat of acquisition by will. The first point which here calls for exposition is the mode in which wills are made.

TITLE X

OF THE EXECUTION OF WILLS

The term testament is derived from two words which mean a signifying of intention.

1 Lest the antiquities of this branch of law should be entirely forgotten, it should be known that originally two kinds of testaments were in use, one of which our ancestors employed in times of peace and quiet, and which was called the will made in the *comitia calata,* while the other was resorted to when they were setting out to battle, and was called *procinctum.* More recently a third kind was introduced, called the will by bronze and balance, because it was made by mancipation, which was a sort of fictitious sale, in the presence of five witnesses and a balance holder, all Roman citizens above the age of puberty, together with the person who was called the purchaser of the family. The two first-mentioned kinds of testament, however, went out of use even in ancient times, and even the third, or will by bronze and balance, though it has remained in vogue longer than they, 2 has become partly disused. All these three kinds of will which we have mentioned belonged to the civil law, but later still a fourth form was introduced by the praetor's edict; for the new law of the praetor, or *ius honorarium,* dispensed

with mancipation, and rested content with the seals of seven witnesses, whereas the seals of witnesses were not required by the civil law. When, however, by a gradual process the 3 civil and praetorian laws, partly by usage, partly by definite changes introduced by constitutions, came to be combined into a harmonious whole, it was enacted that a will should be valid which was wholly executed at one time and in the presence of seven witnesses (these two points being required, in a way, by the old civil law), to which the witnesses signed their names—a new formality imposed by imperial legisla-tion—and affixed their seals, as had been required by the praetor's edict. Thus the present law of testament seems to be derived from three distinct sources ; the witnesses, and the necessity of their all being present continuously through the execution of the will in order that that execution may be valid, coming from the civil law : the signing of the document by the testator and the witnesses being due to imperial constitutions, and the exact number of witnesses, and the sealing of the will by them, to the praetor's edict. An 4 additional requirement imposed by our constitution, in order to secure the genuineness of testaments and prevent forgery, is that the name of the heir shall be written by either the testator or the witnesses, and generally that everything shall be done according to the tenor of that enactment.

The witnesses may all seal the testament with the same 5 seal ; for, as Pomponius remarks, what if the device on all seven seals were the same ? It is also lawful for a witness to use a seal belonging to another person. Those persons only 6 can be witnesses who are legally capable of witnessing a tes-tament. Women, persons below the age of puberty, slaves, lunatics, persons dumb or deaf, and those who have been interdicted from the management of their property, or whom the law declares worthless and unfitted to perform this office, cannot witness a will. In cases where one of the 7 witnesses to a will was thought free at the time of its execu-tion, but was afterwards discovered to be a slave, the Emperor Hadrian, in his rescript to Catonius Verus, and afterwards the Emperors Severus and Antoninus declared that of their goodness they would uphold such a will as validly made ;

for, at the time when it was sealed, this witness was admitted by all to be free, and, as such, had had his civil position 8 called in question by no man. A father and a son in his power, or two brothers who are both in the power of one father, can lawfully witness the same testament, for there can be no harm in several persons of the same family witnessing 9 together the act of a man who is to them a stranger. No one, however, ought to be among the witnesses who is in the testator's power, and if a son in power makes a will of military peculium after his discharge, neither his father nor any one in his father's power is qualified to be a witness; for it is not allowed to support a will by the evidence of 10 persons in the same family with the testator. No will, again, can be witnessed by the person instituted heir, or by any one in his power, or by a father in whose power he is, or by a brother under the power of the same father: for the execution of a will is considered at the present day to be purely and entirely a transaction between the testator and the heir. Through mistaken ideas on this matter the whole law of testamentary evidence fell into confusion: for the ancients, though they rejected the evidence of the purchaser of the family and of persons connected with him by the tie of power, allowed a will to be witnessed by the heir and persons similarly connected with him, though it must be admitted that they accompanied this privilege with urgent cautions against its abuse. We have, however, amended this rule, and enacted in the form of law what the ancients expressed in the form only of advice, by assimilating the heir to the old purchaser of the family, and have rightly forbidden the heir, who now represents that character, and all other persons connected with him by the tie referred to, to bear witness in a matter in which, in a sense, they would be witnesses in their own behalf. Accordingly, we have not allowed earlier constitutions on this subject to be inserted 11 in our Code. Legatees, and persons who take a benefit under a will by way of trust, and those connected with them, we have not forbidden to be witnesses, because they are not universal successors of the deceased: indeed, by one of our constitutions we have specially granted this privilege to them, and, *a fortiori,* to persons in their power, or in whose power they are.

It is immaterial whether the will be written on a tablet, 12 paper, parchment, or any other substance : and a man may 13 execute any number of duplicates of his will, for this is sometimes necessary, though in each of them the usual formalities must be observed. For instance, a person setting out upon a voyage may wish to take a statement of his last wishes along with him, and also to leave one at home ; and numberless other circumstances which happen to a man, and over which he has no control, will make this desirable. So 14 far of written wills. When, however, one wishes to make a will binding by the civil law, but not in writing, he may summon seven witnesses, and in their presence orally declare his wishes ; this, it should be observed, being a form of will which has been declared by constitutions to be perfectly valid by civil law.

TITLE XI

OF SOLDIERS' WILLS

Soldiers, in consideration of their extreme ignorance of law, have been exempted by imperial constitutions from the strict rules for the execution of a testament which have been described. Neither the legal number of witnesses, nor the observance of the other rules which have been stated, is necessary to give force to their wills, provided, that is to say, that they are made by them while on actual service ; this last qualification being a new though wise one introduced by our constitution. Thus, in whatever mode a soldier's last wishes are declared, whether in writing or orally, this is a binding will, by force of his mere intention. At times, however, when they are not employed on actual service, but are living at home or elsewhere, they are not allowed to claim this privilege : they may make a will, even though they be sons in power, in virtue of their service, but they must observe the ordinary rules, and are bound by the forms which we described above as requisite in the execution of the wills of civilians. Respecting the testaments of soldiers the Emperor 1 Trajan sent a rescript to Statilius Severus in the following terms : ' The privilege allowed to soldiers of having their wills upheld, in whatever manner they are made, must be understood to be limited by the necessity of first proving that a will has been made at all ; for a will can be made without writing even by civilians. Accordingly, with reference to the inheritance which is the subject of the action before you, if it can be shown that the soldier who left it, did in the presence of witnesses, collected expressly for the purpose, declare orally who he wished to be his heir, and on what slaves he wished to confer liberty, it may well be maintained that in this way he made an unwritten testament, and his wishes therein declared ought to be carried out. But if, as is so common in ordinary conversation, he said to some one, " I make you my heir ", or, " I leave you all my property ", such expressions cannot be held to amount to a testament, and the interest of the very soldiers, who are privileged in the way described, is the principal ground for rejecting such a precedent. For if it were admitted, it would be easy, after a soldier's death, to procure witnesses to affirm that they had heard him say he left his property to any one they pleased to name, and in this way it would be impossible to 2 discover the true intentions of the deceased.' A soldier too 3 may make a will though dumb or deaf. This privilege, however, which we have said soldiers enjoy, is allowed them by imperial constitutions only while they are engaged on actual service, and in camp life. Consequently, if veterans wish to make a will after their discharge, or if soldiers actually serving wish to do this away from camp, they must observe the forms prescribed for all citizens by the general law ; and a testament executed in camp without formalities, that is to say, not according to the form prescribed by law, will remain valid only for one year after the testator's discharge. Supposing then that the testator died within a year, but that a condition, subject to which the heir was instituted, was not fulfilled within the year, would it be feigned that the testator was a soldier at the date of his decease, and the testament consequently be upheld? and this question we answer in the 4 affirmative. If a man, before going on actual service, makes an invalid will, and then during a campaign opens it, and adds some new disposition, or cancels one already made, or in some other way makes it clear that he wishes it to be his testament, it must be pronounced valid, as being, in fact, a new will made by the man as a soldier. Finally, if a 5 soldier is adrogated, or, being a son in power, is emancipated, his previously executed will remains good by the fiction of a new expression of his wishes as a soldier, and is not deemed to be avoided by his loss of status.

It is, however, to be observed that earlier statutes and 6 imperial constitutions allowed to children in power in certain cases a civil peculium after the analogy of the military peculium, which for that reason was called quasi-military, and of which some of them were permitted to dispose by will even while under power. By an extension of this principle our constitution has allowed all persons who have a peculium of this special kind to dispose of it by will, though subject to the ordinary forms of law. By a perusal of this constitution the whole law relating to this privilege may be ascertained.

TITLE XII

OF PERSONS INCAPABLE OF MAKING WILLS

Certain persons are incapable of making a lawful will. For instance, those in the power of others are so absolutely incapable that they cannot make a testament even with the permission of their parents, with the exception of those whom we have enumerated, and particularly of children in power who are soldiers, and who are permitted by imperial constitutions to dispose by will of all they may acquire while on actual service. This was allowed at first only to soldiers on active service, by the authority of the Emperors Augustus and Nerva, and of the illustrious Emperor Trajan; afterwards, it was extended by an enactment of the Emperor Hadrian to veterans, that is, soldiers who had received their discharge. Accordingly, if a son in power makes a will of his military peculium, it will belong to the person whom he institutes as heir: but if he dies intestate, leaving no children or brothers surviving him, it will go to the parent in whose power he is, according to the ordinary rule. From this it can be under-

stood, that a parent has no power to deprive a son in his power of what he has acquired on service, nor can the parent's creditors sell or otherwise touch it ; and when the parent dies it is not shared between the soldier's son and his brothers, but belongs to him alone, although by the civil law the peculium of a person in power is always reckoned as part of the property of the parent, exactly as that of a slave is deemed part of the property of his master, except of course such property of the son as by imperial constitutions, and especially our own, the parent is unable to acquire in absolute ownership. Consequently, if a son in power, not having a military or quasi-military peculium, makes a will, it is invalid, even though he is released from power before his decease.
1 Again, a person under the age of puberty is incapable of making a will, because he has no judgement, and so too is a lunatic, because he has lost his reason ; and it is immaterial that the one reaches the age of puberty, and the other re-covers his faculties, before his decease. If, however, a lunatic makes a will during a lucid interval, the will is deemed valid, and one is certainly valid which he made before he lost his reason : for subsequent insanity never avoids a duly executed
2 testament or any other disposition validly made. So too a spendthrift, who is interdicted from the management of his own affairs, is incapable of making a valid will, though one
3 made by him before being so interdicted holds good. The deaf, again, and the dumb cannot always make a will, though here we are speaking not of persons merely hard of hearing, but of total deafness, and similarly by a dumb person is meant one totally dumb, and not one who merely speaks with difficulty ; for it often happens that even men of culture and learning by some cause or other lose the faculties of speech and hearing. Hence relief has been afforded them by our constitution, which enables them, in certain cases and in certain modes therein specified, to make a will and other lawful dispositions. If a man, after making his will, becomes dumb or deaf through ill health or any other cause, it re-
4 mains valid notwithstanding. A blind man cannot make a will, except by observing the forms introduced by a law
5 of our imperial father Justin. A will made by a prisoner

while in captivity with the enemy is invalid, even though he subsequently returns. One made, however, while he was in his own state is valid, if he returns, by the law of postliminium ; if he dies in captivity it is valid by the lex Cornelia.

TITLE XIII

OF THE DISINHERISON OF CHILDREN

The law, however, is not completely satisfied by the observance of the rules hereinbefore explained. A testator who has a son in his power must take care either to institute him heir, or to specially disinherit him, for passing him over in silence avoids the will ; and this rule is so strict, that even if the son die in the lifetime of the father no heir can take under the will, because of its original nullity. As regards daughters and other descendants of either sex by the male line, the ancients did not observe this rule in all its strictness ; for if these persons were neither instituted nor disinherited, the will was not avoided, but they were entitled to come in with the instituted heirs, and to take a certain portion of the inheritance. And these persons the ascendant was not obliged to specially disinherit ; he could disinherit them collectively by a general clause. Special disinherison may 1 be expressed in these terms—' Be Titius my son disinherited ', or in these, ' Be my son disinherited,' without inserting the name, supposing there is no other son. Children born after the making of the will must also be either instituted heirs or disinherited, and in this respect are similarly privileged, that if a son or any other family heir, male or female, born after the making of the will, be passed over in silence, the will, though originally valid, is invalidated by the subsequent birth of the child, and so becomes completely void. Consequently, if the woman from whom a child was expected have an abortive delivery, there is nothing to prevent the instituted heirs from taking the inheritance. It was immaterial whether female family heirs born after the making of the will were disinherited specially or by a general clause, but if the latter mode be adopted, some legacy must be left them in order that they may not seem to have been passed over merely through inadvertence : but male family heirs born after the making of the will, sons and other lineal descendants, are held not to be properly disinherited unless they are disinherited specially, thus: 'Be any son that shall 2 be born to me disinherited.' With children born after the making of the will are classed children who succeed to the place of a family heir, and who thus, by an event analogous to subsequent birth, become family heirs to an ancestor. For instance, if a testator have a son, and by him a grandson or granddaughter in his power, the son alone, being nearer in degree, has the right of a family heir, although the grand-children are in the testator's power equally with him. But if the son die in the testator's lifetime, or is in some other way released from his power, the grandson and granddaughter succeed to his place, and thus, by a kind of subsequent birth, acquire the rights of family heirs. To prevent this subse-quent avoidance of one's will, grandchildren by a son must be either instituted heirs or disinherited, exactly as, to secure the original validity of a testament, a son must be either instituted or specially disinherited; for if the son die in the testator's lifetime, the grandson and granddaughter take his place, and avoid the will just as if they were children born after its execution. And this disinherison was first allowed by the lex Iunia Vellaea, which explains the form which is to be used, and which resembles that employed in disin-3 heriting family heirs born after the making of a will. It is not necessary, by the civil law, to either institute or disinherit emancipated children, because they are not family heirs. But the praetor requires all, females as well as males, unless instituted, to be disinherited, males specially, females col-lectively; and if they are neither appointed heirs nor dis-inherited as described, the praetor promises them possession 4 of goods against the will. Adopted children, so long as they are in the power of their adoptive father, are in precisely the same legal position as children born in lawful wedlock; consequently they must be either instituted or disinherited, according to the rules stated for the disinherison of natural children. When, however, they have been emancipated by their adoptive father, they are no longer regarded as his children either by the civil law or by the praetor's edict.

Conversely, in relation to their natural father, so long as they remain in the adoptive family they are strangers, so that he need neither institute nor disinherit them : but when emancipated by their adoptive father, they have the same rights in the succession to their natural father as they would have had if it had been he by whom they were emancipated. Such was the law introduced by our predecessors. Deeming, 5 however, that between the sexes, to each of which nature assigns an equal share in perpetuating the race of man, there is in this matter no real ground of distinction, and marking that, by the ancient statute of the Twelve Tables, all were called equally to the succession on the death of their ancestor intestate (which precedent the praetors also seem to have subsequently followed), we have by our constitution introduced a simple system of the same kind, applying uniformly to sons, daughters, and other descendants by the male line, whether born before or after the making of the will. This requires that all children, whether family heirs or emancipated, shall be specially disinherited, and declares that their pretermission shall have the effect of avoiding the will of their parent, and depriving the instituted heirs of the inheritance, no less than the pretermission of children who are family heirs or have been emancipated, whether already born, or born after, though conceived before the making of the will. In respect of adoptive children we have introduced a distinction, which is explained in our constitution on adoptions. If a soldier engaged on actual service makes a testament 6 without specially disinheriting his children, whether born before or after the making of the will, but simply passing them over in silence, though he knows that he has children, it is provided by imperial constitutions that his silent pretermission of them shall be equivalent to special disinherison. A mother or maternal grandfather is not bound to institute 7 her or his children or grandchildren ; they may simply omit them, for silence on the part of a mother, or of a maternal grandfather or other ascendant, has the same effect as actual disinherison by a father. For neither by the civil law, nor by that part of the praetor's edict in which he promises children who are passed over possession of goods against the will, is a mother obliged to disinherit her son or daughter if she does not institute them heirs, or a maternal grandfather to be equally precise with reference to grandchildren by a daughter: though such children and grandchildren, if omitted, have another remedy, which will shortly be explained.

TITLE XIV

OF THE INSTITUTION OF THE HEIR

A man may institute as his heirs either free men or slaves, and either his own slaves or those of another man. If he wished to institute his own slave it was formerly necessary, according to the more common opinion, that he should expressly give him his liberty in the will: but now it is lawful, by our constitution, to institute one's own slave without this express manumission—a change not due to any spirit of innovation, but to a sense of equity, and one whose principle was approved by Atilicinus, as is stated by Paulus in his books on Masurius Sabinus and on Plautius. Among a testator's own slaves is to be reckoned one of whom he is bare owner, the usufruct being vested in some other person. There is, however, one case in which the institution of a slave by his mistress is void, even though freedom be given him in the will, as is provided by a constitution of the Emperors Severus and Antoninus in these terms: 'Reason demands that no slave, accused of criminal intercourse with his mistress, shall be capable of being manumitted, before his sentence is pronounced, by the will of the woman who is accused of participating in his guilt: accordingly if he be instituted heir by that mistress, the institution is void.' Among 'other persons' slaves' is reckoned one in whom the testator has 1 a usufruct. If a slave is instituted heir by his own master, and continues in that condition until his master's decease, he becomes by the will both free, and necessary heir. But if the testator himself manumits him in his lifetime, he may use his own discretion about acceptance; for he is not a necessary heir, because, though he is named heir to the testament, it was not by that testament that he became free. If he has been alienated, he must have the order of his new master to accept, and then his master becomes heir through him, while he personally becomes neither heir nor free, even though his freedom was expressly given him in the testament, because by alienating him his former master is presumed to have renounced the intention of enfranchising him. When another person's slave is instituted heir, if he continues in the same condition he must have the order of his master to accept ; if alienated by him in the testator's lifetime, or after the testator's death but before acceptance, he must have the order of the alienee to accept ; finally, if manumitted in the testator's lifetime, or after the testator's death but before acceptance, he may accept or not at his own discretion. A 2 slave who does not belong to the testator may be instituted heir even after his master's decease, because slaves who belong to an inheritance are capable of being instituted or made legatees; for an inheritance not yet accepted represents not the future heir but the person deceased. Similarly, the slave of a child conceived but not yet born may be instituted heir. If a slave belonging to two or more joint owners, both or all 3 of whom are legally capable of being made heirs or legatees, is instituted heir by a stranger, he acquires the inheritance for each and all of the joint owners by whose orders he accepts it in proportion to the respective shares in which they own him.

A testator may institute either a single heir, or as many 4 as he pleases. An inheritance is usually divided into twelve 5 ounces, and is denoted in the aggregate by the term *as*, and each fraction of this aggregate, ranging from the ounce up to the *as* or pound, has its specific name, as follows : *sextans* $(\frac{1}{6})$, *quadrans* $(\frac{1}{4})$, *triens* $(\frac{1}{3})$, *quincunx* $(\frac{5}{12})$, *semis* $(\frac{1}{2})$, *septunx* $(\frac{7}{12})$, *bes* $(\frac{2}{3})$, *dodrans* $(\frac{3}{4})$, *dextans* $(\frac{5}{6})$, *deunx* $(\frac{11}{12})$, and *as*. It is not necessary, however, that there should always be twelve ounces, for for the purposes of testamentary distribution an *as* may consist of as many ounces as the testator pleases ; for instance, if a testator institutes only a single heir, but declares that he is to be heir *ex semisse,* or to one half of the inheritance, this half will really be the whole, for no one can die partly testate and partly intestate, except soldiers, in the carrying out of whose wills the intention is the only thing regarded. Conversely, a testator may divide his inheritance

6 into as large a number of ounces as he pleases. If more heirs than one are instituted, it is unnecessary for the testator to assign a specific share in the inheritance to each, unless he intends that they shall not take in equal portions ; for it is obvious that if no shares are specified they divide the inheritance equally between them. Supposing, however, that specific shares are assigned to all the instituted heirs except one, who is left without any express share at all, this last heir will be entitled to any fraction of the *as* which has not been disposed of ; and if there are two or more heirs to whom no specific shares have been assigned, they will divide this unassigned fraction equally between them. Finally, if the whole *as* has been assigned in specific shares to some of the heirs, the one or more who have no specific shares take half the inheritance, while the other half is divided among the rest according to the shares assigned to them ; and it is immaterial whether the heir who has no specified share comes first or last in the institution, or occupies some intermediate place ; for such share is presumed to be given to him as is

7 not in some other way disposed of. Let us now see how the law stands if some part remains undisposed of, and yet each heir has his share assigned to him—if, for instance, there are three heirs instituted, and each is assigned a quarter of the inheritance. It is evident that in this case the part undisposed of will go to them in proportion to the share each has assigned to him by the will, and it will be exactly as if they had each been originally instituted to a third. Conversely, if each heir is given so large a fraction that the *as* will be exceeded, each must suffer a proportionate abatement ; thus if four heirs are instituted, and to each is assigned a third of the inheritance, it will be the same as if each had been originally instituted to

8 a quarter. If more than twelve ounces are distributed among some of the heirs only, one being left without a specific share, he will have what is wanting to complete the second *as* ; and the same will be done if more than twenty-four ounces are distributed, leaving him shareless ; but all these ideal sums are afterwards reduced to the single *as*, whatever be the number of ounces they comprise.

9　The institution of the heir may be either absolute or conditional, but no heir can be instituted from, or up to, some definite date, as, for instance, in the following form—'be so and so my heir after five years from my decease', or 'after the calends of such a month', or 'up to and until such calends'; for a time limitation in a will is considered a superfluity, and an heir instituted subject to such a time limitation is treated as heir absolutely. If the institution of an heir, a legacy, 10 a fiduciary bequest, or a testamentary manumission is made to depend on an impossible condition, the condition is deemed unwritten, and the disposition absolute. If an institution is 11 made to depend on two or more conditions, conjunctively expressed,—as, for instance, 'if this and that shall be done'— all the conditions must be satisfied : if they are expressed in the alternative, or disjunctively—as 'if this or that shall be done'—it is enough if one of them alone is satisfied.

A testator may institute as his heir a person whom he has 12 never seen, for instance, nephews who have been born abroad and are unknown to him : for want of this knowledge does not invalidate the institution.

TITLE XV

OF ORDINARY SUBSTITUTION

A testator may institute his heirs, if he pleases, in two or more degrees, as, for instance, in the following form : 'If A shall not be my heir, then let B be my heir'; and in this way he can make as many substitutions as he likes, naming in the last place one of his own slaves as necessary heir, in default of all others taking. Several may be substituted in place of 1 one, or one in place of several, or to each heir may be substituted a new and distinct person, or, finally, the instituted heirs may be substituted reciprocally in place of one another. If heirs who are instituted in equal shares are reciprocally 2 substituted to one another, and the shares which they are to have in the substitution are not specified, it is presumed (as was settled by a rescript of the Emperor Pius) that the testator intended them to take the same shares in the substitution as they took directly under the will. If a third 3 person is substituted to one heir who himself is substituted to his co-heir, the Emperors Severus and Antoninus have

decided by rescript that this third person is entitled to the
4 shares of both without distinction. If a testator institutes
another man's slave, supposing him to be an independent
person, and substitutes Maevius in his place to meet the case
of his not taking the inheritance, then, if the slave accepts by
the order of his master, Maevius is entitled to a half. For,
when applied to a person whom the testator knows to be in
the power of another, the words 'if he shall not be my heir'
are taken to mean 'if he shall neither be heir himself nor
cause another to be heir'; but when applied to a person
whom the testator supposes to be independent, they mean
'if he shall not acquire the inheritance either for himself, or
for that person to whose power he shall subsequently become
subject', and this was decided by Tiberius Caesar in the case
of his slave Parthenius.

TITLE XVI

OF PUPILLARY SUBSTITUTION

To children below the age of puberty and in the power of
the testator, not only can such a substitute as we have described be appointed, that is, one who shall take on their
failing to inherit, but also one who shall be their heir if, after
inheriting, they die within the age of puberty; and this may
be done in the following terms, 'Be my son Titius my heir;
and if he does not become my heir, or, after becoming my
heir, die before becoming his own master (that is, before
reaching puberty), then be Seius my heir.' In which case, if
the son fails to inherit, the substitute is the heir of the
testator; but if the son, after inheriting, dies within the age
of puberty, he is the heir of the son. For it is a rule of
customary law, that when our children are too young to make
wills for themselves, their parents may make them for them.
1 The reason of this rule has induced us to insert in our Code
a constitution, providing that if a testator has children, grandchildren, or great-grandchildren who are lunatics or idiots, he
may, after the analogy of pupillary substitution, substitute
certain definite persons to them, whatever their sex or the
nearness of their relationship to him, and even though they
have reached the age of puberty; provided always that on

their recovering their faculties such substitution shall at once
become void, exactly as pupillary substitution proper ceases
to have any operation after the pupil has reached puberty.
Thus, in pupillary substitution effected in the form described, 2
there are, so to speak, two wills, the father's and the son's,
just as if the son had personally instituted an heir to himself;
or rather, there is one will dealing with two distinct matters,
that is, with two distinct inheritances. If a testator be appre- 3
hensive that, after his own death, his son, while still a pupil,
may be exposed to the danger of foul play, because another
person is openly substituted to him, he ought to make the
ordinary substitution openly, and in the earlier part of the
testament, and write the other substitution, wherein a man is
named heir on the succession and death of the pupil, separately on the lower part of the will; and this lower part he
should tie with a separate cord and fasten with a separate
seal, and direct in the earlier part of the will that it shall not
be opened in the lifetime of the son before he attains the
age of puberty. Of course a substitution to a son under
the age of puberty is none the less valid because it is an integral
part of the very will in which the testator has instituted him
his heir, though such an open substitution may expose the
pupil to the danger of foul play. Not only when we leave our 4
inheritance to children under the age of puberty can we make
such a substitution, that if they accept the inheritance, and
then die under that age, the substitute is their heir, but we
can do it when we disinherit them, so that whatever the
pupil acquires by way of inheritance, legacy or gift from his
relatives or friends, will pass to the substitute. What has been
said of substitution to children below the age of puberty,
whether instituted or disinherited, is true also of substitution
to afterborn children. In no case, however, may a man make 5
a will for his children unless he makes one also for himself;
for the will of the pupil is but a complementary part of the
father's own testament; accordingly, if the latter is void, the
former will be void also. Substitution may be made either 6
to each child separately, or only to such one of them as shall
last die under the age of puberty. The first is the proper
plan, if the testator's intention is that none of them shall die

intestate: the second, if he wishes that, as among them, the order of succession prescribed by the Twelve Tables shall be 7 strictly preserved. The person substituted in the place of a child under the age of puberty may be either named individually—for instance, Titius—or generally described, as by the words 'whoever shall be my heir'; in which latter case, on the child dying under the age of puberty, those are called to the inheritance by the substitution who have been instituted heirs and have accepted, their shares in the substitution being proportionate to the shares in which they succeeded the 8 father. This kind of substitution may be made to males up to the age of fourteen, and to females up to that of twelve years; when this age is once passed, the substitution 9 becomes void. To a stranger, or a child above the age of puberty whom a man has instituted heir, he cannot appoint a substitute to succeed him if he take and die within a certain time: he has only the power to bind him by a trust to convey the inheritance to another either wholly or in part; the law relating to which subject will be explained in its proper place.

TITLE XVII

OF THE MODES IN WHICH WILLS BECOME VOID

A duly executed testament remains valid until either re-1 voked or rescinded. A will is revoked when, though the civil condition of the testator remains unaltered, the legal force of the will itself is destroyed, as happens when, after making his will, a man adopts as his son either an independent person, in which case the adoption is effected by imperial decree, or a person already in power, when it is done through the agency of the praetor according to our constitution. In both these cases the will is revoked, precisely as it would be by the 2 subsequent birth of a family heir. Again, a subsequent will duly executed is a revocation of a prior will, and it makes no difference whether an heir ever actually takes under it or not; the only question is whether one might conceivably have done so. Accordingly, whether the person instituted declines to be heir, or dies in the lifetime of the testator, or after his death but before accepting the inheritance, or is excluded by failure of the condition under which he was instituted—in all these cases the testator dies intestate; for the earlier will is revoked by the later one, and the later one is inoperative, as no heir takes under it. If, after duly making 3 one will, a man executes a second one which is equally valid, the Emperors Severus and Antoninus decided by rescript that the first is revoked by the second, even though the heir instituted in the second is instituted to certain things only. The terms of this enactment we have ordered to be inserted here, because it contains another provision. 'The Emperors Severus and Antoninus to Cocceius Campanus. A second will, although the heir named therein be instituted to certain things only, is just as valid as if no mention of the things had been made: but the heir is bound to content himself with the things given him, or with such further portion of the inheritance as will make up the fourth part to which he is entitled under the lex Falcidia, and (subject thereto) to transfer the inheritance to the persons instituted in the earlier will: for the words inserted in the later will undoubtedly contain the expression of a wish that the earlier one shall remain valid.' This accordingly is a mode in which a testament may be revoked. There is another event by which a 4 will duly executed may be invalidated, namely, the testator's undergoing a loss of status: how this may happen was explained in the preceding Book. In this case the will may be 5 said to be rescinded, though both those that are revoked, and those that are not duly executed, may be said to become or be rescinded; and similarly too those which are duly executed but subsequently rescinded by loss of status may be said to be revoked. However, as it is convenient that different grounds of invalidity should have different names to distinguish them, we say that some wills are unduly executed from the commencement, while others which are duly executed are either revoked or rescinded. Wills, however, which, 6 though duly executed, are subsequently rescinded by the testator's undergoing loss of status are not altogether inoperative: for if the seals of seven witnesses are attached, the instituted heir is entitled to demand possession in accordance with the will, if only the testator were a citizen of Rome

and independent at the time of his decease; but if the cause
of the rescission was the testator's subsequent loss of citizenship or of freedom, or his adoption, and he dies an alien, or
slave, or subject to his adoptive father's power, the instituted
heir is barred from demanding possession in accordance with
7 the will. The mere desire of a testator that a will which he
has executed shall no longer have any validity is not, by
itself, sufficient to avoid it ; so that, even if he begins to make
a later will, which he does not complete because he either
dies first, or changes his mind, the first will remains good ;
it being provided in an address of the Emperor Pertinax
to the Senate that one testament which is duly executed
is not revoked by a later one which is not duly and completely executed ; for an incomplete will is undoubtedly null.
8 In the same address the Emperor declared that he would
accept no inheritance to which he was made heir on account
of a suit between the testator and some third person, nor
would he uphold a will in which he was instituted in order
to screen some legal defect in its execution, or accept an
inheritance to which he was instituted merely by word of
mouth, or take any testamentary benefit under a document
defective in point of law. And there are numerous rescripts
of the Emperors Severus and Antoninus to the same purpose :
' for though,' they say, ' the laws do not bind us, yet we live
in obedience to them.'

TITLE XVIII

OF AN UNDUTEOUS WILL

Inasmuch as the disinherison or omission by parents of
their children has generally no good reason, those children
who complain that they have been wrongfully disinherited or
passed over have been allowed to bring an action impeaching
the will as unduteous, under the pretext that the testator was
of unsound mind at the time of its execution. This does not
mean that he was really insane, but that the will, though
legally executed, bears no mark of that affection to which
a child is entitled from a parent: for if a testator is really
1 insane, his will is void. Parents may impeach the wills of
their children as unduteous, as well as children those of their

parents. Brothers and sisters of the testator are by imperial
constitutions preferred to infamous persons who are instituted
to their exclusion, so that it is in these cases only that they
can bring this action. Persons related to the testator in
a further degree than as brothers or sisters can in no case
bring the action, or at any rate succeed in it when brought.
Children fully adopted, in accordance with the distinction 2
drawn in our constitution, can bring this action as well as
natural children, but neither can do so unless there is no
other mode in which they can obtain the property of the
deceased : for those who can obtain the inheritance wholly
or in part by any other title are barred from attacking a will
as unduteous. Afterborn children too can employ this remedy,
if they can by no other means recover the inheritance. That 3
they may bring the action must be understood to mean,
that they may bring it only if absolutely nothing has been
left them by the testator in his will : a restriction introduced
by our constitution out of respect for a father's natural rights.
If, however, a part of the inheritance, however small, or even
a single thing is left them, the will cannot be impeached, but
the heir must, if necessary, make up what is given them to
a fourth of what they would have taken had the testator died
intestate, even though the will does not direct that this fourth
is to be made up by the assessment of an honest and reliable
man. If a guardian accepts, under his own father's will, 4
a legacy on behalf of the pupil under his charge, the father
having left nothing to him personally, he is in no way
debarred from impeaching his father's will as unduteous on
his own account. On the other hand, if he impeaches the 5
will of his pupil's father on the pupil's behalf, because nothing
has been left to the latter, and is defeated in the action, he
does not lose a legacy given in the same will to himself
personally. Accordingly, that a person may be barred from 6
the action impeaching the will, it is requisite that he should
have a fourth of what he would have taken on intestacy,
either as heir, legatee direct or fiduciary, donee in contemplation of death, by gift from the testator in his lifetime (though
gift of this latter kind bars the action only if made under any
of the circumstances mentioned in our constitution) or in

any of the other modes stated in the imperial legislation.
7 In what we have said of the fourth we must be understood
to mean that whether there be one person only, or more
than one, who can impeach the will as unduteous, one-fourth
of the whole inheritance may be given them, to be divided
among them all proportionately, that is to say, to each
person a fourth of what he would have had if the testator
had died intestate.

Title XIX

OF THE KINDS OF AND DIFFERENCES BETWEEN HEIRS

Heirs are of three kinds, that is to say, they are either
1 necessary, family heirs and necessary, or external. A necessary heir is a slave of the testator, whom he institutes as
heir : and he is so named because, willing or unwilling, and
without any alternative, he becomes free and necessary heir
immediately on the testator's decease. For when a man's
affairs are embarrassed, it is common for one of his slaves
to be instituted in his will, either in the first place, or as
a substitute in the second or any later place, so that, if the
creditors are not paid in full, the heir may be insolvent rather
than the testator, and his property, rather than the testator's,
may be sold by the creditors and divided among them. To
balance this disadvantage he has this advantage, that his
acquisitions after the testator's decease are for his own sole
benefit ; and although the estate of the deceased is insufficient
to pay the creditors in full, the heir's subsequent acquisitions
2 are never on that account liable to a second sale. Heirs who
are both family heirs and necessary are such as a son or
a daughter, a grandchild by a son, and further similar lineal
descendants, provided that they are in the ancestor's power
at the time of his decease. To make a grandson or granddaughter a family heir it is, however, not sufficient for them
to be in the grandfather's power at the moment of his decease : it is further requisite that their own father shall, in
the lifetime of the grandfather, have ceased to be family heir
himself, whether by death or by any other mode of release
from power : for by this event the grandson and granddaughter succeed to the place of their father. They are

called family heirs, because they are heirs of the house, and even in the lifetime of the parent are to a certain extent deemed owners of the inheritance : wherefore in intestacy the first right of succession belongs to the children. They are called necessary heirs because they have no alternative, but, willing or unwilling, both where there is a will and where there is not, they become heirs. The praetor, however, permits them, if they wish, to abstain from the inheritance, and leave the parent to become insolvent rather than themselves.

Those who were not subject to the testator's power are 3 called external heirs. Thus children of ours who are not in our power, if instituted heirs by us, are deemed external heirs ; and children instituted by their mother belong to this class, because women never have children in their power. Slaves instituted heirs by their masters, and manumitted subsequently to the execution of the will, belong to the same class. It is necessary that external heirs should have testamentary 4 capacity, whether it is an independent person, or some one in his power, who is instituted : and this capacity is required at two times ; at the time of the making of the will, when, without it, the institution would be void ; and at the time of the testator's decease, when, without it, the institution would have no effect. Moreover, the instituted heir ought to have this capacity also at the time when he accepts the inheritance, whether he is instituted absolutely or subject to a condition; and indeed it is especially at this time that his capacity to take ought to be looked to. If, however, the instituted heir undergoes a loss of status in the interval between the making of the will and the testator's decease, or the satisfaction of the condition subject to which he was instituted, he is not thereby prejudiced : for, as we said, there are only three points of time which have to be regarded. Testamentary capacity thus does not mean merely capacity to make a will ; it also means capacity to take for oneself, or for the father or master in whose power one is, under the will of another person : and this latter kind of testamentary capacity is quite independent of the capacity to make a will oneself. Accordingly, even lunatics, deaf persons, after-born children, infants, children in power, and other persons' slaves are said to have testamentary

capacity ; for though they cannot make a valid will, they can
acquire for themselves or for another under a will made by
5 some one else. External heirs have the privilege of de-
liberating whether they will accept or disclaim an inheritance.
But if a person who is entitled to disclaim interferes with the
inheritance, or if one who has the privilege of deliberation
accepts it, he no longer has the power of relinquishing it,
unless he is a minor under the age of twenty-five years, for
minors obtain relief from the praetor when they incautiously
accept a disadvantageous inheritance, as well as when they
6 take any other injudicious step. It is, however, to be observed
that the Emperor Hadrian once relieved even a person who
had attained his majority, when, after his accepting the inheritance, a great debt, unknown at the time of acceptance,
had come to light. This was but the bestowal of an
especial favour on a single individual ; the Emperor Gordian
subsequently extended the privilege, but only to soldiers,
to whom it was granted as a class. We, however, in our
benevolence have placed this benefit within the reach of
all our subjects, and drafted a constitution as just as it is
splendid, under which, if heirs will but observe its terms, they
can accept an inheritance without being liable to creditors
and legatees beyond the value of the property. Thus so
far as their liability is concerned there is no need for them
to deliberate on acceptance, unless they fail to observe the
procedure of our constitution, and prefer deliberation, by
which they will remain liable to all the risks of acceptance
7 under the older law. An external heir, whether his right
accrue to him under a will or under the civil law of intestate
succession, can take the inheritance either by acting as heir,
or by the mere intention to accept. By acting as heir is
meant, for instance, using things belonging to the inheritance
as one's own, or selling them, or cultivating or giving leases
of the deceased's estates, provided only one expresses in any
way whatsoever, by deed or word, one's intention to accept
the inheritance, so long as one knows that the person with
whose property one is thus dealing has died testate or intestate, and that one is that person's heir. To act as heir,
in fact, is to act as owner, and the ancients often used the

term 'heir' as equivalent to the term 'owner'. And just as the mere intention to accept makes an external heir heir, so too the mere determination not to accept bars him from the inheritance. Nothing prevents a person who is born deaf or dumb, or who becomes so after birth, from acting as heir and thus acquiring the inheritance, provided only he knows what he is doing.

TITLE XX

OF LEGACIES

Let us now examine legacies :—a kind of title which seems foreign to the matter in hand, for we are expounding titles whereby aggregates of rights are acquired ; but as we have treated in full of wills and heirs appointed by will, it was natural in close connexion therewith to consider this mode of acquisition.

Now a legacy is a kind of gift left by a person deceased; 1 and formerly they were of four kinds, namely, legacy by vin- 2 dication, by condemnation, by permission, and by preception, to each of which a definite form of words was appropriated by which it was known, and which served to distinguish it from legacies of the other kinds. Solemn forms of words of this sort, however, have been altogether abolished by imperial constitutions ; and we, desiring to give greater effect to the wishes of deceased persons, and to interpret their expressions with reference rather to those wishes than to their strict literal meaning, have issued a constitution, composed after great reflection, enacting that in future there shall be but one kind of legacy, and that, whatever be the terms in which the bequest is couched, the legatee may sue for it no less by real or hypothecary than by personal action. How carefully and wisely this constitution is worded may be ascertained by a perusal of its contents. We have determined, however, 3 to go even beyond this enactment ; for, observing that the ancients subjected legacies to strict rules, while the rules which they applied to fiduciary bequests, as springing more directly from the deceased person's wishes, were more liberal, we have deemed it necessary to assimilate the former completely to the latter, so that any features in which legacies are inferior to fiduciary bequests may be supplied to them from the latter, and the latter themselves may in future possess any superiority which has hitherto been enjoyed by legacies only. In order, however, to avoid perplexing students in their first essays in the law by discussing these two forms of bequest together, we have thought it worth while to treat them separately, dealing first with legacies, and then with fiduciary bequests, so that the reader, having first learnt their respective natures in a separate treatment, may, when his legal education is more advanced, be able easily to comprehend their treatment in combination.

4 A legacy may be given not only of things belonging to the testator or heir, but also of things belonging to a third person, the heir being bound by the will to buy and deliver them to the legatee, or to give him their value if the owner is unwilling to sell them. If the thing given be one of those of which private ownership is impossible, such, for instance, as the Campus Martius, a basilica, a church, or a thing devoted to public use, not even its value can be claimed, for the legacy is void. In saying that a thing belonging to a third person may be given as a legacy we must be understood to mean that this may be done if the deceased knew that it belonged to a third person, and not if he was ignorant of this: for perhaps he would never have given the legacy if he had known that the thing belonged neither to him nor to the heir, and there is a rescript of the Emperor Pius to this effect. It is also the better opinion that the plaintiff, that is the legatee, must prove that the deceased knew he was giving as a legacy a thing which was not his own, rather than that the heir must prove the contradictory : for the general rule of law is that the burden of proof lies on the plaintiff.

5 If the thing which a testator bequeaths is in pledge to a creditor, the heir is obliged to redeem it, subject to the same distinction as has been drawn with reference to a legacy of a thing not belonging to the testator ; that is to say, the heir is bound to redeem only if the deceased knew the thing to be in pledge : and the Emperors Severus and Antoninus have decided this by rescript. If, however, the deceased expresses his intention that the legatee should redeem the thing him-

self, the heir is under no obligation to do it for him. If a 6
legacy is given of a thing belonging to another person, and
the legatee becomes its owner during the testator's lifetime
by purchase, he can obtain its value from the heir by action
on the will: but if he gives no consideration for it, that is to
say, gets it by way of gift or by some similar title, he cannot
sue ; for it is settled law that where a man has already got
a thing, giving no consideration in return, he cannot get its
value by a second title of the same kind. Accordingly, if
a man is entitled to claim a thing under each of two distinct
wills, it is material whether he gets the thing, or merely its
value, under the earlier one: for if he gets the thing itself,
he cannot sue under the second will, because he already has
the thing without giving any consideration, whereas he has a
good right of action if he has merely got its value. A thing 7
which does not yet exist, but will exist, may be validly bequeathed :—for instance, the produce of such and such land,
or the child of such and such female slave. If the same 8
thing is given as a legacy to two persons, whether jointly or
severally, and both claim it, each is entitled to only a half ;
if one of them does not claim it, because either he does not
care for it, or has died in the testator's lifetime, or for some
other reason, the whole goes to his co-legatee. A joint legacy
is given in such words as the following : ' I give and bequeath
my slave Stichus to Titius and Seius ': a several legacy thus,
' I give and bequeath my slave Stichus to Titius : I give and
bequeath Stichus to Seius': and even if the testator says
'the same slave Stichus' the legacy is still a several one.
If land be bequeathed which belongs to some one other than 9
the testator, and the intended legatee, after purchasing the
bare ownership therein, obtains the usufruct without consideration, and then sues under the will, Julian says that this
action for the land is well grounded, because in a real action
for land a usufruct is regarded merely as a servitude ; but it is
part of the duty of the judge to deduct the value of the usufruct from the sum which he directs to be paid as the value
of the land. A legacy by which something already belong- 10
ing to the legatee is given him is void, for what is his own
already cannot become more his own than it is : and even

though he alienates it before the testator's death, neither it nor
11 its value can be claimed. If a testator bequeaths something
belonging to him, but which he thought belonged to another
person, the legacy is good, for its validity depends not on
what he thought, but on the real facts of the case : and it is
clearly good if he thought it already belonged to the legatee,
12 because his expressed wish can thus be carried out. If, after
making his will, a testator alienates property which he has
therein given away as a legacy, Celsus is of opinion that the
legatee may still claim it unless the testator's intention was
thereby to revoke the bequest, and there is a rescript of the
Emperors Severus and Antoninus to this effect, as well as
another which decides that if, after making his will, a testator
pledges land which he had therein given as a legacy, he is not
to be deemed to have thereby revoked the bequest, and that
consequently the legatee can enforce by action the heir's
obligation to redeem the pledge. And if a testator alienates
part of a thing which he has given as a legacy, the part
which has not been alienated can in any case be claimed, and
the alienated part as well if the alienor's intention was not to
13 revoke the legacy. If a man bequeaths to his debtor a discharge from his debt, the legacy is good, and the testator's
heir cannot sue either the debtor himself, or his heir, or any
one who occupies the position of heir to him, and the debtor
can even compel the testator's heir to formally release him.
Moreover, a testator can also forbid his heir to claim payment
14 of a debt before a certain time has elapsed. Contrariwise, if
a debtor leaves his creditor a legacy of what he owes him, the
legacy is void, if it includes no more than the debt, for
the creditor is thus in no way benefited ; but if the debtor
unconditionally bequeaths a sum of money which the creditor
cannot claim until a definite date has arrived or a condition
has been satisfied, the legacy is good, because it confers on
the creditor a right to earlier payment. And, even if the
day arrives, or the condition is satisfied, during the testator's
lifetime, Papinian decides, and rightly, that the legacy is
nevertheless a good one, because it was good when first
written ; for the opinion that a legacy becomes void, because
something happens to deprive it of all material effect, is now

rejected. If a man leaves his wife a legacy of her dowry, the 15 gift is good, because the legacy is worth more than a mere right of action for the dowry. If, however, he has never received the dowry which he bequeaths, the Emperors Severus and Antoninus have decided by rescript that the legacy is void, provided the general term 'dowry' is used, but good, if in giving it to the wife a definite sum or thing is specified, or described generally by reference to the dowry deed. If 16 a thing bequeathed perishes through no act of the heir, the loss falls on the legatee : thus if a slave belonging to another person, who is given in this way, is manumitted through no act of the heir, the latter is not bound. If, however, the slave belongs to the heir, who manumits him, Julian says that he is bound, and it is immaterial whether he knew or not that the slave had been bequeathed away from him ; and he is also bound if the slave be manumitted by another person to whom he has given him, even though he was unaware that he had been bequeathed away from him. If a testator gives 17 a legacy of female slaves along with their offspring, the legatee can claim the latter even if the mothers are dead, and so again if a legacy is given of ordinary slaves along with their *vicarii* or subordinates, the latter can be claimed even if the former are dead. But if the legacy be of a slave along with his peculium, and the slave is dead, or has been manumitted or alienated, the legacy of the peculium is extinguished ; and similarly, if the legacy be of land with everything upon it, or with all its instruments of tillage, by the alienation of the land the legacy of the instruments of tillage is extinguished. If a flock be given as a legacy, 18 which is subsequently reduced to a single sheep, this single survivor can be claimed ; and Julian says that in a legacy of 19 a flock are comprised sheep which are added to it after the making of the will, a flock being but one aggregate composed of distinct members, just as a house is but one aggregate composed of distinct stones built together. So if the legacy consist of a house, we hold that pillars or marbles added to it after the making of the will pass under the bequest. If a 20 slave's peculium be given as a legacy, the legatee undoubtedly profits by what is added to it, and is a loser by what is taken

from it, during the testator's lifetime. Whatever the slave
acquires in the interval between the testator's death and the
acceptance of the inheritance belongs, according to Julian, to
the legatee, if that legatee be the slave himself who is manumitted by the will, because a legacy of this kind vests from
the acceptance of the inheritance : but if the legatee be a
stranger, he is not entitled to such acquisitions, unless they
are made by means of the peculium itself. A slave manumitted by a will is not entitled to his peculium unless it is
expressly bequeathed to him, though, if the master manumits him in his lifetime, it is enough if it be not expressly
taken from him, and to this effect the Emperors Severus and
Antoninus have decided by rescript : as also, that a legacy of
his peculium to a slave does not carry with it the right to sue
for money which he has expended on his master's account,
and that a legacy of a peculium may be inferred from directions in a will that a slave is to be free so soon as he has
made a statement of his accounts and made up any balance,
21 which may be against him, from his peculium. Incorporeal
as well as corporeal things can be bequeathed : thus a man
can leave a legacy even of a debt which is owed to him, and
the heir can be compelled to transfer to the legatee his rights
of action, unless the testator has exacted payment in his lifetime, in which case the legacy is extinguished. Again, such
a legacy as the following is good : ' be my heir bound to repair
22 so and so's house, or to pay so and so's debts.' If a legacy be
a general one, as of a slave or some other thing not specifically
determined, the legatee is entitled to choose what slave, or
what thing, he will have, unless the testator has expressed
23 a contrary intention. A legacy of selection, that is, when a
testator directs the legatee to select one from among his
slaves, or any other class of things, was held to be given
subject to an implied condition that the legatee should make
the choice in person ; so that if he died before doing so the
legacy did not pass to his heir. By our constitution, however,
we have made an improvement in this matter, and allowed the
legatee's heir to exercise the right of selection, although the
legatee has not done so personally in his lifetime ; which
enactment, through our careful attention to the subject,

contains the further provision, that if there are either several co-legatees to whom a right of selection has been bequeathed, and who cannot agree in their choice, or several co-heirs of a single legatee, who differ through some wishing to choose this thing and others that, the question shall be decided by fortune—the legacy not being extinguished, which many of the jurists in an ungenerous spirit wished to make the rule—; that is to say, that lots shall be drawn, and he on whom the lot falls shall have a priority of choice over the rest.

Those persons only can be legatees who have testamentary 24 capacity, that is, who are legally capable of taking under a will. Formerly it was not allowed to leave either legacies 25 or fiduciary bequests to uncertain persons, and even soldiers, as the Emperor Hadrian decided by rescript, were unable to benefit uncertain persons in this way. An uncertain person was held to be one of whom the testator had no certain conception, as the legatee in the following form : ' Whoever bestows his daughter in marriage on my son, do thou, my heir, give him such or such land.' So too a legacy left to the first consuls designate after the writing of the will was held to be given to an uncertain person, and many others that might be instanced : and so it was held that freedom could not be bequeathed to an uncertain person, because it was settled that slaves ought to be enfranchised by name, and an uncertain person could not be appointed guardian. But a legacy given with a certain demonstration, that is, to an uncertain member of a certain class, was valid, for instance, the following : ' Whoever of all my kindred now alive shall first marry my daughter, do thou, my heir, give him such or such thing.' It was, however, provided by imperial constitutions that legacies or fiduciary bequests left to uncertain persons and paid by mistake could not be recovered back. An after-born stranger again could not take a legacy ; an 26 after-born stranger being one who on his birth will not be a family heir to the testator ; thus a grandson by an emancipated son was held to be an after-born stranger to his grandfather. These parts of the law, however, have not been left 27 without due alteration, a constitution having been inserted in our Code by which we have in these respects amended the

rules relating to legacies and fiduciary bequests no less than
to inheritances, as will be made clear by a perusal of the
enactment, which, however, still maintains the old rule that an
uncertain person cannot be appointed guardian: for when
a testator is appointing a guardian for his issue, he ought
to be quite clear as to the person and character of the party
28 he selects. An after-born stranger could and still can be
instituted heir, unless conceived of a woman who cannot by
29 law be a man's wife. If a testator makes a mistake in any
of the names of the legatee, the legacy is nevertheless valid
provided there is no doubt as to the person he intended, and
the same rule is very properly observed as to heirs as well as
legatees; for names are used only to distinguish persons, and
if the person can be ascertained in other ways a mistake in
30 the name is immaterial. Closely akin to this rule is another,
namely, that an erroneous description of the thing bequeathed
does not invalidate the bequest; for instance, if a testator
says, 'I give and bequeath Stichus my born slave,' the legacy
is good, if it is quite clear who is meant by Stichus, even
though it turn out that he was not born the testator's slave,
but was purchased by him. Similarly, if he describe Stichus
as 'the slave I bought from Seius', whereas in fact he bought
him from some one else, the legacy is good, if it is clear what
31 slave he intended to give. Still less is a legacy invalidated
by a wrong motive being assigned by the testator for giving
it: if, for instance, he says, 'I give and bequeath Stichus to
Titius, because he looked after my affairs while I was away,'
or 'because I was acquitted on a capital charge through his
undertaking my defence', the legacy is still good, although
in point of fact Titius never did look after the testator's
affairs, or never did, through his advocacy, procure his acquittal. But the law is different if the testator expresses his
motive in the guise of a condition, as: 'I give and bequeath
such and such land to Titius, if he has looked after my affairs.'
32 It is questioned whether a legacy to a slave of the heir is
valid. It is clear that such a legacy is void if given unconditionally, even though the slave ceases to belong to the
heir during the testator's lifetime: for a legacy which would
be void if the testator died immediately after making his will

ought not to become valid by the simple fact of the testator's
living longer. Such a legacy, however, is good if given subject
to a condition, the question then being, whether at the vesting
of the legacy the slave has ceased to belong to the heir. On 33
the other hand, there is no doubt that even an absolute
legacy to the master of a slave who is instituted heir is good:
for, even supposing that the testator dies immediately after
making the will, the right to the legacy does not necessarily
belong to the person who is heir ; for the inheritance and the
legacy are separable, and a different person from the legatee
may become heir through the slave ; as happens if, before the
slave accepts the inheritance at his master's bidding, he is
conveyed to another person, or is manumitted and thus
becomes heir himself; in both of which cases the legacy is
valid. But if he remains in the same condition, and accepts
at his master's bidding, the legacy is extinguished. A legacy 34
given before an heir was appointed was formerly void, because
a will derives its operation from the appointment of an heir,
and accordingly such appointment is deemed the beginning
and foundation of the whole testament, and for the same
reason a slave could not be enfranchised before an heir was
appointed. Yet even the old lawyers themselves disapproved
of sacrificing the real intentions of the testator by too strictly
following the order of the writing : and we accordingly have
deemed these rules unreasonable, and amended them by our
constitution, which permits a legacy, and much more freedom,
which is always more favoured, to be given before the appointment of an heir, or in the middle of the appointments, if there
are several. Again, a legacy to take effect after the death 35
of the heir or legatee, as in the form : 'After my heir's death
I give and bequeath,' was formerly void, as also was one
to take effect on the day preceding the death of the heir or
legatee. This too, however, we have corrected, by making
such legacies as valid as they would be were they fiduciary
bequests, lest in this point the latter should be found to have
some superiority over the former. Formerly too the gift, 36
revocation, and transference of legacies by way of penalty
was void. A penal legacy is one given in order to coerce
the heir into doing or not doing something ; for instance, the

following: 'If my heir gives his daughter in marriage to Titius,' or, conversely, 'if he does not give her in marriage to Titius, let him pay ten *aurei* to Seius'; or again, 'if my heir parts with my slave Stichus,' or, conversely, 'if he does not part with him, let him pay ten *aurei* to Titius'. And so strictly was this rule observed, that it is declared in a large number of imperial constitutions that even the Emperor will accept no legacy by which a penalty is imposed on some other person: and such legacies were void even when given by a soldier's will, in which as a rule so much trouble was taken to carry out exactly the testator's wishes. Moreover, Sabinus was of opinion that a penal appointment of a co-heir was void, as exemplified in the following: 'Be Titius my heir: if Titius gives his daughter in marriage to Seius, be Seius my heir also'; the ground of the invalidity being that it made no difference in what way Titius was constrained, whether by a legacy being left away from him, or by some one being appointed co-heir. Of these refinements, however, we disapproved, and have consequently enacted generally that bequests, even though given, revoked, or transferred in order to penalize the heir, shall be treated exactly like other legacies, except where the event on which the penal legacy is contingent is either impossible, illegal, or immoral: for such testamentary dispositions as these the opinion of my times will not permit.

TITLE XXI

OF THE ADEMPTION AND TRANSFERENCE OF LEGACIES

Legacies may be revoked either in a later clause of the will or by codicils, and the revocation may be made either in words contrary to those of the gift, as the gift thus 'I give and bequeath', the revocation thus 'I do not give and bequeath', or in words not contrary, that is to say, in any words 1 whatsoever. A legacy may also be transferred from one person to another, as thus: 'I give and bequeath to Seius the slave Stichus whom I bequeathed to Titius,' and this may be done either by a later clause of the will or by codicils; the result being that the legacy is taken away from Titius and simultaneously given to Seius.

TITLE XXII
OF THE LEX FALCIDIA

We have finally to consider the lex Falcidia, the most recent enactment limiting the amount which can be given in legacies. The statute of the Twelve Tables had conferred complete liberty of bequest on testators, by which they were enabled to give away their whole patrimony in legacies, that statute having enacted : ' let a man's testamentary disposition of his property be regarded as valid.' This complete liberty of bequest, however, it was thought proper to limit in the interest of testators themselves, for intestacy was becoming common through the refusal of instituted heirs to accept inheritances from which they received little or no advantage at all. The lex Furia and the lex Voconia were enactments designed to remedy the evil, but as both were found inadequate to the purpose, the lex Falcidia was finally passed, providing that no testator should be allowed to dispose of more than three-quarters of his property in legacies, or in other words, that whether there was a single heir instituted, or two or more, he or they should always be entitled to at least a quarter of the inheritance. If two heirs, say Titius 1 and Seius, are instituted, and Titius's share of the inheritance is either wholly exhausted in legacies specifically charged thereon, or burdened beyond the limit fixed by the statute, while no legacies at all are charged on Seius, or at any rate legacies which exhaust it only to the extent of one half or less, the question arose whether, as Seius has at least a quarter of the whole inheritance, Titius was or was not entitled to retain anything out of the legacies which had been charged upon him : and it was settled that he could keep an entire fourth of his share of the inheritance ; for the calculation of the lex Falcidia is to be applied separately to the share of each of several heirs in the inheritance. The amount of the 2 property upon which the calculation is brought to bear is its amount at the moment of the testator's decease. Thus, to illustrate by an example, a testator who is worth a hundred *aurei* at his decease gives the whole hundred away in legacies : here, if before the heir accepts, the inheritance is so much augmented through slaves who belong to it, or by births of

children from such of them as are females, or by the young of
cattle, that, even after paying away a hundred *aurei* in legacies,
the heir will still have a clear fourth of the inheritance, the
legatee's position is in no way improved, but a quarter of
the sum given in legacies may still be deducted for himself by
the heir. Conversely, if only seventy-five *aurei* are given in
legacies, and before acceptance the inheritance is so much
diminished in value, say by fire, shipwreck, or death of slaves,
that no more or even less than seventy-five *aurei* are left, the
legatees can claim payment of their legacies in full. In this
latter case, however, the heir is not prejudiced, for he is quite
free to refuse the inheritance: consequently, the legatees
must come to terms with him, and content themselves with
a portion of their legacies, lest they lose all through no one's
3 taking under the will. When the calculation of the lex
Falcidia is made, the testator's debts and funeral expenses
are first deducted, and the value of slaves whom he has
manumitted in the will or directed to be manumitted is not
reckoned as part of the inheritance ; the residue is then
divided so as to leave the heirs a clear fourth, the other three
quarters being distributed among the legatees in proportion
to the amount of the legacies given them respectively in the
will. Thus, if we suppose four hundred *aurei* to have been
given in legacies, and the value of the inheritance, out of
which they are to be paid, to be exactly that sum, each
legatee must have his legacy abated by one-fourth ; if three
hundred and fifty have been given in legacies, each legacy
will be diminished by one-eighth ; if five hundred, first a fifth,
and then a fourth, must be deducted: for when the amount
given in legacies actually exceeds the sum of the inheritance,
there must be struck off first the excess, and then the share
which the heir is entitled to retain.

TITLE XXIII
OF TRUST INHERITANCES

We now proceed to fiduciary bequests or trusts; and let
us begin with trust inheritances.
1   Legacies or inheritances given by trust had originally no
binding legal force, because no one could be compelled against

his will to do what he was merely asked to do. As there were certain classes of persons to whom testators were unable to leave inheritances or legacies, when they wished to effect these objects they used to trust to the good faith of some one who had this kind of testamentary capacity, and whom they asked to give the inheritance, or the legacy, to the intended beneficiary; hence the name 'trusts', because they were not enforced by legal obligation, but only by the transferor's sense of honesty. Subsequently the Emperor Augustus, either out of regard for various favourites of his own, or because the request was said to have been made in the name of the Emperor's safety, or moved thereto by individual and glaring cases of perfidy, commanded the consuls in certain cases to enforce the duty by their authority. And this being deemed equitable, and being approved by the people, there was gradually developed a new and permanent jurisdiction, and trusts became so popular that soon a special praetor was appointed to hear suits relating to them, who was called the trust praetor.

The first requisite is an heir directly instituted, in trust 2 to transfer the inheritance to another, for the will is void without an instituted heir in the first instance. Accordingly, when a testator has written: 'Lucius Titius, be thou my heir,' he may add: 'I request you, Lucius Titius, as soon as you can accept my inheritance, to convey and transfer it to Gaius Seius'; or he can request him to transfer a part. So a trust may be either absolute or conditional, and to be performed either immediately or on a specified future day.

After the transfer of the inheritance the transferor continues 3 heir, the transferee being sometimes regarded as quasi-heir, sometimes as quasi-legatee. But during the reign of Nero, 4 in the consulate of Trebellius Maximus and Annaeus Seneca, a senatusconsult was passed providing that, when an inheritance is transferred in pursuance of a trust, all the actions which the civil law allows to be brought by or against the heir shall be maintainable by and against the transferee: and after this enactment the praetor used to give indirect or fictitious actions to and against the transferee as quasi-heir. However, as the instituted heirs, when (as so often was the 5

case) they were requested to transfer the whole or nearly
the whole of an inheritance, declined to accept for what was
no benefit, or at most a very slight benefit, to themselves, and
this caused a failure of the trusts, afterwards, in the time
of the Emperor Vespasian, and during the consulate of
Pegasus and Pusio, the senate decreed that an heir who
was requested to transfer the inheritance should have the
same right to retain a fourth thereof as the lex Falcidia
gives to an heir charged with the payment of legacies, and
gave a similar right of retaining the fourth of any specific
thing left in trust. After the passing of this senatusconsult
the heir, wherever it came into operation, was sole administrator, and the transferee of the residue was in the position
of a partiary legatee, that is, of a legatee of a certain specified
portion of the estate under the kind of bequest called partici-
pation, so that the stipulations which had been usual between
an heir and a partiary legatee were now entered into by the
heir and transferee, in order to secure a rateable division
of the gains and losses arising out of the inheritance.
6 Accordingly, after this, if no more than three-fourths of the
inheritance was in trust to be transferred, then the SC. Trebellianum governed the transfer, and both were liable to be
sued for the debts of the inheritance in rateable portions, the
heir by civil law, the transferee, as quasi-heir, by that enactment. But if more than three-fourths, or even the whole was
left in trust to be transferred, the SC. Pegasianum came
into operation, and when once the heir had accepted, of
course voluntarily, he was the sole administrator whether
he retained one-fourth or declined to retain it: but if he
did, he entered into stipulations with the transferee similar
to those usual between the heir and a partiary legatee, while
if he did not, but transferred the whole inheritance, he
covenanted with him as quasi-purchaser. If an instituted
heir refuse to accept an inheritance from a suspicion that
the liabilities exceed the assets, it is provided by the SC.
Pegasianum that, on the petition of the person to whom he is
requested to transfer, he shall be ordered by the praetor to
accept and transfer it, whereupon the transferee shall be as
capable of suing and being sued as the transferee under the

SC. Trebellianum. In this case no stipulations are necessary, because by a concurrent operation of the two senatusconsults both the transferor is protected, and all actions relating to the inheritance pass to and against the transferee. As, how- 7 ever, the covenants which had become necessary through the SC. Pegasianum were disliked even by the older lawyers, and are in certain cases considered injurious by the eminent jurist Papinian, and it being our desire that our statute book should be clear and simple rather than complicated, we have, after placing these two senatusconsults side by side and examining their points of resemblance and difference, resolved to repeal the SC. Pegasianum, as the later enactment, and to give exclusive authority to the SC. Trebellianum, under which in future all trust inheritances are to be transferred, whether the testator has freely given his heir a fourth of the property, or more or less, or even nothing at all: provided always, that when the heir has either nothing or less than a fourth, it shall be lawful for him, under our authority expressed in this statute, to retain a fourth, or so much as will make his portion equal to a fourth, or to recover it by action if he has already paid it over, the heir and the transferee being capable both of suing and being sued in proportion to their shares in the inheritance, after the analogy of the SC. Trebellianum; and provided also, that if the heir voluntarily transfers the whole inheritance, the transferee shall be able to sue and be sued on all actions relating to the inheritance whatsoever. Moreover, we have transferred to the SC. Trebellianum the leading provision of the SC. Pegasianum, whereby it was enacted that when an instituted heir refused to accept an inheritance offered to him, he could be compelled to accept and transfer the whole inheritance if the intended transferee so desired, and that all actions should pass to and against the latter: so that it is under the SC. Trebellianum alone that the heir, if unwilling to accept, is now obliged to do so, if the intended transferee desire the inheritance, though to him personally no loss or profit can accrue under the transaction. It makes no difference whether it is a sole 8 or part heir who is under a trust to transfer, or whether what he is requested to transfer is the whole or only a part of that to which he is heir; for we direct that the same rules shall be applied in the case of a part being transferred as we have said are observed in the transference of a whole inheritance. 9 If the request addressed to the heir is to transfer the inheritance after deducting or reserving some specific thing which is equal in value to a fourth part thereof, such as land or anything else, the conveyance will be made under the SC. Trebellianum, exactly as if he had been asked after retaining a fourth part of the inheritance to transfer the residue. There is, however, some difference between the two cases; for in the first, where the inheritance is transferred after deducting or reserving some specific thing, the senatusconsult has the effect of making the transferee the only person who can sue or be sued in respect of the inheritance, and the part retained by the heir is free from all encumbrances, exactly as if he had received it under a legacy; whereas in the second, where the heir, after retaining a fourth part of the inheritance, transfers the rest as requested, the actions are divided, the transferee being able to sue and be sued in respect of three-fourths of the inheritance, and the heir in respect of the rest. Moreover, if the heir is requested to transfer the inheritance after deducting or reserving only a single specific thing, which, however, in value is equivalent to the greater part of the inheritance, the transferee is still the only person who can sue and be sued, so that he ought well to weigh whether it is worth his while to take it: and the case is precisely the same, whether what the heir is directed to deduct or reserve before transferring is two or more specific things, or a definite sum which in fact is equivalent to a fourth or even the greater part of the inheritance. What we have said of a sole heir is equally true of one who is instituted only to a part. 10 Moreover, a man about to die intestate can charge the person to whom he knows his property will go by either the civil or praetorian law to transfer to some one else either his whole inheritance, or a part of it, or some specific thing, such as land, a slave, or money: but legacies have no validity 11 unless given by will. The transferee may himself be charged by the deceased with a trust to transfer to some other person either the whole or a part of what he receives, or even some-

thing different. As has been already observed, trusts in 12
their origin depended solely on the good faith of the heir,
from which early history they derived both their name and
their character: and it was for that reason that the Emperor
Augustus made them legally binding obligations. And we,
in our desire to surpass that prince, have recently made
a constitution, suggested by a matter brought before us by
the eminent Tribonian, quaestor of our sacred palace, by
which it is enacted, that if a testator charges his heir with
a trust to transfer the whole inheritance or some specific
thing, and the trust cannot be proved by writing or by
the evidence of five witnesses—five being, as is known, the
number required by law for the proof of oral trusts—through
there having been fewer witnesses than five, or even none at
all, and if the heir, whether it be his own son or some one
else whom the testator has chosen to trust, and by whom
he desired the transfer to be made, perfidiously refuses to
execute the trust, and in fact denies that he was ever charged
with it, the alleged beneficiary, having previously sworn to
his own good faith, may put the heir upon his oath: whereupon the heir may be compelled to swear that no trust
was ever charged upon him, or, in default, to transfer the
inheritance or the specific thing, as the case may be, in
order that the last wishes of the testator, the fulfilment of
which he has left to the honour of his heir, may not be
defeated. We have also prescribed the same procedure
where the person charged with a trust is a legatee or already
himself a transferee under a prior trust. Finally, if the person
charged admits the trust, but tries to shelter himself behind legal
technicalities, he may most certainly be compelled to perform
his obligation.

TITLE XXIV

OF TRUST BEQUESTS OF SINGLE THINGS

Single things can be left in trust as well as inheritances;
land, for instance, slaves, clothing, gold, silver, and coined
money; and the trust may be imposed either on an heir
or on a legatee, although a legatee cannot be charged with
a legacy. Not only the testator's property, but that of an 1
heir, or legatee, or person already benefited by a trust, or any

one else may be given by a trust. Thus a legatee, or a person
in whose favour the testator has already created a trust, may
be asked to transfer either a thing left to him, or any other
thing belonging to himself or a stranger, provided always
that he is not charged with a trust to transfer more than
he takes by the will, for in respect of such excess the trust
would be void. When a person is charged by a trust to
transfer a thing belonging to some one else, he must either
2 purchase and deliver it, or pay its value. Liberty can be
left to a slave by a trust charging an heir, legatee, or other
person already benefited by a trust of the testator's, with his
manumission, and it makes no difference whether the slave
is the property of the testator, of the heir, of the legatee or
of a stranger : for a stranger's slave must be purchased and
manumitted ; and on his master's refusal to sell (which refusal
is allowable only if the master has taken nothing under the
will) the trust to enfranchise the slave is not extinguished, as
though its execution had become impossible, but its execution
is merely postponed ; because it may become possible to free
him at some future time, whenever an opportunity of purchasing him presents itself. A trust of manumission makes the
slave the freedman, not of the testator, though he may have
been his owner, but of the manumitter, whereas a direct
bequest of liberty makes a slave the freedman of the testator,
whence too he is called '*orcinus*'. But a direct bequest of
liberty can be made only to a slave who belongs to the
testator both at the time of making his will and at that
of his decease ; and by a direct bequest of liberty is to be
understood the case where the testator desires him to become
free in virtue, as it were, of his own testament alone, and so
3 does not ask some one else to manumit him. The words most
commonly used to create a trust are I beg, I request, I wish,
I commission, I trust to your good faith ; and they are just as
binding when used separately as when united.

TITLE XXV

OF CODICILS

It is certain that codicils were not in use before the time of
Augustus, for Lucius Lentulus, who was also the originator

of trusts, was the first to introduce them, in the following manner. Being on the point of death in Africa, he executed codicils, confirmed by his will, by which he begged Augustus to do something for him as a trust; and on the Emperor's fulfilling his wishes, other persons followed the precedent and discharged trusts created in this manner, and the daughter of Lentulus paid legacies which could not have been legally claimed from her. It is said that Augustus called a council of certain jurists, among them Trebatius, who at that time enjoyed the highest reputation, and asked them whether the new usage could be sanctioned, or did not rather run counter to the received principles of law, and that Trebatius recommended their admission, remarking 'how convenient and even necessary the practice was to citizens', owing to the length of the journeys which were taken in those early days, and upon which a man might often be able to make codicils when he could not make a will. And subsequently, after codicils had been made by Labeo, nobody doubted their complete validity.

Not only can codicils be made after a will, but a man 1 dying intestate can create trusts by codicils, though Papinian says that codicils executed before a will are invalid unless confirmed by a later express declaration that they shall be binding. But a rescript of the Emperors Severus and Antoninus decides that the performance of a trust imposed by codicils written before a will may in any case be demanded, if it appears that the testator had not abandoned the intention expressed in them. An inheritance can neither be given 2 nor taken away by codicils, nor, accordingly, can a child be disinherited in this way: for, if it were otherwise, the law of wills and of codicils would be confounded. By this it is meant that an inheritance cannot directly be given or taken away by codicils; for indirectly, by means of a trust, one can very well be given in this manner. Nor again can a condition be imposed on an instituted heir, or a direct substitution be effected, by codicils. A man can make any 3 number of codicils, and no solemnities are required for their execution.

BOOK III

OF THE DEVOLUTION OF INHERITANCES ON INTESTACY

A MAN is said to die intestate who either has made no will at all, or has made one which is invalid, or if one which has been duly executed has been subsequently revoked or rescinded, or finally, if no one accepts as heir under the testament.

1   The inheritances of intestate persons go first, by the statute
2 of the Twelve Tables, to family heirs; and family heirs, as we said above, are those who were in the power of the deceased at the time of his death, such as a son or daughter, a grandchild by a son, or a great-grandchild by such grandchild if a male, and this whether the relationship be natural or adoptive. Among them must also be reckoned children who, though not born in lawful wedlock, have been inscribed members of the *curia* according to the tenor of the imperial constitutions relating to them, and thus acquire the rights of family heirs, or who come within the terms of our constitutions by which we have enacted that, if any one shall cohabit with a woman whom he might have lawfully married, but for whom he did not at first feel marital affection, and shall after begetting children by her begin to feel such affection and formally marry her, and then have by her sons or daughters, not only shall those be lawful children and in their father's power who were born after the settlement of the dowry, but also those born before, to whom in reality the later born ones owed their legitimacy; and we have provided that this rule shall hold even though no children are born after the execution of the dowry deed, or if, having been born, they are dead. It is to be observed, however, that a grandchild or great-grandchild is not a family heir, unless the person in the preceding degree has ceased to be in the power of the parent, either through having died, or by some

other means, such as emancipation ; for if at the time of
a man's decease a son is in his power, a grandson by that son
cannot be a family heir, and the case is exactly the same with
more remote descendants. Children too who are born after
the ancestor's death, and who would have been in his power
had they been born during his lifetime, are family heirs.
Family heirs succeed even though ignorant of their title, and 3
they can take upon an intestacy even though insane, because
whenever the law vests property in a person, even when he is
ignorant of his title, it equally vests it in him if insane.
Thus, immediately on the parent's death, the ownership is
as it were continued without any break, so that pupils who
are family heirs do not require their guardian's sanction in
order to succeed, for inheritances go to such heirs even though
ignorant of their title ; and similarly an insane family heir
does not require his curator's consent in order to succeed, but
takes by operation of law. Sometimes, however, a family heir 4
succeeds in this way to his parent, even though not in the
latter's power at the time of his decease, as where a person
returns from captivity after his father's death, this being the
effect of the law of postliminium. And sometimes conversely 5
a man is not a family heir although in the power of the
deceased at the time of his death, as where the latter after
his death is adjudged to have been guilty of treason, and his
memory is thereby branded with infamy : such a person is
unable to have a family heir, for his property is confiscated to
the treasury, though one who would otherwise have succeeded
him may be said to have in law been a family heir, and
ceased to be such. Where there is a son or daughter, and a 6
grandchild by another son, these are called together to the
inheritance, nor does the nearer in degree exclude the more
remote, for it seems just that grandchildren should represent
their father and take his place in the succession. Similarly
a grandchild by a son, and a great-grandchild by a grandson
are called to the inheritance together. And as it was thought
just that grandchildren and great-grandchildren should represent their father, it seemed consistent that the inheritance
should be divided by the number of stems, and not by the
number of individuals, so that a son should take one-half, and

grandchildren by another son the other : or, if two sons left
children, that a single grandchild, or two grandchildren by
one son, should take one-half, and three or four grandchildren
7 by the other son the other. In ascertaining whether, in any
particular case, so and so is a family heir, one ought to regard
only that moment of time at which it first was certain that
the deceased died intestate, including hereunder the case of
no one's accepting under the will. For instance, if a son be
disinherited and a stranger instituted heir, and the son die
after the decease of his father, but before it is certain that
the heir instituted in the will either will not or cannot take the
inheritance, a grandson will take as family heir to his grandfather, because he is the only descendant in existence when
first it is certain that the ancestor died intestate ; and of this
8 there can be no doubt. A grandson born after, though conceived before, his grandfather's death, whose father dies in the
interval between the grandfather's decease and desertion of
the latter's will through failure of the instituted heir to take,
is family heir to his grandfather ; though it is obvious that
if (other circumstances remaining the same) he is conceived
as well as born after the grandfather's decease, he is no family
heir, because he was never connected with his grandfather
by any tie of relationship ; exactly as a person adopted by
an emancipated son is not among the children of, and therefore cannot be family heir to, the latter's father. And such
persons, not being children in relation to the inheritance,
cannot apply either for possession of the goods of the deceased as next of kin. So much for family heirs.
9   As to emancipated children, they have, by the civil law, no
right to succeed to an intestate ; for, having ceased to be in
the power of their parent, they are not family heirs, nor are
they called by any other title in the statute of the Twelve
Tables. The praetor, however, following natural equity,
gives them possession of the goods of the deceased merely as
children, exactly as if they had been in his power at the time
of his death, and this whether they stand alone or whether
there are family heirs as well. Consequently, if a man die
leaving two children, one emancipated, and the other in his
power at the time of his decease, the latter is sole heir

by the civil law, as being the only family heir ; but through
the former's being admitted to part of the inheritance by the
indulgence of the praetor, the family heir becomes heir to
part of the inheritance only.   Emancipated children, however, 10
who have given themselves in adoption are not thus admitted,
under the title of children, to share the property of their
natural father, if at the time of his decease they are in
their adoptive family ; though it is otherwise if they are emancipated during his lifetime by their adoptive father, for then
they are admitted as if they had been emancipated by him
and had never been in an adoptive family, while, conversely, as
regards their adoptive father, they are henceforth regarded
as strangers.   If, however, they are emancipated by the adoptive after the death of the natural father, as regards the
former they are strangers all the same, and yet do not acquire
the rank of children as regards succession to the property of
the latter ; the reason of this rule being the injustice of putting
it within the power of an adoptive father to determine to whom
the property of the natural father shall belong, whether to his
children or to his agnates.   Adoptive are thus not so well off 11
as natural children in respect of rights of succession : for by
the indulgence of the praetor the latter retain their rank as
children even after emancipation, although they lose it by the
civil law ; while the former, if emancipated, are not assisted
even by the praetor.   And there is nothing wrong in their
being thus differently treated, because civil changes can affect
rights annexed to a civil title, but not rights annexed to
a natural title, and natural descendants, though on emancipation they cease to be family heirs, cannot cease to be children
or grandchildren ; whereas on the other hand adoptive
children are regarded as strangers after emancipation, because
they lose the title and name of son or daughter, which they
have acquired by a civil change, namely adoption, by another
civil change, namely emancipation.   And the rule is the same 12
in the possession of goods against the will which the praetor
promises to children who are passed over in their parent's
testament, that is to say, are neither instituted nor duly
disinherited ; for the praetor calls to this possession children
who were in their parent's power at the time of his decease,

or emancipated, but excludes those who at that time were in
an adoptive family: still less does he here admit adoptive
children emancipated by their adoptive father, for by emanci-
13 pation they cease entirely to be children of his. We should
observe, however, that though children who are in an adoptive
family, or who are emancipated by their adoptive after the
decease of their natural father, are not admitted on the death
of the latter intestate by that part of the edict by which
children are called to the possession of goods, they are called
by another part, namely that which admits the cognates of
the deceased, who, however, come in only if there are no
family heirs, emancipated children, or agnates to take before
them : for the praetor prefers children, whether family heirs
or emancipated, to all other claimants, ranking in the second
degree statutory successors, and in the third cognates, or next
14 of kin.   All these rules, however, which to our predecessors
were sufficient, have received some emendation by the constitution which we have enacted relative to persons who have
been given in adoption to others by their natural fathers ; for
we found cases in which sons by entering an adoptive family
forfeited their right of succeeding their natural parents, and
then, the tie of adoption being easily broken by emancipation,
lost all title to succeed their adoptive parents as well. We
have corrected this, in our usual manner, by a constitution
which enacts that, when a natural father gives his son in
adoption to another person, the son's rights shall remain the
same in every particular as if he had continued in the power
of his natural father, and the adoption had never taken place,
except only that he shall be able to succeed his adoptive
father should he die intestate. If, however, the latter makes
a will, the son cannot obtain any part of the inheritance
either by the civil or by the praetorian law, that is to say,
either by impeaching the will as unduteous or by applying
for possession against the will ; for, being related by no tie of
blood, the adoptive father is not bound either to institute
him heir or to disinherit him, even though he has been
adopted, in accordance with the SC. Afinianum, from among
three brothers ; for, even under these circumstances, he is not
entitled to a fourth of what he might have taken on intestacy,

nor has he any action for its recovery. We have, however, by our constitution excepted persons adopted by natural ascendants, for between them and their adopters there is the natural tie of blood as well as the civil tie of adoption, and therefore in this case we have preserved the older law, as also in that of an independent person giving himself in adrogation : all of which enactment can be gathered in its special details from the tenor of the aforesaid constitution.

By the ancient law too, which favoured the descent through 15 males, those grandchildren only were called as family heirs, and preferred to agnates, who were related to the grandfather in this way : grandchildren by daughters, and great-grand-children by granddaughters, whom it regarded only as cog-nates, being called after the agnates in the succession to their maternal grandfather or great-grandfather, or their grand-mother or great-grandmother, whether paternal or maternal. But the Emperors would not allow so unnatural a wrong to endure without sufficient correction, and accordingly, as people are, and are called, grandchildren and great-grandchildren of a person whether they trace their descent through males or through females, they placed them altogether in the same rank and order of succession. In order, however, to bestow some privilege on those who had in their favour the provisions of the ancient law as well as natural right, they determined that grandchildren, great-grandchildren, and others who traced their descent through a female should have their portion of the inheritance diminished by receiving less by one-third than their mother or grandmother would have taken, or than their father or grandfather, paternal or maternal, when the deceased, whose inheritance was in question, was a woman ; and they excluded the agnates, if such descendants claimed the in-heritance, even though they stood alone. Thus, exactly as the statute of the Twelve Tables calls the grandchildren and great-grandchildren to represent their deceased father in the succession to their grandfather, so the imperial legislation substitutes them for their deceased mother or grandmother, subject to the aforesaid deduction of a third part of the share which she personally would have taken. As, however, there 16 was still some question as to the relative rights of such

grandchildren and of the agnates, who on the authority of
a certain constitution claimed a fourth part of the deceased's
estate, we have repealed the said enactment, and not
permitted its insertion in our Code from that of Theodosius.
By the constitution which we have published, and by which
we have altogether deprived it of validity, we have provided
that in case of the survival of grandchildren by a daughter,
great-grandchildren by a granddaughter, or more remote
descendants related through a female, the agnates shall have
no claim to any part of the estate of the deceased, that
collaterals may no longer be preferred to lineal descendants ;
which constitution we hereby re-enact with all its force from
the date originally determined : provided always, as we
direct, that the inheritance shall be divided between sons
and grandchildren by a daughter, or between all the grandchildren, and other more remote descendants, according to
stocks, and not by counting heads, on the principle observed
by the ancient law in dividing an inheritance between sons
and grandchildren by a son, the issue obtaining without any
diminution the portion which would have belonged to their
mother or father, grandmother or grandfather : so that if, for
instance, there be one or two children by one stock, and three
or four by another, the one or two, and the three or four,
shall together take respectively one moiety of the inheritance.

TITLE II

OF THE STATUTORY SUCCESSION OF AGNATES

If there is no family heir, nor any of those persons called
to the succession along with family heirs by the praetor or
the imperial legislation, to take the inheritance in any way,
it devolves, by the statute of the Twelve Tables, on the
1 nearest agnate. Agnates, as we have observed in the first
book, are those cognates who trace their relationship through
males, or, in other words, who are cognate through their
respective fathers. Thus, brothers by the same father are
agnates, whether by the same mother or not, and are called
consanguinei ; an uncle is agnate to his brother's son, and vice
versa ; and the children of brothers by the same father, who
are called *consobrini*, are one another's agnates, so that it is

easy to arrive at various degrees of agnation. Children
who are born after their father's decease acquire the rights
of kinship exactly as if they had been born before that
event. But the law does not give the inheritance to all the
agnates, but only to those who were nearest in degree at
the moment when it first was certain that the deceased died
intestate. The relation of agnation can also be established 2
by adoption, for instance, between a man's own sons and
those whom he has adopted, all of whom are properly called
consanguinei in relation to one another. So too, if your
brother, or your paternal uncle, or even a more remote
agnate, adopts any one, that person undoubtedly becomes one
of your agnates. Male agnates have reciprocal rights of suc- 3
cession, however remote the degree of relationship : but the
rule as regards females, on the other hand, was that they
could not succeed as agnates to any one more remotely
related to them than a brother, while they themselves could
be succeeded by their male agnates, however distant the connexion : thus you, if a male, could take the inheritance of a
daughter either of your brother or of your paternal uncle,
or of your paternal aunt, but she could not take yours ; the
reason of this distinction being the seeming expediency of
successions devolving as much as possible on males. But as
it was most unjust that such females should be as completely
excluded as if they were strangers, the praetor admits them
to the possession of goods promised in that part of the edict
in which mere natural kinship is recognized as a title to
succession, under which they take provided there is no
agnate, or other cognate of a nearer degree of relationship.
Now these distinctions were in no way due to the statute
of the Twelve Tables, which, with the simplicity proper to all
legislation, conferred reciprocal rights of succession on all
agnates alike, whether males or females, and excluded no
degree by reason merely of its remoteness, after the analogy
of family heirs ; but it was introduced by the jurists who came
between the Twelve Tables and the imperial legislation, and
who with their legal subtleties and refinements excluded
females other than sisters altogether from agnatic succession.
And no other scheme of succession was in those times heard

of, until the praetors, by gradually mitigating to the best
of their ability the harshness of the civil law, or by filling
up voids in the old system, provided through their edicts
a new one. Mere cognation was thus in its various degrees
recognized as a title to succession, and the praetors gave relief
to such females through the possession of goods, which they
promised to them in that part of the edict by which cognates
are called to the succession. We, however, have followed the
Twelve Tables in this department of law, and adhered to their
principles: and, while we commend the praetors for their
sense of equity, we cannot hold that their remedy was adequate;
for when the degree of natural relationship was the same, and
when the civil title of agnation was conferred by the older law
on males and females alike, why should males be allowed
to succeed all their agnates, and women (except sisters) be
debarred from succeeding any? Accordingly, we have restored the old rules in their integrity, and made the law on
this subject an exact copy of the Twelve Tables, by enacting,
in our constitution, that all 'statutory' successors, that is,
persons tracing their descent from the deceased through males,
shall be called alike to the succession as agnates on an intestacy,
whether they be males or females, according to their proximity
of degree; and that no females shall be excluded on the pretence that none but sisters have the right of succeeding by
4 the title of kinship. By an addition to the same enactment
we have deemed it right to transfer one, though only one,
degree of cognates into the ranks of those who succeed by
a statutory title, in order that not only the children of a brother
may be called, as we have just explained, to the succession of
their paternal uncle, but that the children of a sister too, even
though only of the half blood on either side (but not her more
remote descendants), may share with the former the inheritance
of their uncle; so that, on the decease of a man who is paternal
uncle to his brother's children, and maternal uncle to those of
his sister, the nephews and nieces on either side will now
succeed him alike, provided, of course, that the brother and
sister do not survive, exactly as if they all traced their relationship through males, and thus all had a statutory title. But if
the deceased leaves brothers or sisters who accept the inherit-

ance, the remoter degrees are altogether excluded, the division
in this case being made individually, that is to say, by counting
heads, not stocks. If there are several degrees of agnates, 5
the statute of the Twelve Tables clearly calls only the nearest,
so that if, for instance, the deceased leaves a brother, and a
nephew by another brother deceased, or a paternal uncle, the
brother is preferred. And although that statute, in speaking
of the nearest agnate, uses the singular number, there is no
doubt that if there are several of the same degree they are all
admitted: for though properly one can speak of ' the nearest
degree ' only when there are several, yet it is certain that even
though all the agnates are in the same degree the inheritance
belongs to them. If a man dies without having made a will 6
at all, the agnate who takes is the one who was nearest at
the time of the death of the deceased. But when a man dies,
having made a will, the agnate who takes (if one is to take at
all) is the one who is nearest when first it becomes certain
that no one will accept the inheritance under the testament ;
for until that moment the deceased cannot properly be said
to have died intestate at all, and this period of uncertainty is
sometimes a long one, so that it not unfrequently happens
that through the death, during it, of a nearer agnate, another
becomes nearest who was not so at the death of the testator.
In agnatic succession the established rule was that the right 7
of accepting the inheritance could not pass from a nearer to
a more remote degree ; in other words, that if the nearest
agnate, who, as we have described, is called to the inheritance,
either refuses it or dies before acceptance, the agnates of the
next grade have no claim to admittance under the Twelve
Tables. This hard rule again the praetors did not leave
entirely without correction, though their remedy, which con-
sisted in the admission of such persons, since they were
excluded from the rights of agnation, in the rank of cognates,
was inadequate. But we, in our desire to have the law as
complete as possible, have enacted in the constitution which
in our clemency we have issued respecting the rights of
patrons, that in agnatic succession the transference of the
right to accept from a nearer to a remoter degree shall not be
refused : for it was most absurd that agnates should be denied

a privilege which the praetor had conferred on cognates especially as the burden of guardianship fell on the second degree of agnates if there was a failure of the first, the principle which we have now sanctioned being admitted so far as it imposed burdens, but rejected so far as it conferred a boon.

8　To statutory succession the ascendant too is none the less called who emancipates a child, grandchild, or remoter descendant under a fiduciary agreement, which by our constitution is now implied in every emancipation. Among the ancients the rule was different, for the parent acquired no rights of succession unless he had entered into a special agreement of trust to that effect prior to the emancipation.

Title III

OF THE SENATUSCONSULTUM TERTULLIANUM

So strict were the rules of the statute of the Twelve Tables in preferring the issue of males, and excluding those who traced their relationship through females, that they did not confer reciprocal rights of inheritance even on a mother and her children, though the praetors called them to succeed one another as next of kin by promising them the possession

1 of goods in the class of cognates. But this narrowness of the law was afterwards amended, the Emperor Claudius being the first to confer on a mother, as a consolation for the loss

2 of her children, a statutory right to their inheritance, and afterwards, very full provisions were made by the SC. Tertullianum, enacted in the time of the Emperor Hadrian, and relating to the melancholy succession of children by their mothers, though not by their grandmothers, whereby it was provided that a freeborn woman who had three or a freedwoman who had four children should be entitled to succeed to the goods of her children who died intestate, even though herself under paternal power; though, in this latter case, she cannot accept the inheritance except by the direction of the

3 person in whose power she is. Children of the deceased who are or who rank as family heirs, whether in the first or any other degree, are preferred to the mother, and even where the deceased is a woman her children by imperial constitutions have a prior claim to the mother, that is, to their own

grandmother. Again, the father of the deceased is preferred to the mother, but not so the paternal grandfather or great-grandfather, at least when it is between them only that the question arises who is entitled. A brother by the same father excluded the mother from the succession to both sons and daughters, but a sister by the same father came in equally with the mother ; and where there were both a brother and a sister by the same father, as well as a mother who was entitled by number of children, the brother excluded the mother, and divided the inheritance in equal moieties with the sister. By a constitution, however, which we have placed 4 in the Code made illustrious by our name, we have deemed it right to afford relief to the mother, in consideration of natural justice, of the pains of childbirth, and of the danger and even death which mothers often incur in this manner ; for which reason we have judged it a sin that they should be prejudiced by a circumstance which is entirely fortuitous. For if a free-born woman had not borne three, or a freedwoman four children, she was undeservedly defrauded of the succession to her own offspring ; and yet what fault had she committed in bearing few rather than many children ? Accordingly, we have conferred on mothers a full statutory right of succession to their children, whether they be freeborn or freedwomen, although they may not have given birth to three or four children, and even if they have had no other child than the one in question deceased. The earlier constitutions, in their 5 review of statutory rights of succession, were in some points favourable, in others unfavourable, to mothers ; thus in some cases they did not call them to the whole inheritance of their children, but deducted a third in favour of certain other persons with a statutory title, while in others they did exactly the opposite. We, however, have determined to follow a straight-forward and simple path, and, preferring the mother to all other persons with a statutory title, to give her the entire succession of her sons, without deduction in favour of any other persons except a brother or sister, whether by the same father as the deceased, or possessing rights of cognation only ; so that, as we have preferred the mother to all with a statu-tory title, so we call to the inheritance, along with her, all brothers and sisters of the deceased, whether statutorily entitled or not: provided that, if the only surviving relatives of the deceased are sisters, agnatic or cognatic, and a mother, the latter shall have one-half, and all the sisters together the other half of the inheritance; if a mother and a brother or brothers, with or without sisters agnatic or cognatic, the inheritance shall be divided among mother, brothers, and sisters 6 in equal portions.   But, while we are legislating for mothers, we ought also to bestow some thought on their offspring; and accordingly mothers should observe that if they do not apply within a year for guardians for their children, either originally or in lieu of those who have been removed or excused, they will forfeit their title to succeed such children if they die under 7 the age of puberty.   A mother can succeed her child under the SC. Tertullianum even though the child be illegitimate.

TITLE IV
OF THE SENATUSCONSULTUM ORFITIANUM

Conversely, children were admitted to succeed their mother on her death intestate by the SC. Orfitianum, passed in the time of the Emperor Marcus, when Orfitus and Rufus were consuls: by which a statutory right of succession was conferred on both sons and daughters, even though in the power of another, in preference to their deceased mother's brothers 1 and sisters and other agnates.   As, however, grandsons were not called by this senatusconsult with a statutory title to the succession of their grandmothers, this was subsequently amended by imperial constitutions, providing that grand- 2 children should be called to inherit exactly like children. It is to be observed that rights of succession such as those conferred by the SC[a]. Tertullianum and Orfitianum are not extinguished by loss of status, owing to the rule that rights of succession conferred by later statutes are not destroyed in this way, but only such as are conferred by the statute of the 3 Twelve Tables; and finally that under the latter of these two enactments even illegitimate children are admitted to their mother's inheritance.

4   If there are several heirs with a statutory title, some of whom do not accept, or are prevented from doing so by death

or some other cause, their shares accrue in equal proportions to those who do accept the inheritance, or to their heirs, supposing they die before the failure of the others to take.

TITLE V

OF THE SUCCESSION OF COGNATES

After family heirs, and persons who by the praetor and the imperial legislation are ranked as such, and after persons statutorily entitled, among whom are the agnates and those whom the aforesaid senatusconsults and our constitution have raised to the rank of agnates, the praetor calls the nearest cognates. In this class or order natural or blood relationship 1 alone is considered: for agnates who have undergone loss of status and their children, though not regarded as having a statutory title under the statute of the Twelve Tables, are called by the praetor in the third order of succession. The sole exceptions to this rule are emancipated brothers and sisters (not, however, including their children), who are admitted by the statute of Anastasius to the statutory succession of a brother or sister along with other brothers and sisters, though not in equal shares with them, but with some deduction, the amount of which can easily be ascertained from the terms of the constitution itself. But to other agnates of remoter degrees, even though they have not undergone loss of status, and still more to cognates, they are preferred by the aforesaid statute. Again, 2 collateral relations connected with the deceased only by the female line are called to the succession by the praetor in the third order as cognates; and children who are in an adoptive 3 family are admitted in this order to the inheritance of their natural parent. It is clear that illegitimate children can have 4 no agnates, for in law they have no father, and it is through the father that agnatic relationship is traced, while cognatic relationship is traced through the mother as well. On the same principle they cannot be held to be *consanguinei* of one another, for *consanguinei* are in a way agnatically related: consequently, they are connected with one another only as cognates, and in the same way too with the cognates of their mother. Accordingly, they can succeed to the possession of goods under that part of the Edict in which cognates are

5 called by the title of mere kinship. In this place too we should observe that a person who claims as an agnate can be admitted to the inheritance, even though ten degrees removed from the deceased, both by the statute of the Twelve Tables, and by the Edict in which the praetor promises the possession of goods to heirs statutorily entitled : but on the ground of mere natural kinship the praetor promises possession of goods to those cognates only who are within the sixth degree ; the only persons in the seventh degree whom he admits as cognates being the children of a second cousin of the deceased.

Title VI

OF THE DEGREES OF COGNATION

It is here necessary to explain the way in which the degrees of natural relationship are reckoned. In the first place it is to be observed that they can be counted either upwards, or downwards, or crosswise, that is to say, collaterally. Relations in the ascending line are parents, in the descending line, children : collateral relations are brothers and sisters, their children, and similarly uncles and aunts paternal and maternal. In the ascending and descending lines a man's nearest cognate may be related to him in the first degree ; in the collateral line he cannot be nearer to him than the second.
1 Relations in the first degree, reckoning upwards, are the father and mother ; reckoning downwards, the son and
2 daughter. Those in the second degree, upwards, are grandfather and grandmother ; downwards, grandson and grand-
3 daughter ; and in the collateral line brother and sister. In the third degree, upwards, are the great-grandfather and great-grandmother ; downwards, the great-grandson and great-granddaughter ; in the collateral line, the sons and daughters of a brother or sister, and also uncles and aunts paternal and maternal. The father's brother is called *patruus*, in Greek πατρῷος, the mother's brother *avunculus*, in Greek specifically μητρῷος, though the term θεῖος is used indifferently to indicate either. The father's sister is called *amita*, the mother's *matertera* ; both go in Greek by the name θεία, or, with some,
4 τιτθίς. In the fourth degree, upwards, are the great-great-

grandfather and the great-great-grandmother; downwards, the great-great-grandson and the great-great-granddaughter; in the collateral line, the paternal great-uncle and great-aunt, that is to say, the grandfather's brother and sister : the same relations on the grandmother's side, that is to say, her brother and sister : and first cousins male and female, that is, children of brothers and sisters in relation to one another. The children of two sisters, in relation to one another, are properly called *consobrini*, a corruption of *consororini*; those of two brothers, in relation to one another, *fratres patrueles*, if males, *sorores patrueles*, if females; and those of a brother and a sister, in relation to one another, *amitini*; thus the sons of your father's sister call you *consobrinus*, and you them *amitini*. In the fifth degree, upwards, are the grandfather's great- 5 grandfather and great-grandmother, downwards, the great-grandchildren of one's own grandchildren, and in the collateral line the grandchildren of a brother or sister, a great-grandfather's or great-grandmother's brother or sister, the children of one's first cousins, that is, of a *frater* or *soror patruelis*, of a *consobrinus* or *consobrina*, of an *amitinus* or *amitina*, and first cousins once removed, that is to say, the children of a great-uncle or great-aunt paternal or maternal. In the sixth degree, upwards, are the great-grandfather's 6 great-grandfather and great-grandmother; downwards, the great-grandchildren of a great-grandchild, and in the collateral line the great-grandchildren of a brother or sister, as also the brother and sister of a great-great-grandfather or great-great-grandmother, and second cousins, that is to say, the children of *fratres* or *sorores patrueles*, of *consobrini*, or of *amitini*. This will be enough to show how the degrees of 7 relationship are reckoned ; for from what has been said it is easy to understand how we ought to calculate the remoter degrees also, each generation always adding one degree : so that it is far easier to say in what degree any one is related to some one else than to indicate his relationship by the proper specific term. The degrees of agnation are also reckoned in 8 the same manner ; but as truth is fixed in the mind of man 9 much better by the eye than by the ear, we have deemed it necessary, after giving an account of the degrees of relationship, to have a table of them inserted in the present book, that so the youth may be able by both ears and eyes to gain a most perfect knowledge of them.

10   It is certain that the part of the Edict in which the possession of goods is promised to the next of kin has nothing to do with the relationships of slaves with one another, nor is there any old statute by which such relationships were recognized. However, in the constitution which we have issued with regard to the rights of patrons—a subject which up to our times had been most obscure, and full of difficulties and confusion—we have been prompted by humanity to grant that if a slave shall beget children by either a free woman or another slave, or conversely if a slave woman shall bear children of either sex by either a freeman or a slave, and both the parents and the children (if born of a slave woman) shall become free, or if the mother being free, the father be a slave, and subsequently acquire his freedom, the children shall in all these cases succeed their father and mother, and the patron's rights lie dormant. And such children we have called to the succession not only of their parents, but also of one another reciprocally, by this enactment, whether those born in slavery and subsequently manumitted are the only children, or whether there be others conceived after their parents had obtained their freedom, and whether they all have the same father or mother, or the same father and different mothers, or vice versa ; the rules applying to children born in lawful wedlock being applied here also.

11   To sum up all that we have said, it appears that persons related in the same degree of cognation to the deceased are not always called together, and that even a remoter is sometimes preferred to a nearer cognate. For as family heirs and those whom we have enumerated as equivalent to family heirs have a priority over all other claimants, it is clear that a great-grandson or great-great-grandson is preferred to a brother, or the father or mother of the deceased; and yet the father and mother, as we have remarked above, are in the first degree of cognation, and the brother is in the second, while the great-grandson and great-great-grandson are only in the third and fourth respectively. And it is immaterial

whether the descendant who ranks among family heirs was in the power of the deceased at the time of his death, or out of it through having been emancipated or through being the child of an emancipated child or of a child of the female sex. When there are no family heirs, and none of those persons 12 who we have said rank as such, an agnate who has lost none of his agnatic rights, even though very many degrees removed from the deceased, is usually preferred to a nearer cognate; for instance, the grandson or great-grandson of a paternal uncle has a better title than a maternal uncle or aunt. Accordingly, in saying that the nearest cognate is preferred in the succession, or that, if there are several cognates in the nearest degree, they are called equally, we mean that this is the case if no one is entitled to priority, according to what we have said, as either being or ranking as a family heir, or as being an agnate; the only exceptions to this being emancipated brothers and sisters of the deceased who are called to succeed him, and who, in spite of their loss of status, are preferred to other agnates in a remoter degree than themselves.

TITLE VII

OF THE SUCCESSION TO FREEDMEN

Let us now turn to the property of freedmen. These were originally allowed to pass over their patrons in their wills with impunity: for by the statute of the Twelve Tables the inheritance of a freedman devolved on his patron only when he died intestate without leaving a family heir. If he died intestate, but left a family heir, the patron was not entitled to any portion of this property, and this, if the family heir was a natural child, seemed to be no grievance; but if he was an adoptive child, it was clearly unfair that the patron should be debarred from all right to the succession. Accordingly 1 this injustice of the law was at a later period corrected by the praetor's Edict, by which, if a freedman made a will, he was commanded to leave his patron half his property; and, if he left him nothing at all, or less than a half, possession of such half was given to him against the testament. If, on the other hand, he died intestate, leaving as family heir an adoptive son, the patron could obtain even against the latter possession of the goods of the deceased to the extent of one-half. But the freedman was enabled to exclude the patron if he left natural children, whether in his power at the time of his death, or emancipated or given in adoption, provided that he made a will in which he instituted them heirs to any part of the succession, or that, being passed over, they demanded possession against the will under the Edict :

2 if disinherited, they did not avail to bar the patron. At a still later period the lex Papia Poppaea augmented the rights of patrons who had more wealthy freedmen. By this it was enacted that, whenever a freedman left property amounting in value to a hundred thousand sesterces and upwards, and not so many as three children, the patron, whether he died testate or intestate, should be entitled to a portion equal to that of a single child. Accordingly, if the freedman left a single son or daughter as heir, the patron could claim half the property, exactly as if he had died without leaving any children : if he left two children as heirs, the patron could claim a third : if he left three, the patron was excluded altogether.

3 In our constitution, however, which we have drawn up in a convenient form and in the Greek language, so as to be known by all, we have established the following rules for application to such cases. If the freedman or freedwoman is less than a *centenarius*, that is, has a fortune of less than a hundred *aurei* (which we have reckoned as equivalent to the sum of a hundred thousand sesterces fixed by the lex Papia), the patron shall have no right to any share in the succession if they make a will; while, if they die intestate without leaving any children, we have retained unimpaired the rights conferred on the patron by the Twelve Tables. If they are possessed of more than a hundred *aurei*, and leave a descendant or descendants of either sex and any degree to take the inheritance civil or praetorian, we have given to such child or children the succession to their parents, to the exclusion of every patron and his issue. If, however, they leave no children, and die intestate, we have called the patron or patroness to their whole inheritance : while if they make a will, passing over their patron or patroness, and leaving no

children, or having disinherited such as they have, or (supposing them to be mothers or maternal grandfathers) having passed them over without leaving them the right to impeach the testament as unduteous, then, under our constitution, the patron shall succeed, by possession against the will, not, as before, to one-half of the freedman's estate, but to one-third, or, if the freedman or freedwoman has left him less than this third in his or her will, to so much as will make up the difference. But this third shall be free from all charges, even from legacies or trust bequests in favour of the children of the freedman or freedwoman, all of which are to fall on the patron's co-heirs. In the same constitution we have gathered together the rules applying to many other cases, which we deemed necessary for the complete settlement of this branch of law: for instance, a title to the succession of freedmen is conferred not only on patrons and patronesses, but on their children and collateral relatives to the fifth degree : all of which may be ascertained by reference to the constitution itself. If, however, there are several descendants of a patron or patroness, or of two or several, the nearest in degree is to take the succession of the freedman or freedwoman, which is to be divided, not among the stocks, but by counting the heads of those nearest in degree. And the same rule is to be observed with collaterals : for we have made the law of succession to freedmen almost identical with that relating to freeborn persons. All that has been 4 said relates nowadays to freedmen who are Roman citizens, for *dediticii* and *Latini Iuniani* having been together abolished there are now no others. As to a statutory right of succession to a Latin, there never was any such thing ; for men of this class, though during life they lived as free, yet as they drew their last breath they lost their liberty along with their life, and under the lex Iunia their manumitters kept their property, like that of slaves, as a kind of peculium. It was subsequently provided by the SC. Largianum that the manumitter's children, unless expressly disinherited, should be preferred to his external heirs in succession to the goods of a Latin ; and this was followed by the edict of the Emperor Trajan, providing that a Latin who contrived, without the knowledge or consent of his patron, to obtain by imperial

favour a grant of citizenship should live a citizen, but die a
Latin. Owing, however, to the difficulties accompanying these
changes of condition, and others as well, we have determined
by our constitution to repeal for ever the lex Iunia, the SC.
Largianum, and the edict of Trajan, and to abolish them
along with the Latins themselves, so as to enable all freedmen to enjoy the citizenship of Rome : and we have converted
in a wonderful manner the modes in which persons became
Latins, with some additions, into modes of attaining Roman
citizenship.

Title VIII

OF THE ASSIGNMENT OF FREEDMEN

Before we leave the subject of succession to freedmen,
we should observe a resolution of the Senate, to the effect
that, though the property of freedmen belongs in equal portions to all the patron's children who are in the same degree,
it shall yet be lawful for a parent to assign a freedman to one
of his children, so that after his own death the assignee shall
be considered his sole patron, and the other children who,
had it not been for such assignment, would be admitted
equally with him, shall have no claim to the succession whatever : though they recover their original rights if the assignee
1 dies without issue.   It is lawful to assign freedwomen as
well as freedmen, and to daughters and granddaughters no
2 less than to sons and grandsons ; and the power of assignment is conferred on all who have two or more children in
their power, and enables them to assign a freedman or freedwoman to such children while so subject to them.   Accordingly the question arose, whether the assignment becomes
void, if the parent subsequently emancipates the assignee?
and the affirmative opinion, which was held by Julian and
3 many others, has now become settled law.   It is immaterial
whether the assignment is made in a testament or not, and
indeed patrons are enabled to exercise this power in any
terms whatsoever, as is provided by the senatusconsult passed
in the time of Claudius, when Suillus Rufus and Ostorius
Scapula were consuls.

TITLE IX

OF POSSESSION OF GOODS

The law as to the possession of goods was introduced by the praetor by way of amending the older system, and this not only in intestate succession, as has been described, but also in cases where deceased persons have made a will. For instance, although the posthumous child of a stranger, if instituted heir, could not by the civil law .enter upon the inheritance, because his institution would be invalid, he could with the assistance of the praetor be made possessor of the goods by the praetorian law. Such a one can now, however, by our constitution be lawfully instituted, as being no longer unrecognized by the civil law. Sometimes, however, the 1 praetor promises the possession of goods rather in confirmation of the older law than for the purpose of correcting or impugning it; as, for instance, when he gives possession in accordance with a duly executed will to those who have been instituted heirs therein. Again, he calls family heirs and agnates to the possession of goods on an intestacy; and yet, even putting aside the possession of goods, the inheritance belongs to them already by the civil law. Those whom the 2 praetor calls to a succession do not become heirs in the eye of law, for the praetor cannot make an heir, because persons become heirs by a statute only, or some similar ordinance such as a senatusconsult or an imperial constitution : but as the praetor gives them the possession of goods they become quasi heirs, and are called 'possessors of goods'. And several additional grades of grantees of possession were recognized by the praetor in his anxiety that no one might die without a successor; the right of entering upon an inheritance, which had been confined by the statute of the Twelve Tables within very narrow limits, having been conferred more extensively by him in the spirit of justice and equity. The following are the kinds of testamentary 3 possession of goods. First, the so-called 'contratabular' possession, given to children who are merely passed over in the will. Second, that which the praetor promises to all duly instituted heirs, and which is for that reason called

'*secundum tabulas*'. Then, having spoken of wills, the praetor
passes on to cases of intestacy, in which, firstly, he gives the
possession of goods which is called *unde liberi* to family
heirs and those who in his Edict are ranked as such.
Failing these, he gives it, secondly, to successors having a
statutory title : thirdly, to the ten persons whom he preferred
to the manumitter of a free person, if a stranger in relation
to the latter, namely the latter's father and mother, grand-
parents paternal and maternal, children, grandchildren by
daughters as well as by sons, and brothers and sisters whether
of the whole or of the half blood only. The fourth degree of
possession is that given to the nearest cognates : the fifth is
that called *tum quam ex familia* : the sixth, that given to the
patron and patroness, their children and parents : the seventh,
that given to the husband or wife of the deceased ; the eighth,
4 that given to the cognates of the manumitter. Such was the
system established by the praetorian jurisdiction. We, however, who have been careful to pass over nothing, but correct
all defects by our constitutions, have retained, as necessary,
the possession of goods called *contra tabulas* and *secundum tabulas,* and also the kinds of possession upon intestacy
5 known as *unde liberi* and *unde legitimi.* The possession, however, which in the praetor's Edict occupied the fifth place, and
was called *unde decem personae,* we have with benevolent
intentions and with a short treatment shown to be superfluous.
Its effect was to prefer to the extraneous manumitter the ten
persons specified above ; but our constitution, which we have
made concerning the emancipation of children, has in all
cases made the parent implicitly the manumitter, as previously
under a fiduciary contract, and has attached this privilege to
every such manumission, so as to render superfluous the
aforesaid kind of possession of goods. We have therefore
removed it, and put in its place the possession which the
praetor promises to the nearest cognates, and which we have
6 thus made the fifth kind instead of the sixth. The possession
of goods which formerly stood seventh in the list, which was
called *tum quam ex familia,* and that which stood eighth,
namely, the possession entitled *unde liberi patroni patronaeque
et parentes eorum,* we have altogether suppressed by our

constitution respecting the rights of patrons. For, having assimilated the succession to freedmen to the succession to freeborn persons, with this sole exception—in order to preserve some difference between the two classes—that no one has any title to the former who is related more distantly than the fifth degree, we have left them sufficient remedies in the 'contratabular' possession, and in those called *unde legitimi* and *unde cognati*, wherewith to vindicate their rights, so that thus all the subtleties and inextricable confusion of these two kinds of possession of goods have been abolished. We have 7 preserved in full force another possession of goods, which is called *unde vir et uxor*, and which occupied the ninth place in the old classification, and have given it a higher place, namely, the sixth. The tenth kind, which was called *unde cognati manumissoris*, we have very properly abolished for reasons which have been already stated : thus leaving in full operation only six ordinary kinds of possession of goods. The seventh, which follows them, was introduced with most 8 excellent reason by the praetors, whose Edict finally promised the possession of goods to those persons expressly entitled to it by any statute, senatusconsult, or imperial constitution ; but this was not permanently incorporated by the praetor with either the intestate or the testamentary kinds of possession, but was accorded by him, as circumstances demanded, as an extreme and extraordinary remedy to those persons who claim, either under a will or on an intestacy, under statutes, senatusconsults, or the more recent legislation of the emperors. The praetor, having thus introduced many 9 kinds of successions, and arranged them in a system, fixed a definite time within which the possession of goods must be applied for, as there are often several persons entitled in the same kind of succession, though related in different degrees to the deceased, in order to save the creditors of the estate from delay in their suits, and to provide them with a proper defendant to sue ; and with the object also of making it less easy for them to obtain possession of the property of the deceased, as in bankruptcy, wherein they consulted their own advantage only. He allowed to children and parents, adoptive no less than natural, an interval of a

year, and to all other persons one hundred days, within
10 which to make the application. If a person entitled does not
apply for the possession of goods within the time specified,
his portion goes by accrual to those in the same degree or
class with himself: or, if there be none, the praetor promises
by his successory edict the possession to those in the next
degree, exactly as if the person in the preceding one were
non-existent. If any one refuses the possession of goods
which he has the opportunity of accepting, it is not usual to
wait until the aforesaid interval, within which possession must
be applied for, has elapsed, but the next degree is admitted
11 immediately under the same edict. In reckoning the interval,
only those days are considered upon which the persons
12 entitled could have made application. Earlier emperors,
however, have judiciously provided that no one need trouble
himself expressly to apply for the possession of goods, but
that, if he shall within the prescribed time in any manner
have signified his intention to accept, he shall have the full
benefit of such tacit acceptance.

TITLE X

OF ACQUISITION BY ADROGATION

There is another kind of universal succession which owes
its introduction neither to the statute of the Twelve Tables
nor to the praetor's Edict, but to the law which is based
1 upon custom and consent. When an independent person
gives himself in adrogation, all his property, corporeal and
incorporeal, and all debts due to him formerly passed in full
ownership to the adrogator, except such rights as are extinguished by loss of status, for instance, bounden services of
freedmen and rights of agnation. Use and usufruct, though
formerly enumerated among such rights, have now been saved
by our constitution from extinction by the least loss of status.
2 But we have now confined acquisition by adrogation within
the same limits as acquisition through their children by
natural parents; that is to say, adoptive as well as natural
parents acquire no greater right in property which comes to
children in their power from any extraneous source than a
mere usufruct; the ownership is vested in the children them-

selves. But if a son who has been adrogated dies in his adoptive family, the whole of his property vests in the adrogator, failing those persons who, under our constitution, are preferred to the father in succession to property which is not acquired immediately from him. Conversely, the adrogator 3 is not, by strict law, suable for the debts of his adoptive son, but an action may be brought against him as his representative; and if he declines to defend the latter, the creditors are allowed, by an order of the magistrates having jurisdiction in such cases, to take possession of the property of which the usufruct as well as the ownership would have belonged to the son, had he not subjected himself to the power of another, and to dispose of it in the mode prescribed by law.

TITLE XI

OF THE ADJUDICATION OF A DECEASED PERSON'S ESTATE TO PRESERVE GIFTS OF LIBERTY

A new form of succession was added by a constitution of the Emperor Marcus, which provided that if slaves, who have received a bequest of liberty from their master in a will under which no heir takes, wish to have his property adjudged to them, in order that effect may be given to the gift of freedom, their application shall be entertained. Such is the 1 substance of a rescript addressed by the Emperor Marcus to Popilius Rufus, which runs as follows: 'If there is no successor to take on the intestacy of Virginius Valens, who by his will has conferred freedom on certain of his slaves, and if, consequently, his property is in danger of being sold, the magistrate who has cognizance of such matters shall on application entertain your desire to have the property adjudged to you, in order to give effect to the bequests of liberty, direct and fiduciary, provided you give proper security to the creditors for payment of their claims in full. Slaves to whom liberty has been directly bequeathed shall become free exactly as if the inheritance had been actually accepted, and those whom the heir was requested to manumit shall obtain their liberty from you; provided that if you will have the property adjudged to you only upon the condition, that even the slaves who have received a direct bequest of liberty shall become your freedmen, and if they, whose status is now in question, agree to this, we are ready to authorize compliance with your wishes. And lest the benefit afforded by this our rescript be rendered ineffectual in another way, by the Treasury laying claim to the property, be it hereby known to those engaged in our service that the cause of liberty is to be preferred to pecuniary advantage, and that they must so effect such seizures as to preserve the freedom of those who could have obtained it had the inheritance been accepted

2 under the will.' This rescript was a benefit not only to slaves thus liberated, but also to the deceased testators themselves, by saving their property from being seized and sold by their creditors ; for it is certain that such seizure and sale cannot take place if the property has been adjudged on this account, because some one has come forward to defend the deceased, and a satisfactory defender too, who gives the creditors full

3 security for payment. Primarily, the rescript is applicable only where freedom is conferred by a will. How then will the case stand, if a man who dies intestate makes gifts of freedom by codicils, and on the intestacy no one accepts the inheritance ? We answer, that the boon conferred by the constitution ought not here to be refused. No one can doubt that liberty given, in codicils, by a man who dies having

4 made a will, is effectual. The terms of the constitution show that it comes into application when there is no successor on an intestacy ; accordingly, it is of no use so long as it is uncertain whether there will be one or not ; but, when this has been determined in the negative, it at once becomes

5 applicable. Again, it may be asked whether, if a person who abstains from accepting an inheritance can claim a judicial restoration of rights, the constitution can still be applied, and the goods adjudged under it ? And what, if such person obtains a restoration after they have been actually adjudged in order to give effect to the bequest of freedom ? We reply that gifts of liberty to which effect has once been given

6 cannot possibly be recalled. The object with which this constitution was enacted was to give effect to bequests of liberty, and accordingly it is quite inapplicable where no such bequests are made. Supposing, however, that a man

manumits certain slaves in his lifetime, or in contemplation of death, and, in order to prevent any questions arising whether the creditors have thereby been defrauded, the slaves are desirous of having the property adjudged to them, should this be permitted? and we are inclined to say that it should, though the point is not covered by the terms of the constitution. Perceiving, however, that the enactment was want- 7 ing in many minute points of this kind, we have ourselves issued a very full constitution, in which have been collected many conceivable cases by which the law relating to this kind of succession has been completed, and with which any one can become acquainted by reading the constitution itself.

TITLE XII

OF UNIVERSAL SUCCESSIONS, NOW OBSOLETE, IN SALE OF GOODS UPON BANKRUPTCY, AND UNDER THE SC. CLAUDIANUM.

There were other kinds of universal succession in existence prior to that last before mentioned; for instance, the ' purchase of goods ' which was introduced with many prolixities of form for the sale of insolvent debtors' estates, and which remained in use under the so-called ' ordinary ' system of procedure. Later generations adopted the 'extraordinary' procedure, and accordingly sales of goods became obsolete along with the ordinary procedure of which they were a part. Creditors are now allowed to take possession of their debtor's property only by the order of a judge, and to dispose of it as to them seems most advantageous; all of which will appear more perfectly from the larger books of the Digest. There was 1 too a miserable form of universal acquisition under the SC. Claudianum, when a free woman, through indulgence of her passion for a slave, lost her freedom by the senatusconsult, and with her freedom her property. But this enactment we deemed unworthy of our times, and have ordered its abolition in our Empire, nor allowed it to be inserted in our Digest.

Title XIII

OF OBLIGATIONS

Let us now pass on to obligations. An obligation is a legal bond, with which we are bound by a necessity of per-
1 forming some act according to the laws of our State. The leading division of obligations is into two kinds, civil and praetorian. Those obligations are civil which are established by statute, or at least are sanctioned by the civil law; those are praetorian which the praetor has established by his own
2 jurisdiction, and which are also called honorary. By another division they are arranged in four classes, contractual, quasi-contractual, delictal, and quasi-delictal. And, first, we must examine those which are contractual, and which again fall into four species, for contract is concluded either by delivery, by a form of words, by writing, or by consent: each of which we will treat in detail.

Title XIV

OF REAL CONTRACTS, OR THE MODES IN WHICH OBLIGATIONS ARE CONTRACTED BY DELIVERY

Real contracts, or contracts concluded by delivery, are exemplified by loan for consumption, that is to say, loan of such things as are estimated by weight, number, or measure, for instance, wine, oil, corn, coined money, copper, silver, or gold: things in which we transfer our property on condition that the receiver shall transfer to us, at a future time, not the same things, but other things of the same kind and quality: and this contract is called *mutuum*, because thereby *meum* or mine becomes *tuum* or thine. The action to which it gives
1 rise is called a condiction. Again, a man is bound by a real obligation if he takes what is not owed him from another who pays him by mistake; and the latter can, as plaintiff, bring a condiction against him for its recovery, after the analogy of the action whose formula ran 'if it be proved that he ought to convey', exactly as if the defendant had received a loan from him. Consequently a pupil who, by mistake, is paid something which is not really owed him without his guardian's authority, will be no more bound by a condiction for the

recovery of money not owed than by one for money received as a loan: though this kind of liability does not seem to be founded on contract; for a payment made in order to discharge a debt is intended to extinguish, not to create, an obligation. So too a person to whom a thing is lent for use is laid under 2 a real obligation, and is liable to the action on a loan for use. The difference between this case and a loan for consumption is considerable, for here the intention is not to make the object lent the property of the borrower, who accordingly is bound to restore the same identical thing. Again, if the receiver of a loan for consumption loses what he has received by some accident, such as fire, the fall of a building, shipwreck, or the attack of thieves or enemies, he still remains bound : but the borrower for use, though responsible for the greatest care in keeping what is lent him—and it is not enough that he has shown as much care as he usually bestows on his own affairs, if only some one else could have been more diligent in the charge of it—has not to answer for loss occasioned by fire or accident beyond his control, provided it did not occur through any fault of his own. Otherwise, of course, it is different: for instance, if you choose to take with you on a journey a thing which has been lent to you for use, and lose it by being attacked by enemies or thieves, or by a shipwreck, it is beyond question that you will be liable for its restoration. A thing is not properly said to be lent for use if any recompense is received or agreed upon for the service ; for where this is the case, the use of the thing is held to be hired, and the contract is of a different kind, for a loan for use ought always to be gratuitous. Again, the obligation incurred by 3 a person with whom a thing is deposited for custody is real, and he can be sued by the action of deposit; he too being responsible for the restoration of the identical thing deposited, though only where it is lost through some positive act of commission on his part: for for carelessness, that is to say, inattention and negligence, he is not liable. Thus a person from whom a thing is stolen, in the charge of which he has been most careless, cannot be called to account, because, if a man entrusts property to the custody of a careless friend, he has no one to blame but himself for his want of caution.

K 2

4 Finally, the creditor who takes a thing in pledge is under a real obligation, and is bound to restore the thing itself by the action of pledge. A pledge, however, is for the benefit of both parties ; of the debtor, because it enables him to borrow more easily, and of the creditor, because he has the better security for repayment ; and accordingly, it is a settled rule that the pledgee cannot be held responsible for more than the greatest care in the custody of the pledge ; if he shows this, and still loses it by some accident, he himself is freed from all liability, without losing his right to sue for the debt.

TITLE XV

OF VERBAL OBLIGATION

An obligation is contracted by question and answer, that is to say, by a form of words, when we stipulate that property shall be conveyed to us, or some other act be performed in our favour. Such verbal contracts ground two different actions, namely condiction, when the stipulation is certain, and the action on stipulation, when it is uncertain ; and the name is derived from *stipulum*, a word in use among the ancients to mean 'firm', coming possibly from *stipes*, the trunk of a tree.

1   In this contract the following forms of words were formerly sanctioned by usage : 'Do you engage yourself to do so and so?' 'I do engage myself.' 'Do you promise?' 'I do promise.' 'Do you pledge your credit?' 'I pledge my credit.' 'Do you guarantee?' 'I guarantee.' 'Will you convey?' 'I will convey.' 'Will you do?' 'I will do.' Whether the stipulation is in Latin, or Greek, or any other language, is immaterial, provided the two parties understand one another, so that it is not necessary even that they should both speak in the same tongue, so long as the answer corresponds to the question, and thus two Greeks, for instance, may contract an obligation in Latin. But it was only in former times that the solemn forms referred to were in use : for subsequently, by the enactment of Leo's constitution, their employment was rendered unnecessary, and nothing was afterwards required except that the parties should understand

each other, and agree to the same thing, the words in which such agreement was expressed being immaterial.

The terms of a stipulation may be absolute, or performance 2 may either be postponed to some future time, or be made subject to a condition. An absolute stipulation may be ex- emplified by the following : ' Do you promise to give five *aurei*?' and here (if the promise be made) that sum may be instantly sued for. As an instance of a stipulation '*in diem*', as it is called where a future day is fixed for payment, we may take the following : ' Do you promise to give ten *aurei* on the first of March?' In such a stipulation as this, an immediate debt is created, but it cannot be sued upon until the arrival of the day fixed for payment : and even on that very day an action cannot be brought, because the debtor ought to have the whole of it allowed to him for payment ; for otherwise, unless the whole day on which payment was promised is past, it cannot be certain that default has been made. If the terms of your stipulation run ' Do you promise 3 to pay me ten *aurei* a year so long as I live?' the obliga- tion is deemed absolute, and the liability perpetual, for a debt cannot be owed till a certain time only ; though if the pro- misee's heir sues for payment, he will be successfully met by the plea of contrary agreement. A stipulation is conditional, 4 when performance is made to depend on some uncertain event in the future, so that it becomes actionable only on something being done or omitted : for instance, ' Do you promise to give five *aurei* if Titius is made consul?' If, how- ever, a man stipulates in the form ' Do you promise to give so and so, if I do not go up to the Capitol?' the effect is the same as if he had stipulated for payment to himself at the time of his death. The immediate effect of a conditional stipulation is not a debt, but merely the expectation that at some time there will be a debt : and this expectation devolves on the stipulator's heir, supposing he dies himself before fulfil- ment of the condition. It is usual in stipulations to name a 5 place for payment ; for instance, ' Do you promise to give at Carthage?' Such a stipulation as this, though in its terms absolute, implies a condition that enough time shall be allowed to the promisor to enable him to pay the money

at Carthage. Accordingly, if a man at Rome stipulates thus,
'Do you promise to pay to-day at Carthage?' the stipulation
is void, because the performance of the act to be promised
6 is a physical impossibility. Conditions relating to past or
present time either make the obligation void at once, or have
no suspensive operation whatever. Thus, in the stipulation
'Do you promise to give so and so, if Titius has been consul,
or if Maevius is alive?' the promise is void, if the condition is
not satisfied; while if it is, it is binding at once: for events
which in themselves are certain do not suspend the binding
force of an obligation, however uncertain we ourselves may be
about them.

7   The performance or non-performance of an act may be the
object of a stipulation no less than the delivery of property,
though where this is the case, it will be best to connect the
non-performance of the act to be performed, or the performance of the act to be omitted, with a pecuniary penalty to be
paid in default, lest there be a doubt as to the value of the
act or omission, which will make it necessary for the plaintiff
to prove to what damages he is entitled. Thus, if it be a
performance which is stipulated for, some such penalty should
be added as in the following: 'If so and so is not done, do
you promise to pay ten *aurei* as a penalty?' And if the performance of some acts, and the non-performance of others,
are bargained for in the same stipulation, a clause of the
following kind should be added, 'If any default is made,
either as contrary to what is agreed upon, or by way of non-
performance, do you promise to pay a penalty of ten *aurei*?'

TITLE XVI

OF STIPULATIONS IN WHICH THERE ARE TWO CREDITORS OR TWO DEBTORS

There may be two or more parties on either side in a stipulation, that is to say, as promisors or promisees. Joint
promisees are so constituted by the promisor answering,
'I promise,' after they have all first asked the question; for
instance, if after two promisees have separately stipulated
from him, he answers, 'I promise to give so and so to each of
you.' But if he first promises to Titius, and then, on another's

putting the question to him, promises to him too, there will be
two distinct obligations, namely, one between him and each of
the promisees, and they are not considered joint promisees at
all. The usual form to constitute two or more joint promisors
is as follows,—'Maevius, do you promise to give five *aurei*?
Seius, do you promise to give the same five *aurei*?' and in
answer they reply separately, 'I promise.' In obligations of 1
this kind each joint promisee is owed the whole sum, and
the whole sum can be claimed from each joint promisor;
and yet in both cases but one payment is due, so that if
one joint promisee receives the debt, or one joint promisor
pays it, the obligation is thereby extinguished for all, and all
are thereby released from it. Of two joint promisors one may 2
be bound absolutely, while performance by the other is postponed to a future day, or made to depend on a condition;
but such postponement or such condition in no way prevents
the stipulator from at once suing the one who was bound
absolutely.

Title XVII

OF STIPULATIONS MADE BY SLAVES

From his master's legal capacity a slave derives ability to
be promisee in a stipulation. Thus, as an inheritance in most
matters represents the legal 'person' of the deceased, whatever a slave belonging to it stipulates for, before the inheritance is accepted, he acquires for the inheritance, and so for
the person who subsequently becomes heir. All that a slave 1
acquires by a stipulation he acquires for his master only,
whether it was to that master, or himself, or his fellow slave, or no
one in particular that performance was to be made under the
contract; and the same principle applies to children in power,
so far as they now are instruments of acquisition for their father.
When, however, what is stipulated for is permission to do some 2
specific act, that permission cannot extend beyond the person
of the promisee: for instance, if a slave stipulates for permission to cross the promisor's land, he cannot himself be denied
passage, though his master can. A stipulation by a slave 3
belonging to joint owners enures to the benefit of all of them
in proportion to the shares in which they own him, unless he

stipulated at the bidding, or expressly in favour, of one of them only, in which case that one alone is benefited. Where a jointly owned slave stipulates for the transfer of property which cannot be acquired for one of his two masters, the contract enures to the benefit of the other only: for instance, where the stipulation is for the transfer of a thing which already belongs to one of them.

TITLE XVIII

OF THE DIFFERENT KINDS OF STIPULATIONS

Stipulations are either judicial, praetorian, conventional, or common : by the latter being meant those which are both
1 praetorian and judicial. Judicial stipulations are those which it is simply part of the judge's duty to require ; for instance, security against fraud, or for the pursuit of a runaway slave,
2 or (in default) for payment of his value. Those are praetorian, which the praetor is bound to exact simply in virtue of his magisterial functions ; for instance, security against apprehended damage, or for payment of legacies by an heir. Under praetorian stipulations we must include also those directed by the aedile, for these too are based upon jurisdic-
3 tion. Conventional stipulations are those which arise merely from the agreement of the parties, apart from any direction of a judge or of the praetor, and which one may almost say are of as many different kinds as there are conceivable objects to
4 a contract. Common stipulations may be exemplified by that by which a guardian gives security that his ward's property will not be squandered or misappropriated, which he is sometimes required to enter into by the praetor, and sometimes also by a judge when the matter cannot be managed in any other way ; or, again, we might take the stipulation by which an agent promises that his acts shall be ratified by his principal.

TITLE XIX

OF INVALID STIPULATIONS

Anything, whether movable or immovable, which admits of private ownership, may be made the object of a stipulation ;
1 but if a man stipulates for the delivery of a thing which either

does not or cannot exist, such as Stichus, who is dead but whom he thought alive, or an impossible creature, like a hippocentaur, the contract will be void. Precisely the same 2 principle applies where a man stipulates for the delivery of a thing which is sacred or religious, but which he thought was a subject of human ownership, or of a thing which is public, that is to say, devoted in perpetuity to the use and enjoyment of the people at large, like a forum or theatre, or of a free man whom he thought a slave, or of a thing which he is incapable of owning, or which is his own already. And the fact that a thing which is public may become private property, that a free man may become a slave, that the stipulator may become capable of owning such and such a thing, or that such and such a thing may cease to belong to him, will not avail to merely suspend the force of the stipulation in these cases, but it is void from the outset. Conversely, a stipulation which originally was perfectly good may be avoided by the thing, which is its object, acquiring any of the characters just specified through no fault of the promisor. And a stipulation, such as 'do you promise to convey Lucius Titius when he shall be a slave?' and others like it, are also void from the beginning; for objects which by their very nature cannot be owned by man cannot either in any way be made the object of an obligation. If one man promises that another shall convey, or 3 do so and so, as, for instance, that Titius shall give five *aurei*, he will not be bound, though he will if he promises to get Titius to give them. If a man stipulates for conveyance to, 4 or performance in favour of, another person who is not his paterfamilias, the contract is void; though of course performance to a third person may be bargained for (as in the stipulation 'do you promise to give to me or to Seius?'); where, though the obligation is created in favour of the stipulator only, payment may still be lawfully made to Seius, even against the stipulator's will, the result of which, if it is done, being that the promisor is entirely released from his obligation, while the stipulator can sue Seius by the action of agency. If a man stipulates for payment of ten *aurei* to himself and another who is not his paterfamilias, the contract will be good, though there has been much doubt whether in such a case the stipulator can sue for the whole sum agreed upon, or only half; the law is now settled in favour of the smaller sum. If you stipulate for performance in favour of one in your power, all benefit under the contract is taken by yourself, for your words are as the words of your son, as his words are as yours, in all cases in which he is merely an 5 instrument of acquisition for you. Another circumstance by which a stipulation may be avoided is want of correspondence between question and answer, as where a man stipulates from you for payment of ten *aurei*, and you promise five, or vice versa ; or where his question is unconditional, your answer conditional, or vice versa, provided only that in this latter case the difference is express and clear ; that is to say, if he stipulates for payment on fulfilment of a condition, or on some determinate future day, and you answer: 'I promise to pay to-day,' the contract is void ; but if you merely answer : 'I promise,' you are held by this laconic reply to have undertaken payment on the day, or subject to the condition specified ; for it is not essential that every word used by the stipulator should 6 be repeated in the answer of the promise. Again, no valid stipulation can be made between two persons of whom one is in the power of the other. A slave indeed cannot be under an obligation to either his master or anybody else : but children in power can be bound in favour of any one except their own 7 paterfamilias. The dumb, of course, cannot either stipulate or promise, nor can the deaf, for the promisee in stipulation must hear the answer, and the promisor must hear the question ; and this makes it clear that we are speaking of persons only who are stone deaf, not of those who (as it is said) are hard of 8 hearing. A lunatic cannot enter into any contract at all, 9 because he does not understand what he is doing. On the other hand a pupil can enter into any contract, provided that he has his guardian's authority, when necessary, as it is for incurring an obligation, though not for imposing an obligation 10 on another person. This concession of legal capacity of disposition is manifestly reasonable in respect of children who have acquired some understanding, for children below the age of seven years, or who have just passed that age, resemble lunatics in want of intelligence. Those, however, who have

just completed their seventh year are permitted, by a bene-
ficent interpretation of the law, in order to promote their
interests, to have the same capacity as those approaching the
age of puberty ; but a child below the latter age, who is in
paternal power, cannot bind himself even with his father's
sanction. An impossible condition annexed to an obligation 11
invalidates the stipulation. An impossible condition is one
which, according to the course of nature, cannot be fulfilled, as,
for instance, if one says : ' Do you promise to give if I touch
the sky with my finger ? ' But if the stipulation runs : ' Do
you promise to give if I do not touch the sky with my
finger ? ' it is considered unconditional, and accordingly can be
sued upon at once. Again, a verbal obligation made between 12
persons who are not present with one another is void. This
rule, however, afforded contentious persons opportunities of
litigation, by alleging, after some interval, that they, or their
adversaries, had not been present on the occasion in question ;
and we have therefore issued a constitution, addressed to the
advocates of Caesarea, in order with the more dispatch to
settle such disputes, whereby it is enacted that written documents in evidence of a contract which recite the presence of
the parties shall be taken to be indisputable proof of the fact,
unless the person, who resorts to allegations usually so dis-
graceful, proves by the clearest evidence, either documentary
or borne by credible witnesses, that he or his adversary was
elsewhere than alleged during the whole day on which the
document is stated to have been executed. Formerly, a man 13
could not stipulate that a thing should be conveyed to him
after his own death, or after that of the promisor ; nor could
one person who was in another's power even stipulate for
conveyance after that other's death, because he was deemed
to speak with the voice of his parent or master ; and stipulations for conveyance the day before the promisee's or promisor's decease were also void. Stipulations, however, as has
already been remarked, derive their validity from the consent
of the contracting parties, and we therefore introduced a necessary emendation in respect also of this rule of law, by providing that a stipulation shall be good which bargains for
performance either after the death, or the day before the

14 death, of either promisee or promisor. Again, a stipulation in
the form : 'Do you promise to give to-day, if such or such a
ship arrives from Asia to-morrow?' was formerly void, as
being preposterous in its expression, because what should
come last is put first. Leo, however, of famous memory held
that a preposterous stipulation in the settlement of a dowry
ought not to be rejected as void, and we have determined to
allow it perfect validity in every case, and not merely in that
15 in which it was formerly sanctioned. A stipulation, say by
Titius, in the form : 'Do you promise to give when I shall
die' or 'when you shall die'? is good now, as indeed it always
16 was even under the older law. So too a stipulation for per-
17 formance after the death of a third person is good. If a document in evidence of a contract states that so and so promised,
the promise is deemed to have been given in answer to a
18 preceding question. When several acts of conveyance or
performance are comprised in a single stipulation, if the promisor simply answer : 'I promise to convey,' he becomes
liable on each and all of them, but if he answers that he will
convey only one or some of them, he incurs an obligation in
respect of those only which are comprised in his answer, there
being in reality several distinct stipulations of which only one
or some are considered to have acquired binding force : for for
each act of conveyance or performance there ought to be a
19 separate question and a separate answer. As has been already
observed, no one can validly stipulate for performance to a
person other than himself, for the purpose of this kind of
obligation is to enable persons to acquire for themselves that
whereby they are profited, and a stipulator is not profited
if the conveyance is to be made to a third person. Hence,
if it be wished to make a stipulation in favour of any such
third person, a penalty should be stipulated for, to be paid, in
default of performance of that which is in reality the object
of the contract, to the party who otherwise would have no
interest in such performance ; for when one stipulates for a
penalty, it is not his interest in what is the real contract
which is considered, but only the amount to be forfeited to
him upon non-fulfilment of the condition. So that a stipulation for conveyance to Titius, but made by some one else,

is void: but the addition of a penalty, in the form 'If you do not convey, do you promise to pay me so many *aurei*?' makes it good and actionable. But where the promisee stipu- 20 lates in favour of a third person, having himself an interest in the performance of the promise, the stipulation is good. For instance, if a guardian, after beginning to exercise his tutorial functions, retires from their exercise in favour of his fellow guardian, taking from him by stipulation security for the due charge of the ward's property, he has a sufficient interest in the performance of this promise, because the ward could have sued him in case of maladministration, and therefore the obligation is binding. So too a stipulation will be good by which one bargains for delivery to one's agent, or for payment to one's creditor, for in the latter case one may be so far interested in the payment that, if it be not made, one will become liable to a penalty or to having a foreclosure of estates which one has mortgaged. Conversely, he who promises that 21 another shall do so and so is not bound unless he promises a penalty in default; and, again, a man cannot validly stipulate 22 that property which will hereafter be his shall be conveyed to him as soon as it becomes his own. If the stipulator 23 and the promisor mean different things, there is no contractual obligation, but it is just as if no answer had been made to the question; for instance, if one stipulates from you for Stichus, and you think he means Pamphilus, whose name you believed to be Stichus. A promise made for an illegal or 24 immoral purpose, as, for instance, to commit a sacrilege or homicide, is void.

If a man stipulates for performance on the fulfilment of a 25 condition, and dies before such fulfilment, his heir can sue on the contract when it occurs: and the heir of the promisor can be sued under the same circumstances. A stipulation for a con- 26 veyance this year, or this month, cannot be sued upon until the whole year, or the whole month, has elapsed: and simi- 27 larly the promisee cannot sue immediately upon a stipulation for the conveyance of an estate or a slave, but only after allowing a sufficient interval for the conveyance to be made.

Title XX

OF FIDEJUSSORS OR SURETIES

Very often other persons, called fidejussors or sureties, are bound for the promisor, being taken by promisees as addi-

1 tional security. Such sureties may accompany any obligation, whether real, verbal, literal or consensual: and it is immaterial even whether the principal obligation be civil or natural, so that a man may go surety for the obligation of a slave

2 either to a stranger or to his master. A fidejussor is not only bound himself, but his obligation devolves also on his heir;

3 and the contract of suretyship may be entered into before no

4 less than after the creation of the principal obligation. If there are several fidejussors to the same obligation, each of them, however many they are, is liable for the whole amount, and the creditor may sue whichever he chooses for the whole; but by the letter of Hadrian he may be compelled to sue for only an aliquot part, determined by the number of sureties who are solvent at the commencement of the action: so that if one of them is insolvent at that time the liability of the rest is proportionately increased. Thus, if one fidejussor pay the whole amount, he alone suffers by the insolvency of the principal debtor; but this is his own fault, as he might have availed himself of the letter of Hadrian, and required that the

5 claim should be reduced to his rateable portion. Fidejussors cannot be bound for more than their principal, for their obligation is but accessory to the latter's, and the accessory cannot contain more than the principal; but they can be bound for less. Thus, if the principal debtor promised ten *aurei*, the fidejussor can well be bound for five, but not vice versa; and if the principal's promise is absolute, that of the fidejussor may be conditional, though a conditional promise cannot be absolutely guaranteed, for more and less is to be understood of time as well as of quantity, immediate payment

6 being regarded as more, and future payment as less. For the recovery of anything paid by him for the principal the fide-

7 jussor can sue the latter by the action on agency. A fidejussor may be taken in Greek, by using the expressions τῇ ἐμῇ πίστει κελεύω, λέγω, θέλω, or βούλομαι; and φημί will be taken as

equivalent to λέγω. It is to be observed that in the stipulations 8 of fidejussors the general rule is that whatever is stated in writing to have been done is taken to have really been done; and, accordingly, it is settled law that if a man signs his name to a paper stating that he became a fidejussor, all formalities are presumed to have been duly observed.

TITLE XXI

OF LITERAL OBLIGATION

Formerly there was a kind of obligation made by writing, and said to be contracted by the entry of a debt in a ledger; but such entries have nowadays gone out of use. Of course, if a man states in writing that he owes money which has never been paid over to him, he cannot be allowed, after a considerable interval, to defend himself by the plea that the money was not, in fact, advanced; for this is a point which has frequently been settled by imperial constitutions. The consequence is, that even at the present day a person who is estopped from this plea is bound by his written signature, which (even of course where there is no stipulation) is ground for a condiction. The length of time after which this defence could not be pleaded was formerly fixed by imperial constitutions at five years; but it has been reduced by our constitution, in order to save creditors from a more extended risk of being defrauded of their money, so that now it cannot be advanced after the lapse of two years from the date of the alleged payment.

TITLE XXII

OF OBLIGATION BY CONSENT

Obligations contracted by mere consent are exemplified by sale, hire, partnership and agency, which are called consensual contracts because no writing, nor the presence of the parties, nor any delivery is required to make the obligation actionable, but the consent of the parties is sufficient. Parties who are not present together, therefore, can form these contracts by letter, for instance, or by messenger: and they are in their nature bilateral, that is, both parties incur a reciprocal obligation to perform whatever is just and fair, whereas verbal contracts are unilateral, one party being promisee, and the other alone promisor.

Title XXIII

OF PURCHASE AND SALE

The contract of purchase and sale is complete immediately the price is agreed upon, and even before the price or as much as any earnest is paid: for earnest is merely evidence of the completion of the contract. In respect of sales unattested by any written evidence this is a reasonable rule, and so far as they are concerned we have made no innovations. By one of our constitutions, however, we have enacted, that no sale effected by an agreement in writing shall be good or binding, unless that agreement is written by the contracting parties themselves, or, if written by some one else, is at least signed by them, or finally, if written by a notary, is duly drawn by him and executed by the parties. So long as any of these requirements is unsatisfied, there is room to retract, and either purchaser or vendor may withdraw from the agreement with impunity—provided, that is to say, that no earnest has been given. Where earnest has been given, and either party refuses to perform the contract, that party, whether the agreement be in writing or not, if purchaser forfeits what he has given, and if vendor is compelled to restore double what he has received, even though there has been no express agreement in the matter of earnest.

1 It is necessary that the price should be settled, for without a price there can be no purchase and sale, and it ought to be a fixed and certain price. For instance, where the parties agreed that the thing should be sold at a price to be subsequently fixed by Titius, the older jurists doubted much whether this was a valid contract of sale or not. The doubt has been settled in the following way by our decision; if the third person named actually fixes the price, it must certainly be paid, as settled by him, and the thing must be delivered, in order to give effect to the sale; the purchaser (if not fairly treated) suing by the action on purchase, and the vendor by the action on sale. But if the third person named will not or

cannot fix the price, the sale will be void, because no price has been settled. This rule, which we have adopted with regard to sales, may reasonably be extended also to contracts of hire. The price, too, should be in money; for it used to be **2** much disputed whether anything else, such as a slave, a piece of land, or a robe, could be treated as price. Sabinus and Cassius held the affirmative, explaining thus the common theory that exchange is a species, and the oldest species, of purchase and sale; and in their support they quoted the lines of Homer, who says in a certain passage that the army of the Greeks procured themselves wine by giving other things in exchange, the actual words being as follow: 'then the long-haired Greeks bought themselves wine, some with bronze, some with shining iron, some with hides, some with live oxen, some with slaves.'[1] The other school maintained the negative, and distinguished between exchange on the one hand, and purchase and sale on the other: for if an exchange were the same thing as a sale, it would be impossible to determine which is the thing sold, and which is the price, and both things cannot be regarded in each of these characters. The opinion, however, of Proculus, who affirmed that exchange was a species of contract apart by itself, and distinct from sale, has deservedly prevailed, as it is confirmed by other lines from Homer, and by still more cogent reasons, and this has been admitted by preceding Emperors, and is fully stated in our Digest. As soon as the **3** contract of sale is concluded—that is, as we have said, as soon as the price is agreed upon, if the contract is not in writing—the thing sold is immediately at the risk of the purchaser, even though it has not yet been delivered to him. Accordingly, if a slave dies, or is injured in any part of his body, or if a house is either totally or partially burnt down, or if a piece of land is wholly or partially swept away by a river flood, or is reduced in acreage by an inundation, or made of less value by a storm blowing down some of its trees, the loss falls on the purchaser, who must pay the price even though he has not got what he purchased. The vendor is not responsible and does not suffer for anything not due to any design or fault of his own. If, however, after the purchase of a piece of

[1] Il. vii. 472 sqq.

land, it receives an increase by alluvion, it is the purchaser
who profits thereby: for the profit ought to belong to him
who also bears the risk. And if a slave who has been sold
runs away, or is stolen, without any design or fault of the
vendor, one should look to see whether the latter expressly
undertook to keep him safely until delivery was made; for,
if he did this, the loss falls upon him, though otherwise he
incurs no liability: and this is a rule which applies to all
animals and other objects whatsoever. The vendor, however,
will be bound to transfer to the purchaser all his rights of
action for the recovery of the object or damages, for, not having
yet delivered it to the purchaser, he still remains its owner,
and the same holds good of the penal actions on theft and on
4 unlawful damage. A sale may be made conditionally as well
as absolutely. The following is an example of a conditional
sale: 'If Stichus meets with your approval within a certain
5 time, he shall be purchased by you for so many *aurei*.' If
a man buys a piece of land which is sacred, religious, or public,
such as a forum or basilica, knowing it to be such, the purchase is void. But if the vendor has fraudulently induced him
to believe that what he was buying was not sacred, or was
private property, as he cannot legally have what he contracted
for, he can bring the action on purchase to recover damages
for what he has lost by the fraud; and the same rule applies
to the purchase of a free man represented by the vendor to
be a slave.

TITLE XXIV

OF LETTING AND HIRING

The contract of hire resembles very closely the contract of
sale, and the same rules of law apply to both. Thus, as the
contract of sale is concluded as soon as the price is agreed
upon, so the contract of hire is held to be concluded as soon
as the sum to be paid for the hiring is settled, and from that
moment the letter has an action on the letting, and the hirer
1 on the hiring. What we have said above as to a sale in
which the price is left to be fixed by a third person must be
understood to apply also to a contract of hire in which the
amount to be paid for hire is left to be fixed in the same
way. Consequently, if a man gives clothes to a fuller to

clean or finish, or to a tailor to mend, and the amount of hire is not fixed at the time, but left to subsequent agreement between the parties, a contract of hire cannot properly be said to have been concluded, but an action is given on the circumstances, as amounting to an innominate contract. Again, 2 a question often arose in connexion with the contract of hire similar to that which was so common, namely, whether an exchange was a sale. For instance, what is the nature of the transaction if a man gives you the use or enjoyment of a thing, and receives in return the use or enjoyment of another thing from you? It is now settled that this is not a contract of hire, but a kind of contract apart by itself. Thus, if a man had one ox, and his neighbour another, and they agreed that each should in turn lend the other his ox for ten days to make use of, and then one of the oxen died while working for the man to whom it did not belong, an action cannot be brought on hire, nor on a loan for use, for a loan for use ought to be gratuitous : but an action should be brought as on an innominate contract. So nearly akin, indeed, is purchase and 3 sale to letting and hiring, that in some cases it is a question to which class of the two a contract belongs. As an instance may be taken those lands which are delivered over to be enjoyed for ever, upon the terms, that is to say, that so long as the rent is paid to the owner it shall not be lawful for the latter to take the lands away from either the original hirer, or his heir, or any one else to whom he or his heir has conveyed them by sale, gift, dowry, or in any other way whatsoever. The questionings of the earlier lawyers, some of whom thought this kind of contract a hiring, and others a sale, occasioned the enactment of the statute of Zeno, which determined that this contract of *emphyteusis*, as it is called, was of a peculiar nature, and should not be included under either hire or sale, but should rest on the terms of the agreement in each particular case : so that if anything were agreed upon between the parties, this should bind them exactly as if it were inherent in the very nature of the contract ; while if they did not agree expressly at whose risk the land should be, it should be at that of the owner in case of total destruction, and at that of the tenant, if the injury were merely partial.

4 And these rules we have adopted in our legislation. Again, if a goldsmith agrees to make Titius rings of a certain weight and pattern out of his own gold for, say, ten *aurei*, it is a question whether the contract is purchase and sale or letting and hiring. Cassius says the material is bought and sold, the labour let and hired ; but it is now settled that there is only a purchase and sale. But if Titius provided the gold, and agreed to pay him for his work, the contract is clearly a letting and hiring.

5 The hirer ought to observe all the terms of the contract, and in the absence of express agreement his obligations should be ascertained by reference to what is fair and equitable. Where a man has either given or promised hire for the use of clothes, silver, or a beast of burden, he is required in his charge of it to show as much care as the most diligent father of a family shows in his own affairs ; if he do this, and still accidentally lose it, he will be under no obligation to re-

6 store either it or its value. If the hirer dies before the time fixed for the termination of the contract has elapsed, his heir succeeds to his rights and obligations in respect thereof.

TITLE XXV

OF PARTNERSHIP

A partnership either extends to all the goods of the partners, when the Greeks call it by the special name of κοινο-πραξία, or is confined to a single sort of business, such as the

1 purchase and sale of slaves, oil, wine, or grain. If no express agreement has been made as to the division of the profit and loss, an equal division of both is understood to be intended, but if it has, such agreement ought to be carried into effect ; and there has never been any doubt as to the validity of a contract between two partners that the one shall take two-thirds of the profits, and bear two-thirds of the loss, and that the remaining third shall be taken and borne respectively by

2 the other. If Titius and Seius agreed that the former should take two-thirds of the profits, and bear only one-third of the loss, and that the latter should bear two-thirds of the loss, and take only one-third of the profits, it has been made a question whether such an agreement ought to be held valid. Quintus

Mucius thought such an arrangement contrary to the very nature of partnership, and therefore not to be supported : but Servius Sulpicius, whose opinion has prevailed, was of a different view, because the services of a particular partner are often so valuable that it is only just to admit him to the business on more favourable terms than the rest. It is certain that a partnership may be formed on the terms that one partner shall contribute all the capital, and that the profits shall be divided equally, for a man's services are often equivalent to capital. Indeed, the opinion of Quintus Mucius is now so generally rejected, that it is admitted to be a valid contract that a partner shall take a share of the profits, and bear no share in the loss, which indeed Servius, consistently with his opinion, maintained himself. This of course must be taken to mean that if there is a profit on one transaction, and a loss on another, a balance should be struck, and only the net profit be considered as profits. It is quite clear that if the 3 shares are expressed in one event only, as for instance in the event of profit, but not in the event of loss, or vice versa, the same proportions must be observed, in the event of which no mention has been made, as in the other. The continuance of 4 partnership depends on the continuing consent of the members ; it is dissolved by notice of withdrawal from any one of them. But of course if the object of a partner in withdrawing from the partnership is to fraudulently keep for himself some accruing gain—for instance, if a partner in all goods succeeds to an inheritance, and withdraws from the partnership in order to have exclusive possession thereof—he will be compelled to divide this gain with his partners ; but what he gains undesignedly after withdrawing he keeps to himself, and his partner always has the exclusive benefit of whatever accrues to him after such withdrawal. Again, a partnership is dis- 5 solved by the death of a partner, for when a man enters into a contract of partnership, he selects as his partner a definite person. Accordingly, a partnership based on the agreement of even several persons is dissolved by the death of one of them, even though several others survive, unless when the contract was made it was otherwise agreed. So too a partner- 6 ship formed for the attainment of some particular object is

7 terminated when that object is attained. It is clear too that
a partnership is dissolved by the forfeiture of the property of
one of the partners, for such an one, as he is replaced by a
8 successor, is reckoned civilly dead. So again, if one of the
partners is in such embarrassed circumstances as to surrender
all his property to his creditors, and all that he possessed is
sold to satisfy the public or private claims upon him, the
partnership is dissolved, though if the members still agree
to be partners, a new partnership would seem to have begun.
9 It has been doubted whether one partner is answerable to
another on the action of partnership for any wrong less than
fraud, like the bailee in a deposit, or whether he is not suable
also for carelessness, that is to say, for inattention and negligence ; but the latter opinion has now prevailed, with this
limitation, that a partner cannot be required to satisfy the
highest standard of carefulness, provided that in partnership
business he shows as much diligence as he does in his own
private affairs: the reason for this being that if a man chooses
as his partner a careless person, he has no one to blame but
himself.

TITLE XXVI

OF AGENCY

Of the contract of agency there are five modes. A man
gives you a commission either for his own exclusive benefit,
or for his own and yours together, or for that of some third
person, or for his own and the third person's, or for the third
person's and yours. A commission given simply for the sake
of the agent gives rise in reality to no relation of agency, and
accordingly no obligation comes into existence, and therefore
1 no action. A commission is given solely for the benefit of
the principal when, for instance, the latter instructs you to
manage his business, to buy him a piece of land, or to enter
2 into a stipulation as surety for him. It is given for your
benefit and for that of your principal together when he, for
instance, commissions you to lend money at interest to a
person who borrows it for your principal's benefit ; or where,
on your wishing to sue him as surety for some one else, he
commissions you to sue his principal, himself undertaking all

risk : or where, at his risk, you stipulate for payment from a person whom he substitutes for himself as your debtor. It 3 is given for the benefit of a third person when, for instance, some one commissions you to look after Titius's affairs as general agent, or to buy Titius a piece of land, or to go surety for him. It. is for the benefit of the principal and a third 4 person when, for instance, some one instructs you to look after affairs common to himself and Titius, or to buy an estate for himself and Titius, or to go surety for them jointly. It 5 is for the benefit of yourself and a third person when, for instance, some one instructs you to lend money at interest to Titius ; if it were to lend money free of interest, it would be for the benefit of the third person only. It is for your benefit 6 alone if, for instance, some one commissions you to invest your money in the purchase of land rather than to lend it at interest, or vice versa. But such a commission is not really so much a commission in the eye of the law as a mere piece of advice, and consequently will not give rise to an obligation, for the law holds no one responsible as on agency for mere advice given, even if it turns out ill for the person advised, for every one can find out for himself whether what he is advised to do is likely to turn out well or ill. Consequently, if you have money lying idle in your cash-box, and on so and so's advice buy something with it, or put it out at interest, you cannot sue that person by the action on agency, although your purchase or loan turns out a bad speculation ; and it has even been questioned, on this principle, whether a man is suable on agency who commissions you to lend money to Titius ; but the prevalent opinion is that of Sabinus, that so specific a recommendation is sufficient to support an action, because (without it) you would never have lent your money to Titius at all. So too instructions to commit an unlawful 7 or immoral act do not create a legal obligation—as if Titius were to instigate you to steal, or to do an injury to the property or person of some one else ; and even if you act on his instructions, and have to pay a penalty in consequence, you cannot recover its amount from Titius.

An agent ought not to exceed the terms of his commission. 8 Thus, if some one commission you to purchase an estate for

him, but not to exceed the price of a hundred *aurei*, or to go
surety for Titius up to that amount, you ought not in either
transaction to exceed the sum specified : for otherwise you
will not be able to sue him on the agency. Sabinus and
Cassius even thought that in such a case you could not successfully sue him even for a hundred *aurei*, though the leaders
of the opposite school differed from them, and the latter
opinion is undoubtedly less harsh. If you buy the estate for
less, you will have a right of action against him, for a direction
to buy an estate for a hundred *aurei* is regarded as an implied
direction to buy, if possible, for any smaller sum.

9   The authority given to an agent duly constituted can be
annulled by revocation before he commences to act upon it.

10 Similarly, the death of either the principal or the agent
before the latter commences to act extinguishes the agent's
authority ; but equity has so far modified this rule that if,
after the death of a principal and without having notice of
his decease, an agent executes his commission, he can sue on
the agency : for otherwise the law would be penalizing a
reasonable and unavoidable ignorance. Similar to this is
the rule, that debtors who pay a manumitted steward, say,
of Titius, without notice of his manumission, are discharged
from liability, though by the strict letter of the law they are
not discharged, because they have not paid the person whom

11 they were bound to pay. It is open to every one to decline
a commission of agency, but acceptance must be followed by
execution, or by a prompt resignation, in order to enable the
principal to carry out his purpose either personally or by the
appointment of another agent. Unless the resignation is made
in such time that the principal can attain his object without
suffering any prejudice, an action will lie at his suit, in default
of proof by the agent that he could not resign before, or that
his resignation, though inconvenient, was justifiable.

12   A commission of agency may be made to take effect from
a specified future day, or may be subject to a condition.

13 Finally, it should be observed that unless the agent's services
are gratuitous, the relation between him and the principal
will not be agency proper, but some other kind of contract ;
for if a remuneration is fixed, the contract is one of hiring.

And generally we may say that in all cases where, supposing a man's services are gratuitous, there would be a contract of agency or deposit, there is held to be a contract of hiring if remuneration is agreed upon; consequently, if you give clothes to a fuller to clean or to finish, or to a tailor to mend, without agreeing upon or promising any remuneration, you can be sued by the action on agency.

TITLE XXVII

OF QUASI-CONTRACTUAL OBLIGATIONS

Having enumerated the different kinds of contracts, let us now examine those obligations also which do not originate, properly speaking, in contract, but which, as they do not arise from a delict, seem to be quasi-contractual. Thus, if one 1 man has managed the business of another during the latter's absence, each can sue the other by the action on uncommissioned agency; the direct action being available to him whose business was managed, the contrary action to him who managed it. It is clear that these actions cannot properly be said to originate in a contract, for their peculiarity is that they lie only where one man has come forward and managed the business of another without having received any commission so to do, and that other is thereby laid under a legal obligation even though he knows nothing of what has taken place. The reason of this is the general convenience; otherwise people might be summoned away by some sudden event of pressing importance, and without commissioning any one to look after and manage their affairs, the result of which would be that during their absence those affairs would be entirely neglected: and of course no one would be likely to attend to them if he were to have no action for the recovery of any outlay he might have incurred in so doing. Conversely, as the uncommissioned agent, if his management is good, lays his principal under a legal obligation, so too he is himself answerable to the latter for an account of his management; and herein he must show that he has satisfied the highest standard of carefulness, for to have displayed such carefulness as he is wont to exercise in his own affairs is not enough, if only a more diligent person could have managed the business better. Guardians again, 2

who can be sued by the action on guardianship, cannot properly be said to be bound by contract, for there is no contract between guardian and ward: but their obligation, as it certainly does not originate in delict, may be said to be quasi-contractual. In this case too each party has a remedy against the other: not only can the ward sue the guardian directly on the guardianship, but the guardian can also sue the ward by the contrary action of the same name, if he has either incurred any outlay in managing the ward's property, or bound himself on his behalf, or pledged his own property as security for
3 the ward's creditors. Again, where persons own property jointly without being partners, by having, for instance, a joint bequest or gift made to them, and one of them is liable to be sued by the other in a partition suit because he alone has taken its fruits, or because the plaintiff has laid out money on it in necessary expenses: here the defendant cannot properly be said to be bound by contract, for there has been no contract made between the parties; but as his obligation is not based on delict, it may be said to be quasi-contractual.
4 The case is exactly the same between joint heirs, one of whom is liable to be sued by the other on one of these grounds in
5 an action for partition of the inheritance. So, too, the obligation of an heir to discharge legacies cannot properly be called contractual, for it cannot be said that the legatee has contracted at all with either the heir or the testator: yet, as the heir is not bound by a delict, his obligation would seem to
6 be quasi-contractual. Again, a person to whom money not owed is paid by mistake is thereby laid under a quasi-contractual obligation; an obligation, indeed, which is so far from being contractual, that, logically, it may be said to arise from the extinction rather than from the formation of a contract; for when a man pays over money, intending thereby to discharge a debt, his purpose is clearly to loose a bond by which he is already bound, not to bind himself by a fresh one. Still, the person to whom money is thus paid is laid under an obligation exactly as if he had taken a loan for consumption,
7 and therefore he is liable to a condiction. Under certain circumstances money which is not owed, and which is paid by mistake, is not recoverable; the rule of the older lawyers on

this point being that wherever a defendant's denial of his obligation is punished by duplication of the damages to be recovered—as in actions under the lex Aquilia, and for the recovery of a legacy—he cannot get the money back on this plea. The older lawyers, however, applied this rule only to such legacies of specific sums of money as were given by condemnation; but by our constitution, by which we have assimilated legacies and trust bequests, we have made this duplication of damages on denial an incident of all actions for their recovery, provided the legatee or beneficiary is a church, or other holy place honoured for its devotion to religion and piety. Such legacies, although paid when not due, cannot be reclaimed.

Title XXVIII

OF PERSONS THROUGH WHOM WE CAN ACQUIRE OBLIGATIONS

Having thus gone through the classes of contractual and quasi-contractual obligations, we must remark that rights can be acquired by you not only on your own contracts, but also on those of persons in your power—that is to say, your slaves and children. What is acquired by the contracts of your slaves becomes wholly yours; but the acquisitions of children in your power by obligations must be divided on the principle of ownership and usufruct laid down in our constitution : that is to say, of the material results of an action brought on an obligation made in favour of a son the father shall have the usufruct, though the ownership is reserved to the son himself: provided, of course, that the action is brought by the father, in accordance with the distinction drawn in our recent constitution. Freemen also, and the slaves of another person, acquire 1 for you if you possess them in good faith, but only in two cases, namely, when they acquire by their own labour, or in dealing with your property. A usufructuary or usuary slave 2 acquires under the same conditions for him who has the usufruct or use. It is settled law that a slave jointly owned 3 acquires for all his owners in the proportion of their property in him, unless he names one exclusively in a stipulation, or in the delivery of property to himself, in which case he acquires for him alone; as in the stipulation 'do you promise to convey to Titius, my master?' If it was by the direction of one of his joint owners only that he entered into a stipulation, the effect was formerly doubted ; but now it has been settled by our decision that (as is said above) under such circumstances he acquires for him only who gave him the order.

TITLE XXIX

OF THE MODES IN WHICH OBLIGATIONS ARE DISCHARGED

An obligation is always extinguished by performance of what is owed, or by performance of something else with the creditor's assent. It is immaterial from whom the performance proceeds—be it the debtor himself, or some one else on his behalf: for on performance by a third person the debtor is released, whether he knows of it or not, and even when it is against his will. Performance by the debtor releases, besides himself, his sureties, and conversely performance by a surety 1 releases, besides himself, the principal debtor. Acceptilation is another mode of extinguishing an obligation, and is, in its nature, an acknowledgement of a fictitious performance. For instance, if something is due to Titius under a verbal contract, and he wishes to release it, it can be done by his allowing the debtor to ask 'that which I promised thee hast thou received?' and by his replying 'I have received it'. An acceptilation can be made in Greek, provided the form corresponds to that of the Latin words, as ἔχεις λαβὼν δηνάρια τόσα; ἔχω λαβών. This process, as we said, discharges only obligations which arise from verbal contract, and no others, for it seemed only natural that where words can bind words may also loose: but a debt due from any other cause may be transformed into a debt by stipulation, and then released by an imaginary verbal payment or acceptilation. So, too, as a debt can be lawfully discharged 2 in part, so acceptilation may be made of part only. A stipulation has been invented, commonly called Aquilian, by which an obligation of any kind whatsoever can be clothed in stipulation form, and then extinguished by acceptilation; for by this process any kind of obligation may be novated. Its terms, as settled by Gallus Aquilius, are as follow : 'Whatever, and on whatsoever ground, you are or shall be compellable to convey to or do for me, either now or on a future specified day, and for whatsoever I have or shall have against you an action personal or real, or any extraordinary remedy, and whatsoever of mine you hold or possess naturally or civilly, or would possess, or now fail to possess through some wilful fault of your own—as the value of each and all of these claims Aulus Agerius stipulated for the payment of such and such a sum, and payment was formally promised by Numerius Negidius.' Then conversely, Numerius Negidius asked Aulus Agerius, ' hast thou received the whole of what I have to-day engaged, by the Aquilian stipulation, to pay thee ? ' to which Aulus Agerius replied ' I have it, and account it received '. Novation 3 is another mode of extinguishing an obligation, and takes place when you owe Seius a sum, and he stipulates for payment thereof from Titius ; for the intervention of a new person gives birth to a new obligation, and the first obligation is transformed into the second, and ceases to exist. Sometimes indeed the first stipulation is avoided by novation even though the second is of no effect : for instance, if you owe Titius a sum, and he stipulates for payment thereof from a pupil without his guardian's authority, he loses his claim altogether, for you, the original debtor, are discharged, and the second obligation is unenforceable. The same does not hold if one stipulate from a slave ; for then the former debtor continues bound as fully as if one had stipulated from no one. But when the original debtor is the promisor, a second stipulation produces a novation only if it contains something new—if a condition, for instance, or a term, or a surety be added, or taken away— though, supposing the addition of a condition, we must be understood to mean that a novation is produced only if the condition is accomplished : if it fails, the prior obligation continues in force. Among the older lawyers it was an established rule, that a novation was effected only when it was with that intention that the parties entered into the second obligation ; but as this still left it doubtful when the intention was present and when absent, various presumptions were established as to the matter by different persons in different cases. We therefore issued our constitution, enacting most clearly that no novation shall take place unless the contracting parties

expressly state their intention to be the extinction of the prior
obligation, and that in default of such statement, the first
obligation shall subsist, and have the second also added to it :
the result being two obligations resting each on its own
independent ground, as is prescribed by the constitution, and
4 as can be more fully ascertained by perusing the same. Moreover, those obligations which are contracted by consent alone
are dissolved by a contrary agreement. For instance, if Titius
and Seius agree that the latter shall buy an estate at Tusculum
for a hundred *aurei*, and then before execution on either side
by payment of the price or delivery of the estate they arrange
to abandon the sale, they are both released. The case is the
same with hire and the other contracts which are formed by
consent alone.

BOOK IV

TITLE I

OF OBLIGATIONS ARISING FROM DELICT

HAVING treated in the preceding Book of contractual and quasi-contractual obligations, it remains to inquire into obligations arising from delict. The former, as we remarked in the proper place, are divided into four kinds; but of these latter there is but one kind, for, like obligations arising from real contracts, they all originate in some act, that is to say, in the delict itself, such as a theft, a robbery, wrongful damage, or an injury.

Theft is a fraudulent dealing with property, either in itself, 1 or in its use, or in its possession: an offence which is prohibited by natural law. The term *furtum*, or theft, is derived either 2 from *furvum*, meaning 'black', because it is effected secretly and under cover, and usually by night: or from *fraus*, or from *ferre*, meaning 'carrying off'; or from the Greek word φώρ, thief, which indeed is itself derived from φέρειν, to carry off. There are two kinds of theft, theft detected in the commission, 3 and simple theft: the possession of stolen goods discovered upon search, and the introduction of stolen goods, are not (as will appear below) so much specific kinds of theft as actionable circumstances connected with theft. A thief detected in the commission is termed by the Greeks ἐπ' αὐτοφώρῳ; in this kind is included not only he who is actually caught in the act of theft, but also he who is detected in the place where the theft is committed; for instance, one who steals from a house, and is caught before he has got outside the door; or who steals olives from an olive garden, or grapes from a vineyard, and is caught while still in the olive garden or vineyard. And the definition of theft detected in the commission must be even further extended, so as to include the thief who is caught or even seen with the stolen goods still in his hands, whether the place be public or private, and whether the person who sees

or catches him be the owner of the property, or some third
person, provided he has not yet escaped to the place where he
intended to take and deposit his booty : for if he once escapes
there, it is not theft detected in the commission, even if he be
found with the stolen goods upon him. What is simple theft
is clear from what has been said : that is to say, it is all theft
4 which is not detected in the commission. The offence of discovery of stolen goods occurs when a person's premises are
searched in the presence of witnesses, and the stolen property
is found thereon ; this makes him liable, even though innocent
of theft, to a special action for receiving stolen goods. To introduce stolen goods is to pass them off to a man, on whose
premises they are discovered, provided this be done with the
intent that they shall be discovered on his premises rather than
on those of the introducer. The man on whose premises they
are found may sue the latter, though innocent of theft, in an
action for the introduction of stolen goods. There is also an
action for refusal of search, available against him who prevents
another who wishes to look in the presence of witnesses for
stolen property ; and finally, by the action for non-production
of stolen goods, a penalty is imposed by the praetor's edict
on him who has failed to produce stolen property which is
searched for and found on his premises. But the last-named
actions, namely, those for receiving stolen goods, for intro-
ducing them, for refusal of search, and for non-production,
have now become obsolete : for the search for such property is
no longer made in the old fashion, and accordingly these
actions went out of use also. It is obvious, however, that
any one who knowingly receives and hides stolen property
5 may be sued by the action for simple theft. The penalty for
theft detected in the commission is four times the value, and
for simple theft twice the value, of the property stolen,
whether the thief be a slave or a free person.
6   Theft is not confined to carrying away the property of
another with intent of appropriation, but comprises also all
corporeal dealing with the property of another against the will
of the owner. Thus, for a pawnee to use the thing which he
has in pawn, or to use a thing committed to one's keeping as
a deposit, or to put a thing which is lent for use to a different

use than that for which it was lent, is theft ; to borrow plate, for instance, on the representation that the borrower is going to entertain his friends, and then to carry it away into the country: or to borrow a horse for a drive, and then to take it out of the neighbourhood, or like the man in the old story, to take it into battle. With regard, however, to those persons 7 who put a thing lent for use to a different purpose than the lender contemplated, the rule is that they are guilty of theft only if they know it to be contrary to the will of the owner, and that if he had notice he would refuse permission ; but if they believe that he would give permission, it is not theft : and the distinction is just, for there is no theft without unlawful intention. It is also said not to be theft if a man turns 8 a thing lent for use to a use other than he believes its owner would sanction, though in point of fact its owner is consenting. Whence arose the following question : if Titius solicits the slave of Maevius to steal property of the latter, and convey it to him, and the slave informs Maevius of it, who, wishing to detect Titius in the very act, allows the slave to convey the property to him ; can an action of theft, or for corrupting the slave, or neither, be maintained against Titius? The case was submitted to us, and we examined the conflicting opinions of the earlier jurists on the matter: some of whom thought that neither action lay, and others, that Maevius might sue on theft only. But we, in order to put an end to such quibbles, have enacted by our decision that in such a case both the action on theft and that for corrupting a slave shall lie. It is true that the slave has not been corrupted by the advances made to him, so that the case does not come within the rules which introduced the action for such corruption : yet the would-be corrupter's intention was to make him dishonest, so that he is liable to a penal action, exactly as if the slave had actually been corrupted, lest his immunity from punishment should encourage others to perpetrate a similar wrong on a slave less strong to resist temptation. A free man too may be the 9 subject of a theft—for instance, a child in my power, if secretly removed from my control. So too a man some- 10 times steals his own property—for instance, a debtor who purloins the goods which he has pledged to a creditor.

11   Theft may be chargeable on a person who is not the perpetrator; on him, namely, by whose aid and abetment a theft is committed. Among such persons we may mention the man who knocks money out of your hand for another to pick up, or who stands in your way that another may snatch something from you, or scatters your sheep or your oxen, that another may steal them, like the man in the old books, who waved a red cloth to frighten a herd. If the same thing were done as a frolic, without the intention of assisting a theft, the proper action is not theft, but on the case. Where, however, Titius commits theft with the aid of Maevius, both are liable to an action on theft. A man, too, is held to have aided and abetted a theft who places a ladder under a window, or breaks open a window or a door, in order that another may steal, or who lends tools for the breaking of them open, or a ladder to place under a window, if he knows the object for which they are borrowed. It is clear that a man is not liable on theft, who, though he advises and instigates the offence, does **12** not actually aid in its commission. If a child in power, or a slave, steal property of his father or master, it is theft, and the property is deemed stolen, so that no one can acquire it by usucapion until it has returned into the hands of the owner; but no action will lie on the theft, because between a son in power and his father, or between a slave and his master, no action will lie on any ground whatsoever. But if the offender is aided and abetted by a third person, the latter is liable to an action on theft, because a theft has in fact been committed, and by his aid and abetment.

13   The action on theft will lie at the suit of any person interested in the security of the property, even though he be not its owner: indeed, even the owner cannot maintain **14** the action unless he suffers damage from the loss. Hence, when a pawn is stolen the pawnee can sue, even though his debtor be perfectly able to pay the debt; for it is more advantageous to him to rely on the pledge, than to bring a personal action: and this rule is so unbending that even the pawnor who steals a pawn is suable for theft by the pawnee. **15** So, if clothes are delivered to be cleaned or finished or mended for a certain remuneration, and then are stolen, it is the fuller

or tailor who can sue on the theft, and not the owner ; for the
owner suffers nothing by the loss, having the action of letting
against the fuller or tailor for the recovery of his property.
Similarly a purchaser in good faith, even though a good title
as owner is not given to him, can bring the action of theft
if the property is stolen, exactly like the pawnee. The action
is, however, not maintainable at the suit of a fuller or tailor,
unless he is solvent, that is to say, unless he is able to fully
indemnify the owner ; if he is insolvent, the owner cannot
recover from him, and so can maintain an action against the
thief, being, on this hypothesis, interested in the recovery
of the property. Where the fuller or tailor is only partly
instead of wholly solvent the rule is the same. The older 16
lawyers held that what has been said of the fuller and tailor
applied also to the borrower for use, on the ground that as
the remuneration which the fuller receives makes him responsible for custody, so the advantage which the borrower
derives from the use requires him to keep it safely at his
peril. Our wisdom, however, has amended the law in this
particular in our decisions, by allowing the owner the option
of suing either the borrower by action on the loan, or the
thief by action of theft ; though when his choice has been
determined he cannot change his mind, and resort to the other
action. If he prefers to sue the thief, the borrower is absolutely released from liability ; but if he proceeds against the
borrower, he cannot in any way himself sue the thief on the
stealing, though this may be done by the borrower, who
is defendant in the other action, provided that the owner
knew, at the time when he began his action against the
borrower, that the thing had been stolen. If he is ignorant
of this, or even if he is merely doubtful whether the borrower
still has the property in his possession or not, and sues him
on the loan, he may, on subsequently learning the facts, and if
he wishes to drop the action which he has commenced, and
sue the thief instead, adopt this course, in which case no
obstacle is to be thrown in his way, because it was in ignorance
that he took action and sued the borrower on the loan. If,
however, the owner has been indemnified by the borrower, in
no case can he bring the action of theft against the thief, as

his rights of action pass to the person who has compensated him for the loss of his property. Conversely it is clear, that if, at the outset, the owner began an action on the loan against the borrower, not knowing that the property had been stolen, and subsequently, on learning this, proceeded against the thief instead, the borrower is absolutely released from liability, whatever may be the result of the owner's action against the thief; the rule being the same, whether the borrower be wholly

17 or only partially solvent. As a depositary is not answerable for the safe keeping of the thing deposited, but only for fraud, and, if it is stolen, is not compellable to make restitution by action of deposit, he has no interest if it is lost, and therefore the action of theft is maintainable only by the depositor.

18 Finally, it has been a question whether a child below the age of puberty, who carries away the property of another, is guilty of theft. The answer is that, as theft depends on intention, obligation by theft is not incurred unless the child is near

19 puberty, and so understands its delinquency. The object of the action on theft, whether it be for double or quadruple the value of the goods stolen, is merely the recovery of the penalty; to recover the goods themselves or their value the owner has an independent remedy by vindication or condiction. The former is the proper remedy when it is known who is in possession of the goods, whether this be the thief or any one else: the latter lies against the thief or his heir, whether in possession of the stolen property or not.

TITLE II

OF ROBBERY

Robbery is chargeable also as theft; for who deals with the property of another more against that other's will than the robber? And thus the description of the robber as an audacious thief is a good one. However, as a special remedy for this offence the praetor has introduced the action for robbery, or rapine with violence, which may be brought within a year for four times the value, after a year for simple damages, and which lies even when only a single thing of the slightest value has been taken with violence. This fourfold value, however, is not all penalty, nor is there an independent action for the recovery of the property or its value, as we observed was the case in the action of theft detected in the commission; but the thing or its value is included in the four-fold, so that, in point of fact, the penalty is three times the value of the property, and this whether the robber be taken in the act or not; for it would be absurd to treat a robber more lightly than one who carries off property merely secretly. This action is maintainable only where the robbery is attended 1 with wrongful intention; consequently, if a man by mistake thought that property was his own, and, in his ignorance of law, forcibly carried it off in the belief that it was lawful for an owner to take away, even by force, a thing belonging to himself from a person in whose possession it was, he cannot be held liable to this action; and similarly on principle he would not in such a case be suable for theft. Lest, however, robbers, under the cloak of such a plea, should discover a method of gratifying a grasping habit with impunity, the law has been amended upon this point by imperial constitutions, by which it is enacted that it shall not be lawful for any one to forcibly carry off movable property, inanimate or animate, even though he believe it to belong to him; and that whosoever disobeys this shall forfeit the property, if, in fact, it be his, and if it be not, shall restore it, and along with it its value in money. And by the said constitutions it is also declared that this provision relates not only to movables (of which alone robbery can be committed), but also to forcible entries on land and houses, so as to deter men from all violent seizing upon property whatsoever under the cloak of such excuses. In 2 order to support this action it is not necessary that the goods of which robbery has been committed should belong to the plaintiff, provided they were taken from among his property. Thus, if a thing be let, or lent, or pledged to Titius, or even deposited with him under such circumstances that he has an interest in its not being carried off—for instance, by his having undertaken the entire responsibility for its safe custody;—or if he possesses it in good faith, or has a usufruct or any other right in it whereby he suffers loss or incurs liability through its being forcibly taken from him, the action will be maintainable by him; not necessarily in order to restore to him the ownership, but only to compensate him for what it is alleged he has lost by its being taken from his goods or withdrawn from his means. In fact, it may be said generally that where, supposing property to be taken secretly, the action of theft will lie, the action on robbery will lie at suit of the same person, if it be taken with violence.

TITLE III

OF THE LEX AQUILIA

Unlawful damage is actionable under the lex Aquilia, whose first chapter provides that if a slave of another man, or a quadruped from his flocks or herds, be unlawfully killed, the offender shall pay to the owner whatever was the highest value thereof

1 within the year next immediately preceding. From the fact that this enactment does not speak of quadrupeds simply, but only of such quadrupeds as are usually included under the idea of flocks and herds, it is to be inferred that it has no application to wild animals or to dogs, but only to such beasts as can properly be said to graze in herds, namely horses, mules, asses, oxen, sheep, and goats. It is settled, too, that swine come under its operation, for they are comprehended in 'herds' because they feed in this manner; thus Homer in his Odyssey, as quoted by Aelius Marcianus in his Institutes, says, 'You will find him sitting among his swine, and they are feeding by the

2 Rock of Corax, over against the spring Arethusa.'[1] To kill unlawfully is to kill without any right; thus a man who kills a robber is not liable to this action, if he could in no other way

3 escape the danger by which he was threatened. So, too, where one man kills another by misadventure, he is not liable under this statute, provided there is no fault or carelessness on his part; otherwise it is different, for under this statute care-

4 lessness is as punishable as wilful wrong-doing. Accordingly, if a man, while playing or practising with javelins, runs your slave through as he passes by, a distinction is drawn. If it be done by a soldier in his exercising ground, that is to say, where such practice is usually conducted, he is in no way to blame; but if it be done by some one else, his carelessness will make him liable; and so it is with the soldier, if he do it in

[1] Od. xiii. 407, 8.

some place other than that appropriated to military exercises.
So, too, if a man is trimming a tree, and kills your slave as he 5
passes by with a bough which he lets fall, he is guilty of
negligence, if it is near a public way, or a private path belonging to a neighbour, and he does not call out to give people
warning; but if he calls out, and the slave takes no pains to
get out of the way, he is not to blame. Nor would such a
man be liable, if he was cutting a tree far away from a road,
or in the middle of a field, even if he did not call out; for
strangers had no business to be there. Again, if a surgeon 6
operates on your slave, and then neglects altogether to attend
to his cure, so that the slave dies in consequence, he is liable
for his carelessness. Sometimes, too, unskilfulness is undis- 7
tinguishable from carelessness—as where a surgeon kills your
slave by operating upon him unskilfully, or by giving him
wrong medicines; and similarly, if your slave is run over by 8
a team of mules, which the driver has not enough skill to hold,
the latter is suable for carelessness; and the case is the same
if he was simply not strong enough to hold them, provided
they could have been held by a stronger man. The rule also
applies to runaway horses, if the running away is due to the
rider's deficiency either in skill or in strength. The meaning 9
of the words of the statute 'whatever was the highest value
thereof within the year' is that if any one, for instance,
kills a slave of yours, who at the moment of his death is
lame, or maimed, or blind of one eye, but within the year was
sound and worth a price, the person who kills him is answerable not merely for his value at the time of his death, but for
his highest value within the year. It is owing to this that the
action under this statute is deemed to be penal, because a
defendant is sometimes bound to pay a sum not merely
equivalent to the damage he has done, but far in excess of it;
and consequently, the right of suing under the statute does not
pass against the heir, though it would have done so if the
damages awarded had never exceeded the actual loss sustained by the plaintiff. By juristic construction of the statute, 10
though not so enacted in its terms, it has been settled that
one must not only take account, in the way we have described,
of the value of the body of the slave or animal killed, but must

also consider all other loss which indirectly falls upon the plaintiff through the killing. For instance, if your slave has been instituted somebody's heir, and, before he has by your order accepted, he is slain, the value of the inheritance you have missed must be taken into consideration; and so, too, if one of a pair of mules, or one of four chariot horses, or one of a company of slave players is killed, account is to be taken not only of what is killed, but also of the extent to which the
11 others have been depreciated. The owner whose slave is killed has the option of suing the wrongdoer for damages in a private action under the lex Aquilia, or of accusing him on a capital charge by indictment.

12 The second chapter of the lex Aquilia is now obsolete; the
13 third makes provision for all damage which is not covered by the first. Accordingly, if a slave, or some quadruped which comes within its terms, is wounded, or if a quadruped which does not come within its terms, such as a dog or wild animal, is wounded or killed, an action is provided by this chapter; and if any other animal or inanimate thing is unlawfully damaged, a remedy is herein afforded; for all burning, breaking, and crushing is hereby made actionable, though, indeed, the single word 'breaking' covers all these offences, denoting as it does every kind of injury, so that not only crushing and burning, but any cutting, bruising, spilling, destroying, or deteriorating is hereby denominated. Finally, it has been decided that if one man mixes something with another's wine or oil, so as to spoil its natural goodness, he is liable under this
14 chapter of the statute. It is obvious that, as a man is liable under the first chapter only where a slave or quadruped is killed by express design or through negligence on his part, so, too, he is answerable for all other damage under this chapter only where it results from some wilful act or carelessness of his. Under this chapter, however, it is not the highest value which the thing had within a year, but that which it had within the last thirty days, which is chargeable on the author
15 of the mischief. It is true that here the statute does not expressly say 'the *highest* value', but Sabinus rightly held that the damages must be assessed as if the words 'highest value' occurred also in this chapter; the Roman people, who enacted

this statute on the proposal of Aquilius the tribune, having thought it sufficient to use them in the first chapter only.

It is held that a direct action lies under this statute only 16 when the body of the offender is substantially the instrument of mischief. If a man occasions loss to another in any other way, a modified action will usually lie against him; for instance, if he shuts up another man's slave or quadruped, so as to starve him or it to death, or drives his horse so hard as to knock him to pieces, or drives his cattle over a precipice, or persuades his slave to climb a tree or go down a well, who, in climbing the one or going down the other, is killed or injured in any part of his body, a modified action is in all these cases given against him. But if a slave is pushed off a bridge or bank into a river, and there drowned, it is clear from the facts that the damage is substantially done by the body of the offender, who is consequently liable directly under the lex Aquilia. If damage be done, not by the body or to a body, but in some other form, neither the direct nor the modified Aquilian action will lie, though it is held that the wrongdoer is liable to an action on the case; as, for instance, where a man is moved by pity to loose another's slave from his fetters, and so enables him to escape.

TITLE IV

OF INJURIES

By injury, in a general sense, is meant anything which is done without any right. Besides this, it has three special significations; for sometimes it is used to express outrage, the proper word for which—contumely—is derived from the verb 'to contemn', and so is equivalent to the Greek $\ddot{v}\beta\rho\iota s$: sometimes it means culpable negligence, as where damage is said to be done (as in the lex Aquilia) 'with injury', where it is equivalent to the Greek $\dot{a}\delta\iota\kappa\eta\mu a$; and sometimes iniquity and injustice, which the Greeks express by $\dot{a}\delta\iota\kappa\iota a$; thus a litigant is said to have received an 'injury' when the praetor or judge delivers an unjust judgement against him. An injury or out- 1 rage is inflicted not only by striking with the fist, a stick, or a whip, but also by vituperation for the purpose of collecting a crowd, or by taking possession of a man's effects on the ground that he was in one's debt ; or by writing, composing, or publishing defamatory prose or verse, or contriving the doing of any of these things by some one else; or by constantly following a matron, or a young boy or girl below the age of puberty, or attempting anybody's chastity ; and, in 2 a word, by innumerable other acts. An outrage or injury may be suffered either in one's own person, or in the person of a child in one's power, or even, as now is generally allowed, in that of one's wife. Accordingly, if you commit an ' outrage ' on a woman who is married to Titius, you can be sued not only in her own name, but also in those of her father, if she be in his power, and of her husband. But if, conversely, it be the husband who is outraged, the wife cannot sue ; for wives should be protected by their husbands, not husbands by their wives. Finally, a father-in-law may sue on an outrage committed on his daughter-in-law, if the son to whom she is married is in 3 his power. Slaves cannot be outraged themselves, but their master may be outraged in their person, though not by all the acts by which an outrage might be offered to him in the person of a child or wife, but only by aggravated assaults or such insulting acts as clearly tend to dishonour the master himself : for instance, by flogging the slave, for which an action lies ; but for mere verbal abuse of a slave, or for 4 striking him with the fist, the master cannot sue. If an outrage is committed on a slave owned by two or more persons jointly, the damages to be paid to these severally should be assessed with reference not to the shares in which they own him, but to their rank or position, as it is to the reputation 5 and not to property that the injury is done ; and if an outrage is committed on a slave belonging to Maevius, but in whom Titius has a usufruct, the injury is deemed to be done to the 6 former rather than to the latter. But if the person outraged is a free man who believes himself to be your slave, you have no action unless the object of the outrage was to bring you into contempt, though he can sue in his own name. The principle is the same when another man's slave believes himself to belong to you ; you can sue on an outrage committed on him only when its object is to bring contempt on you.

7   The penalty prescribed for outrage in the Twelve Tables

was, for a limb disabled, retaliation, for a bone merely broken
a pecuniary mulct proportionate to the great poverty of the
age. The praetors, however, subsequently allowed the person
outraged to put his own estimate on the wrong, the judge
having a discretion to condemn the defendant either in the
sum so named by the plaintiff, or in a less amount ; and of
these two kinds of penalties that fixed by the Twelve Tables
is now obsolete, while that introduced by the praetors, which
is also called ' honorary ', is most usual in the actual practice
of the courts. Thus the pecuniary compensation awarded
for an outrage rises and falls in amount according to the rank
and character of the plaintiff, and this principle is not im-
properly followed even where it is a slave who is outraged ;
the penalty where the slave is a steward being different from
what it is when he is an ordinary menial, and different again
when he is condemned to wear fetters. The lex Cornelia 8
also contains provisions as to outrages, and introduced an
action on outrage, available to a plaintiff who alleges that he
has been struck or beaten, or that a forcible entry has been
made upon his house ; the term 'his house' including not
only one which belongs to him and in which he lives, but also
one which is hired by him, or in which he is received gratuitously as a guest. An outrage becomes ' aggravated ' either 9
from the atrocious character of the act, as where a man is
wounded or beaten with clubs by another ; or from the place
where it is committed, for instance, in the theatre or forum, or
in full sight of the praetor ; or from the rank of the person
outraged,—if it be a magistrate, for instance, or if a senator be
outraged by a person of low condition, or a parent by his
child, or a patron by his freedman ; for such an injury done to
a senator, a parent, or a patron has a higher pecuniary compensation awarded for it than one done to a mere stranger, or
to a person of low condition. Sometimes too the position of
the wound makes an outrage aggravated, as where a man
is struck in the eye. Whether the person on whom such an
outrage is inflicted is independent or in the power of another
is almost entirely immaterial, it being considered aggravated
in either case. Finally, it should be observed that a person 10
who has been outraged always has his option between the

civil remedy and a criminal indictment. If he prefers the
former, the penalty which is imposed depends, as we have
said, on the plaintiff's own estimate of the wrong he has
suffered ; if the latter, it is the judge's duty to inflict an extraordinary penalty on the offender. It should be remembered,
however, that by a constitution of Zeno persons of illustrious
or still higher rank may bring or defend such criminal actions
on outrage by an agent, provided they comply with the requirements of the constitution, as may be more clearly as-
11 certained by a perusal of the same. Liability to an action
on outrage attaches not only to him who commits the act,—
the striking of a blow, for instance—but also to those who
maliciously counsel or abet in the commission, as, for in-
12 stance, to a man who gets another struck in the face. The
right of action on outrage is lost by condonation ; thus, if
a man be outraged, and takes no steps to obtain redress, but
at once lets the matter, as it is said, slip out of his mind, he
cannot subsequently alter his intentions, and resuscitate an
affront which he has once allowed to rest.

TITLE V

OF QUASI-DELICTAL OBLIGATIONS

The obligation incurred by a judge who delivers an unjust
or partial decision cannot properly be called delictal, and
yet it does not arise from contract ; consequently, as he
cannot but be held to have done a wrong, even though it may
be due to ignorance, his liability would seem to be quasi-
delictal, and a pecuniary penalty will be imposed on him at
1 the judge's discretion. Another case of quasi-delictal obligation is that of a person from whose residence, whether it be
his own, or rented, or gratuitously lent him, anything is
thrown or poured out whereby another is injured ; the reason
why his liability cannot properly be called delictal being
that it is usually incurred through the fault of some other
person, such as a slave or a freedman. Of a similar character
is the obligation of one who keeps something placed or hung
over a public way, which might fall and injure any one. In
this last case the penalty has been fixed at ten *aurei* ; in that
of things thrown or poured out of a dwelling-house the action

is for damages equivalent to double the loss sustained, though if a free man be thereby killed the penalty is fixed at fifty *aurei*, and even if he be merely injured he can sue for such damages as the judge shall in his discretion award; and here the latter should take into account the medical and other expenses of the plaintiff's illness, as well as the loss which he has sustained through being disabled from work. If a son in power 2 lives apart from his father, and anything is thrown or poured out of his place of residence, or if he has anything so placed or hung as to be dangerous to the public, it is the opinion of Julian that no action lies against the father, but that the son should be made sole defendant; and the same principle should be applied to a son in power who is made a judge, and delivers an unjust or partial decision. Similarly ship-owners, inn and 3 stable keepers are liable as on a quasi-delict for wilful damage or theft committed in their ships, inns, or stables, provided the act be done by some or one of their servants there employed, and not by themselves; for the action which is given in such cases is not based on contract, and yet as they are in some sense in fault for employing careless or dishonest servants, their liability would seem to be quasi-delictal. In such circumstances the action which is given is on the case, and lies at suit of the injured person's heir, though not against the heir of the ship-owner, inn or stable keeper.

TITLE VI

OF ACTIONS

The subject of actions still remains for discussion. An action is nothing else than the right of suing before a judge for what is due to one.

The leading division of all actions whatsoever, whether 1 tried before a judge or a referee, is into two kinds, real and personal; that is to say, the defendant is either under a contractual or delictal obligation to the plaintiff, in which case the action is personal, and the plaintiff's contention is that the defendant ought to convey something to, or do something for him, or of a similar nature; or else, though there is no legal obligation between the parties, the plaintiff asserts a ground of action against some one else relating to some thing, in which case the action is real. Thus, a man may be in possession of some corporeal thing, in which Titius claims a right of property, and which the possessor affirms belongs to him; here, if Titius sues for its recovery, the action is real.

2 It is real also if a man asserts that he has a right of usufruct over a landed estate or a house, or a right of going or driving cattle over his neighbour's land, or of drawing water from the same; and so too are the actions relating to urban servitudes, as, for instance, where a man asserts a right to raise his house, to have an uninterrupted prospect, to project some building over his neighbour's land, or to rest the beams of his own house in his neighbour's wall. Conversely, there are actions relating to usufructs, and to rustic and urban servitudes, of a contrary import, which lie at the suit of plaintiffs who deny their opponent's right of usufruct, of going or driving cattle, of drawing water, of raising their house, of having an uninterrupted view, of projecting some building over the plaintiff's land, or of resting the beams of their house in the plaintiff's wall. These actions too are real, but negative, and never occur in disputes as to corporeal things, in which the plaintiff is always the party out of possession; and there is no action by which the possessor can (as plaintiff) deny that the thing in question belongs to his adversary, except in one case only, as to which all requisite information can be gathered from the

3 fuller books of the Digest. The actions which have hitherto been mentioned, and others which resemble them, are either of statutory origin, or at any rate belong to the civil law. There are other actions, however, both real and personal, which the praetor has introduced in virtue of his jurisdiction, and of which it is necessary to give examples. For instance, he will usually, under the circumstances to be mentioned, allow a real action to be brought with a fictitious allegation—namely, that the plaintiff has acquired a title by usucapion where this, in fact, is not the case; or, conversely, he will allow a fictitious plea on the part of the defendant, to the effect that the plaintiff has not acquired such title where, in point of

4 fact, he has. Thus, if possession of some object be delivered on a ground sufficient to legally transfer the same—for instance, under a sale or gift, as part of a dowry, or as a legacy

—and the transferee has not yet acquired a complete title by
usucapion, he has no direct real action for its recovery, if he
accidentally loses possession, because by the civil law a real
action lies at the suit of the owner only. But as it seemed
hard that in such a case there should be no remedy, the
praetor introduced an action in which the plaintiff, who has
lost possession, fictitiously alleges that he has acquired a full
title by usucapion, and thus claims the thing as his own. This
is called the Publician action, because it was first placed in
the Edict by a praetor called Publicius. Conversely, if a 5
person, while absent in the service of the State, or while in the
power of an enemy, acquires by usucapion property belonging to some one resident at home, the latter is allowed, within
a year from the cessation of the possessor's public employment, to sue for a recovery of the property by a rescission of
the usucapion : by fictitiously alleging, in other words, that
the defendant has not thus acquired it ; and the praetor from
motives of equity allows this kind of action to be brought in
certain other cases, as to which information may be gathered
from the larger work of the Digest or Pandects. Similarly, 6
if a person conveys away his property in fraud of creditors,
the latter, on obtaining from the governor of the province a
decree vesting in them possession of the debtor's estate, are
allowed to avoid the conveyance, and sue for the recovery of
the property ; in other words, to allege that the conveyance
has never taken place, and that the property consequently
still belongs to the debtor. Again, the Servian and quasi- 7
Servian actions, the latter of which is also called 'hypothecary', are derived merely from the praetor's jurisdiction. The
Servian action is that by which a landlord sues for his tenant's
property, over which he has a right in the nature of mortgage
as security for his rent; the quasi-Servian is a similar remedy,
open to every pledgee or hypothecary creditor. So far then
as this action is concerned, there is no difference between a
pledge and a hypothec : and indeed whenever a debtor and
a creditor agree that certain property of the former shall be
the latter's security for his debt, the transaction is called a
pledge or a hypothec indifferently. In other points, however,
there is a distinction between them ; for the term ' pledge ' is

properly used only where possession of the property in question is delivered to the creditor, especially if that property be
movable : while a hypothec is, strictly speaking, such a right
created by mere agreement without delivery of possession.
8 Besides these, there are also personal actions which the praetor has introduced in virtue of his jurisdiction, for instance,
that brought to enforce payment of money already owed, and
the action on a banker's acceptance, which closely resembled
it. By our constitution, however, the first of these actions has
been endowed with all the advantages which belonged to
the second, and the latter, as superfluous, has therefore been
deprived of all force and expunged from our legislation. To
the praetor is due also the action claiming an account of the
peculium of a slave or child in power, that in which the issue
9 is whether a plaintiff has made oath, and many others. The
action brought to enforce payment of money already owed is
the proper remedy against a person who, by a mere promise,
without stipulation, has engaged to discharge a debt due
either from himself or from some third party. If he has
10 promised by stipulation, he is liable by the civil law. The
action claiming an account of a *peculium* is a remedy introduced by the praetor against a master or a father. By strict
law, such persons incur no liability on the contracts of their
slaves or children in power ; yet it is only equitable that
damages should be recoverable against them to the extent of
the *peculium*, in which children in power and slaves have a
11 sort of property. Again, if a plaintiff, on being challenged
by the defendant, deposes on oath that the latter owes him
the money which is the object of the action, and payment is
not made to him, the praetor most justly grants to him an
action in which the issue is, not whether the money is owing,
12 but whether the plaintiff has sworn to the debt. There is also
a considerable number of penal actions which the praetor has
introduced in the exercise of his jurisdiction ; for instance,
against those who in any way injure or deface his album ;
or who summon a parent or patron without magisterial sanction ; or who violently rescue persons summoned before himself, or who compass such a rescue ; and others innumerable.
13 'Prejudicial' actions would seem to be real, and may be

exemplified by those in which it is inquired whether a man is free born, or has become free by manumission, or in which the question relates to a child's paternity. Of these the first alone belongs to the civil law: the others are derived from the praetor's jurisdiction. The kinds of actions having been 14 thus distinguished, it is clear that a plaintiff cannot demand his property from another in the form ' if it be proved that the defendant is bound to convey '. It cannot be said that what already belongs to the plaintiff ought to be conveyed to him, for conveyance transfers ownership, and what is his cannot be made more his than it is already. Yet for the prevention of theft, and multiplication of remedies against the thief, it has been provided that, besides the penalty of twice or four times the value of the property stolen, the property itself, or its value, may be recovered from the thief by a personal action in the form ' if it be proved that the defendant ought to convey ', as an alternative for the real action which is also available to the plaintiff, and in which he asserts his ownership of the stolen property. We call a real action a 15 ' vindication ', and a personal action, in which the contention is that some property should be conveyed to us, or some service performed for us, a ' condiction ', this term being derived from *condicere*, which has an old meaning of 'giving notice'. To call a personal action, in which the plaintiff contends that the defendant ought to convey to him, a condiction, is in reality an abuse of the term, for nowadays there is no such notice as was given in the old action of that name.

Actions may next be divided into those which are purely 16 reparative, those which are purely penal, and those which are mixed, or partly reparative, partly penal. All real 17 actions are purely reparative. Of personal actions those which spring from contract are nearly all of the same character ; for instance, the actions on loans of money, or stipulations, on loans for use, on deposit, agency, partnership, sale, and hire. If, however, the action be on a deposit occasioned by a riot, a fire, the fall of a building, or a shipwreck, the praetor enables the depositor to recover double damages, provided he sues the bailee in person ; he cannot recover double damages from the bailee's heir, unless he can prove

personal fraud against the latter.   In these two cases the
18 action, though on contract, is mixed.   Actions arising from
delict are sometimes purely penal, sometimes are partly penal
and partly reparative, and consequently mixed.   The sole
object of the action of theft is the recovery of a penalty,
whether that penalty be four times the value of the property
stolen, as in theft detected in the commission, or only twice
that value, as in simple theft.   The property itself is recoverable by an independent action in which the person from whom
it has been stolen claims it as his own, whether it be in the
possession of the thief himself or of some third person ; and
against the thief himself he may even bring a condiction, to
19 recover the property or its value.   The action on robbery is
mixed, for the damages recoverable thereunder are four times
the value of the property taken, three-fourths being pure
penalty, and the remaining fourth compensation for the loss
which the plaintiff has sustained.   So too the action on unlawful damage under the lex Aquilia is mixed, not only
where the defendant denies his liability, and so is sued for
double damages, but also sometimes where the claim is for
simple damages only ; as where a lame or one-eyed slave is
killed, who within the year previous was sound and of large
value ; in which case the defendant is condemned to pay his
greatest value within the year, according to the distinction
which has been drawn above.   Persons too who are under an
obligation as heirs to pay legacies or trust bequests to our
holy churches or other venerable places, and neglect to do so
until sued by the legatee, are liable to a mixed action, by
which they are compelled to give the thing or pay the money
left by the deceased, and, in addition, an equivalent thing or
sum as penalty, the condemnation being thus in twice the
value of the original claim.

20   Some actions are mixed in a different sense, being partly
real, partly personal.   They are exemplified by the action for
the division of a ' family ', by which one of two or more joint
heirs can enforce against the other or rest a partition of the
inheritance, and by the actions for the division of common
property, and for rectification of boundaries between adjoining landed proprietors.   In these three actions the judge has

power, according as shall to him seem fair and equitable, to adjudge any part of the joint property, or of the land in dispute, to any one of the parties, and to order any one of them who seems to have an undue advantage in the partition or rectification to pay a certain sum of money to the other or the rest as compensation. The damages recoverable in an 21 action may be either once, twice, three, or four times the value of the plaintiff's original interest; there is no action by which more than fourfold damages can be claimed. Single 22 damages only are recoverable in the actions on stipulation, loan for consumption, sale, hire, agency, and many others besides. Actions claiming double damages are exemplified 23 by those on simple theft, on unlawful damage under the lex Aquilia, on certain kinds of deposit, and for corruption of a slave, which lies against any one by whose instigation and advice another man's slave runs away, or becomes disobedient to his master, or takes to dissolute habits, or becomes worse in any way whatsoever, and in which the value of property which the runaway slave has carried off is taken into account. Finally, as we remarked above, the action for the recovery of legacies left to places of religion is of this character. An 24 action for triple damages is grounded when a plaintiff makes an overstatement of his claim in the writ of summons, in consequence of which the officers of the court take too large a fee from the defendant. In such a case the latter will be able to recover from the plaintiff three times the loss which he sustains by the overcharge, including in these damages simple compensation for the sum paid in excess of the proper fee. This is provided by a distinguished constitution in our Code, under which a statutory condiction clearly lies for the damages in question. Quadruple damages are recoverable by the 25 action on theft detected in the commission, by the action on intimidation, and by the action grounded on the giving of money in order to induce one man to bring a vexatious suit against another, or to desist from a suit when brought. Under our constitution too a statutory condiction lies for the recovery of fourfold damages from officers of the court, who exact money from defendants in excess of its provisions. There is this difference between the actions on simple theft 26

and for the corruption of a slave, and the other of which we
spoke in connexion with them, that by the two former double
damages are recoverable under any circumstances ; the latter,
namely the action on unlawful damage under the lex Aquilia,
and that on certain kinds of deposit, entail double damages
on the defendant only if he denies his liability ; if he admits
it, simple damages alone can be recovered. The damages
are double under an action for recovery of legacies left to
religious places not only when the liability is denied, but also
when the defendant delays payment until sued by the order
of a magistrate ; if he admits his liability, and pays before
being so sued, he cannot be compelled to pay more than the
27 original debt. The action on intimidation also differs from
the others which we mentioned in the same connexion, in
that it contains in its very nature an implied condition that
the defendant is entitled to acquittal if, on being so ordered
by the judge, he restores to the plaintiff the property of
which the latter has been deprived. In other actions of the
same class this is not so ; for instance, in the action on theft
detected in the commission, the defendant has under any
28 circumstances to pay fourfold damages. Again, some actions
are equitable, others are actions of strict law. To the former
class belong the actions on sale, hire, unauthorized agency,
agency proper, deposit, partnership, guardianship, loan for
use, mortgage, division of a 'family', partition of joint property, those on the innominate contracts of sale by commission
and exchange, and the suit for recovery of an inheritance.
Until quite recently it was a moot point whether the last-
named was properly an equitable action, but our constitution
29 has definitely decided the question in the affirmative. Formerly too the action for the recovery of a dowry was an
equitable action : but as we found that the action on stipulation was more convenient, we have, while establishing many
distinctions, attached all the advantages which the former
remedy possessed to the action on stipulation, when employed
for the recovery of a dowry. The former action being thus
by a judicious reform abolished, that on stipulation, by which
it has been replaced, has deservedly been invested with all the
characteristics of an equitable action, so far as and whenever

it is brought for the recovery of a dowry. We have also given persons entitled to sue for such recovery a tacit hypothec over the husband's property, but this right is not to give any priority over other hypothecary creditors except where it is the wife herself who sues to recover her dowry; it being in her interest only that we have made this new provision. In 30 equitable actions the judge has full power to assess on good and fair grounds the amount due to the plaintiff, and in so doing to take into account counterclaims of the defendant, condemning the latter only in the balance. Even in actions of strict law counterclaims have been permitted since a rescript of the Emperor Marcus, the defendant meeting the plaintiff's claim by a plea of fraud. By our constitution, however, a wider field has been given to the principle of set-off, when the counterclaim is clearly established, the amount claimed in the plaintiff's action, whether real or personal, or whatever its nature, being reduced by operation of law to the extent of the defendant's counterclaim. The only exception to this rule is the action on deposit, against which we have deemed it no less than dishonest to allow any counterclaim to be set up; for if this were permitted persons might be fraudulently prevented from recovering property deposited under the pretence of a set-off. There are some actions again which 31 we call arbitrary, because their issue depends on an ' *arbitrium* ' or order of the judge. Here, unless on such order the defendant satisfies the plaintiff's claim by restoring or producing the property, or by performing his obligation, or in a noxal action by surrendering the guilty slave, he ought to be condemned. Some of such actions are real, others personal. The former are exemplified by the Publician action, the Servian action for the recovery of a tenant farmer's stock, and the quasi-Servian or so-called hypothecary action; the latter by the actions on intimidation and on fraud, by that for the recovery of a thing promised at a particular place, and by the action claiming production of property. In all these actions, and others of a similar nature, the judge has full power to determine on good and just grounds, according to the circumstances of each particular case, the form in which reparation ought to be made to the plaintiff.

32   It is the judge's duty, in delivering judgement, to make his
award as definite as is possible, whether it relate to the payment of money or the delivery of property, and this even when
the plaintiff's claim is altogether unliquidated.

33   Formerly, if the plaintiff, in his statement of claim, demanded more than he was entitled to, his case fell to the
ground, that is, he lost even that which was his due, and in
such cases the praetor usually declined to restore him to his
previous position, unless he was a minor ; for in this matter
too the general rule was observed of giving relief to minors
after inquiry made, if it were proved that they had made an
error owing to their lack of years.   If, however, the mistake
was entirely justifiable, and such as to have possibly misled
even the discreetest of men, relief was afforded even to persons
of full age, as in the case of a man who sues for the whole of
a legacy, of which part is found to have been taken away by
codicils subsequently discovered ; or where such subsequently
discovered codicils give legacies to other persons, so that, the
total amount given in legacies being reduced under the lex
Falcidia, the first legatee is found to have claimed more than
the three-fourths allowed by that statute.   Over-statement of
claim takes four forms ; that is, it may relate either to the
object, the time, the place, or the specification.   A plaintiff
makes an over-claim in the object when, for instance, he sues
for twenty *aurei* while only ten are owing to him, or when,
being only part owner of property, he sues to recover the
whole or a greater portion of it than he is entitled to.   Over-
claim in respect of time occurs when a man sues for money
before the day fixed for payment, or before the fulfilment of
a condition on which payment was dependent ; for exactly as
one who pays money only after it falls due is held to pay less
than his just debt, so one who makes his demand prematurely
is held to make an over-claim.   Over-claim in respect of place
is exemplified by a man suing at one place for performance of
a promise which it was expressly agreed was to be performed
at another, without any reference, in his claim, to the latter : as,
for instance, if a man, after stipulating thus, ' Do you promise to
pay at Ephesus ? ' were to claim the money as due at Rome,
without any addition as to Ephesus.   This is an over-claim,

because by alleging that the money is due at Rome simply, the plaintiff deprives his debtor of the advantage he might have derived from paying at Ephesus. On this account an arbitrary action is given to a plaintiff who sues at a place other than that agreed upon for payment, in which the advantage which the debtor might have had in paying at the latter is taken into consideration, and which usually is greatest in connexion with commodities which vary in price from district to district, such as wine, oil, or grain; indeed even the interest on loans of money is different in different places. If, however, a plaintiff sues at Ephesus—that is, in our example, at the place agreed upon for the payment—he need do no more than simply allege the debt, as the praetor too points out, because the debtor has all the advantage which payment in that particular place gives him. Over-claim in respect of specification closely resembles over-claim in respect of place, and may be exemplified by a man's stipulating from you 'do you promise to convey Stichus or ten *aurei*?' and then suing for the one or the other—that is to say, either for the slave only, or for the money only. The reason why this is an over-claim is that in stipulations of this sort it is the promisor who has the election, and who may give the slave or the money, whichever he prefers; consequently if the promisee sues, alleging that either the money alone, or the slave alone, ought to be conveyed to him, he deprives his adversary of his election, and thereby puts him in a worse position, while he himself acquires an undue advantage. Other cases of this form of over-claim occur where a man, having stipulated in general terms for a slave, for wine, or for purple, sues for the particular slave Stichus, or for the particular wine of Campania, or for Tyrian purple; for in all of these instances he deprives his adversary of his election, who was entitled, under the terms of the stipulation, to discharge his obligation in a mode other than that which is required of him. And even though the specific thing for which the promisee sues be of little or no value, it is still an over-claim: for it is often easier for a debtor to pay what is of greater value than what is actually demanded of him. Such were the rules of the older law, which, however, has been made more liberal by our own and Zeno's statutes. Where the

over-claim relates to time, the constitution of Zeno prescribes
the proper procedure ; if it relates to quantity, or assumes any
other form, the plaintiff, as we have remarked above, is to be
condemned in a sum equivalent to three times any loss which
34 the defendant may have sustained thereby. If the plaintiff in
his statement of claim demands less than is his due, as for
instance by alleging a debt of five *aurei*, when in fact he is
owed ten, or by claiming only half of an estate the whole of
which really belongs to him, he runs no risk thereby, for, by
the constitution of Zeno of sacred memory, the judge will in
the same action condemn the defendant in the residue as well
35 as in the amount actually claimed. If he demands the wrong
thing in his statement of claim, the rule is that he runs no
risk ; for if he discovers his mistake, we allow him to set it
right in the same action. For instance, a plaintiff who is
entitled to the slave Stichus may claim Eros ; or he may
allege that he is entitled to a conveyance under a will, when
his right is founded in reality upon a stipulation.
36   There are again some actions in which we do not always
recover the whole of what is due to us, but in which we sometimes get the whole, sometimes only part. For instance, if the
fund to which our claim looks for satisfaction be the *peculium*
of a son in power or a slave, and it is sufficient in amount to
meet that claim, the father or master is condemned to pay
the whole debt ; but if it is not sufficient, the judge condemns
him to pay only so far as it will go. Of the mode of ascertaining
the amount of a *peculium* we will speak in its proper place.
37 So too if a woman sues for the recovery of her dowry, the rule
is that the husband is to be condemned to restore it only so
far as he is able, that is, so far as his means permit. Accordingly, if his means will enable him to restore the dowry in
full, he will be condemned to do so ; if not, he will be condemned to pay only so much as he is able. The amount of
the wife's claim is also usually lessened by the husband's right
of retaining some portion for himself, which he may do to the
extent of any outlay he has made on dowry property, according
to the rule, stated in the larger work of the Digest, that a
dowry is diminished by operation of law to the extent of all
38 necessary outlay thereon. Again, if a man goes to law with

his parent or patron, or if one partner brings an action of partnership against another, he cannot get judgement for more than his adversary is able to pay. The rule is the same when a man is sued on a mere promise to give a present. Very often 39 too a plaintiff obtains judgement for less than he was owed through the defendant's pleading a set-off: for, as has already been observed, the judge, acting on equitable principles, would in such a case take into account the cross demand in the same transaction of the defendant, and condemn him only in the residue. So too if an insolvent person, who 40 surrenders all his effects to his creditors, acquires fresh property of sufficient amount to justify such a step, his creditors may sue him afresh, and compel him to satisfy the residue of their claims so far as he is able, but not to give up all that he has; for it would be inhuman to condemn a man to pay his debts in full who has already been once deprived of all his means.

TITLE VII

OF CONTRACTS MADE WITH PERSONS IN POWER

As we have already mentioned the action in respect of the *peculium* of children in power and slaves, we must now explain it more fully, and with it the other actions by which fathers and masters are sued for the debts of their sons or slaves. Whether the contract be made with a slave or with a child in power, the rules to be applied are much the same; and therefore, to make our statements as short as possible, we will speak only of slaves and masters, premising that what we say of them is true also of children and the parents in whose power they are; where the treatment of the latter differs from that of the former, we will point out the divergence.

If a slave enters into a contract at the bidding of his 1 master, the praetor allows the latter to be sued for the whole amount: for it is on his credit that the other party relies in making the contract. On the same principle the praetor 2 grants two other actions, in which the whole amount due may be sued for; that called *exercitoria*, to recover the debt of a ship-master, and that called *institoria*, to recover the debt of a manager or factor. The former lies against a master who has appointed a slave to be captain of a ship, to recover a debt incurred by the slave in his character of captain, and it is called *exercitoria*, because the person to whom the daily profits of a ship belong is termed an *exercitor*. The latter lies against a man who has appointed a slave to manage a shop or business, to recover any debt incurred in that business; it is called *institoria*, because a person appointed to manage a business is termed an *institor*. And these actions are granted by the praetor even if the person whom one sets over a ship, a shop, or any other business, be a free man or another man's slave, because equity requires their application in these latter cases 3 no less than in the former. Another action of the praetor's introduction is that called *tributoria*. If a slave, with the knowledge of his master, devotes his *peculium* to a trade or business, the rule which the praetor follows, in respect of contracts made in the course of such trade or business, is that the *peculium* so invested and its profits shall be divided between the master, if anything is due to him, and the other creditors in the ratio of their claims. The distribution of these assets is left to the master, subject to this provision, that any creditor who complains of having received less than his proper 4 share can bring this action against him for an account. There is also an action in respect of *peculium* and of what has been converted to the uses of the master, under which, if a debt has been contracted by a slave without the consent of his master, and some portion thereof has been converted to his uses, he is liable to that extent, while if no portion has been so converted, he is liable to the extent of the slave's *peculium*. Conversion to his uses is any necessary expenditure on his account, as repayment to his creditors of money borrowed, repair of his falling house, purchase of corn for his slaves, or of an estate for him, or any other necessary. Thus, if out of ten *aurei* which your slave borrows from Titius, he pays your creditor five, and spends the remainder in some other way, you are liable for the whole of the five, and for the remainder to the extent of the *peculium*: and from this it is clear that if the whole ten were applied to your uses Titius could recover the whole from you. Thus, though it is but a single action which is brought in respect of *peculium* and of conversion to

uses, it has two condemnatory clauses. The judge by whom
the action is tried first looks to see whether there has been
any application to the uses of the master, and does not proceed
to ascertain the amount of the *peculium* unless there has been
no such application, or a partial application only. In ascertaining the amount of the *peculium* deduction is first made of
what is owed to the master or any person in his power, and
the residue only is treated as *peculium* ; though sometimes
what a slave owes to a person in his master's power is not
deducted, for instance, where that person is another slave who
himself belongs to the *peculium* ; thus, where a slave owes a
debt to his own vicarial slave, its amount is not deducted from
the *peculium*. There is no doubt that a person with whom 5
a slave enters into a contract at the bidding of his master, or
who can sue by the actions *exercitoria* or *institoria*, may in
lieu thereof bring an action in respect of the *peculium* and of
conversion to uses ; but it would be most foolish of him to
relinquish an action by which he may with the greatest ease
recover the whole of what is owing to him under the contract,
and undertake the trouble of proving a conversion to uses, or
the existence of a *peculium* sufficient in amount to cover the
whole of the debt.   So too a plaintiff who can sue by the action
called *tributoria* may sue in respect of *peculium* and conversion
to uses, and sometimes the one action is the more advisable,
sometimes the other.   The former has this advantage, that in
it the master has no priority ; there is no deduction of debts
owing to him, but he and the other creditors stand on precisely
the same footing ; while in the action in respect of *peculium*
deduction is first made of debts owing to the master, who is
condemned to pay over to the creditors only what then
remains.   On the other hand, the advantage of the action in
respect of *peculium* is that in it the slave's whole *peculium* is
liable to his creditors, whereas in the action called *tributoria*
only so much of it is liable as is invested in the trade or
business ; and this may be only a third, a fourth, or even a less
fraction, because the slave may have the rest invested in land
or slaves, or out on loan.   A creditor ought therefore to select
the one or the other action by considering their respective
advantages in each particular case ; though he certainly ought

to choose that in respect of conversion to uses, if he can prove
6 such conversion. What we have said of the liability of a master
on the contracts of his slave is equally applicable where the
contract is made by a child or grandchild in the power of his
7 or her father or grandfather. A special enactment in favour
of children in power is found in the senatusconsult of Macedo,
which has prohibited the giving of loans of money to such
persons, and refused an action to the lender both against the
child, whether he be still in power, or has become independent
by death of the ancestor or emancipation, and against the
parent, whether he still retains the child in his power, or has
emancipated him. This enactment was made by the Senate
because it was found that persons in power, when dragged
down by the burden of loans which they had squandered in
profligacy, often plotted against the lives of their parents.
8   Finally, it should be observed that where a contract has
been entered into by a slave or son in power at his master's or
parent's bidding, or where there has been a conversion to his
uses, a condiction may be brought directly against the parent
or master, exactly as if he had been the original contracting
party in person. So too, wherever a man is suable by either
of the actions called *exercitoria* and *institoria*, he may, in lieu
thereof, be sued directly by a condiction, because in effect the
contract in such cases is made at his bidding.

TITLE VIII

OF NOXAL ACTIONS

Where a delict, such as theft, robbery, unlawful damage, or
outrage, is committed by a slave, a noxal action lies against
the master, who on being condemned has the option of paying
the damages awarded, or surrendering the slave in satis-
1 faction of the injury. The wrongdoer, that is, the slave,
is called '*noxa*'; '*noxia*' is the term applied to the wrong
2 itself, that is, the theft, damage, robbery, or outrage. This
principle of noxal surrender in lieu of paying damages
awarded is based on most excellent reason, for it would be
unjust that the misdeed of a slave should involve his master
3 in any detriment beyond the loss of his body. If a master is
sued by a noxal action on the ground of his slave's delict, he

is released from all liability by surrendering the slave in satisfaction of the wrong, and by this surrender his right of ownership is permanently transferred ; though if the slave can procure enough money to compensate the surrenderee in full for the wrong he did him, he can, by applying to the praetor, get himself manumitted even against the will of his new master. Noxal actions were introduced partly by statute, 4 partly by the Edict of the praetor ; for theft, by the statute of the Twelve Tables ; for unlawful damage, by the lex Aquilia ; for outrage and robbery, by the Edict. Noxal actions always 5 follow the person of the wrongdoer. Thus, if your slave does a wrong while in your power, an action lies against you ; if he becomes the property of some other person, that other is the proper person to be sued ; and if he is manumitted, he becomes directly and personally liable, and the noxal action is extinguished. Conversely, a direct action may change into noxal ; thus, if an independent person has done a wrong, and then becomes your slave (as he may in several ways described in the first Book), a noxal action lies against you in lieu of the direct action which previously lay against the wrongdoer in person. But no action lies for an offence committed by a 6 slave against his master, for between a master and a slave in his power there can be no obligation ; consequently, if the slave becomes the property of some other person, or is manumitted, neither he nor his new master can be sued ; and on the same principle, if another man's slave commits a wrong against you, and then becomes your property, the action is extinguished, because it has come into a condition in which an action cannot exist ; the result being that even if the slave passes again out of your power you cannot sue. Similarly, if a master commits a wrong against his slave, the latter cannot sue him after manumission or alienation. These rules 7 were applied by the ancients to wrongs committed by children in power no less than by slaves ; but the feeling of modern times has rightly rebelled against such inhumanity, and noxal surrender of children under power has quite gone out of use. Who could endure in this way to give up a son, still more a daughter, to another, whereby the father would be exposed to greater anguish in the person of a son than even the latter himself, while mere decency forbids such treatment in the case of a daughter? Accordingly, noxal actions are permitted only where the wrongdoer is a slave, and indeed we find it often laid down by old legal writers that sons in power may be sued personally for their own delicts.

TITLE IX

OF PAUPERIES, OR DAMAGE DONE BY QUADRUPEDS

A noxal action was granted by the statute of the Twelve Tables in cases of mischief done through wantonness, passion, or ferocity, by irrational animals; it being by an enactment of that statute provided, that if the owner of such an animal is ready to surrender it as compensation for the damage, he shall thereby be released from all liability. Examples of the application of this enactment may be found in kicking by a horse, or goring by a bull, known to be given that way; but the action does not lie unless in causing the damage the animal is acting contrary to its natural disposition; if its nature be to be savage, this remedy is not available. Thus, if a bear runs away from its owner, and causes damage, the quondam owner cannot be sued, for immediately with its escape his ownership ceased to exist. The term *pauperies*, or 'mischief', is used to denote damage done without there being any wrong in the doer of it, for an unreasoning animal cannot be said to have done a wrong. Thus far as to the noxal action.

1   It is, however, to be observed that the Edict of the aedile forbids dogs, boars, bears, or lions to be kept near where there is a public road, and directs that if any injury be caused to a free man through disobedience of this provision, the owner of the beast shall be condemned to pay such sum as to the judge shall seem fair and equitable: in case of any other injury the penalty is fixed at double damages. Besides this aedilician action, that on *pauperies* may also be sometimes brought against the same defendant; for when two or more actions, especially penal ones, may be brought on one and the same ground, the bringing of one does not debar the plaintiff from subsequently bringing the other.

TITLE X

OF PERSONS THROUGH WHOM WE CAN BRING AN ACTION

We must now remark that a man may sue either for himself, or for another as attorney, guardian, or curator : whereas formerly one man could not sue for another except in public suits, as an assertor of freedom, and in certain actions relating to guardianship. The lex Hostilia subsequently permitted the bringing of an action of theft on behalf of persons who were in the hands of an enemy, or absent on State employment, and their pupils. It was, however, found extremely inconvenient to be unable to either bring or defend an action on behalf of another, and accordingly men began to employ attorneys for this purpose ; for people are often hindered by ill-health, age, unavoidable absence, and many other causes from attending to their own business. For the appointment 1 of an attorney no set form of words is necessary, nor need it be made in the presence of the other party, who indeed usually knows nothing about it ; for in law any one is your attorney whom you allow to bring or defend an action on your behalf. The modes of appointing guardians and curators 2 have been explained in the first Book.

TITLE XI

OF SECURITY

The old system of taking security from litigants differed from that which has more recently come into use.

Formerly the defendant in a real action was obliged to give security, so that if judgement went against him, and he neither gave up the property which was in question, nor paid the damages assessed, the plaintiff might be able to sue either him or his sureties : and this is called security for satisfaction of judgement, because the plaintiff stipulates for payment to himself of the sum at which the damages are assessed. And there was all the more reason for compelling the defendant in a real action to give security if he was merely the representative of another. From the plaintiff in a real action no security was required if it was on his own account that he sued, but if he was merely an attorney, he was required to give security for the ratification of his proceedings by his principal, owing to the possibility of the latter's subsequently suing in person on the same claim. Guardians and curators were required by the Edict to give the same security as attorneys; but when they appeared as plaintiffs they were sometimes excused.

1 So much for real actions. In personal actions the same rules applied, so far as the plaintiff was concerned, as we have said obtained in real actions. If the defendant was repre- sented by another person, security had always to be given, for no one is allowed to defend another without security; but if the defendant was sued on his own account, he was not compelled to give security for satisfaction of judgement.

2 Nowadays, however, the practice is different; for if the de- fendant is sued on his own account, he is not compelled to give security for payment of the damages assessed, whether the action be real or personal; all that he has to do is to enter into a personal engagement that he will subject himself to the jurisdiction of the court down to final judgement; the mode of making such engagement being either a promise under oath, which is called a sworn recognizance, or a bare promise, or giving of sureties, according to the defendant's

3 rank and station. But the case is different where either plaintiff or defendant appears by an attorney. If the plaintiff does so, and the attorney's appointment is not enrolled in the records, or confirmed by the principal personally in court, the attorney must give security for ratification of his proceedings by his principal; and the rule is the same if a guardian, curator, or other person who has undertaken the management

4 of another's affairs brings an action through an attorney. If a defendant appears, and is ready to appoint an attorney to defend the action for him, he can do this either by coming personally into court, and confirming the appointment by the solemn stipulations employed when security is given for satisfaction of judgement, or by giving security out of court whereby, as surety for his attorney, he guarantees the observ- ance of all the clauses of the so-called security for satisfaction of judgement. In all such cases he is obliged to give a right

of hypothec over all his property, whether the security be given in or out of court, and this right avails against his heirs no less than against himself. Finally, he has to enter into a personal engagement or recognizance to appear in court when judgement is delivered; and in default of such appearance his surety will have to pay all the damages to which he is condemned, unless notice of appeal is given. If, however, 5 the defendant for some reason or other does not appear, and another will defend for him, he may do so, and it is immaterial whether the action be real or personal, provided he will give security for satisfaction of the judgement in full; for we have already mentioned the old rule, that no one is allowed to defend another without security. All this will appear 6 more clearly and fully by reference to the daily practice of the courts, and to actual cases of litigation: and it is 7 our pleasure that these rules shall hold not only in this our royal city, but also in all our provinces, although it may be that through ignorance the practice elsewhere was different; for it is necessary that the provinces generally shall follow the lead of the capital of all our empire, that is, of this royal city, and observe its usages.

TITLE XII

OF ACTIONS PERPETUAL AND TEMPORAL, AND WHICH MAY BE BROUGHT BY AND AGAINST HEIRS

It should be here observed that actions founded on statutes, senatusconsults, and imperial constitutions could be brought at any length of time from the accrual of the cause of action, until certain limits were fixed for actions both real and personal by imperial enactments; while actions which were introduced by the praetor in the exercise of his jurisdiction could, as a rule, be brought only within a year, that being the duration of his authority. Some praetorian actions, however, are perpetual, that is to say, can be brought at any time which does not exceed the limit fixed by the enactments referred to; for instance, those granted to 'possessors of goods' and other persons who are fictitiously represented as heirs. So, too, the action for theft detected in the commission, though praetorian, is perpetual, the praetor having judged it absurd

1 to limit it by a year. Actions which will lie against a man under either the civil or the praetorian law will not always lie against his heir, the rule being absolute that for delict—for instance, theft, robbery, outrage, or unlawful damage—no penal action can be brought against the heir. The heir of the person wronged, however, may bring these actions, except in outrage, and similar cases, if any. Sometimes, even an action on contract cannot be brought against the heir; this being the case where the testator has been guilty of fraud, and his heir has not profited thereby. If, however, a penal action, such as those we have mentioned, has been actually commenced by the original parties, it is transmitted to the heirs of each.

2 Finally, it must be remarked that if, before judgement is pronounced, the defendant satisfies the plaintiff, the judge ought to absolve him, even though he was liable to condemnation at the time when the action was commenced; this being the meaning of the old dictum, that all actions involve the power of absolution.

TITLE XIII

OF EXCEPTIONS

We have next to examine the nature of exceptions. Exceptions are intended for the protection of the defendant, who is often in this position, that though the plaintiff's case is a good one in the abstract, yet as against him, the particular

1 defendant, his contention is inequitable. For instance, if you are induced by duress, fraud, or mistake to promise Titius by stipulation what you did not owe him, it is clear that by the civil law you are bound, and that the action on your promise is well grounded; yet it is inequitable that you should be condemned, and therefore in order to defeat the action you are allowed to plead the exception of duress, or of fraud, or

2 one framed to suit the circumstances of the case. So too, if, as a preliminary to an advance of money, one stipulates from you for its repayment, and then never advances it after all, it is clear that he can sue you for the money, and you are bound by your promise to give it; but it would be iniquitous that you should be compelled to fulfil such an engagement, and therefore you are permitted to defend yourself by the

exception that the money, in point of fact, was never advanced. The time within which this exception can be pleaded, as we remarked in a former Book, has been shortened by our constitution. Again, if a creditor agrees with his debtor not to 3 sue for a debt, the latter still remains bound, because an obligation cannot be extinguished by a bare agreement; accordingly, the creditor can validly bring against him a personal action claiming payment of the debt, though, as it would be inequitable that he should be condemned in the face of the agreement not to sue, he may defend himself by pleading such agreement in the form of an exception. Similarly, if at 4 his creditor's challenge a debtor affirms on oath that he is not under an obligation to convey, he still remains bound; but as it would be unfair to examine whether he has perjured himself, he can, on being sued, set up the defence that he has sworn to the non-existence of the debt. In real actions, too, exceptions are equally necessary; thus, if on the plaintiff's challenge the defendant swears that the property is his, there is nothing to prevent the former from persisting in his action; but it would be unfair to condemn the defendant, even though the plaintiff's contention that the property is his be well founded. Again, an obligation still subsists even after judge- 5 ment in an action, real or personal, in which you have been defendant, so that in strict law you may be sued again on the same ground of action; but you can effectually meet the claim by pleading the previous judgement. These examples 6 will have been sufficient to illustrate our meaning; the multitude and variety of the cases in which exceptions are necessary may be learnt by reference to the larger work of the Digest or Pandects. Some exceptions derive their force from 7 statutes or enactments equivalent to statutes, others from the jurisdiction of the praetor; and some are said to be perpetual 8 or peremptory, others to be temporary or dilatory. Perpetual 9 or peremptory exceptions are obstructions of unlimited duration, which practically destroy the plaintiff's ground of action, such as the exceptions of fraud, intimidation, and agreement never to sue. Temporary or dilatory exceptions are merely 10 temporary obstructions, their only effect being to postpone for a while the plaintiff's right to sue; for example, the plea of

an agreement not to sue for a certain time, say, five years; for at the end of that time the plaintiff can effectually pursue his remedy. Consequently persons who would like to sue before the expiration of the time, but are prevented by the plea of an agreement to the contrary, or something similar, ought to postpone their action till the time specified has elapsed; and it is on this account that such exceptions are called dilatory. If a plaintiff brought his action before the time had expired, and was met by the exception, this would debar him from all success in those proceedings, and formerly he was unable to sue again, owing to his having rashly brought the matter into court, whereby he consumed his right of action, and lost all chance of recovering what was his due. Such unbending rules, however, we do not at the present day approve. Plaintiffs who venture to commence an action before the time agreed upon, or before the obligation is yet actionable, we subject to the constitution of Zeno, which that most sacred legislator enacted as to over-claims in respect of time; whereby, if the plaintiff does not observe the stay which he has voluntarily granted, or which is implied in the very nature of the action, the time during which he ought to have postponed his action shall be doubled, and at its termination the defendant shall not be suable until he has been reimbursed for all expenses hitherto incurred. So heavy a penalty it is hoped will induce plaintiffs
11 in no case to sue until they are entitled. Moreover, some personal incapacities produce dilatory exceptions, such as those relating to agency, supposing that a party wishes to be represented in an action by a soldier or a woman; for soldiers may not act as attorneys in litigation even on behalf of such near relatives as a father, mother, or wife, not even in virtue of an imperial rescript, though they may attend to their own affairs without committing a breach of discipline. We have sanctioned the abolition of those exceptions, by which the appointment of an attorney was formerly opposed on account of the infamy of either attorney or principal, because we found that they no longer were met with in actual practice, and to prevent the trial of the real issue being delayed by disputes as to their admissibility and operation.

TITLE XIV
OF REPLICATIONS

Sometimes an exception, which *prima facie* seems just to the defendant, is unjust to the plaintiff, in which case the latter must protect himself by another allegation called a replication, because it parries and counteracts the force of the exception. For example, a creditor may have agreed with his debtor not to sue him for money due, and then have subsequently agreed with him that he shall be at liberty to do so; here if the creditor sues, and the debtor pleads that he ought not to be condemned on proof being given of the agreement not to sue, he bars the creditor's claim, for the plea is true, and remains so in spite of the subsequent agreement; but as it would be unjust that the creditor should be prevented from recovering, he will be allowed to plead a replication, based upon that agreement. Sometimes again a replication, though *prima* **1** *facie* just, is unjust to the defendant; in which case he must protect himself by another allegation called a rejoinder: and **2** if this again, though on the face of it just, is for some reason unjust to the plaintiff, a still further allegation is necessary for his protection, which is called a surrejoinder. And some- **3** times even further additions are required by the multiplicity of circumstances under which dispositions are made, or by which they are subsequently affected; as to which fuller information may easily be gathered from the larger work of the Digest. Exceptions which are open to a defendant are **4** usually open to his surety as well, as indeed is only fair: for when a surety is sued the principal debtor may be regarded as the real defendant, because he can be compelled by the action on agency to repay the surety whatsoever he has disbursed on his account. Accordingly, if the creditor agrees with his debtor not to sue, the latter's sureties may plead this agreement, if sued themselves, exactly as if the agreement had been made with them instead of with the principal debtor. There are, however, some exceptions which, though pleadable by a principal debtor, are not pleadable by his surety; for instance, if a man surrenders his property to his creditors as an insolvent, and one of them sues him for his debt in full, he can effectually protect himself by pleading the surrender ; but this cannot be done by his surety, because the creditor's main object, in accepting a surety for his debtor, is to be able to have recourse to the surety for the satisfaction of his claim if the debtor himself becomes insolvent.

TITLE XV

OF INTERDICTS

We have next to treat of interdicts or of the actions by which they have been superseded. Interdicts were formulae by which the praetor either ordered or forbad some thing to be done, and occurred most frequently in case of litigation about possession or quasi-possession.

1   The first division of interdicts is into orders of abstention, of restitution, and of production. The first are those by which the praetor forbids the doing of some act—for instance, the violent ejection of a bona fide possessor, forcible interference with the interment of a corpse in a place where that may lawfully be done, building upon sacred ground, or the doing of anything in a public river or on its banks which may impede its navigation. The second are those by which he orders restitution of property, as where he directs possession to be restored to a 'possessor of goods' of things belonging to an inheritance, and which have hitherto been in the possession of others under the title of heir, or without any title at all; or where he orders a person to be reinstated in possession of land from which he has been forcibly ousted. The third are those by which he orders the production of persons or property ; for instance, the production of a person whose freedom is in question, of a freedman whose patron wishes to demand from him certain services, or of children on the application of the parent in whose power they are. Some think that the term interdict is properly applied only to orders of abstention, because it is derived from the verb *interdicere*, meaning to denounce or forbid, and that orders of restitution or production are properly termed decrees ; but in practice they are all called interdicts, because they are given *inter*
2 *duos*, between two parties. The next division is into inter-

dicts for obtaining possession, for retaining possession, and for recovering possession.   Interdicts for obtaining possession are 3 exemplified by the one given to a 'possessor of goods', which is called *Quorum bonorum*, and which enjoins that whatever portion of the goods, whereof possession has been granted to the claimant, is in the hands of one who holds by the title of heir or as mere possessor only, shall be delivered up to the grantee of possession.   A person is deemed to hold by the title of heir who thinks he is an heir; he is deemed to hold as mere possessor who relies on no title at all, but holds a portion of the whole of the inheritance, knowing that he is not entitled.   It is called an interdict for obtaining possession, because it is available only for initiating possession; accordingly, it is not granted to a person who has already had and lost possession.   Another interdict for obtaining possession is that named after Salvius, by which the landlord gets possession of the tenant's property which has been hypothecated as a security for rent.   The interdicts *Uti possidetis* and 4 *Utrubi* are interdicts for retaining possession, and are employed when two parties claim ownership in anything, in order to determine which shall be defendant and which plaintiff; for no real action can be commenced until it is ascertained which of the parties is in possession, because law and reason both require that one of them shall be in possession and shall be sued by the other.   As the rôle of defendant in a real action is far more advantageous than that of plaintiff, there is almost invariably a keen dispute as to which party is to have possession pending litigation: the advantage consisting in this, that, even if the person in possession has no title as owner, the possession remains to him unless and until the plaintiff can prove his own ownership: so that where the rights of the parties are not clear, judgement usually goes against the plaintiff.   Where the dispute relates to the possession of land or buildings, the interdict called *Uti possidetis* is employed; where to movable property, that called *Utrubi*. Under the older law their effects were very different.   In *Uti possidetis* the party in possession at the issue of the interdict was the winner, provided he had not obtained that possession from his adversary by force, or clandestinely, or by permission ; whether he had obtained it from some one else in any of these modes was immaterial. In *Utrubi* the winner was the party who had been in possession the greater portion of the year next immediately preceding, provided that possession had not been obtained by force, or clandestinely, or by permission, from his adversary. At the present day, however, the practice is different, for as regards the right to immediate possession the two interdicts are now on the same footing ; the rule being, that whether the property in question be movable or immovable, the possession is adjudged to the party who has it at the commencement of the action, provided he had not obtained it by force, or clandestinely, or 5 by permission, from his adversary. A man's possession includes, besides his own personal possession, the possession of any one who holds in his name, though not subject to his power ; for instance, his tenant. So also a depositary or borrower for use may possess for him, as is expressed by the saying that we retain possession by any one who holds in our name. Moreover, mere intention suffices for the retention of possession ; so that although a man is not in actual possession either himself or through another, yet if it was not with the intention of abandoning the thing that he left it, but with that of subsequently returning to it, he is deemed not to have parted with the possession. Through what persons we can obtain possession has been explained in the second Book ; and it is agreed on all hands that for obtaining possession 6 intention alone does not suffice. An interdict for recovering possession is granted to persons who have been forcibly ejected from land or buildings ; their proper remedy being the interdict *Unde vi*, by which the ejector is compelled to restore possession, even though it had been originally obtained from him by the grantee of the interdict by force, clandestinely, or by permission. But by imperial constitutions, as we have already observed, if a man violently seizes on property to which he has a title, he forfeits his right of ownership ; if on property which belongs to some one else, he has not only to restore it, but also to pay the person whom he has violently dispossessed a sum of money equivalent to its value. In cases of violent dispossession the wrongdoer is liable under the lex

Iulia relating to private or public violence, by the former being meant unarmed force, by the latter dispossession effected with arms; and the term 'arms' must be taken to include not only shields, swords, and helmets, but also sticks and stones. Thirdly, interdicts are divided into simple and 7 double. Simple interdicts are those wherein one party is plaintiff and the other defendant, as is always the case in orders of restitution or production; for he who demands restitution or production is plaintiff, and he from whom it is demanded is defendant. Of interdicts which order abstention some are simple, others double. The simple are exemplified by those wherein the praetor commands the defendant to abstain from desecrating consecrated ground, or from obstructing a public river or its banks; for he who demands such order is the plaintiff, and he who is attempting to do the act in question is defendant. Of double interdicts we have examples in *Uti possidetis* and *Utrubi*; they are called double because the footing of both parties is equal, neither being exclusively plaintiff or defendant, but each sustaining the double rôle.

To speak of the procedure and result of interdicts under 8 the older law would now be a waste of words; for when the procedure is what is called 'extraordinary', as it is nowadays in all actions, the issue of an interdict is unnecessary, the matter being decided without any such preliminary step in much the same way as if it had actually been taken, and a modified action had arisen on it.

TITLE XVI

OF THE PENALTIES FOR RECKLESS LITIGATION

It should here be observed that great pains have been taken by those who in times past had charge of the law to deter men from reckless litigation, and this is a thing that we too have at heart. The best means of restraining unjustifiable litigation, whether on the part of a plaintiff or of a defendant, are money fines, the employment of the oath, and the fear of infamy. Thus, under our constitution, the oath 1 has to be taken by every defendant, who is not permitted even to state his defence until he swears that he resists the plaintiff's claim because he believes that his cause is a good one. In certain cases where the defendant denies his liability the action is for double or treble the original claim, as in proceedings on unlawful damage, and for recovery of legacies bequeathed to religious places. In various actions the damages are multiplied at the outset ; in an action on theft detected in the commission they are quadrupled ; for simple theft they are doubled ; for in these and some other actions the damages are a multiple of the plaintiff's loss, whether the defendant denies or admits the claim. Vexatious litigation is checked on the part of the plaintiff also, who under our constitution is obliged to swear on oath that his action is commenced in good faith ; and similar oaths have to be taken by the advocates of both parties, as is prescribed in other of our enactments. Owing to these substitutes the old action of dishonest litigation has become obsolete. The effect of this was to penalize the plaintiff in a tenth part of the value he claimed by action ; but, as a matter of fact, we found that the penalty was never exacted, and therefore its place has been taken by the oath above mentioned, and by the rule that a plaintiff who sues without just cause must compensate his opponent for all losses incurred, and also pay the costs of the

2 action. In some actions condemnation carries infamy with it, as in those on theft, robbery, outrage, fraud, guardianship, agency, and deposit, if direct, not contrary ; also in the action on partnership, which is always direct, and in which infamy is incurred by any partner who suffers condemnation. In actions on theft, robbery, outrage, and fraud, it is not only infamous to be condemned, but also to compound, as indeed is only just ; for obligation based on delict differs widely from obligation based on contract.

3   In commencing an action, the first step depends upon that part of the Edict which relates to summons ; for before anything else is done, the adversary must be summoned, that is to say, must be called before the judge who is to try the action. And herein the praetor takes into consideration the respect due to parents, patrons, and the children and parents of patrons, and refuses to allow a parent to be summoned by his

child, or a patron by his freedman, unless permission so to do has been asked of and obtained from him ; and for non-observance of this rule he has fixed a penalty of fifty *solidi*.

TITLE XVII

OF THE DUTIES OF A JUDGE

Finally, we have to treat of the duties of a judge; of which the first is not to judge contrary to statutes, the imperial laws, and custom. Accordingly, if he is trying a noxal action, and 1 thinks that the master ought to be condemned, he should be careful to word his judgement thus : ' I condemn Publius Maevius to pay ten *aurei* to Lucius Titius, or to surrender to him the slave that did the wrong.' If the action is real, and he 2 finds against the plaintiff, he ought to absolve the defendant ; if against the latter, he ought to order him to give up the property in question, along with its fruits. If the defendant pleads that he is unable to make immediate restitution and applies for execution to be stayed, and such application appears to be in good faith, it should be granted upon the terms of his finding a surety to guarantee payment of the damages assessed, if restitution be not made within the time allowed. If the subject of the action be an inheritance, the same rule applies as regards fruits as we laid down in speaking of actions for the recovery of single objects. If the defendant is a mala fide possessor, fruits which but for his own negligence he might have gathered are taken into account in much the same way in both actions ; but a bona fide possessor is not held answerable for fruits which he has not consumed or has not gathered, except from the moment of the commencement of the action, after which time account is taken as well of fruits which might have been gathered but for his negligence as of those which have been gathered and consumed. If the 3 object of the action be production of property, its mere pro-duction by the defendant is not enough, but it must be ac-companied by every advantage derived from it ; that is to say, the plaintiff must be placed in the same position he would have been in if production had been made immediately on the commencement of the action. Accordingly if, during the

delay occasioned by trial, the possessor has completed a
title to the property by usucapion, he will not be thereby
saved from being condemned. The judge ought also to take
into account the mesne profits, or fruits produced by the
property in the interval between the commencement of the
action and judgement. If the defendant pleads that he is
unable to make immediate production, and applies for a
stay, and such application appears to be in good faith, it
should be granted on his giving security that he will render
up the property. If he neither complies at once with the
judge's order for production, nor gives security for doing so
afterwards, he ought to be condemned in a sum representing
the plaintiff's interest in having production at the commence-
4 ment of the proceedings. In an action for the division of a
'family' the judge ought to assign to each of the heirs specific
articles belonging to the inheritance, and if one of them is
unduly favoured, to condemn him, as we have already said, to
pay a fixed sum to the other as compensation. Again, the
fact that one only of two joint-heirs has gathered the fruits of
land comprised in the inheritance, or has damaged or consumed something belonging thereto, is ground for ordering
him to pay compensation to the other ; and it is immaterial,
so far as this action is concerned, whether the joint-heirs are
5 only two or more in number. The same rules are applied in
an action for partition of a number of things held by joint-
owners. If such an action be brought for the partition of a
single object, such as an estate, which easily admits of division,
the judge ought to assign a specific portion to each joint-
owner, condemning such one as seems to be unduly favoured
to pay a fixed sum to the other as compensation. If the
property cannot be conveniently divided—as a slave, for
instance, or a mule—it ought to be adjudged entirely to one
only of the joint-owners, who should be ordered to pay a fixed
6 sum to the other as compensation. In an action for rectification of boundaries the judge ought to examine whether an
adjudication of property is actually necessary. There is only
one case where this is so ; where, namely, convenience requires
that the line of separation between fields belonging to different
owners shall be more clearly marked than heretofore, and

where, accordingly, it is requisite to adjudge part of the one's field to the owner of the other, who ought, in consequence, to be ordered to pay a fixed sum as compensation to his neighbour. Another ground for condemnation in this action is the commission of any malicious act, in respect of the boundaries, by either of the parties, such as removal of landmarks, or cutting down boundary trees: as also is contempt of court, expressed by refusal to allow the fields to be surveyed in accordance with a judge's order. Wherever property is adjudged to a 7 party in any of these actions, he at once acquires a complete title thereto.

TITLE XVIII

OF PUBLIC PROSECUTIONS

Public prosecutions are not commenced as actions are, nor indeed is there any resemblance between them and the other remedies of which we have spoken; on the contrary, they differ greatly both in the mode in which they are commenced, and in the rules by which they are conducted. They are 1 called public because as a general rule any citizen may come forward as prosecutor in them. Some are capital, others not. 2 By capital prosecutions we mean those in which the accused may be punished with the extremest severity of the law, with interdiction from water and fire, with deportation, or with hard labour in the mines: those which entail only infamy and pecuniary penalties are public, but not capital. The follow- 3 ing statutes relate to public prosecutions. First, there is the lex Iulia on treason, which includes any design against the Emperor or State; the penalty under it is death, and even after decease the guilty person's name and memory are branded with infamy. The lex Iulia, passed for the repression 4 of adultery, punishes with death not only defilers of the marriage-bed, but also those who indulge in criminal intercourse with those of their own sex, and inflicts penalties on any who without using violence seduce virgins or widows of respectable character. If the seducer be of reputable condition, the punishment is confiscation of half his fortune; if a mean person, flogging and relegation. The lex Cornelia on 5 assassination pursues those persons, who commit this crime, with the sword of vengeance, and also all who carry weapons for the purpose of homicide. By a 'weapon', as is remarked by Gaius in his commentary on the statute of the Twelve Tables, is ordinarily meant some missile shot from a bow, but it also signifies anything thrown with the hand; so that stones and pieces of wood or iron are included in the term. '*Telum,*' in fact, or 'weapon', is derived from the Greek τηλοῦ, and so means anything thrown to a distance. A similar connexion of meaning may be found in the Greek word βέλος, which corresponds to our *telum*, and which is derived from βάλλεσθαι, to throw, as we learn from Xenophon, who writes, 'they carried with them βέλη, namely spears, bows and arrows, slings, and large numbers of stones.' *Sicarius*, or assassin, is derived from *sica*, a long steel knife. This statute also inflicts punishment of death on poisoners, who kill men by their hateful arts of poison 6 and magic, or who publicly sell deadly drugs. A novel penalty has been devised for a most odious crime by another statute, called the lex Pompeia on parricide, which provides that any person who by secret machination or open act shall hasten the death of his parent, or child, or other relation whose murder amounts in law to parricide, or who shall be an instigator or accomplice of such crime, although a stranger, shall suffer the penalty of parricide. This is not execution by the sword or by fire, or any ordinary form of punishment, but the criminal is sewn up in a sack with a dog, a cock, a viper, and an ape, and in this dismal prison is thrown into the sea or a river, according to the nature of the locality, in order that even before death he may begin to be deprived of the enjoyment of the elements, the air being denied him while alive, and interment in the earth when dead. Those who kill persons related to them by kinship or affinity, but whose murder is not parricide, will suffer the penalties of the lex Cornelia on 7 assassination. The lex Cornelia on forgery, otherwise called the statute of wills, inflicts penalties on all who shall write, seal, or read a forged will or other document, or shall substitute the same for the real original, or who shall knowingly and feloniously make, engrave, or use a false seal. If the criminal be a slave, the penalty fixed by the statute is death, as in the statute relating to assassins and poisoners: if a free man, de-

portation. The lex Iulia, relating to public or private violence, 8
deals with those persons who use force armed or unarmed.
For the former, the penalty fixed by the statute is deportation ;
for the latter, confiscation of one third of the offender's
property. Ravishment of virgins, widows, persons professed
in religion, or others, and all assistance in its perpetration, is
punished capitally under the provisions of our constitution, by
reference to which full information on this subject is obtainable.
The lex Iulia on embezzlement punishes all who steal money 9
or other property belonging to the State, or devoted to the
maintenance of religion. Judges who during their term of
office embezzle public money are punishable with death, as
also are their aiders and abettors, and any who receive such
money knowing it to have been stolen. Other persons who
violate the provisions of this statute are liable to deportation.
A public prosecution may also be brought under the lex Fabia 10
relating to manstealing, for which a capital penalty is sometimes inflicted under imperial constitutions, sometimes a lighter
punishment. Other statutes which give rise to such prosecu- 11
tions are the lex Iulia on bribery, and three others, which are
similarly entitled, and which relate to judicial extortion, to
illegal combinations for raising the price of corn, and to
negligence in the charge of public moneys. These deal with
special varieties of crime, and the penalties which they inflict
on those who infringe them in no case amount to death, but
are less severe in character.

We have made these remarks on public prosecutions only to 12
enable you to have the merest acquaintance with them, and as
a kind of guide to a fuller study of the subject, which, with the
assistance of Heaven, you may make by reference to the
larger volume of the Digest or Pandects.

INDEX

(The references are to the respective Books, Titles, and Sections.)

A.

M.

N.

THE END.

Oxford : Printed at the Clarendon Press by HORACE HART, M.A.

The prices of the following books now are :

GAISFORD'S Paroemiographi Graeci. 8s. 6d. net.

EUSEBII Evangelicae Preparationis Libri XV, Tomi IV, recensuit T. Gaisford. 42s. net.

NORRIS'S Ancient Cornish Drama. 2 vols. 8vo. 21s. net.

HARPOCRATIONIS LEXICON. Ex recensione G. Dindorfii. Tomi II. 21s. net.

PLOTINUS. Edidit F. Creuzer. Tomi III. 42s. net.

WYCLIF'S Select English Works. 3 vols. 21s. net.

Oxford
March 1907

CONTENTS

Clarendon Press Books

B

ENGLISH
Dictionaries and Philological Works
The Oxford Dictionary

A new English Dictionary on historical principles. Founded mainly on the materials collected by the Philological Society, and edited by J. A. H. MURRAY. Imperial 4to.

The Worshipful Company of Goldsmiths has contributed Five Thousand Pounds towards the cost of Volume VI.

In ten Volumes or twenty Half-volumes

ALREADY PUBLISHED

Volumes I–V (A–K): in half morocco. Each £2 12s. 6d.
Half-volumes: I–XI and XIII in half persian. Each £1 7s. 6d.

The remaining half of the work, edited by Dr. MURRAY, Dr. BRADLEY and Mr. CRAIGIE, is in active preparation: it can be supplied as published in Volumes, Half-volumes, or in Parts or Sections.

In Sections

A Section of 64 pages at 2s. 6d., or now usually a double Section of 128 pages at 5s., is issued quarterly. A treble Section of P will be published on April 1, 1907.

ALREADY PUBLISHED

In Vol. VI, by Dr. BRADLEY

L–Lap 2s. 6d.; Lap-Leisurely 5s.; Leisureness–Lief 2s. 6d.; Lief–Lock 5s.; Lock–Lyyn 5s. — L as a half-volume £1 7s. 6d.

M–Mandragon 5s. Mandragora–Matter 5s. Matter–Mesnalty 5s. Mesne–Misbirth 5s.

N–Niche, by Mr. Craigie, 5s.

In Vol. VII, by Dr. MURRAY

O–Onomastic 5s.; Onomastical–Outing 5s.; Outjet–Ozyat (100 pp.) 2s. 6d.; P–Pargeted 5s,; Pargeter–Pennached 7s. 6d.; Pennage–Pfennig 5s. — P–Pf as a half-volume £1 7s. 6d.

Ph–Piper 5s.

In Vol. VIII, by Mr. CRAIGIE

Q (80 pages) 2s. 6d. R–Reactive (112 pages) 5s. Reactively–Ree 5s. Ree–Reign 2s. 6d. Reign–Reserve 5s.

In Parts

A Part (which as a rule is the equivalent of five Sections and is priced at 12s. 6d.) is issued whenever ready. Pennage–Plat, by Dr. Murray, was published on January 1, 1907.

Nearly all the Sections and Parts in which Volumes I–V were originally issued are still obtainable with their separate prefaces and in their original covers.

Reissue

Beginning with the letter A in monthly numbers of 88 pages: 3s. 6d. each. Published as far as the middle of the letter M, all O, and as far as the middle of the letter P and part of the letter R.

Dr. MURRAY's Romanes Lecture

The Evolution of English Lexicography. 8vo. 2s.

Other English Dictionaries

An Anglo-Saxon Dictionary. Based on the MS. collections of the late Joseph Bosworth, edited and enlarged by T. N. TOLLER. In four parts, 4to, stiff covers, £3 12s., or separately I–III 15s. each, IV in two sections 8s. 6d. and 18s. 6d. A supplement is in the press.

The Student's Dictionary of Anglo-Saxon. By H. SWEET. Small 4to. 8s. 6d. net.

Stratmann's Middle English Dictionary of words used by English writers from the twelfth to the fifteenth century; a new edition, rearranged, revised, and enlarged by H. BRADLEY. Small 4to, half morocco. £1 11s. 6d.

A Concise Dictionary of Middle English. From A.D. 1150 to A.D. 1580: intended to be used as a glossary to the Clarendon Press Specimens of English Literature, etc.: by A. L. MAYHEW and W. W. SKEAT. Crown 8vo, quarter roan. 7s. 6d.

[For Professor SKEAT's Etymological Dictionaries, see below.]

Professor Skeat's Etymological Works

An Etymological Dictionary of the English language, arranged on an historical basis. Third edition. 4to. £2 4s.
A supplement to the first edition of the above. 4to. 2s. 6d.

A Concise Etymological Dictionary of the English language. New edition (1901): rewritten and rearranged alphabetically. Crown 8vo. 5s. 6d.

Principles of English Etymology. Crown 8vo.
1. The Native Element. Second edition. 10s. 6d.
2. The Foreign Element. 10s. 6d.

Notes on English Etymology. Chiefly reprinted from the transactions of the Philological Society: with a portrait of the Author. Crown 8vo. 8s. 6d. net.

English words compared with Icelandic. Being an appendix to *Cleasby-Vigfússon's* Dictionary. Stitched. 2s.

A Student's Pastime. Being a select series of articles reprinted from *Notes and Queries.* Crown 8vo. 7s. 6d. net.

A Primer of English Etymology. Fourth and revised edition. Extra fcap 8vo, stiff covers. 1s. 6d.

A Primer of Classical and English Philology. Extra fcap 8vo, cloth. 2s.

Dr. Henry Sweet's Philological Works

The Student's Dictionary of Anglo-Saxon. See p. 3.

New English Grammar: logical and historical.
Part I: Introduction, Phonology, & Accidence. Crown 8vo. 10s. 6d.
Part II: Syntax. Crown 8vo. 3s. 6d.

Short Historical English Grammar. Extra fcap 8vo. 4s. 6d.

Primer of Historical English Grammar. Extra fcap 8vo. 2s.

History of English Sounds from the earliest period, with full word lists. 8vo. 14s.

Primer of Phonetics. Third edition (1906). Extra fcap 8vo. 3s. 6d.

Primer of Spoken English. 3rd ed. revised. Extra fcap 8vo. 3s. 6d.

Elementarbuch des Gesprochenen Englisch. Grammatik, Texte, und Glossar. Third edition. Extra fcap 8vo, stiff covers. 2s. 6d.

Manual of Current Shorthand. Orthographic and phonetic. Crown 8vo. 4s. 6d.

Other Philological Works. Extra fcap 8vo

The Philology of the English Tongue. By J. EARLE. 5th ed. 8s. 6d.

A Book for the Beginner in Anglo-Saxon. By J. EARLE. Fourth edition. 2s. 6d.

Synopsis of Old English Phonology. By A. L. MAYHEW. 8s. 6d.

Elementary English Grammar and Exercise Book. By O. W. TANCOCK. Third edition. 1s. 6d.

An English Grammar and Reading Book. For lower Forms in classical Schools: by the same. Fourth edition. 3s. 6d.

Sentence Analysis for the Lower Forms of Public Schools. By one of the Authors of 'The King's English.' Crown 8vo. 1s. 6d.

An English Miscellany. Presented to Dr. FURNIVALL in honour of his seventy-fifth birthday, 1901: with portrait of Dr. Furnivall and many illustrations; containing twelve papers by W. P. KER, W. W. SKEAT, H. C. BEECHING, SIDNEY LEE, and others. £1 1s.

Twelve Facsimiles of Old English Manuscripts. With transcriptions and an introduction: edited by W. W. SKEAT. 4to, paper covers. 7s. 6d.

Dr. Sweet's series of Primers and Readers
Extra fcap 8vo

First Steps in Anglo-Saxon. 2s. 6d.

Anglo-Saxon Primer. With grammar and glossary. 8th edition. 2s. 6d.

Anglo-Saxon Reader in prose and verse. With grammatical introduction, notes, and glossary. 7th ed., revised and enlarged. Cr. 8vo. 9s. 6d.

A Second Anglo-Saxon Reader. 4s. 6d.

Old English Reading Primers.
> I : Selected Homilies of Ælfric. Second edition. 2s.
> II : Extracts from Alfred's Orosius. Second edition. 2s.

First Middle English Primer. With grammar and glossary. Second edition. 2s. 6d.

Second Middle English Primer. Extracts from Chaucer, with grammar and glossary. Second edition. 2s. 6d.

Icelandic

An Icelandic-English Dictionary, based on the MS collections of RICHARD CLEASBY, by G. VIGFÚSSON. 4to. £3 13s. 6d. net.

An Icelandic Primer. With grammar, notes, and glossary, by HENRY SWEET. Second edition. Extra fcap 8vo. 3s. 6d.

Icelandic Prose Reader. With notes, grammar, and glossary, by G. VIGFÚSSON and F. YORK POWELL. Extra fcap 8vo. 10s. 6d.

Corpus Poeticum Boreale. By G. VIGFÚSSON and F. YORK POWELL. Two volumes 8vo. £3 3s. (A few copies only remain.)

Sturlunga Saga, including the Islendinga Saga of Lawman Sturla Thordsson and other works, edited by G. VIGFÚSSON. 2 vols. 8vo. £2 2s.

Origines Islandicae : the more important Sagas and other native writings relating to the Settlement and Early History of Iceland. By GUD-BRAND VIGFÚSSON and F. YORK POWELL. Two volumes 8vo. £2 2s. net.

Sturla the Historian : being the Romanes Lecture for 1906. By W. P. KER. 8vo. Paper covers. 1s. net.

Old High German and Gothic

An Old High German Primer. Extra fcap 8vo. With grammars, notes, and glossaries. By JOSEPH WRIGHT. 3s. 6d.

A Middle High German Primer. Second edition. 3s. 6d.

A Primer of the Gothic Language, containing St. Mark, Selections from the other Gospels, and Timothy II. Second edition. 4s. 6d.

Ancient Cornish Drama. By E. NORRIS, with sketch of Cornish grammar (separately 2s. 6d.), vocabulary, &c. 2 vols. 8vo. £1 1s.

Old and Middle English

Two of the Saxon Chronicles Parallel, with supplementary extracts from the others. A revised text, edited, with introduction, notes, appendices, and glossary, by C. PLUMMER and J. EARLE. Two volumes, crown 8vo, leather back. Vol. I : Text, Appendices, and Glossary. 10s. 6d. Vol. II : Introduction, Notes, and Index. 12s. 6d.

The Saxon Chronicles 781–1000 A.D. Crown 8vo, stiff covers. 3s.

The Deeds of Beowulf. An English epic of the eighth century, done into modern prose : with introduction and notes by J. EARLE. Cr. 8vo. 8s. 6d.

King Alfred's Version of Boethius' de Consolatione Philosophiae. Edited by W. J. SEDGEFIELD. Crown 8vo. 10s. 6d.

> **The same done into Modern English.** With an introduction by the same. Extra fcap 8vo. 3s. 6d. net.

The Ormulum. With the notes and glossary of R. M. WHITE: edited by R. HOLT. Two volumes. Extra fcap 8vo. £1 1s.

Laurence Minot's Poems. Edited, with introduction and notes, by J. HALL. Second edition. Extra fcap 8vo. 4s. 6d.

The Dream of the Rood. An old English Poem attributed to Cynewulf. Edited by ALBERT S. COOK. Extra fcap 8vo. 3s. 6d.

Gospel of St. Luke in Anglo-Saxon. Edited, with introduction and glossary, by J. W. BRIGHT. Extra fcap 8vo. 5s.

Gower's Confessio Amantis, selections edited with notes, etc., by G. C. MACAULAY. Extra fcap 8vo. 4s. 6d.

Editions by Professor Skeat

Specimens of Early English : with introd., notes, and glossary.
Part I : From *Old English Homilies* to *King Horn* (A.D. 1150 to A.D. 1300) : by R. MORRIS. Second edition. 9s.
Part II : From *Robert of Gloucester* to *Gower* (A.D. 1298 to A.D. 1393): by R. MORRIS and W. W. SKEAT. Fourth edition, revised. 7s. 6d.
Part III : (A.D. 1394 to A.D. 1579), see p. 12.

William Langland's Piers the Plowman. Eighth edition. 4s. 6d.

The Tale of Gamelyn. With notes and glossary. Second edition, revised. Stiff covers. 1s. 6d.

Wycliffe's Bible. Job, Psalms, Proverbs, Ecclesiastes, and the Song of Solomon. With introduction and glossaries. 3s. 6d. The New Testament. 6s.

The Lay of Havelok the Dane. With introduction, glossarial index, index of names, and two illustrations. 4s. 6d.

Pierce the Ploughman's Crede (about 1394 A.D.**).** Collated with MS. Bibl. Reg. 18. B. xvii, and with the text of 1553. 2s.

The Chaucer Series

Library editions, 14 vols., demy 8vo, in uniform binding

The Works of Geoffrey Chaucer. Edited from numerous manuscripts, with introductions and notes, by W. W. SKEAT. In six volumes, with portrait and facsimiles. Each volume, 16s.

Chaucerian and other pieces, being a supplement to the above. Edited from numerous manuscripts by W. W. SKEAT. 18s.

The Vision of William concerning Piers the Plowman, in three parallel texts, together with Richard the Redeless, by William Langland. Edited from numerous manuscripts, with preface, notes, and glossary, by W. W. SKEAT. Two volumes. £1 11s. 6d.

The Complete Works of John Gower. Edited from the manuscripts, with introductions, notes, glossaries, and facsimiles, by G. C. MACAULAY. Each volume 16s. Vol. I : The French Works. Vols. II and III : The English Works. Vol. IV : The Latin Works.

King Horn, a romance of the thirteenth century. Edited from the manuscripts by JOSEPH HALL. 12s. 6d.

Prof. Skeat's smaller editions of Chaucer

In crown 8vo

The Oxford Chaucer, containing in one volume the complete text of Chaucer's works ; with introduction, portrait, and glossarial index. Crown 8vo. 3s. 6d. Glossarial index separately. Limp cloth. 1s. 6d.

The Minor Poets. With notes, etc. Second edition. 10s. 6d.

The Hous of Fame. Paper boards. 2s.

The Legend of Good Women. 6s.

The Chaucer Canon. With a discussion of the works associated with the name of Geoffrey Chaucer. 3s. 6d. net.

In extra fcap 8vo

The Prologue, the Knightes Tale, the Nonne Prestes Tale, from the Canterbury Tales. R. MORRIS's edition, re-edited by W. W. SKEAT. 2s. 6d.

The Prologue. (School edition.) Third edition. Paper boards. 1s.

The Prioresses Tale, Sir Thopas, the Monkes Tale, the Clerkes Tale, the Squieres Tale, etc. Ninth edition. 4s. 6d.

The Tale of the Man of Lawe, the Pardoneres Tale, the Second Nonnes Tale, the Chanouns Yemannes Tale, from the Canterbury Tales. New edition revised (1904). 4s. 6d.

English Drama

The Mediaeval Stage, from classical times through folk-play and minstrelsy to Elizabethan drama. By E. K. CHAMBERS. With two illustrations. 8vo. £1 5s. net.

York Plays, performed by the Crafts or Mysteries of York, in the fourteenth to the sixteenth centuries. Edited, with introduction and glossary, by L. TOULMIN SMITH. 8vo. £1 1s.

Miracle Plays, Moralities and Interludes, being specimens of the pre-Elizabethan drama. Edited, with introduction, notes, and glossary, by A. W. POLLARD. Fourth edition, with ten illustrations. Crown 8vo. 7s. 6d.

The Pilgrimage to Parnassus, with the two parts of the Return from Parnassus, being three comedies performed in St. John's College, Cambridge, A.D. 1597-1601. Edited by W. D. MACRAY. Medium 8vo, gilt top. 8s. 6d.

Specimens of the Elizabethan Drama. From Lyly to Shirley, A.D. 1580-A.D. 1642. Edited, with introduction and notes, by W. H. WILLIAMS. Crown 8vo. 7s. 6d.

Marlowe's Edward II. With introduction and notes by O. W. TANCOCK. Third edition. Extra fcap 8vo, stiff covers, 2s. ; cloth 3s.

Marlowe's Dr. Faustus and **Greene's Friar Bacon and Friar Bungay.** Edited by A. W. WARD. Fourth edition. Crown 8vo. 6s. 6d.

Scenes from Old Play Books. Arranged as an Introduction to Shakespeare. By P. SIMPSON. Crown 8vo. With reproduction of the Swan Theatre. 3s. 6d.

Ancient Classical Drama. A study in Literary Evolution. By R. G. MOULTON. Crown 8vo. 8s. 6d.

New uniform editions of the Dramatists

The Works of Thomas Kyd. Edited, with facsimile letters and title-pages, by F. S. BOAS. 8vo. 15s. net.

The Works of John Lyly. Edited by R. W. BOND. In three volumes 8vo, with collotype and facsimile title-pages. 42s. net.

The Plays and Poems of Robert Greene. Edited, with a collotype and seven facsimile title-pages, by J. CHURTON COLLINS. In two volumes 8vo. 18s. net.

The Works of Ben Jonson. Edited by C. H. HERFORD and P. SIMPSON. [In preparation.

Shakespeare

The Oxford Shakespeare. New large type edition. Mr. W. J. Craig's
Text, with portrait and glossary, in one volume. 1350 pages ; cloth 3s. 6d.,
leather from 6s. On Oxford India paper, cloth 7s. 6d., leather from 9s.

Shakespeare's Poems and Pericles. Collotype facsimile, with
introductions by Sidney Lee, of the earliest editions of Pericles and
the four volumes of poems—Venus and Adonis, Lucrece, Sonnets, and the
Passionate Pilgrim. In five volumes, not sold separately, either (a) in real
vellum with kid leather ties (the precise form of the original binding), at
£7 7s. net the set; or (b) in paper boards imitating vellum, with ties, after
the original manner of binding, at £4 4s. net the set. Or in a single volume,
(c) in rough calf, at £4 14s. 6d. net ; or (d) in paper boards, at £3 13s. 6d. net.

Select Plays of Shakespeare. In extra fcap 8vo, stiff covers.

Edited by W. G. Clark and W. Aldis Wright.

Hamlet. 2s.	Merchant of Venice. 1s.
Macbeth. 1s. 6d.	Richard the Second. 1s. 6d.

Edited by W. Aldis Wright.

As You Like It. 1s. 6d.	King John. 1s. 6d.
Coriolanus. 2s. 6d.	King Lear. 1s. 6d.
Henry the Eighth. 2s.	Midsummer Night's Dream. 1s. 6d.
Henry the Fifth. 2s.	Much Ado about Nothing. 1s. 6d.
Henry the Fourth, Part I. 2s.	Richard the Third. 2s. 6d.
Julius Caesar. 2s.	Tempest. 1s. 6d.

Twelfth Night. 1s. 6d.

Shakespeare as a Dramatic Artist. By R. G. Moulton. Third
edition, enlarged. Crown 8vo, 7s. 6d.

Chapters on Macbeth, being an extract from the above. 9d. net.

North's Plutarch. Lives of Coriolanus, Caesar, Brutus, and Antonius.
Edited, with introduction and notes, by R. H. Carr. Crown 8vo. 3s. 6d.
Coriolanus, separately, 1s. 6d.

Tudor and Stuart Library, 1906-7

Linen rag paper, printed with the types given to the University
by Dr. Fell, 1660. Sm. 4to and crown 8vo.

Knyvett's Defence of the Realme. With an introduction by
C. Hughes. 5s. net.

Howell's Devises. With an introduction by W. A. Raleigh. 5s. net.

Peacham's Compleat Gentleman. With an introduction by G. S.
Gordon. 5s. net.

Greville's Life of the Renowned Sir Philip Sidney. With
an introduction by Nowell Smith. 5s. net.

Evelyn's Sculptura. With an introduction by C. F. Bell. 5s. net.

Pepys' Memoires of the Royal Navy. With an introduction by
J. R. Tanner. 5s. net.

Historians and Philosophers
Annotated editions
Three volumes, leather backs, demy 8vo

More's Utopia. Edited by J. H. LUPTON. 10s. 6d. net.

Bacon's Essays. Edited by S. H. REYNOLDS. 12s. 6d.

Selden's Table Talk. Edited by S. H. REYNOLDS. 8s. 6d.

Hooker's Complete Works, with Walton's Life. Arranged by J. Keble. 7th ed., revised by R. W. CHURCH and F. PAGET. 3 vols. medium 8vo. 12s. each. Vol. II contains Book V of the Ecclesiastical Polity.

Introduction to Book V. By F. PAGET. Medium 8vo. 7s. 6d.

Clarendon's History. Re-edited from a fresh collation of the original MS. in the Bodleian Library, with marginal dates and occasional notes, by W. DUNN MACRAY. Six volumes, crown 8vo. £2 5s.

Locke's Essay concerning Human Understanding. Collated and annotated with Prolegomena, Biographical, Critical, and Historical, by A. CAMPBELL FRASER. Two volumes. 8vo. £1 12s.

Locke's Conduct of the Understanding. Edited by T. FOWLER. Fifth edition. Extra fcap 8vo. 2s. 6d.

Berkeley's Works. Edited, with an account of his life, by A. CAMPBELL FRASER. New edition. Four volumes. Crown 8vo. 24s.

Hume's Treatise. Reprinted from the original edition in three volumes, and edited by L. A. SELBY-BIGGE. Second edition. Crown 8vo. 6s. net.

Enquiries. Edited by L. A. SELBY-BIGGE. Uniform with the Treatise and Berkeley's works. Second edition. Crown 8vo. 6s. net.

Letters to Strahan. Edited by G. BIRKBECK HILL. 8vo. 12s. 6d.

Butler's Works. Edited by W. E. GLADSTONE. Vol. I. The Analogy. Vol. II. Sermons. Medium 8vo, 14s. each; crown 8vo, Vol. I, 5s. 6d.; II, 5s.

Chesterfield's Letters to his Godson. Edited from the Originals, with a Memoir of Lord Chesterfield, by the late Earl of CARNARVON. Second ed. With appendix and additional correspondence. Royal 8vo. £1 1s.

Older editions

Clarendon's History and his Life, written by himself, in which is included a Continuation of his History of the Grand Rebellion. Royal 8vo. £1 2s.

Clarendon's History, with the notes of Bishop WARBURTON. 1849. Seven volumes, medium 8vo. £2 10s.

Clarendon's Life, including a Continuation of his History. 1857. Two volumes medium 8vo. £1 2s.

Butler's Works. 1875. Two volumes, 8vo. 5s. 6d. each.

Other Library editions

Seven volumes, uniformly bound in cloth, with paper labels.
The texts carefully collated with the original editions

The Shirburn Ballads, 1585–1616. Edited from the MS. by
ANDREW CLARK. 8vo, with thirty-nine illustrations from black-letter copies.
10s. 6d. net.

Milton's Poetical Works : edited by H. C. BEECHING; with two
collotypes, and nine facsimile title-pages. 8vo. 7s. 6d. net.

Caroline Poets. Edited by GEORGE SAINTSBURY. 8vo. Vol. I, containing
Chamberlayne's *Pharonnida* and *England's Jubilee*, Benlowes' *Theophila* and
the Poems of Katherine Philips and Patrick Hannay. 10s. 6d. net. Vol. II.
10s. 6d. net.

Blake's Poetical Works. A new and verbatim text from the MS.
engraved and letterpress originals, with variorum readings and bibliographical
notes and prefaces. By JOHN SAMPSON. 8vo. 10s. 6d. net.

Shelley's Poetical Works, including materials never before printed in
any edition of the Poems; edited, with textual notes and bibliographical list
of editions, by THOMAS HUTCHINSON. 8vo, with portrait of Shelley and two
other collotype illustrations. 7s. 6d. net.

Keats's Poetical Works. Edited, with an Introduction and Textual
Notes, by H. BUXTON FORMAN, C.B. 8vo, with five illustrations. 7s. 6d. net.

Dr. Birkbeck Hill's Johnson and Boswell

The set of thirteen uniform volumes, medium 8vo, quarter-roan,
£7 net, cloth £6 net

Johnson's Lives of the Poets. Edited by G. BIRKBECK HILL. With
a memoir of Dr. Birkbeck Hill, by his nephew HAROLD SPENCER SCOTT, and
a full index. Three vols. Quarter-roan £2 2s. net; cloth, £1 16s. net.

Letters. Two volumes. Quarter-roan £1 4s. net; cloth, £1 1s. net.

Miscellanies. Two volumes. Quarter-roan £1 4s. net; cloth, £1 1s. net.

Boswell's Life of Johnson : including the Tour to the Hebrides, and
JOHNSON's Diary of a Journey into North Wales. Edited by G. BIRKBECK HILL.
Six volumes. With portraits and facsimiles. Quarter-roan £2 10s. net; cloth,
£2 2s. net.

Walpole's Letters. Edited by Mrs. PAGET TOYNBEE, with over 100
letters hitherto unpublished and 50 photogravure portraits of Walpole and his
circle. 16 vols. Vol. XVI contains Indexes, compiled at the Press, of
Persons (revised by ANDREW CLARK), of Places, and of Subjects. In three
styles, viz. limited edition of 260 copies, in demy 8vo, on hand-made paper,
cloth, £16 net: Crown 8vo, on Oxford India paper, in 8 double volumes,
£6 16s. net: in 16 volumes, on ordinary paper, £4 16s. net.

Annotated editions

MORE to CLARENDON

Specimens of English Literature from the Ploughman's Crede to the Shepheardes Calender (A.D. 1394 to A.D. 1579). With introduction, notes, and glossarial index by W. W. SKEAT. Forming Part III of Specimens of English ; see p. 6. Sixth edition. Extra fcap 8vo. 7s. 6d.

More's Utopia. Edited, with introduction, notes, and glossary, by J. CHURTON COLLINS. Crown 8vo. 3s. 6d.

Hooker's Ecclesiastical Polity, Book I. Edited by R. W. CHURCH. Extra fcap 8vo. 2s.

Elizabethan Critical Essays. Edited, with an introduction and notes, by G. GREGORY SMITH. Crown 8vo. 2 Vols. 12s. net.

Hakluyt's Principal Navigations: being narratives of the Voyages of the Elizabethan Seamen to America. Selection edited by E. J. PAYNE. Crown 8vo, with portraits. First and second series. Second edition. 5s. each.

Spenser's Faery Queene. Bks. I and II. With introd. and notes by G. W. KITCHIN, glossary by A. L. MAYHEW. Extra fcap 8vo. 2s. 6d. each.

Bacon's Advancement of Learning. Ed. by W. ALDIS WRIGHT. Cr. 8vo. 3s. 6d.

Milton's Poems. Edited by R. C. BROWNE. Extra fcap 8vo. Two volumes, 6s. 6d. : or separately, vol. I, 4s. ; vol. II, 3s.

In paper covers, extra fcap 8vo
Lycidas, 3d. ; Comus, 6d. : edited by R. C. BROWNE.
Lycidas, 6d.; L'Allegro, 4d.; Il Penseroso, 4d.; Comus, 1s.: ed. by O. ELTON.

Paradise Lost. Book I. H. C. BEECHING. 1s. 6d. Book II. E. K. CHAMBERS. 1s. 6d. Together, 2s. 6d.

Samson Agonistes. J. CHURTON COLLINS. 1s.

Areopagitica. Edited by J. W. HALES. Extra fcap 8vo. 3s.

Bunyan's Pilgrim's Progress, and Grace Abounding. Edited by E. VENABLES. Second ed. revised by MABEL PEACOCK. Cr. 8vo, with portrait. 3s. 6d.

Bunyan's Holy War and the Heavenly Footman. Edited by M. PEACOCK. Extra fcap 8vo. 3s. 6d.

Selections from Fuller, by AUGUSTUS JESSOPP. Crown 8vo. 6s.

Clarendon's History of the Rebellion, Book VI. Edited by T. ARNOLD. Second edition. Crown 8vo. 5s.

Selections from Clarendon, being Characters and Episodes of the Great Rebellion. Edited by the late Dean BOYLE. Crown 8vo. 7s. 6d.

The Oxford Milton. The Poetical works, in the original spelling, edited by H. C. BEECHING. Crown 8vo, cloth. 3s. 6d.

The Oxford Pilgrim's Progress. In Crown 8vo, cloth, with Cruikshank's illustrations. 2s.

DRYDEN to JOHNSON

Dryden's Essays. Edited by W. P. KER. 2 vols. cr. 8vo. 10s. 6d.

Selections from Dryden, including Astraea Redux, Annus Mirabilis, Absalom and Achitophel, Religio Laici and The Hind and the Panther. Edited by W. D. CHRISTIE. Fifth edition, revised by C. H. FIRTH. Extra fcap 8vo. 3s. 6d.

Dryden's Dramatic Poesy. Edited, with notes, by T. ARNOLD. Third edition, revised (1904) by W. T. ARNOLD. Extra fcap 8vo. 3s. 6d.

Selections from Addison's papers in the Spectator. By T. ARNOLD. Extra fcap 8vo. 4s. 6d.

Selections from Steele, being papers from the Tatler, Spectator, and Guardian. Edited by AUSTIN DOBSON. Second edition. Crown 8vo. 7s. 6d.

Selections from Swift. Edited, with biographical introduction and notes, by Sir HENRY CRAIK. Two volumes, crown 8vo, 15s., or 7s. 6d. each.

Selections from Pope. With introduction and notes by MARK PATTISON. Extra fcap 8vo. *Essay on Man*, sixth edition, 1s. 6d.
                    Satires and Epistles, fourth edition, 2s.

Parnell's Hermit. Paper covers. 2d.

Thomson's Seasons and Castle of Indolence. Edited by J. LOGIE ROBERTSON. Extra fcap 8vo. 4s. 6d. *Castle of Indolence* separately. 1s. 6d.

Selections from Chesterfield. By G. BIRKBECK HILL. Crown 8vo. 6s.

Selections from Goldsmith. Edited, with introduction and notes, by AUSTIN DOBSON. Extra fcap 8vo. 3s. 6d.
    The Traveller. Edited by G. BIRKBECK HILL. Stiff covers. 1s.
    The Deserted Village. Paper covers. 2d.

Johnson's Rasselas. Edited, with introduction and notes, by G. BIRKBECK HILL. Cloth flush, 2s. ; also 4s. 6d.

Rasselas, and Lives of Dryden and Pope. Edited by A. MILNES. 4s. 6d. *Lives* separately. Stiff covers. 2s. 6d.

Life of Milton. Edited by C. H. FIRTH. Cloth, 2s. 6d. ; stiff covers, 1s. 6d.

Vanity of Human Wishes. Edited by E. J. PAYNE. Paper covers. 4d.

Selections from Johnson. Edited by G. BIRKBECK HILL. Cr. 8vo. 7s. 6d.

The Oxford Boswell. Crown 8vo, two volumes, 2s. each. Also on India paper; 2 vols. 3s. net each ; together, 5s. net.

The Oxford Goldsmith. Crown 8vo. 3s. 6d. ; also at 2s, A. DOBSON.

GRAY to CAMPBELL.

Selections from Gray. Edited by EDMUND GOSSE. Extra fcap 8vo. Parchment. 3s. With additional notes for schools by F. WATSON. Stiff covers. 1s. 6d.

Elegy and Ode on Eton College. Paper covers. 2d.

Selections from Cowper. Edited, with a life, introduction, and notes, by H. T. GRIFFITH.

Vol. I : Didactic Poems of 1782, with some minor pieces 1779–1783. 3s.

Vol. II : The Task, with Tirocinium and some minor poems 1784–1799. Third edition. 3s.

Selections from Burke. Edited by E. J. PAYNE. Second Edition.

I : Thoughts on the Present Discontents : Speeches on America. 4s. 6d.

II : Reflections on the French Revolution. 5s.

III : Letters on the proposed Regicide peace. 5s.

Selections from Burns. Edited, with introduction, notes, and glossary, by J. LOGIE ROBERTSON. Second edition. Extra fcap 8vo. 3s. 6d.

Keats's Odes. Edited by A. C. DOWNER. With four illustrations. 3s. 6d. net.

Hyperion, Book I. With notes by W. T. ARNOLD. Paper covers. 4d.

Byron's Childe Harold. Edited by H. F. TOZER. Third edition. 3s. 6d.

Scott's Lady of the Lake. Edited by W. MINTO. 3s. 6d.

Lay of the Last Minstrel. By the same editor. Second edition. 1s. 6d. Separately, introduction and Canto I. 6d.

Lord of the Isles. By T. BAYNE. Cloth, 2s. 6d. ; stiff covers, 2s.

Ivanhoe. Edited by C. E. THEODOSIUS. Crown 8vo. 2s.

Marmion. By the same editor. 3s. 6d.

Old Mortality. Edited by H. B. GEORGE. Crown 8vo. 2s.

Quentin Durward. Edited by P. F. WILLERT. Crown 8vo. 2s.

Talisman. Edited by H. B. GEORGE. Crown 8vo. 2s.

Shelley's Adonais. Edited by W. M. ROSSETTI and A. O. PRICKARD. Second edition. Crown 8vo. 3s. 6d. and 5s.

Campbell's Gertrude of Wyoming. Edited by H. M. FITZGIBBON. Second edition. 1s.

Crown 8vo, 3s. 6d. each. Also at 2s.

The Oxford Cowper. H. S. MILFORD.

The Oxford Burns. J. LOGIE ROBERTSON.

The Oxford Byron.

The Oxford Keats. H. BUXTON FORMAN, C.B. (3s. 6d. only.)

The Oxford Shelley. T. HUTCHINSON. (3s. 6d. only.)

The Oxford Scott. J. LOGIE ROBERTSON.

WORDSWORTH to BRIDGES.

Wordsworth's White Doe of Rylstone, &c. Edited by WILLIAM KNIGHT. 2s. 6d.

Kingsley's Water-Babies. Slightly abridged. Edited by JANET HORACE-SMITH and MARION L. MILFORD. Crown 8vo, with five full-page illustrations by JANET ROBERTSON. 2s. 6d.

Demeter : a Mask. By ROBERT BRIDGES. Paper covers, 1s. net ; cloth, 1s. 6d. net.   Music by W. H. HADOW. Crown 4to, 2s. 6d. net.

Greek Classics for English Readers

Matthew Arnold's Merope, with the *Electra* of Sophocles translated by R. WHITELAW. Edited by J. CHURTON COLLINS. Crown 8vo. 3s. 6d.

Euripides' Alcestis, translated by H. KYNASTON. With introduction and notes by J. CHURTON COLLINS. Extra fcap 8vo. 1s. net.

Sophocles' Antigone, translated by R. WHITELAW. With Introduction and Notes by J. CHURTON COLLINS. Extra fcap 8vo. 1s. net.

Anthologies

The Oxford Book of English Verse, A.D. 1250-1900. Chosen and edited by A. T. QUILLER-COUCH. 1096 pages. In two editions. Crown 8vo, gilt top, 7s. 6d. Fcap 8vo, on Oxford India paper, cloth extra, gilt top, 10s. 6d. Also in leather bindings.

The Oxford Treasury of English Literature. By G. E. HADOW and W. H. HADOW. Crown 8vo.
> Vol. I. Old English to Jacobean. 3s. 6d.
> Vol. II. Growth of the Drama. 3s. 6d.

Poems of English Country Life. Selected and edited by H. B. GEORGE and W. H. HADOW. Crown 8vo. 2s.

Typical Selections from the best English writers, with introductory notices. Second edition. Extra fcap 8vo. 3s. 6d. each.
> Vol. I : Latimer to Berkeley.   Vol. II : Pope to Macaulay.

Selections from the English Poets. Edited by Professor ARBER. Crown 8vo, cloth extra. Illustrated, 3s. 6d. each. Without illustrations, 2s. 6d. each. Also in leather bindings.
> 1. Dunbar, 1401-1508. 2. Surrey and Wyatt, 1509-1547. 3. Spenser, 1548-1591. 4. Shakespeare, 1592-1616. 5. Jonson, 1617-1637. 6. Milton, 1638-1674. 7. Dryden, 1675-1700. 8. Pope, 1701-1744. 9. Goldsmith, 1745-1774. 10. Cowper, 1775-1800.

Crown 8vo. 3s. 6d. each. Also at 2s.

The Oxford Wordsworth. T. HUTCHINSON.

The Oxford Hood.

The Oxford Longfellow.

The Oxford Elizabeth B. Browning.

The Oxford Browning.

The Oxford Tennyson.

The Oxford Whittier. W. GARRETT HORDER.

Critical and Miscellaneous Works

Keats's Hyperion. A Facsimile of Keats's Autograph manuscript: with the *Fall of Hyperion, A Dream*; with introductions and notes by ERNEST DE SÉLINCOURT. £2 12s. 6d. net in boards and £3 13s. 6d. net in leather.

Shelley MSS. in the Bodleian; collated by C. D. LOCOCK. Small 4to. With a facsimile. 7s. 6d. net.

Milton's Prosody. By R. BRIDGES; with Classical Metres in English Verse, by W. J. STONE. In Fell type, on hand-made paper. Cr. 8vo. 5s. net.

Poetry for Poetry's Sake, being A. C. BRADLEY's inaugural lecture, 1901. Second impression. 1s. net.

The Progress of Poesy, being J. W. MACKAIL's inaugural lecture, 1906. 1s. net.

The Romanes Lectures, 1892–1900. Decennial issue I. 8vo. 21s.

The King's English. By H. W. F. and F. G. F. Crown 8vo. 5s. net.

OXFORD LIBRARY OF PROSE AND POETRY

Uniform Volumes, fcap 8vo, cloth, 2s. 6d. net each ; lambskin, thin boards, gilt extra, 3s. 6d. net each. With introductions, notes, and illustrations.

Poems and Extracts chosen by Wordsworth. Introduction by H. LITTLEDALE, and preface by J. R. REES.

Wordsworth's Literary Criticism. NOWELL C. SMITH.

Wordsworth's Guide to the Lakes. E. DE SÉLINCOURT.

The Lyrical Poems of William Blake. Text by JOHN SAMPSON. With an introduction by WALTER RALEIGH.

Jowett's Theological Essays. L. CAMPBELL.

Trelawny's Recollections of Shelley and Byron. With introduction by E. DOWDEN.

Kinglake's Eothen. With Introduction by D. G. HOGARTH. Illustrated.

Mary Wollstonecraft's Original Stories. E. V. LUCAS.

Palgrave's Treasury of Sacred Song.

Sea Songs and Ballads. C. STONE and Admiral Sir CYPRIAN BRIDGE, G.C.B.

Cobbett's Grammar of the English Language. H. L. STEPHEN.

Cobbett's Advice to Young Men.

Selections from The Rambler. W. HALE WHITE.

Jowett's Scripture and Truth. CAMPBELL.

See page 96 for detailed list.

OXFORD LIBRARY OF TRANSLATIONS

Uniform Volumes, extra fcap 8vo, 3s. 6d. net per volume.

The Parallel Psalter : being the Prayer Book version of the Psalms and a new version arranged on opposite pages, with an introduction and Glossaries by S. R. DRIVER. Second edition.

The Four Socratic Dialogues of Plato ; Euthyphro, Apology, Crito, Phaedo, translated by B. JOWETT, with Preface by EDWARD CAIRD.

Aristotle's Politics translated by B. JOWETT, with introduction by H. W. C. DAVIS.

The Works of Lucian translated by H. W. FOWLER and F. G. FOWLER. Four volumes.

Longinus on the Sublime translated by A. O. PRICKARD.

Caesar's Civil War translated by F. P. LONG.

Horace translated by E. C. WICKHAM.

Propertius translated by J. S. PHILLIMORE.

The Meditations of Marcus Aurelius Antoninus translated by JOHN JACKSON, with an Introduction by CHARLES BIGG.

Dante's Divina Commedia translated by H. F. TOZER.

Alfred's Boethius done into modern English by W. J. SEDGEFIELD.

Machiavelli's Prince translated by N. H. THOMSON.

Jowett's Translations.   Medium 8vo, etc

Dialogues of Plato translated by B. JOWETT.   Five volumes.   £4 4s.

Republic of Plato translated by B. JOWETT.   Third edition.   Medium 8vo.   12s. 6d.   Half-roan, 14s.

A Selection of Passages from Plato.   Two volumes.   Crown 8vo. 12s.

The Socratic Dialogues of Plato, from B. JOWETT'S translation, with introduction by E. CAIRD.   Extra fcap 8vo.   3s. 6d. net.

Aristotle's Politics translated by B. JOWETT.   Two volumes.   21s.

Aristotle's Politics translated by B. JOWETT, with an introduction by H. W. C. DAVIS.   Extra fcap 8vo.   3s. 6d. net.

Thucydides translated by B. JOWETT.   Second edition, revised.   2 vols. 8vo.   15s.   Vol. I : Essay on Inscriptions, and Books I–III.   Vol. II : Books IV–VIII, and Historical Index.

C

Art

A Handbook of Anatomy for Art Students, fully illustrated. By ARTHUR THOMSON. Third edition, 1906. 8vo, buckram. 16s. net.

Drawings of Old Masters in the University Galleries, and in the Library at Christ Church, Oxford. Chosen and described by SIDNEY COLVIN. Extra imperial folio. Parts I–V each containing 20 drawings, in portfolio, now ready. Subscription price, £3 3s. net per Part.

Drawings by Raffaelle in the University Galleries, Oxford, drawn on stone by J. FISHER. 21s.

Drawings by Michael Angelo and Raffaelle in the University Galleries, Oxford: a critical account by Sir J. C. ROBINSON. Crown 8vo. 4s.

The Master E. S. and the ' Ars Moriendi,' a Chapter in the History of Engraving during the XVth Century; with facsimiles of Engravings in the University Galleries at Oxford and in the British Museum. By LIONEL CUST. Royal 4to, with 46 Plates, paper boards, 17s. 6d. net.

The Blazon of Episcopacy, being the Arms borne by, or attributed to, the Archbishops and Bishops of England and Wales, with an Ordinary of the Coats described and other Episcopal Arms. By W. K. R. BEDFORD. Second edition, with 1000 illustrations. 4to, buckram, 31s. 6d. net.

Oxford Historical Portraits : Illustrated Catalogues.
Loan Collection of 1904 (Personages who died before 1625). 4to, with forty portraits, 6s. net.
Loan Collection of 1905 (Personages who died between 1625 and 1714). 4to, with sixty portraits, 7s. 6d. net.
Loan Collection of 1906 (Personages who died after 1715). 4to, with sixty portraits, 7s. 6d. net.

Maiolica ; a historical treatise on the glazed and enamelled earthenwares of Italy, etc, with plates, marks, etc. By C. DRURY E. FORTNUM. Small 4to. £2 2s. net.

Descriptive Catalogue of the Maiolica and Kindred Wares in the Ashmolean Museum, Oxford. By the same. Small 4to. 10s. 6d. net.

Catalogue of the Castellani Collection in the University Galleries, Oxford. By W. S. W. VAUX. Crown 8vo, 1s.

A Handbook of Pictorial Art. With illustrations, and a chapter on Perspective by A. MACDONALD. By R. St. J. TYRWHITT. Second edition. 8vo, leather back, 18s.

Wadham College, Oxford ; its Foundation, Architecture, and History. By T. G. JACKSON. 4to, illustrated, half-persian, 42s. net.

The Church of St. Mary the Virgin, Oxford. By the same. Demy 4to, quarter-bound, with many illustrations; buckram, gilt top, 36s. net; or with vellum back, gilt top and morocco labels, etc, 42s. net.

Dalmatia, the Quarnero, and Istria. By the same. Three volumes. 8vo. £2 2s.

Music

Oxford History of Music. Edited by W. H. HADOW. 8vo. 15s. net per volume.

The Polyphonic Period, Part I. By H. E. WOOLDRIDGE.

The Polyphonic Period, Part II. By H. E. WOOLDRIDGE.

The Seventeenth Century. By Sir C. HUBERT H. PARRY.

The Age of Bach and Handel. By J. A. FULLER MAITLAND.

The Viennese School. By W. H. HADOW.

The Romantic Period. By E. DANNREUTHER.

Demeter: a Mask. By ROBERT BRIDGES. Music by W. H. HADOW. Crown 4to. 2s. 6d. net. See p. 15.

The Harmonics of Aristoxenus. By H. S. MACRAN. Crown 8vo. 10s. 6d. net.

Modes of Ancient Greek Music. By D. B. MONRO. 8vo. 12s. 6d. net.

The Natural History of the Musical Bow. Part I, Primitive Types. By HENRY BALFOUR. Royal 8vo. Paper covers, 4s. 6d.

Hymns and Chorales for Schools and Colleges. Edited by JOHN FARMER. With music, 5s. Words only, 2s.

Cultivation of the Speaking Voice. By JOHN HULLAH. Second edition. Extra fcap 8vo. 2s. 6d.

Treatise on Harmony. By Sir F. A. GORE OUSELEY. Third edition. 4to. 10s.

Treatise on Counterpoint, Canon, and Fugue, based upon that of Cherubini. By the same. Second edition. 4to. 16s.

Treatise on Musical Form and General Composition. By the same. Second edition. 4to. 10s.

A Chart of the Rules of Harmony. By A. SOMERVELL. 1s. net.

A Chart of the Rules of Counterpoint. By the same. 1s. net.

Music Primer. By J. TROUTBECK and R. F. DALE. Third edition. Crown 8vo. 1s. 6d.

Style in Musical Art, being Sir C. H. H. PARRY's Inaugural Lecture (1900). 8vo. 1s. (published by Mr. Frowde).

C 2

Learning and Education

Opus Epistolarum Des. Erasmi Roterodami denuo recognitum et auctum per P. S. ALLEN. Medium 8vo. Tom. I, 1484–1514, with four illustrations. 18s. net.

The Universities of Europe in the Middle Ages. By H. RASHDALL. Two volumes. 8vo. With maps and illustrations. [Out of print.]

Statutes of the University of Oxford, codified in the year 1636 under the authority of Archbishop Laud. Edited by JOHN GRIFFITHS. With Introduction by C. L. SHADWELL. 4to, cloth, £1 1s.

Ordinances and Statutes (for Colleges and Halls) of the Oxford University Commissioners, 1863. 8vo, 12s. Colleges separately, 1s. each.

Knight's Life of Dean Colet. 8vo. 7s. 6d.

Essays by Mark Pattison arranged by H. NETTLESHIP. Two vols. 8vo. £1 4s.

Life of Casaubon. By MARK PATTISON. Second edition. 8vo. 16s.

Casauboni Ephemerides ed. J. RUSSELL. Tomi II. 8vo. 15s.

Annals of the Bodleian Library, Oxford, with a notice of the earlier library of the University. By W. D. MACRAY. Second edition, enlarged and continued from 1868 to 1880. Medium 8vo, quarter-bound. £1 5s.

Inaugural Lectures. 8vo. Paper covers, 1s. net each.
A Plea for the Historical Teaching of History. By Professor C. H. FIRTH. Second edition.
The Study of History. By Professor OMAN.
The Claims of the Study of Colonial History By Professor H. E. EGERTON.
The Place of Rural Economy in a University Curriculum. By Professor W. SOMERVILLE.

Education

Lectures on the Method of Science. Edited by T. B. STRONG. (The Lectures are part of a Course on Scientific Method, delivered at the Oxford University Extension Meeting, August, 1905.) 8vo. 7s. 6d. net.

Classical Archaeology in Schools. By P. GARDNER and J. L. MYRES. 8vo. Second edition. Paper covers. 1s. net.

The Educational Systems of Great Britain and Ireland. By GRAHAM BALFOUR. Second edition. 8vo. 7s. 6d. net.

Essays on Secondary Education, ed. by C. COOKSON. Cr. 8vo. 4s. 6d.

Physical Education, a theoretical and practical system. By A. MACLAREN. New edition, enlarged by W. MACLAREN. Crown 8vo. 8s. 6d. net.

Lectures on the Logic of Arithmetic. By M. E. BOOLE. Crown 8vo, 2s., or interleaved with writing paper, 3s.

The Preparation of the Child for Science. By M. E. BOOLE. Crown 8vo, uniform with the above. 2s.

Locke's Conduct of the Understanding. Edited by THOMAS FOWLER. Fifth edition. Extra fcap 8vo. 2s. 6d.

Statutes &c. of the University

Oxford University Sheet Almanack, 1907. 4s. 6d.

The Almanack for 1907 is a collotype of an original drawing by MUIRHEAD BONE, of the Great Gate of the Schools ; that for 1906 an etching of Exeter and Brasenose Colleges, from the Radcliffe Camera, by MUIRHEAD BONE.
Most of the illustrations for back years can be obtained, price 2s. net each.

Oxford University Calendar, 1907. Crown 8vo, cloth, 5s.

The Historical Register, a supplement to the Calendar, with record of University Honours and Distinctions to 1900. Crown 8vo, cloth, 7s. 6d.

The Student's Handbook to the University and Colleges at Oxford. Sixteenth edition. Revised to September, 1906. Crown 8vo, 2s. 6d. net ; by post, 2s. 9d. net. Includes the following as a supplement.

Programme of Special Studies for the Academical Year 1906-7; together with some account of opportunities for Special Work or research existing in Oxford University. Crown 8vo, paper covers. 6d. net.

The Examination Statutes, with the Regulations of the Board of Studies and of Faculties for 1906-1907. 8vo. 1s. net.

Guide for Colonial, Indian, and Foreign Students. 2d. net.

Statuta Universitatis Oxoniensis, 1906. 8vo, cloth, 5s.

Statutes made by Commissioners, 1877. 8vo. 12s. 6d.

Statutes for the University only, stitched, 2s. : for the Colleges, stitched, each 1s.

Supplementary Statutes made by the University and by certain of the Colleges : approved by the Queen in Council, 1888. 8vo. 2s. 6d.

Enactments in Parliament, specially concerning the Universities of Oxford and Cambridge. Collected by JOHN GRIFFITHS. 8vo, cloth, 12s.

The Universities and College Estates Acts, 1858 to 1880, and 1898. Arranged by W. B. GAMLEN. 8vo, stiff covers, 2s. 6d.

Catalogue of Oxford Graduates from 1659 to 1850. 8vo. 7s. 6d.

Index to Wills proved in the Court of the Chancellor of the University of Oxford, etc. By J. GRIFFITHS. Royal 8vo. 3s. 6d.

Oxford University Gazette, containing official notices, lecture-lists, etc ; published weekly during Term and when necessary in Vacation. 7s. 6d. per annum, post free. Bound volumes from 1870-1906 may still be purchased, Folio, cloth, 12s. 6d. net each.

The Oxford Degree Ceremony. By J. WELLS. Illustrated. Fcap 8vo, 1s. 6d. net.

Guide to the Bodleian Library. By A. CLARK. Illustrated. Fcap 8vo, 1s. 6d. net.

Anecdota Oxoniensia

(Crown 4to, stiff covers, with many facsimiles)

I. Classical Series

I. The English Manuscripts of the Nicomachean Ethics. By J. A. STEWART. 3s. 6d.

II. Nonius Marcellus, de Compendiosa Doctrina, Harleian MS 2719. Collated by J. H. ONIONS. 3s. 6d.

III. Aristotle's Physics. Book VII. With Introduction by R. SHUTE. 2s.

IV. Bentley's Plautine Emendations. From his copy of Gronovius. By E. A. SONNENSCHEIN. 2s. 6d.

V. Harleian MS 2610; Ovid's Metamorphoses I, II, III. 1–622; XXIV Latin Epigrams from Bodleian or other MSS; Latin Glosses on Apollinaris Sidonius from MS Digby 172. Collated and Edited by ROBINSON ELLIS. 4s.

VI. A Collation with the Ancient Armenian Versions of the Greek Text of Aristotle's Categories, De Interpretatione, De Mundo, De Virtutibus et Vitiis, and of Porphyry's Introduction. By F. C. CONYBEARE. 14s.

VII. Collations from the Harleian MS of Cicero 2682. By ALBERT C. CLARK. 7s. 6d.

VIII. The Dialogues of Athanasius and Zacchaeus and of Timothy and Aquila. Edited by F. C. CONYBEARE. 7s. 6d.

IX. Collations from the Codex Cluniacensis s. Holkhamicus. By W. PETERSON. 7s. 6d.

X. The Vetus Cluniacensis of Poggio : being a contribution to the textual criticism of Cicero Pro Sex. Roscio, Pro Cluentio, Pro Murena, Pro Caelio, and Pro Milone. By A. C. CLARK. With two Facsimiles. 8s. 6d.

II. Semitic Series

I. A Commentary on Ezra and Nehemiah. By Rabbi Saadiah. Edited by H. J. MATHEWS. 3s. 6d.

II. The Book of the Bee. Edited by ERNEST A. WALLIS BUDGE. 21s.

III. A Commentary on the Book of Daniel. By Japhet Ibn Ali. Edited and translated by D. S. MARGOLIOUTH. 21s.

IV, VI. Mediaeval Jewish Chronicles and Chronological Notes. Edited by AD. NEUBAUER. Part I, 14s. Part II, 18s. 6d.

V. The Palestinian Version of the Holy Scriptures. Edited by G. H. GWILLIAM. 6s.

VII. Churches and Monasteries of Egypt; attributed to Abû Salih. Edited and translated by B. T. A. EVETTS, with Notes by A. J. BUTLER. £1 11s. 6d.

Translation, with map, buckram, £1 1s.

VIII. The Ethiopic Version of the Hebrew Book of Jubilees. Edited by R. H. CHARLES. 12s. 6d. (Sold only as part of a complete set.)

IX. Biblical and Patristic Relics of the Palestinian Syriac Literature. Edited by G. H. GWILLIAM, F. C. BURKITT, and J. F. STENNING. 12s. 6d.

X. The Letters of Abu 'l-'Alā of Ma'arrat Al-Nu'mān. Edited and translated by D. S. MARGOLIOUTH. 15s.

XI. The Ethiopic Version of the Book of Enoch. Edited from twenty-three MSS., together with the fragmentary Greek and Latin Versions, by R. H. CHARLES. 17s. 6d.

III. Aryan Series

I-III. Buddhist Texts from Japan. 1. Va*g*rak*kh*edikâ. Edited by F. Max Müller. 3s. 6d. 2. Sukhâvatî-Vyûha. Edited by F. Max Müller and Bunyiu Nanjio. 7s. 6d. 3. The Ancient Palmleaves containing the Pra*g*ñâ-Pâramitâ-H*r*idaya-Sûtra and the Ush*n*îsha-Vi*g*aya-Dhâra*n*î, edited by F. Max Müller and Bunyiu Nanjio. With Appendix by G. Bühler. 10s.

IV. Kâtyâyana's Sarvânukrama*n*î of the *R*igveda, with Extracts from Vedârthadîpikâ. Edited by A. A. Macdonell. 16s.

V. The Dharma-Sa*m*graha. Edited by Kenjiu Kasawara, F. Max Müller, and H. Wenzel. 7s. 6d.

VII. The Buddha-*K*arita of A*s*vaghosha. Edited by E. B. Cowell. 12s. 6d.

VIII. The Mantrapâtha: being the Prayer Book of the Āpastambins. Edited by M. Winternitz. Part I. 10s. 6d.

IV. Mediaeval and Modern Series

I. Sinonoma Bartholomei. Edited by J. L. G. Mowat. 3s. 6d.

II. Alphita. Edited by J. L. G. Mowat. 12s. 6d.

III. The Saltair Na Rann. Edited by Whitley Stokes. 7s. 6d.

IV. The Cath Finntrága, or Battle of Ventry. Edited by Kuno Meyer. 6s.

V. Lives of Saints, from the Book of Lismore. Edited, with Translation, by Whitley Stokes. £1 11s. 6d.

VI. The Elucidarium and other Tracts in Welsh, from Llyvyr Agkyr Llandewivrevi. Edited by J. Morris Jones and John Rhŷs. 21s.

VII. The Crawford Collection of Early Charters and Documents, now in the Bodleian Library. Edited by A. S. Napier and W. H. Stevenson. Paper covers, 10s. 6d.; cloth, 12s.

VIII. Hibernica Minorca, being a fragment of an Old-Irish Treatise on the Psalter. With Translation and Glossary. Edited by Kuno Meyer. 7s. 6d.

IX. Index Britanniae Scriptorum quos collegit I. Baleus; edited by R. L. Poole and Mary Bateson. Paper covers, 35s.; boards, 37s. 6d.

X. The earliest Translation of the Old Testament into the Basque Language (a Fragment). Edited by Llewelyn Thomas. 18s. 6d.

XI. Old English Glosses, chiefly unpublished. Edited by Arthur S. Napier. Paper covers, 15s.; cloth, 17s. 6d.

XII. Cáin Adamnáin: an Old-Irish Treatise on the Law of Adamnain. Edited and translated by Kuno Meyer. 5s.

Bodleian and College Catalogues

No copies are left for sale if the price is not stated.

A Summary Catalogue of Western Manuscripts. By F. Madan. 8vo.
  Vol. III (Eighteenth Century). Nos. 8717–16669. 1895. 21s.
  Vol. IV (Nineteenth Century). Nos. 16670–24330. 1897. 25s.
  Vol. V (Nineteenth Century). Nos. 24331–31000. 1906. 25s. net.
  Vol. VI. Part I (Accessions, 1890–1904). Nos. 31001–33541. 1906. 7s. 6d. net.
Codd. MSS Orientalium ; fol. : Pars I, a J. Uri. 1788. Partis II Vol. I, ab
  A. Nicoll. 1821. Vol. II, ab E. B. Pusey. 1835.
Codd. MSS ab E. D. Clarke comparatorum, 1812–4.
Codd. cum notis MSS olim D'Orvillianorum. 1806. 4to.
Codd. MSS Borealium a Finno Magno Islando. 1832. 4to.
Codd. MSS Bibliothecae Bodleianae :
  I. Codices Graeci, ab H. O. Coxe. 1853. 4to.
  II. Codices Laudiani, ab H. O. Coxe. 1858. 4to. Index. 1885. 2s.
  III. Codices Graeci et Latini Canoniciani, ab H. O. Coxe. 1854. 4to.
  IV. Codices T. Tanneri, ab A. Hackman. 1860. 4to, 12s.
  V. Codices R. Rawlinson, a Gul. D. Macray : Fasc. I (I, II). 1862. 4to,
    12s. Fasc. II (III). 1878. 4to, 30s. Fasc. III (IV. i). 1893. 4to, 21s.
    Fasc. IV (IV. ii). 1898. 4to, 15s. Fasc. V. 1900. 4to, 21s.
  VI. Codices Syriaci, a R. P. Smith. 1864. 4to.
  VII. Codices Aethiopici, ab A. Dillman, Ph. Doct. 1848. 4to, 6s. 6d.
  VIII. Codices Sanscritici, a Th. Aufrecht. 1859–1864. 4to, 30s.
  IX. Codices Digbeiani, a Gul. D. Macray. 1883. 4to, 10s. 6d.
  X. Ashmole Manuscripts. By W. H. Black. 1845. 4to, 30s. Index, by
    W. D. Macray. 1867. 4to, 10s.
  XI. Codici Canoniciani Italici, dal Conte A. Mortara. 1864. 4to, 10s. 6d.
  XII. Hebrew MSS. with those in the College Libraries, Ad. Neubauer. 4to.
    Vol. I. 1886. 105s. Also separately, Catalogue, £3 13s. 6d. ; Facsimiles,
    £2 12s. 6d. Vol. II. 1906, completed by A. E. Cowley. 30s. net.
  XIII. Persian, Turkish, Hindûstânî, and Pushtû Manuscripts. Part I—The
    Persian Manuscripts. Begun by Ed. Sachau, completed and edited by
    H. Ethé. 4to, 63s.
  XIV. Sanskrit Manuscripts. Begun by M. Winternitz, completed by A. B.
    Keith. With a Preface by E. W. B. Nicholson. 4to. 25s. net.
Librorum impressorum. Tomi IV. 1843–1850. fol. £4.
Dissertationum Academicarum. 1834. fol. 7s.
Chinese Works, by Joseph Edkins. 1876. 4to, 2s. 6d.
Japanese and Chinese Books and MSS. By B. Nanjio. 1881. 4to, 1s. 6d.
Books bequeathed by R. Gough. 1814. 4to, 15s.
Early English Poetry, etc, collected by E. Malone. 1835.
Books and Manuscripts bequeathed by F. Douce. 1840. fol. 15s.
Early Newspapers and Essayists presented by F. W. Hope. 1865. 8vo, 7s. 6d.
Periodicals : Part I. English. 1878. 8vo, 1s. Part III. Foreign. 1880. 8vo, 1s.
Mohammadan Coins. By Stanley Lane-Poole. 1888. 4to, cloth, 12s. 6d.
Calendar of the Clarendon State Papers. In three volumes. 1869–1876.
  Vol. I. From 1523 to 1649. By O. Ogle and W. H. Bliss. 1872. 8vo, 18s.
  Vol. II. From 1649 to 1654. By W. D. Macray. 1869. 8vo, 16s.
  Vol. III. From 1655 to 1657. By W. D. Macray. 1876. 8vo, 14s.
Calendar of Charters and Rolls. By W. H. Turner. 1878. 8vo, 31s. 6d.

Catalogue of Sanskrit and Prākrit MSS in the Indian Institute Library, Oxford.
  Compiled by A. B. Keith. 8vo. 4s. 6d. net.
Codd. MSS in Collegiis Aulisque. H. O. Coxe. Tomi II. 1852. 4to, 40s.
Codd. MSS in Bibl. Aed. Christi. G. W. Kitchin. 1867. 4to, 6s. 6d.
Codicum Graecorum Sinaiticorum. Scripsit V. Gardthausen. With six pages
  of Facsimiles. 8vo, linen, 25s.

MODERN LANGUAGES

Bohemian Grammar. By W. R. MORFILL. Crown 8vo. 6s.

Ancient Cornish Drama. Edited and translated by E. NORRIS, with a sketch of Cornish grammar, a vocabulary, etc. Two volumes 8vo. £1 1s. net. Sketch of Cornish grammar separately. 2s. 6d.

Dano-Norwegian Grammar. By J. Y. SARGENT. Crown 8vo. 7s. 6d.

Finnish Grammar. By Sir CHARLES ELIOT. Crown 8vo, roan, 10s. 6d.

Russian Grammar. By W. R. MORFILL. Crown 8vo. 6s.

For French, German, and Italian Books see below; African Languages, p. 84; Oriental Languages, pp. 78-84.

Studies in European Literature, being the Taylorian Lectures, 1889-1899. Crown 8vo. 7s. 6d.

The Oxford Molière

Les Œuvres complètes de Molière. Crown 8vo. 5s. Also, an India Paper edition, cloth extra, 9s. 6d.; and miniature edition, four volumes, 32mo in case, 14s.

French Dictionaries and Grammars

Brachet's Etymological Dictionary of the French language, translated by G. W. KITCHIN. Third edition. Crown 8vo. 7s. 6d.

Brachet's Historical Grammar of the French language, translated by G. W. KITCHIN. Seventh edition. Extra fcap 8vo. 3s. 6d.

The same, rewritten and enlarged by PAGET TOYNBEE. Crown 8vo. 7s. 6d.

Historical Primer of French Phonetics and Inflection. By M. S. BRITTAIN, with introduction by P. TOYNBEE. Extra fcap 8vo. 2s. 6d.

Concise French Grammar, including phonology, accidence and syntax, for use in upper and middle forms. By A. H. WALL. Cr. 8vo. 4s. 6d.

French Primer, for use in middle and lower forms. By the same. Extra fcap 8vo. 2s.

History of French Versification, with numerous examples from the poets, by L. E. KASTNER. Crown 8vo. 5s. 6d. net.

History of French Literature. Specimens, etc
By Professor SAINTSBURY

A Short History of French Literature. Sixth edition with the section on the Nineteenth Century enlarged. Crown 8vo. 10s. 6d.

A Primer of French Literature. Fourth edition revised. Extra fcap 8vo. 2s.

Specimens of French Literature, from Villon to Hugo. Second edition. Crown 8vo. 9s.

Oxford Modern French Series

EDITED BY LEON DELBOS.

Already Published, crown 8vo, stout cloth

1. **Deux Héroïnes de la Révolution Française,** by Lamartine. Edited by MARY BENTINCK SMITH. pp. 192. 2s. 6d.

2. **La Vendetta and Pierre Grassou,** by Balzac. Edited by MARIE PÉCHINET. pp. 140. 2s.

3. **Bug-Jargal,** by Victor Hugo. Edited by LOUIS SERS. pp. 152. 2s.

4. **Mademoiselle de la Seiglière,** by Sandeau. Edited by A. L. DUPUIS. pp. 214. 2s. 6d.

5. **Mémoires d'Outre-Tombe,** by Chateaubriand. Edited by LOUIS SERS. pp. 164. 2s. 6d.

6. **Voyage autour de mon jardin,** by Karr. Edited by STUART G. HALLAM. pp. 148. 2s.

7. **Le Château de Vaux,** by Gozlan. Edited by A. H. SMITH. pp. 92. 1s. 6d.

8. **Extraits des Voyages d'Alexis de Tocqueville.** Edited by J. E. MANSION. pp. 122. 2s.

9. **Le Serment,** by Jules David. Edited by C. HUGON. pp. 96. 1s. 6d.

10. **Voyage en Espagne,** by Gautier. Edited by G. GOODRIDGE. pp. 200. 2s. 6d.

11. **Les Normands en Angleterre et en Gaule,** by Thierry. Edited by A. H. SMITH. pp. 160. 2s. 6d.

12. **Une Haine à bord,** by de la Landelle. Edited by R. E. A. CHESSEX. pp. 256. 3s.

13. **Histoire de la Révolution Française,** by Mignet. Edited by A. L. DUPUIS. pp. 240. 3s.

14. **Une Ténébreuse Affaire,** by Balzac. Edited by MARIE PÉCHINET. pp. 244. 2s. 6d.

15. **Mémoires d'un touriste,** by Stendhal. Edited by H. J. CHAYTOR. pp. 116. 2s.

16. **Voyage aux Pyrénées,** by Taine. Edited by W. ROBERTSON. pp. 226. 2s. 6d.

17. **Jean Sbogar,** by Nodier. Edited by D. L. SAVORY. pp. 160. 2s.

18. **Les Chouans,** by Balzac. Edited by C. L. FREEMAN. pp. 256. 3s.

19. **Histoire d'un homme du peuple,** by Erckmann-Chatrian. Edited by R. E. A. CHESSEX. pp. 160. 3s.

20. **Feuilletons Choisis.** Edited by C. BRERETON. pp. 130. 2s.

21. **Souvenirs de la Vie Militaire,** by Comte Pierre de Castellane. Edited by W. G. HARTOG. pp. 120. 2s.

Oxford Higher French Series

Edited by LEON DELBOS. Extra fcap. 8vo

The Introductions are a novel feature. Originally they were to be all written in English, but as it was desired that they should be as characteristic as possible, and not merely extracted from reference books, but real studies of the various authors and their works, it was decided that each editor should write his introduction in his native language. The notes are less elementary, and it is hoped brighter and more interesting than is usual, and great care has been taken to adapt them to the character of each volume. So far as possible each volume contains a portrait of the author at the time he wrote his book.

De l'Allemagne, by Madame de Staël. Edited by H.W. EVE. 2s. 6d. net.

Notre-Dame de Paris, by Victor Hugo. Edited by L. DELBOS. 3s. 6d. net.

Trois Grotesques, by Gautier. Edited by H. J. CHAYTOR. 2s. net.

Mémoires de Madame de Campan. Edited by H. C. BRADBY. 2s. 6d. net.

Salammbô, by Flaubert. Edited by E. LAUVRIÈRE. 3s. 6d. net.

Jocelyn, by Lamartine. Edited by E. LEGOUIS. 3s. net.

Racine et Shakespeare, by Stendhal. Edited by L. DELBOS. 3s. net.

De Musset's Poésies Choisies. Edited by C. E. Delbos. 2s. net.

Lettres Parisiennes, by Madame de Girardin. Edited by F. DE BAUDISS. 2s. 6d. net.

Hernani, by Victor Hugo. Edited by C. KEMSHEAD. 2s. net.

Pierrette, by Balzac. Edited by T. DE SÉLINCOURT. 2s. 6d. net.

Volumes in the press

Les Journées de Juin, by Stern. Edited by C. N. NAGEL.

Eugénie Grandet, by Balzac. Edited by H. E. BERTHON.

Sainte-Beuve's Essays. Selection, edited by D. L. SAVORY.

La Mer, by Michelet. Edited by W. ROBERTSON.

John Bull in France : or, French as it is spoken, for use of English and American travellers in France. By LEON DELBOS. Second impression. Fcap 8vo, cloth, 2s. ; on India paper, 2s. 6d.

Ma première visite à Paris. By A. E. C. Being a French reading-book, with twenty-six illustrations. Crown 8vo. 1s. 6d.

Premières Notions de Vocabulaire et de Lecture, par J. E. PICHON. Crown 8vo, with many illustrations. 1s. 6d.

La Lignée des poètes au XIXᵉ siècle, being an anthology of modern French Poetry, by CHARLES BONNIER. Demy 12mo, on hand-made paper, in various cloth bindings. 3s. net.

Annotated editions. Extra fcap 8vo

Beaumarchais's Le Barbier de Séville, by Austin Dobson. 2s. 6d.

Corneille's Cinna. With Molière's *Les Femmes savantes* and Fontonelle's *Life of Corneille.* By G. Masson. 2s. 6d.

Cinna, by G. Masson. Cloth, 2s.; stiff covers, 1s. 6d.

Horace, by George Saintsbury. 2s. 6d.

Gautier's Scenes of Travel, selected and edited by George Saintsbury. Second edition. 2s.

L'Éloquence de la chaire française, by Paul Blouët. 2s. 6d.

Maistre's Voyage autour de ma chambre, by G. Masson. limp. 1s. 6d.

Molière's Plays.

Le Misanthrope, by H. W. G. Markheim. 3s. 6d.
Les Fâcheux, by E. J. Trechmann. 2s.
Les Femmes savantes, by G. Masson. Cloth, 2s.; stiff covers, 1s. 6d.

Les Fourberies de Scapin, with Voltaire's *Life of Molière*, by G. Masson. Stiff covers. 1s. 6d.
Les Précieuses Ridicules, by Andrew Lang. Second edition. 1s. 6d.

Musset's On ne badine pas avec l'amour, and Fantasio, by W. H. Pollock. 2s.

Quinet's Lettres à sa mère, selected and edited by G. Saintsbury. 2s.

Racine's Esther, by George Saintsbury. 2s.

Regnard's Le Joueur, and Brueys and Palaprat's Le Grondeur, edited by G. Masson. 2s. 6d.

Sainte-Beuve. Selections from the Causeries du Lundi, by George Saintsbury. 2s.

Voltaire's Mérope, by George Saintsbury. 2s.

Selections, edited by G. Masson
Extra fcap 8vo

Louis XIV and his Contemporaries; as described in Extracts from the best Memoirs of the Seventeenth Century. With English Notes. Genealogical Tables, etc. 2s. 6d.

Selections from Madame de Sévigné's Correspondence. 3s.

Voyage autour de ma chambre, by Xavier de Maistre; Ourika, by Madame de Duras; Le Vieux Tailleur, by MM. Erckmann-Chatrian; La Veillée de Vincennes, by Alfred de Vigny; Les Jumeaux de l'Hôtel Corneille, by Edmond About; Mésaventures d'un écolier, by Rodolphe Töpffer. Third edition revised. 2s. 6d.

French History

De Tocqueville's L'Ancien Régime et la Révolution. Edited, with introduction and notes, by G. W. HEADLAM. Crown 8vo. 6s.

Documents illustrative of the French Revolution, 1789-1791. By L. G. WICKHAM LEGG. Crown 8vo. Two volumes. 12s. net.

Speeches of the Statesmen and Orators of the French Revolution, 1789-1795. With introductions, notes, etc, by H. MORSE STEPHENS. Two volumes, crown 8vo. £1 1s.

Thiers' Moscow Expedition, edited, with introduction and notes, by H. B. GEORGE. Crown 8vo, with 6 maps. 5s.

A History of France, with numerous maps, plans, and tables, by G. W. KITCHIN. Crown 8vo ; Vol. I (to 1453), revised by F. F. URQUHART ; Vols. II (1624), III (1795) revised by A. HASSALL. 10s. 6d. each volume.

Montesquieu. Romanes Lecture. By Sir COURTENAY ILBERT. 8vo. 2s. net.

Old French

Cest Daucasin et de Nicolete. Reproduced in Photo-facsimile and Type-transliteration from the unique MS in the Bibliothèque Nationale at Paris, and edited by F. W. BOURDILLON. Small quarto half-vellum. 24s. net.

Song of Dermot and the Earl. Edited, with translation, notes, etc, by G. H. ORPEN. Extra fcap 8vo. 8s. 6d.

Specimens of Old French (IX–XV centuries). With introduction, notes and glossaries, by PAGET TOYNBEE. Crown 8vo. 16s.

Gower's French Works, including the Mirour de l'Omme or 'Speculum Meditantis,' a poem of 30,000 lines now first edited by G. C. MACAULAY. (Vol. I of Gower's Complete Works, p. 7.) Demy 8vo. 16s.

The Troubadours of Dante, being selections from the works of the Provençal poets quoted by Dante. By H. J. CHAYTOR. Crown 8vo. 5s. 6d. net.

Perrault's Popular Tales, edited from the original editions with introduction, etc, by ANDREW LANG. Extra fcap 8vo. 5s. 6d.

Old High German and Gothic

An Old High German Primer, with grammar, notes and glossary. By JOSEPH WRIGHT. Extra fcap 8vo. 3s. 6d.

A Middle High German Primer, with grammar, notes and glossary. By the same author. Second edition. Extra fcap 8vo. 3s. 6d.

A Primer of the Gothic Language, containing the Gospel of St. Mark, selections from the other Gospels, and the Second Epistle to Timothy, with grammar, notes and glossary. By the same author. Second Edition. Extra fcap 8vo. 4s. 6d.

History of German Literature. Specimens

The German Classics, from the 4th to the 19th century.
With biographical notices, translations into Modern German, and notes.
By the Right Hon. F. MAX MÜLLER. Vol. II revised by L. ARMITAGE.
Second edition. Two volumes, crown 8vo. Vol. I, 8s. 6d. net; Vol. II,
5s. 6d. net.

Scherer's History of German Literature, translated by Mrs.
F. C. CONYBEARE. Edited by the Right Hon. F. MAX MÜLLER. Two volumes
8vo, 15s. net.   Crown 8vo edition, without Appendices and
Bibliographies, two volumes, 3s. 6d. net each volume.

Dr. BUCHHEIM's German Classics

Edited, with biographical, historical and critical introductions
arguments (to the Dramas), and complete commentaries
by the late C. A. BUCHHEIM. Extra fcap 8vo

Becker's Friedrich der Grosse. With a map. Second edition, revised.
3s. 6d.

Goethe's Dichtung und Wahrheit. Books I-IV. 4s. 6d.

Egmont. Fourth edition. 3s.

Hermann und Dorothea. With an introduction by
EDWARD DOWDEN. 3s.

Iphigenie auf Tauris. Fourth edition, revised. 3s.

Halm's Griseldis. 3s.

Heine's Harzreise. With a map. Third edition. 2s. 6d.

Prosa. Being Selections from Heine's Prose Writings. Second
edition. 4s. 6d.

Lessing's Minna von Barnhelm. Eighth edition, revised and
enlarged. 3s. 6d.

Nathan der Weise. Third edition. 4s. 6d.

Schiller's Historische Skizzen. With a map. Seventh edition,
revised. 2s. 6d.

Jungfrau von Orleans. Second edition. 4s. 6d.

Maria Stuart. 3s. 6d.

Wilhelm Tell. Large edition; with a map. Seventh edition.
3s. 6d. School edition; with a map. Fourth edition. 2s.

Other annotated editions. Extra fcap 8vo

Hoffmann's Heute mir, Morgen dir, by J. H. MAUDE. 2s.

Lessing's Laokoon, by A. HAMANN. Second edition, revised, with an
introduction, by L. E. UPCOTT. 4s. 6d.

Riehl's Seines Vaters Sohn and **Gespensterkampf,** by
H. T. GERRANS. Second edition. 2s.

Elementary German Reading and Exercise Books, with English notes, vocabularies, etc

Kinderfreuden, von A. E. C., being an illustrated German Reading Book for young children. Crown 8vo. 1s. 6d.

Combined German Reader, Writer, and Grammar. By H. G. SPEARING. 8vo. 3s. Test-book of the words occurring in the above. Crown 8vo. Paper covers. 6d. net.

Modern German Reader. A graduated collection of extracts from modern German authors. Edited by C. A. BUCHHEIM.
> Part I : Prose Extracts. Seventh edition. 2s. 6d.
> Part II : Extracts in Prose and Poetry. Third edition. 2s. 6d.

Miss BUCHHEIM's German Series. Extra fcap 8vo

German Poetry for Beginners. 2s.

Niebuhr's Griechische Heroen-Geschichten. Second edition, revised. Cloth, 2s. ; stiff covers, 1s. 6d. Edition A, text in German type. Edition B, text in Roman type.

Short German Plays, for Reading and Acting. First series. With notes and vocabulary. 3s.

Short German Plays. Second Series. Der ungebetene Gast, and other Plays. With notes and vocabulary. 2s. 6d.

Chamisso's Peter Schlemihl's wundersame Geschichte. Edited, with notes and a complete vocabulary. 2s.

Elementary German Prose Composition. Third edition. Cloth, 2s. ; stiff covers, 1s. 6d.

Dr. HERMANN LANGE's German Course. 8vo

Germans at Home. An introduction to German conversation, with the essentials of German grammar. Third edition. 2s. 6d.

Grammar of the German Language. 3s. 6d.

German Manual. A German grammar, reading book, and a handbook of German conversation. Second edition. 7s. 6d.

German Composition. A theoretical and practical guide to the translation of English prose into German. 3rd edition. 4s. 6d. Key, 5s. net.

German Spelling. A record of the changes made in 1880. 6d.

For Candidates for Army and Civil Service Examinations. Extra fcap 8vo

Guide to advanced German Prose Composition, containing selections from modern English authors, notes, and a grammatical introduction, by EDUARD EHRKE. 3s. Key, 5s. net.

Passages for unprepared translation. Selected by EDUARD EHRKE. Stiff covers. 3s.

The Oxford Dante

Tutte le Opere di Dante Alighieri nuovamente rivedute nel testo dal Dr. E. Moore: Con indice dei Nomi Propri e delle Cose Notabili, compilato dal Dr. Paget Toynbee. Crown 8vo. Third edition (1904), 6s. net; on India paper, 8s. net. Miniature (second) edition, on India paper, three volumes in case 10s. 6d., and in leather bindings.

Uniformly bound editions in larger print

La Divina Commedia, nuovamente riveduta nel testo dal Dr. E. Moore: Con indice dei Nomi Propri, compilato dal Dr. Paget Toynbee. Crown 8vo. 6s.

An English Commentary on the Divina Commedia. By H. F. Tozer. Crown 8vo. 8s. 6d. Also in six thin volumes: *Inferno*, text and notes, *Purgatorio*, text and notes, *Paradiso*, text and notes. Text, 2s. net each: Notes, 3s. net each.

The Troubadours of Dante. Being selections from the Provençal poets quoted by Dante, with introductions, notes, concise grammar, and glossary, by H. J. Chaytor. Crown 8vo. 5s. 6d. net.

Concordance to the Italian Prose Works and Canzoniere of Dante. Prepared by members of the Dante Society, Cambridge, Massachusetts, and edited by E. S. Sheldon and A. C. White. Royal 8vo. 36s. net.

A Dictionary of Proper Names and Notable Matters in the Works of Dante. By Paget Toynbee. Small 4to, buckram. £1 5s. net.

Studies in Dante. By E. Moore. Demy 8vo. Vols. I–III. £2 2s. net.

    Vol. I: Scripture and Classical Authors in Dante. [A few copies only remain.]

    Vol. II: Miscellaneous Essays. Separately, 10s. 6d. net.

    Vol. III: Miscellaneous Essays. Separately, 10s. 6d. net.

Divina Commedia, translated into English Prose, by H. F. Tozer. Extra fcap 8vo. 3s. 6d. net.

Selections from the Inferno. By H. B. Cotterill. Extra fcap 8vo. 4s. 6d.

Tasso's La Gerusalemme Liberata. By the same. Cantos i, ii. 2s. 6d.

A Primer of Italian Literature, by F. J. Snell. Extra fcap 8vo. 3s. 6d.

Machiavelli

Il Principe. Edited by L. A. Burd, with an introduction by Lord Acton. Demy 8vo. 14s.

The Prince. Translated by N. H. Thomson. Extra fcap 8vo. 3s. 6d. net.

Selections from Don Quixote. The Adventure of the Wooden Horse, and Sancho Panza's Governorship. By Clovis Bévenot. 2s. 6d.

LATIN AND GREEK
Grammars and Exercise Books
Extra fcap 8vo
Mr. J. B. Allen's Elementary Series

Rudimenta Latina. Comprising accidence and exercises of a very elementary character for the use of beginners. 2s.

An Elementary Latin Grammar. 238th thousand. 2s. 6d.

A First Latin Exercise Book. Eighth edition. 2s. 6d.

A Second Latin Exercise Book. Second edition. 3s. 6d.
Key (see note p. 35) to both Exercise Books. 5s. net.

An Elementary Greek Grammar. Containing accidence and elementary syntax. 3s.

Mr. J. B. Allen's Latin Readers
With notes, maps, vocabularies and English exercises; stiff covers, 1s. 6d. each. These books are of the same and not of graduated difficulty.

Lives from Cornelius Nepos.

Tales of Early Rome.

Tales of the Roman Republic, Part I. ⎫ Adapted from the
Tales of the Roman Republic, Part II. ⎬ Text of Livy.

Tales of the Civil War, edited by W. D. Lowe. 1s. 6d.

Other Latin Readers, etc

Selections from Cicero, with notes, by Henry Walford. In three Parts. Third edition. Part I. Anecdotes from Grecian and Roman History. 1s. 6d. Part II. Omens and Dreams: Beauties of Nature. 1s. 6d. Part III. Rome's Rule of her Provinces. 1s. 6d.

Selections from Livy, with notes and maps, by H. Lee-Warner. Part I. The Caudine Disaster. Part II. Hannibal's Campaign in Italy. Part III. The Macedonian War.

A First Latin Reader, by T. J. Nunns. Third edition. 2s.

An Introduction to Latin Syntax, by W. S. Gibson. 2s.

Mr. C. S. Jerram's Series

Reddenda Minora; or easy passages, Latin and Greek, for unseen translation. For the use of lower forms. Revised and enlarged 1s. 6d.

Anglice Reddenda; or extracts, Latin and Greek, for unseen translation. First Series. Fifth edition. 2s. 6d. Also Vol. I, Latin, 2s. 6d.; Vol. II, Greek, 3s. Second Series. New edition. 3s. Third Series. 3s.

D

Greek Readers and Primers

Greek Reader. Selected and adapted with English Notes from Professor von Wilamowitz-Moellendorff's *Griechisches Lesebuch*, by E. C. MARCHANT. Crown 8vo. Vol. I. 2s. Vol. II. 2s.

Selections from Plutarch's Life of Caesar. Crown 8vo, large type. Edited with notes by R. L. A. DU PONTET. 2s.

Greek Readers; Easy, by EVELYN ABBOTT. In stiff covers. 2s. **First Reader,** by W. G. RUSHBROOKE. Third edition. 2s. 6d. **Second Reader,** by A. M. BELL. Second edition. 3s. **Specimens of Greek Dialects;** being a Fourth Greek Reader. With introductions, etc., by W. W. MERRY. 4s. 6d. **Selections from Homer and the Greek Dramatists;** being a Fifth Greek Reader. With explanatory notes and introductions to the study of Greek Epic and Dramatic Poetry, by EVELYN ABBOTT. 4s. 6d.

A Greek Testament Primer. For the use of students beginning Greek, by E. MILLER. Second edition. Paper covers, 2s. ; cloth, 3s. 6d.

Xenophon (see p. 43)

Easy Selections, with a vocabulary, notes, illustrations carefully chosen from coins, casts and ancient statues, and map, by J. S. PHILLPOTTS and C. S. JERRAM. Third edition. 3s. 6d.

Selections, with notes, illustrations, and maps, by J. S. PHILLPOTTS. Fifth ed. 3s. 6d. Key (see p. 35) to §§ 1–3, 2s. 6d. net.

A Greek Primer, for the use of beginners in that language. By the Right Rev. CHARLES WORDSWORTH. Eighty-sixth thousand. 1s. 6d. Graecae Grammaticae Rudimenta. Nineteenth edition. 4s.

An Introduction to the Comparative Grammar of Greek and Latin. By J. E. KING and C. COOKSON. Extra fcap 8vo. 5s. 6d.

Latin Dictionaries

A Latin Dictionary. Founded on Andrews's edition of Freund's Latin Dictionary. Revised, enlarged, and in great part re-written, by CHARLTON T. LEWIS and CHARLES SHORT. 4to. 25s.

A School Latin Dictionary. By C. T. LEWIS. 4to. 12s. 6d.

Elementary Latin Dictionary. By C. T. LEWIS. Square 8vo. 7s. 6d.

Greek Dictionaries

A Greek-English Lexicon. By H. G. LIDDELL and ROBERT SCOTT. Eighth edition, revised. 4to. 36s.

An Intermediate Greek Lexicon. By the same. 12s. 6d.

An Abridged Greek Lexicon. By the same. 7s. 6d.

Latin and Greek Prose Composition

Mr. J. Y. SARGENT'S Course. Extra fcap 8vo

Primer of Latin Prose Composition. 2s. 6d.

Passages for Translation into Latin Prose. Eighth edition.
2s. 6d. Key (see note below) to the eighth edition 5s. net.

Primer of Greek Prose. 3s. 6d. Key (see note below) 5s. net.

Passages for Translation into Greek Prose. 3s.

Exemplaria Graeca. Select Greek versions of the above. 3s.

Other Prose Composition Books. Extra fcap 8vo

Ramsay's Latin Prose Composition. Fourth edition.
Vol. I : Syntax and Exercises. 4s. 6d. Or Part 1, First Year's Course,
1s. 6d. ; Part 2, Second Year's Course, 1s. 6d. ; Part 3, Syntax and
Appendix, 2s. 6d. Key (see note below) to the volume 5s. net.
Vol. II : Passages for Translation. 4s. 6d.

Jerram's Graece Reddenda. Being exercises for Greek Prose. 2s. 6d.

Unseen Translation

Jerram's Reddenda Minora and Anglice Reddenda. See p. 33.

Fox and Bromley's Models and Exercises in Unseen Translation.
Revised edition. Extra fcap 8vo. 5s. 6d. A Key (see note below) giving
references for the passages contained in the above 6d. net.

Latin and Greek Verse

Lee-Warner's Helps and Exercises for Latin Elegiacs.
3s. 6d. Key (see note below) 4s. 6d. net.

Rouse's Demonstrations in Latin Elegiac Verse. Crown
8vo. 4s. 6d. (Exercises and versions.)

Laurence's Helps and Exercises for Greek Iambic
Verse. 3s. 6d. Key (see note below) 5s. net.

Sargent's Models and Materials for Greek Iambic Verse.
4s. 6d. Key (see note below) 5s. net.

Nova Anthologia Oxoniensis. Edited by ROBINSON ELLIS and A. D.
GODLEY. Crown 8vo buckram extra, 6s. net ; on India paper, 7s. 6d. net.

Musa Clauda. Being translations into Latin Elegiac Verse, by S. G.
OWEN and J. S. PHILLIMORE. Crown 8vo boards, 3s. 6d.

Latin Prose Versions. Contributed by various Scholars, edited by
G. G. RAMSAY. Extra fcap 8vo, 5s.

NOTE AS TO KEYS

Application for all Keys to be made direct to the Secretary, Clarendon
Press, Oxford. Keys can be obtained by teachers, or bona fide private
students, on application to the Secretary, Clarendon Press, Oxford.

Annotated editions of Latin Authors

Aetna. A critical recension of the Text, with prolegomena, translation, commentary, and index verborum. By ROBINSON ELLIS. Crown 8vo. 7s. 6d. net.

Avianus, The Fables. With prolegomena, critical apparatus, commentary, etc. By ROBINSON ELLIS. 8vo. 8s. 6d.

Caesar, De Bello Gallico, I–VII. In two crown 8vo volumes. By St. G. STOCK. Vol. I, Introduction, 5s.; Vol. II, Text and Notes, 6s.

> **The Gallic War.** By C. E. MOBERLY. Second edition. With maps. Books I and II, 2s.; III–V, 2s. 6d.; VI–VIII, 3s. 6d. Books I–III, stiff covers, 2s.

> **The Civil War.** New edition. By the same editor. 3s. 6d.

Catulli Veronensis Liber rec. ROBINSON ELLIS. Second edition, with notes and appendices. 8vo. 18s.

> **Commentary.** By the same. Second edition. 8vo. 16s.

> **Carmina Selecta.** Text only, for Schools. 3s. 6d.

Cicero, de Amicitia. By St. GEORGE STOCK. 3s.

> **de Senectute.** By L. HUXLEY. 2s.

> **in Catilinam.** By E. A. UPCOTT. Third edition. 2s. 6d.

> **in Q. Caecilium Divinatio** and **in C. Verrem Actio Prima.** By J. R. KING. Limp, 1s. 6d.

> **pro Cluentio.** Edited by G. G. RAMSAY. Second ed. 3s. 6d.

> **pro Marcello, pro Ligario, pro Rege Deiotaro.** By W. Y. FAUSSET. Second edition. 2s. 6d.

> **pro Milone.** By A. C. CLARK. 8vo. 8s. 6d. By A. B. POYNTON. Second edition. Crown 8vo. 2s. 6d.

> **Philippic Orations,** I, II, III, V, VII. By J. R. KING. 3s. 6d.

> **pro Roscio.** By St. GEORGE STOCK. 3s. 6d.

> **Select Orations,** viz. in Verrem Actio Prima, de Imperio Gn. Pompeii, pro Archia, Philippica IX. By J. R. KING. Second edition. 2s. 6d.

> **Select Letters.** With introductions, notes, and appendices. By A. WATSON. Fourth edition. 8vo. 18s. Text only of the large edition. By the same. Third edition. Extra fcap 8vo. 4s.

> **Selected Letters.** By C. E. PRICHARD and E. R. BERNARD. Second edition. 3s.

> **De Oratore Libri Tres.** With introduction and notes. By A. S. WILKINS. 8vo. 18s. Or separately, Book I. Third edition. 7s. 6d. Book II. Second edition. 5s. Book III. 6s.

Horace, Odes, Carmen Seculare, and Epodes. By E. C. WICKHAM. 8vo. Third edition. 12s. Crown 8vo. Second edition. 6s.

Satires, Epistles, De Arte Poetica. By the same. Crown 8vo. 6s. Odes, Book I. 2s.
Selected Odes, with Notes for a Fifth Form. By the same. 2nd ed. 2s.

Text only : miniature Oxford edition. On writing-paper for MS notes, 3s. 6d. ; on Oxford India paper, roan, 5s.

For English Readers. By E. C. WICKHAM. Fcap 8vo. 3s. 6d. net.

Iuvenalis ad satiram sextam additi versus xxxvi exscr. E. O. WINSTEDT. With a facsimile. In wrapper, 1s. net.

Thirteen Satires. By C. H. PEARSON and HERBERT A. STRONG. Second edition. Crown 8vo. 9s.

Livy, Book I. With Introduction and Notes. By Sir J. R. SEELEY. Third edition. 8vo. 6s.

Books V–VII. By A. R. CLUER. Revised by P. E. MATHESON. 5s. Separately : Book V, 2s. 6d. ; Book VI, 2s. ; Book VII, 2s.

Books XXI–XXIII. By M. T. TATHAM. Second edition, enlarged. 5s. Separately : Book XXI, 2s. 6d ; Book XXII, 2s. 6d.

Lucretius, Book V. Edited, with Notes for a Fifth Form, by W. D. LOWE. Crown 8vo. 2s.

Noctes Manilianae. Being elucidations of Manilius, with some conjectural emendations of Aratea. By ROBINSON ELLIS. Crown 8vo. 6s.

Martialis Epigrammata Selecta (Text and critical notes). 3s. 6d. On India paper. 5s.

Martial, Books VII–XII. Select Epigrams edited from the Text of Professor Lindsay by R. T. BRIDGE and E. D. C. LAKE. Crown 8vo. 3s. 6d.

Nepos. By OSCAR BROWNING. Third edition, revised by W. R. INGE. 3s.

Nonius Marcellus, de compendiosa doctrina I–III. Edited, with introduction and critical apparatus, by J. H. ONIONS. 8vo. 10s. 6d.

Ovid, Heroides, with the Greek translations of Planudes. Edited by ARTHUR PALMER. 8vo. With a facsimile. 21s.

Ibis. With scholia and commentary. By ROBINSON ELLIS. 8vo. 10s. 6d.

Tristia. Edited by S. G. OWEN. 8vo. 16s. Extra fcap 8vo. Third edition. Book I, 2s. 6d. Book III, 2s.

Selections, with an Appendix on the Roman Calendar by W. RAMSAY. By G. G. RAMSAY. Third edition. 5s. 6d.

Persius, The Satires. With a translation and commentary, by JOHN CONINGTON. Edited by HENRY NETTLESHIP. Third edition. 8vo. 8s. 6d.

Plautus, Captivi. By WALLACE M. LINDSAY. Second edition. 2s. 6d.

Mostellaria. By E. A. SONNENSCHEIN. In the press.

Rudens. By the same. 8vo. 8s. 6d. **Editio minor,** Text with Notes and Appendix on Metre, interleaved. 4s. 6d.

Trinummus. By C. E. FREEMAN and A. SLOMAN. Third edition. 3s.

Pliny, Selected Letters. By C. E. Prichard and E. R. Bernard. Third edition. 3s.

Propertius. Index Verborum. By J. S. Phillimore. Crown 8vo. 4s. 6d. net. **Translation** by the same. Extra fcap 8vo. 3s. 6d. net. **Selections.** See Tibullus.

Quintilian, Institutionis Oratoriae Lib. X. By W. Peterson. 8vo. 12s. 6d. School edition. By the same. Extra fcap 8vo. 2nd edition. 3s. 6d.

Sallust. By W. W. Capes. Second edition. 4s. 6d.

Scriptores Latini Rei Metricae. Edited by T. Gaisford. 8vo. 5s.

Selections from the less known Latin Poets. By North Pinder. 7s. 6d.

Tacitus. Edited, with introductions and notes, by H. Furneaux. 8vo.

> **Annals. Books** I–VI. Second ed. 18s. **Books** XI–XVI. 20s.

> **Annals.** (Text only.) Crown 8vo. 6s.

> **Annals,** Books I–IV. By H. Furneaux. Second edition. 5s. Book I. Limp, 2s. Books XIII–XVI (abridged from Furneaux's 8vo edition). By H. Pitman. 4s. 6d.

> **De Germania. Vita Agricolae.** 6s. 6d. each.

> **Dialogus de Oratoribus.** Edited, with introduction and notes, by W. Peterson. 8vo. 10s. 6d.

Terence, Adelphi. By A. Sloman. Second edition. 3s.

> **Andria.** By C. E. Freeman and A. Sloman. Second edition. 3s.

> **Phormio.** By A. Sloman. Second edition. 3s.

Tibullus and Propertius, Selections. By G. G. Ramsay. Third edition. 6s.

Velleius Paterculus, libri duo ad M. Vinicium. By Robinson Ellis. Crown 8vo. 6s.

Virgil. By T. L. Papillon and A. E. Haigh. Two volumes. Crown 8vo. Cloth, 6s. each ; or stiff covers, 3s. 6d. each.

> **Text only** (including the minor works emended by R. Ellis). Miniature Oxford edition. By the same editors. 32mo. On writing-paper, 3s. 6d. ; on Oxford India paper, roan, 5s.

> **Aeneid,** Books I–III, IV–VI, VII–IX, X–XII. By the same editors. 2s. each part. Book IX, by A. E. Haigh, 1s. 6d. ; in two parts, 2s.

> **Bucolics and Georgics.** By the same editors. 2s. 6d.

> **Bucolics.** 2s. 6d. **Georgics,** Books I, II. 2s. 6d. Books III, IV, 2s. 6d. **Aeneid,** Book I. Limp cloth, 1s. 6d. All by C. S. Jerram.

Latin Works of Reference

Lewis and Short's Latin Dictionaries. See p. 34.

The Latin Language, being an historical account of Latin Sounds, Stems, and Flexions. By W. M. LINDSAY. 8vo. 21s.

Selected Fragments of Roman Poetry. Edited, with introduction and notes, by W. W. MERRY. Second edition. Crown 8vo. 6s. 6d.

Fragments and Specimens of Early Latin. With introductions and notes. By J. WORDSWORTH. 8vo. 18s.

Selections from the less known Latin Poets. By NORTH PINDER. 8vo. 7s. 6d.

Latin Historical Inscriptions, illustrating the history of the Early Empire. By G. McN. RUSHFORTH. 8vo. 10s. net.

Scheller's Latin Dictionary. Revised and translated into English by J. L. RIDDLE. Folio. 21s.

Professor Nettleship's Books

Contributions to Latin Lexicography. 8vo. 21s.

Lectures and Essays. Second Series. Edited by F. HAVERFIELD. With portrait and memoir. Crown 8vo. 7s. 6d. (The first series is out of print.)

The Roman Satura. 8vo. Sewed. 1s.

Ancient Lives of Vergil. 8vo. Sewed. 1s.

Professor Sellar's Books

Roman Poets of the Republic. Third edition. Crown 8vo. 10s.

Roman Poets of the Augustan Age. Crown 8vo. viz.: **Virgil.** Third edition. 9s., and **Horace and the Elegiac Poets,** with a memoir of the Author, by ANDREW LANG. Second edition. 7s. 6d.

(A limited number of copies of the first edition of *Horace*, containing a portrait of the Author, can still be obtained in Demy 8vo, price 14s.)

The Principles of Sound and Inflexion, as illustrated in the Greek and Latin Languages. By J. E. KING and C. COOKSON. 8vo. 18s.

Manual of Comparative Philology. By T. L. PAPILLON. Third edition. Crown 8vo. 6s.

By Prof. ROBINSON ELLIS; published by Mr. Frowde.

Juvenal, The New Fragments. 8vo. 1s. net.

Phaedrus, The Fables. 8vo. 1s. net.

The Correspondence of Fronto and M. Aurelius. 8vo. 1s. net.

Catullus in the Fourteenth Century. 8vo. 1s. net.

A Bodleian MS. of Copa, Moretum, and other Poems of the Appendix Vergiliana. Crown 8vo. 1s. net.

OXFORD CLASSICAL TEXTS

The prices given of copies on ordinary paper are for copies bound in limp cloth ; uncut copies may be had in paper covers at 6d. less per volume (1s. less for those priced at 6s. in cloth). All volumes are also on sale interleaved with writing-paper and bound in stout cloth ; prices on application.

Greek

Aeschylus. A. Sidgwick. 3s. 6d. (India paper, 4s. 6d.)

Apollonius Rhodius. R. C. Seaton. 3s.

Aristophanes. F. W. Hall, W. M. Geldart. (India paper, 8s. 6d.)

I. Ach., Eq., Nub., Vesp., Pax, Aves. 3s. 6d.
II. Lys., Thesm., Ran., Eccl., Plut., fr. 3s. 6d.

Bucolici Graeci. U. von Wilamowitz-Moellendorff. 3s. (India paper, 4s.)

Demosthenes. S. H. Butcher. I. Orationes I–XIX. 4s. 6d.

Euripides. G. G. A. Murray. Vols. I and II. (India paper, 9s.)

I. Cyc., Alc., Med., Heracl., Hip., Andr., Hec. 3s. 6d.
II. Suppl., Herc., Ion, Tro., El., I. T. 3s. 6d.

Homer, Iliad. D. B. Monro, T. W. Allen. (India paper, 7s.)
I. Books 1–12. II. Books 13–24. 3s. each.

Hyperides. F. G. Kenyon. (Immediately.)

Longinus. A. O. Prickard. 2s. 6d.

Plato. J. Burnet. Vols. I–III, 6s. each (India paper, 7s. each). Vol. IV. 7s. (India paper, 8s. 6d.)

I. Euth., Apol., Crit., Ph. ; Crat., Tht., Soph., Polit.
II. Par., Phil., Symp., Phdr. ; Alc., I, II, Hipp., Am.
III. Thg., Chrm., Lch., Lys. ; Euthd., Prot., Gorg., Men., Hipp. ma., mi., Io, Menex. Also Republic, separately, 6s. ; quarto, 10s. 6d.
IV. Clit., Rep., Tim., Critias.
V. Minos, Leges, Epinomis, Epustolae, Definitiones, Spuria. (Immediately.)

First and fifth tetralogies separately, paper covers, 2s. each.

Thucydides. H. Stuart Jones. (India paper, 8s. 6d.)
I. Books 1–4. II. Books 5–8. 3s. 6d. each.

Xenophon. E. C. Marchant. Vols. I–III.

I. Historia Graeca. 3s.
II. Libri Socratici. 3s. 6d.
III. Anabasis. 3s.

Latin

Asconius. A. C. CLARK. (Immediately.)

Caesar, Commentarii. R. L. A. DU PONTET. (India paper, 7s.)
Bellum Gallicum. 2s. 6d. Bellum Civile. 3s.

Catullus. R. ELLIS. 2s. 6d. (With Tibullus and Propertius, on India paper. 8s. 6d.)

Cicero, Epistulae. L. C. PURSER. (India paper, 21s.)
I. Epp. ad Fam. 6s. ; II, III. ad Atticum 1–8 and 9–16, 4s. 6d. each ; IV. ad Q. F. 3s.

Orationes. A. C. CLARK.
Rosc. Am., I. Pomp., Clu., Cat., Mur., Cael. 3s.
Pro Milone, Caesarianae, Philippicae. 3s.

Rhetorica. A. S. WILKINS. (India paper, 7s. 6d.)
I. De Oratore. 3s. II. Brutus, &c. 3s. 6d.

Horace. E. C. WICKHAM. 3s. (India paper, 4s. 6d.)

Lucretius. C. BAILEY. 3s. (India paper, 4s.)

Martial. W. M. LINDSAY, 6s. (India paper, 7s. 6d.)

Nepos. E. O. WINSTEDT. 2s.

Persius and **Juvenal.** S. G. OWEN. 3s. (India paper, 4s.)

Plautus. W. M. LINDSAY. (India paper, 16s.)
I. Amph.—Merc. II. Miles—fragm. 6s. each.

Propertius. J. S. PHILLIMORE. 3s. (India paper, see Catullus.)

Statius. (Complete on India paper. 10s. 6d.)
Silvae. J. S. PHILLIMORE. 3s. 6d.
Thebais and Achilleis. H. W. GARROD. 6s.

Tacitus, Opera Minora. H. FURNEAUX. 2s.
Annals. C. D. FISHER. 6s.

Terence. R. Y. TYRRELL. 3s. 6d. (India paper, 5s.)

Tibullus. J. P. POSTGATE. 2s. (India paper, see Catullus.)

Vergil. F. A. HIRTZEL. 3s. 6d. (India paper, 4s. 6d.)

Annotated Greek Classics

Extra fcap 8vo.

Aeschylus. By Arthur Sidgwick. New editions with the text of the *Oxford Classical Texts*.

Agamemnon. Sixth edition revised. 3s. **Choephoroi.** New edition revised. 3s. **Eumenides.** Third edition. 3s. **Persae.** 3s. **Septem contra Thebas.** 3s. **Prometheus Vinctus.** By A. O. Prickard. Fourth edition. 2s.

Aristophanes. By W. W. Merry.

Acharnians. Fifth edition. 3s. **Birds.** Third edition. 3s. 6d. **Clouds.** Second edition. 3s. **Frogs.** Fifth edition. 3s. **Knights.** Second edition. 3s. **Peace.** 3s. 6d. **Wasps.** Second edition. 3s. 6d.

Cebes, Tabula. By C. S. Jerram. Stiff covers, 1s. 6d.; cloth, 2s. 6d.

Demosthenes. By Evelyn Abbott and P. E. Matheson.

Against Philip. Vol. I: Philippic I, Olynthiacs I–III. Fourth edition, 3s. Vol. II: De Pace, Philippic II, de Chersoneso, Philippic III. 4s. 6d. Philippics I–III (reprinted from above). 2s. 6d. **On the Crown.** 3s. 6d. **Against Meidias.** By J. R. King. Crown 8vo. 3s. 6d.

Euripides.

Alcestis. By C. S. Jerram. Fifth edition. 2s. 6d. **Bacchae.** By A. H. Cruickshank. 3s. 6d. **Cyclops.** By W. E. Long. 2s. 6d. **Hecuba.** By C. B. Heberden. 2s. 6d. **Helena.** By C. S. Jerram. Second edition. 3s. **Heracleidae.** By C. S. Jerram. 3s. **Ion.** By C. S. Jerram. 3s. **Iphigenia in Tauris.** By C. S. Jerram. New edition revised 3s. **Medea.** By C. B. Heberden. Third edition. 2s.

Herodotus, Book IX. By Evelyn Abbott. 3s.

Selections. With a map. By W. W. Merry. 2s. 6d.

Homer, Iliad. By D. B. Monro. I–XII. With a brief Homeric Grammar. Fifth edition. 6s. Book I, with the Homeric Grammar, separately. Third edition. 1s. 6d.
XIII–XXIV. Fourth edition. 6s. Book III (for beginners), by M. T. Tatham. 1s. 6d. Book XXI. By Herbert Hailstone. 1s. 6d.

Homer, Odyssey. By W. W. Merry. I–XII. Sixty-sixth thousand. 5s. Books I and II, separately, each 1s. 6d. Books VI and VII. 1s. 6d. Books VII–XII. 3s.
XIII–XXIV. Sixteenth thousand. 5s. Books XIII–XVIII. 3s. Books XIX–XXIV. 3s.

Lucian, Vera Historia. By C. S. JERRAM. Second edition. 1s. 6d.

Lysias, Epitaphios. By F. J. SNELL. 2s.

Plato. By St. GEORGE STOCK. The Apology. Third edition. 2s. 6d.
Crito. 2s. Meno. Third edition. 2s. 6d.

Euthydemus. With revised text, introduction, notes, and indices,
by E. H. GIFFORD. Crown 8vo. 3s. 6d.

Menexenus. By J. A. SHAWYER. Crown 8vo. 2s.

Selections. By J. PURVES with preface by B. JOWETT. 2nd ed. 5s.

Plutarch, Lives of the Gracchi. By G. E. UNDERHILL. Crown
8vo. 4s. 6d.

Coriolanus (for Junior Students). With introduction and notes. 2s.

Sophocles. By LEWIS CAMPBELL and EVELYN ABBOTT. New and revised
edition. Two volumes: Vol. I text 4s. 6d. ; Vol. II notes 6s.
Or singly 2s. each (text and notes) Ajax, Antigone, Electra, Oedipus
Coloneus, Oedipus Tyrannus, Philoctetes, Trachiniae.

Scenes from Sophocles, edited by C. E. LAURENCE. With illustrations.
1s. 6d. each. (1) Ajax. (2) Antigone.

Select Fragments of the Greek Comic Poets. By A. W.
PICKARD-CAMBRIDGE. Crown 8vo. 5s.

Golden Treasury of Ancient Greek Poetry. By Sir R. S.
WRIGHT. Second edition. Revised by E. ABBOTT. Extra fcap 8vo. 10s. 6d.

Golden Treasury of Greek Prose. By Sir R. S. WRIGHT and
J. E. L. SHADWELL. Extra fcap 8vo. 4s. 6d.

Theocritus. By H. KYNASTON. Fifth edition. 4s. 6d.

Thucydides, Book I. By W. H. FORBES. With maps. Post 8vo. 8s. 6d.
Book III. By H. F. FOX. Crown 8vo. 3s. 6d.

Xenophon. (See also p. 34.)

Anabasis. Each of the first four Books is now issued in uniform
cloth binding at 1s. 6d. Each volume contains introduction, text, notes,
and a full vocabulary to the Anabasis. Book I. By J. MARSHALL.
Book II. By C. S. JERRAM. Books III and IV. By J. MARSHALL.
And *Vocabulary to the Anabasis*, by J. MARSHALL. 1s.

Cyropaedia, Book I. 2s. Books IV and V. 2s. 6d. By C. BIGG.

Hellenica, Books I, II. By G. E. UNDERHILL. 3s.

Memorabilia. By J. MARSHALL. 4s. 6d.

Editions etc of Greek Authors mostly with English notes

Appian, Book I. Edited with map and appendix on Pompey's passage of the Alps, by J. L. STRACHAN-DAVIDSON. Crown 8vo. 3s. 6d.

Aristophanes, A Concordance to. By H. DUNBAR. 4to. £1 1s.

Aristotle.

Ethica Nicomachea, recognovit brevique adnotatione critica instruxit I. BYWATER. Post 8vo, cloth. 6s. The same, on 4to paper, for marginal notes. 10s. 6d. Also in crown 8vo, paper covers. 3s. 6d.

Contributions to the Textual Criticism of Aristotle's Nicomachean Ethics. By I. BYWATER. Stiff cover. 2s. 6d.

Notes on the Nicomachean Ethics. By J. A. STEWART. 2 vols. Post 8vo. £1 12s.

The English Manuscripts of the Nicomachean Ethics. By J. A. STEWART. Crown 4to. 3s. 6d.

De Arte Poetica Liber recognovit brevique adnotatione critica instruxit I. BYWATER. Post 8vo, stiff covers. 1s. 6d.

Selecta ex Organo Capitula. In usum Scholarum Academicarum. Crown 8vo, stiff covers. 3s. 6d.

The Politics, with introduction, notes, etc., by W. L. NEWMAN. 4 vols. Medium 8vo. 14s. net per volume.

The Politics, translated into English, with introduction, notes, and indices, by B. JOWETT. Medium 8vo. 2 vols. £1 1s.

Aristotelian Studies. On the Structure of the Seventh Book of the Nicomachean Ethics. By J. COOK WILSON. 8vo. 5s.

On the History of the Aristotelian Writings. By R. SHUTE. 8vo. 7s. 6d.

Physics, Book VII.

Greek Theories of Elementary Cognition from Alcmaeon to Aristotle. By J. I. BEARE. 12s. 6d. net.

Aristoxenus. Edited, with introduction, music, translation, and notes, by H. S. MACRAN. Crown 8vo. 10s. 6d. net.

Demosthenes and Aeschines on the Crown. With introductory essays and notes, by G. A. SIMCOX and W. H. SIMCOX. 8vo. 12s.

Heracliti Ephesii Reliquiae. Edited by I. BYWATER, with Diogenes Laertius' Life of Heraclitus, etc. 8vo. 6s.

Herodas. Edited, with full introduction and notes, by J. ARBUTHNOT NAIRN. With facsimiles of the fragments and other illustrations. 8vo. 12s. 6d. net.

Herodotus, Books V and VI. Terpischore and Erato. Edited, with notes and appendices, by E. Abbott. With two maps. Post 8vo. 6s.

Homer, A Concordance to the Odyssey and Hymns; and to the Parallel Passages in the Iliad, Odyssey, and Hymns. By H. Dunbar. 4to. £1 1s.

Odyssey. Books I-XII. Edited, with English notes, appendices, etc, by W. W. Merry and J. Riddell. Second edition. 8vo. 16s.

Books XIII-XXIV. Edited, with English notes, appendices, and illustrations, by D. B. Monro. 8vo. 16s.

Hymni Homerici, codicibus denuo collatis recensuit A. Goodwin. Small folio. With four plates. £1 1s. net.

Scholia Graeca in Iliadem. Edited by W. Dindorf, after a new collation of the Venetian MSS by D. B. Monro. 4 vols. 8vo. £2 10s. See also p. 47.

Opera et Reliquiae, recensuit D. B. Monro. Crown 8vo, on India paper. 10s. 6d. net. 'The Oxford Homer.'

Index Andocideus, Lycurgeus, Dinarcheus. Confectus ab A. L. Forman. 8vo. 7s. 6d.

Menander's Γεωργός, the Geneva Fragment, with text, translation, and notes, by B. P. Grenfell and A. S. Hunt. 8vo, stiff covers. 1s. 6d.

Plato, Philebus. Edited by E. Poste. 8vo. 7s. 6d.

Republic. Edited, with notes and essays, by B. Jowett and L. Campbell. In three volumes. Medium 8vo, cloth. £2 2s.

Sophistes and Politicus. Edited by L. Campbell. 8vo. 10s. 6d.

Theaetetus. Edited by L. Campbell. 2nd ed. 8vo. 10s. 6d.

The Dialogues, translated into English, with analyses and introductions, by B. Jowett. Third edition. Five volumes, medium 8vo. £4 4s. In half-morocco, £5. *The Subject-Index to the second edition of the Dialogues,* by E. Abbott, separately. 8vo, cloth. 2s. 6d.

The Republic, translated into English, by B. Jowett. Third edition. Medium 8vo. 12s. 6d. Half-roan, 14s.

Selections from Jowett's translation, with introductions by M. J. Knight. Two volumes. Crown 8vo. 12s.

Polybius, Selections. Edited by J. L. Strachan-Davidson. With maps. Medium 8vo, buckram. £1 1s.

Sophocles, The Plays and Fragments. Edited by L. Campbell. Vol. I: Oedipus Tyrannus. Oedipus Coloneus. Antigone. 8vo. 16s. Vol. II: Ajax, Electra. Trachiniae. Philoctetes. Fragments. 8vo. 16s.

Strabo, Selections. With an introduction on Strabo's Life and Works. By H. F. Tozer. With maps and plans. Post 8vo, cloth. 12s.

Thucydides. Translated into English by B. Jowett. Second edition, revised. 2 vols. 8vo. 15s.

Vol. I : Essay on Inscriptions, and Books I–III.

Vol. II : Books IV–VIII, and Historical Index.

Book I. Edited, with introduction, notes, and maps, by W. H. Forbes. Post 8vo. 8s. 6d.

Xenophon, Hellenica. Edited, with introduction and appendices, by G. E. Underhill. Crown 8vo. 7s. 6d. Also with the Oxford Classical Text by E. C. Marchant, one volume. 7s. 6d. net.

Older Clarendon Press Editions of Greek Authors

The Greek texts in fine and generally large type ; the Scholia (and some of the texts) have not appeared in any later editions. The annotations are in Latin.

Aeschinem et Isocratem, Scholia Graeca in, edidit G. Dindorfius. 8vo. 4s.

Aeschyli Tragoediae et Fragmenta. Ex rec. G. Dindorfii. Second edition. 8vo. 5s. 6d.

Annotationes G. Dindorfii. Partes II. 8vo. 10s.

Quae supersunt in codice Laurentiano typis descripta edidit R. Merkel. Small folio. £1 1s.

Apsinis et Longini Rhetorica. Recensuit Joh. Bakius. 8vo. 3s.

Aristophanes. J. Caravellae Index. 8vo. 3s.

Comoediae et Fragmenta. Ex rec. G. Dindorfii. Tomi II. 8vo. 11s.

Annotationes G. Dindorfii. Partes II. 8vo. 11s.

Scholia Graeca ex Codicibus aucta et emendata a G. Dindorfio. Partes III. 8vo. £1.

Aristoteles, ex recensione Immanuelis Bekkeri. Accedunt Indices Sylburgiani. Tomi I–XVI. 8vo.

The nine volumes in print (I (Organon) and IX (Ethica) are out of print) may be had separately, price 5s. 6d. each.

Choerobosci Dictata in Theodosii Canones, necnon Epimerismi in Psalmos. Edidit Thomas Gaisford. Tomi III. 8vo. 15s.

Demosthenes, ex recensione G. Dindorfii. Tomi IX. 8vo. £2 6s.

Separately : Textus, £1 1s. Annotationes, 15s. Scholia, 10s.

Etymologicon Magnum. Edited by T. Gaisford. Folio. £2 12s. 6d. net.

Euripidis Tragoediae et Fragmenta. Ex rec. G. Dindorfii. Tomi II. 8vo. 10s.

Annotationes G. Dindorfii. Partes II. 8vo. 10s.

Scholia Graeca ex Codicibus aucta et emendata a G. Dindorfio. Tomi IV. 8vo. £1 16s.

Alcestis. Ex recensione G. Dindorfii. 8vo. 2s. 6d.

Harpocrationis Lexicon. Ex recensione G. Dindorfii. Tomi II.
8vo. 10s. 6d.

Hephaestionis Enchiridion, Terentianus Maurus, Proclus, etc. Edidit
T. Gaisford. Tomi II. 10s.

Homerus

. Ilias, cum brevi annotatione C. G. Heynii. Accedunt Scholia minora.
Tomi II. 8vo. 15s.
Ilias. Ex rec. G. Dindorfii. 8vo. 5s. 6d.
Scholia Graeca in Iliadem. See p. 45.
Scholia Graeca in Iliadem Townleyana, recensuit Ernestus Maass. 2 vols.
8vo. £1 16s.
Odyssea. Ex rec. G. Dindorfii. 8vo. 5s. 6d.
Scholia Graeca in Odysseam. Ed. G. Dindorfius. Tomi II. 8vo. 15s. 6d.
Seberi Index in Homerum. 8vo. 6s. 6d.

Oratores Attici, ex recensione Bekkeri: Vol. III. Isaeus, Æschines,
Lycurgus, etc. 8vo. 7s. Vols. I and II are out of print.

Paroemiographi Graeci. Edidit T. Gaisford. 8vo. 5s. 6d.

Index Graecitatis Platonicae, confecit T. Mitchell. 1832. 2 vols.
8vo. 5s.

Plotinus. Edidit F. Creuzer. Tomi III. 4to. £1 8s.

Plutarchi Moralia, id est, Opera, exceptis Vitis, reliqua. Edidit
D. Wyttenbach. Accedit Index Graecitatis. Tomi VIII. Partes XV.
8vo, cloth. £3 10s.

Sophoclis Tragoediae et Fragmenta. Ex recensione et cum commentarii
G. Dindorfii. Third edition. 2 vols. Fcap 8vo. £1 1s.
Each Play separately, limp, 1s.; text only, 6d.; text on writing-paper, 8s.
Tragoediae et Fragmenta cum annotationibus G. Dindorfii.
Tomi II. 8vo. 10s.
The text, Vol. I, 5s. 6d. The notes, Vol. II, 4s. 6d.

Stobaei Florilegium. Ad MSS fidem emendavit et supplevit T. Gaisford.
Tomi IV. 8vo. £1 net.
Eclogarum Physicarum et Ethicarum libri duo : accedit Hierocli
Commentarius in aurea carmina Pythagoreorum. Recensuit T.
Gaisford. Tomi II. 8vo. 11s.

Suidae Lexicon. Edited by T. Gaisford. Three vols. Folio. Large
paper copies, £5 5s. net.

Xenophon. Ex rec. et cum annotatt. L. Dindorfii.
Historia Graeca. Second edition. 8vo. 10s. 6d.
Expeditio Cyri. Second edition. 8vo. 10s. 6d.
Institutio Cyri. 8vo. 10s. 6d.
Memorabilia Socratis. 8vo. 7s. 6d.
Opuscula Politica Equestria et Venatica cum Arriani Libello de Venatione.
8vo. 10s. 6d.

Greek Drama and Music

The Attic Theatre. A description of the Stage and Theatre of the Athenians. By A. E. HAIGH. 2nd ed. With illustrations. 8vo. 12s. 6d.

The Tragic Drama of the Greeks. With illustrations. By the same. 8vo. 12s. 6d.

The Ancient Classical Drama. A Study in Literary Evolution. By R. G. MOULTON. Second edition. Crown 8vo. 8s. 6d.

Modes of Ancient Greek Music. By D. B. MONRO. 12s. 6d. net. (For ARISTOXENUS, see p. 44.)

Coins and Inscriptions

Historia Numorum. A Manual of Greek Numismatics. By BARCLAY V. HEAD. Royal 8vo, half-bound. £2 2s.

A Manual of Greek Historical Inscriptions. By E. L. HICKS. New edition, revised by G. F. HILL. 8vo. 12s. 6d.
    A few copies of the first edition, containing some additional inscriptions down to the death of Alexander, are still procurable at 10s. 6d.

The Inscriptions of Cos. By W. R. PATON and E. L. HICKS. Royal 8vo. £1 8s.

A Grammar of the Homeric Dialect. By D. B. MONRO. Second edition. 8vo. 14s.

The Sounds and Inflections of Greek Dialects (Ionic). By H. W. SMITH. 8vo. £1 4s.

A Glossary of Greek Birds. By D'ARCY W. THOMPSON, C.B. 8vo, buckram. 10s. net.

Practical Introduction to Greek Accentuation. By H. W. CHANDLER. 8vo. 2nd ed. 10s. 6d. Also an abridgement. Ext. fcap 8vo. 2s. 6d.

Palaeography : Papyri

Plauti Codex Turnebi. By W. M. LINDSAY. 8vo. 21s. net.

Catalogus Codicum Graecorum Sinaiticorum. Scripsit V. GARDTHAUSEN. With facsimiles. 8vo, linen. £1 5s.

On abbreviations in Greek MSS. By T. W. ALLEN. Royal 8vo. 5s.

An Alexandrian erotic fragment and other Greek papyri, chiefly Ptolemaic. Edited by B. P. GRENFELL. Small 4to. 8s. 6d. net.

New classical fragments and other papyri. Edited by B. P. GRENFELL and A. S. HUNT. 12s. 6d. net.

Revenue laws of Ptolemy Philadelphus. Edited by B. P. GRENFELL and J. P. MAHAFFY. £1 11s. 6d. net.

Palaeography of Greek papyri, by F. G. KENYON. With twenty facsimiles and a table of alphabets. 8vo. 10s. 6d.

HISTORY
History, Philosophy, and Law
Greece, Italy, Egypt, etc

Clinton's Fasti Hellenici, from the LVIth to the CXXIIIrd Olympiad. Third edition. 4to. £1 14s. 6d. From the CXXIVth Olympiad to the Death of Augustus. Second edition. 4to. £1 12s. Epitome. 8vo. 6s. 6d.

Clinton's Fasti Romani, from the death of Augustus to the death of Heraclius. Two volumes. 4to. £2 2s. Epitome. 8vo. 7s.

Greswell's Fasti Temporis Catholici. 4 vols. 8vo. £2 10s. Tables and Introduction to Tables. 8vo. 15s. Origines Kalendariae Italicae. 4 vols. 8vo. £2 2s. Origines Kalendariae Hellenicae. 6 vols. 8vo. £4 4s.

A Manual of Greek Historical Inscriptions. By E. L. HICKS. New edition, revised by G. F. HILL. 8vo. 12s. 6d.

Latin Historical Inscriptions, illustrating the history of the Early Empire. By G. McN. RUSHFORTH. 8vo. 10s. net.

Sources for Greek History between the Persian and Peloponnesian Wars. Collected and arranged by G. F. HILL. 8vo. 10s. 6d.

Sources for Roman History, B.C. 133-70. By A. H. J. GREENIDGE and A. M. CLAY. Crown 8vo. 5s. 6d. net.

A Manual of Ancient History. By G. RAWLINSON. 2nd ed. 8vo. 14s.

Finlay's History of Greece from its Conquest by the Romans (B.C. 146) to A.D. 1864. A new edition, revised, and in part re-written, with many additions, by the Author, and edited by H. F. TOZER. 7 vols. 8vo. £3 10s.

The History of Sicily from the earliest times. By E. A. FREEMAN.

    Vols. I and II. [Vol. I. The Native Nations: The Phoenician and Greek Settlements. Vol. II. From the beginning of Greek Settlement to the beginning of Athenian Intervention.] 8vo. £2 2s.

    Vol. III. The Athenian and Carthaginian Invasions. £1 4s.

    Vol. IV. From the Tyranny of Dionysios to the Death of Agathoklês. Edited from posthumous MSS, by A. J. EVANS. £1 1s.

Italy and her Invaders (A.D. 376-814). With plates and maps. Eight volumes. 8vo. By T. HODGKIN.

    Vols. I-II. The Visigothic Invasions. The Hunnish Invasion. The Vandal Invasion, and the Herulian Mutiny. Second edition. £2 2s.

    Vols. III-IV. The Ostrogothic Invasion. The Imperial Restoration. Second edition. £1 16s.

    Vols. V-VI. The Lombard Invasion, and the Lombard Kingdom. £1 16s.

    Vols. VII-VIII. Frankish Invasions, and the Frankish Empire. £1 4s.

The Dynasty of Theodosius; or, Seventy Years' Struggle with the Barbarians. By the same author. Crown 8vo. 6s.

Aetolia; its Geography, Topography, and Antiquities. By W. J. WOODHOUSE. With maps and illustrations. Royal 8vo. £1 1s. net.

The Islands of the Aegean. By H. F. TOZER. Crown 8vo. 8s. 6d.

E

Dalmatia, the Quarnero, and Istria; with Cettigne in Montenegro and the Island of Grado. By T. G. Jackson. Three volumes. With many plates and illustrations. 8vo. £2 2s.

Cramer's Description of Asia Minor. Two volumes. 8vo. 11s.

Description of Ancient Greece. 3 vols. 8vo. 16s. 6d.

The Cities and Bishoprics of Phrygia. By W. M. Ramsay. Royal 8vo. Vol. I, Part I. The Lycos Valley and South-Western Phrygia. 18s. net. Vol. I, Part II. West and West Central Phrygia. £1 1s. net.

Stories of the High Priests of Memphis, the Sethon of Herodotus, and the Demotic Tales of Khamnas. By F. Ll. Griffith. With Portfolio containing seven facsimiles. Royal 8vo. £2 7s. 6d. net.

The Arab Conquest of Egypt. By A. J. Butler. With maps and plans. 8vo. 16s. net.

Baghdad during the Abbasid Caliphate, from contemporary sources. By G. Le Strange. With eight plans. 8vo. 16s. net.

Archaeology

Sacred Sites of the Gospels. By W. Sanday, with the assistance of P. Waterhouse. With 63 full-page illustrations from photographs, maps and plans. 8vo. 13s. 6d. net.

Ancient Coptic Churches of Egypt. By A. J. Butler. 2 vols. 8vo. 30s.

A Catalogue of the Cyprus Museum. By J. L. Myres and Max Ohnefalsch-Richter. 8vo. With eight plates, 7s. 6d. net.

A Catalogue of the Sparta Museum. By M. N. Tod and A. J. B. Wace. 8vo. 10s. 6d. net.

Catalogue of the Greek Vases in the Ashmolean Museum. By P. Gardner. Small folio, linen, with 26 plates. £3 3s. net.

Catalogue of the Coins in the Indian Museum, Calcutta, including the Cabinet of the Asiatic Society of Bengal. Vol. I. By Vincent A. Smith. Royal 8vo, 30s. net ; or separately, Part I. The Early Foreign Dynasties and the Guptas, 15s. net. Part II. Ancient Coins of Indian Types, 6s. net. Part III. Persian, Mediaeval, South Indian, and Miscellaneous Coins, 10s. 6d. net. Vol. II will contain the Muhammadan coins. Section I of Part II is by Sir James Bourdillon, the whole of the remainder by H. Nelson Wright. (Published for the Trustees of the Indian Museum.)

The Cults of the Greek States. By L. R. Farnell. 8vo. Vols. I and II, with 61 plates and over 100 illustrations. £1 12s. net : Vols. III and IV, with 83 plates. Immediately.

Classical Archaeology in Schools. By P. Gardner and J. L. Myres. 8vo. Second edition. Paper covers, 1s. net.

Introduction to Greek Sculpture. By L. E. Upcott. Second edition. Crown 8vo. 4s. 6d.

Marmora Oxoniensia, inscriptiones Graecae ad Chandleri exempla editae, cur. Gul. Roberts, 1791. Crown 8vo. 3s. 6d.

De Antiquis Marmoribus, Blasii Caryophili. 1828. 7s. 6d.

Fragmenta Herculanensia. A Catalogue of the Oxford copies of the Herculanean Rolls, with texts of several papyri. By W. Scott. Royal 8vo. £1 1s. Thirty-six Engravings of Texts and Alphabets from the Herculanean Fragments. Folio. Small paper, 10s. 6d., large paper, £1 1s.

Herculanensium Voluminum Partes II. 1824. 8vo. 10s.

English History : Sources

Opus Epistolarum Das. Erasmi Roterodami denuo recognitum et auctum per P. S. Allen. Medium 8vo. Tom. I, 1484–1514, with four illustrations. 18s. net.

Two of the Saxon Chronicles Parallel; with supplementary extracts from the others. A Revised Text, edited, with introduction, notes, appendices, and glossary, by C. Plummer and J. Earle. Two volumes crown 8vo, half-roan. Vol. I. Text, appendices, and glossary. 10s. 6d. Vol. II. Introduction, notes, and index. 12s. 6d.

The Saxon Chronicles (787–1001 a.d.). Crown 8vo, stiff covers. 3s.

Baedae Opera Historica, edited by C. Plummer. Two volumes. Crown 8vo, half-roan. £1 1s. net.

Handbook to the Land-Charters, and other Saxonic Documents, by J. Earle. Crown 8vo. 16s.

The Crawford Collection of early Charters and Documents, now in the Bodleian Library. Edited by A. S. Napier and W. H. Stevenson. Small 4to, cloth. 12s.

Asser's Life of Alfred, with the Annals of St. Neot, edited by W. H. Stevenson. Crown 8vo. 12s. net.

The Alfred Jewel, an historical essay. With illustrations and a map, by J. Earle. Small 4to, buckram. 12s. 6d. net.

Chronicles of London. Edited, with introduction and notes, by C. L. Kingsford. 8vo. 10s. 6d. net.

Dialogus de Scaccario (De necessariis observantiis Scaccarii dialogus) by Richard, Son of Nigel. Edited by A. Hughes, C. G. Crump, and C. Johnson, with introduction and notes. 8vo. 12s. 6d. net.

The Song of Lewes. Edited from the MS, with introduction and notes, by C. L. Kingsford. Extra fcap 8vo. 5s.

Chronicon Galfridi le Baker de Swynebroke, edited by Sir E. Maunde Thompson, K.C.B. Small 4to, 18s. ; cloth, gilt top, £1 1s.

Passio et Miracula Beati Olaui. Edited from the Twelfth-century MS by F. Metcalfe. Small 4to. 6s.

Gascoigne's Theological Dictionary ('Liber Veritatum'): selected passages, illustrating the condition of Church and State, 1403-1458. With an introduction by J. E. Thorold Rogers. Small 4to. 10s. 6d.

Fortescue's Governance of England : otherwise called The Difference between an Absolute and a Limited Monarchy. A revised text, edited, with introduction, etc, by C. Plummer. 8vo, quarter-bound. 12s. 6d.

The Protests of the Lords, including those which have been expunged, from 1624 to 1874; with historical introductions. By J. E. Thorold Rogers. In three volumes. 8vo. £2 2s.

The Clarendon Press Series of Charters, Statutes, etc

From the earliest times to 1307. By Bishop Stubbs.

Select Charters and other illustrations of English Constitutional History. Eighth edition. Crown 8vo. 8s. 6d.

From 1307 to 1558. In Preparation. By G. W. Prothero.

Select Statutes and other Constitutional Documents.

From 1558 to 1625.

Constitutional Documents of the Reigns of Elizabeth and James I. Third edition. Crown 8vo. 10s. 6d.

From 1625 to 1660. By S. R. Gardiner.

The Constitutional Documents of the Puritan Revolution. Third edition. Crown 8vo. 10s. 6d.

Calendars, etc

Calendar of Charters and Rolls preserved in the Bodleian Library. 8vo. £1 11s. 6d.

Calendar of the Clarendon State Papers, preserved in the Bodleian Library. In three volumes. 1869–76.

    Vol. I. From 1523 to January 1649. 8vo. 18s. Vol. II. From 1649 to 1654. 8vo. 16s. Vol. III. From 1655 to 1657. 8vo. 14s.

Hakluyt's Principal Navigations, being narratives of the Voyages of the Elizabethan Seamen to America. Selection edited by E. J. Payne. Crown 8vo, with portraits. Second edition. First and Second Series, 5s. each.

Aubrey's ' Brief Lives,' set down between the Years 1669 and 1696. Edited from the Author's MSS by A. Clark. Two volumes. 8vo. £1 5s.

Whitelock's Memorials of English Affairs from 1625 to 1660. 4 vols. 8vo. £1 10s.

Ludlow's Memoirs, 1625–1672. Edited, with Appendices of Letters and illustrative documents, by C. H. Firth. Two volumes. 8vo. £1 16s.

Luttrell's Diary. A brief Historical Relation of State Affairs, 1678–1714. Six volumes. 8vo. £1 4s.

Burnet's History of James II. 8vo. 9s. 6d.

Life of Sir M. Hale, with Fell's Life of Dr. Hammond. Small 8vo. 2s. 6d.

Burnet's History of My Own Time. A new edition based on that of M. J. ROUTH. Edited by OSMUND AIRY.
> Vol. I. The Reign of Charles the Second, Part I. 12s. 6d.
> Vol. II. Completing the Reign of Charles the Second, with Index to Vols. I and II. 12s. 6d.
>> **Supplement**, derived from Burnet's Memoirs, Autobiography, etc, all hitherto unpublished. Edited by H. C. FOXCROFT, 1902. 8vo. 16s. net.

Carte's Life of James Duke of Ormond. A new edition carefully compared with the original MSS. Six volumes. 8vo. £1 5s.

The Whitefoord Papers, being the Correspondence and other Manuscripts of Colonel CHARLES WHITEFOORD and CALEB WHITEFOORD, from 1739 to 1810. Edited by W. A. S. HEWINS. 8vo. 12s. 6d.

History of Oxford

A complete list of the Publications of the Oxford Historical Society can be obtained from Mr. Frowde.

Manuscript Materials relating to the History of Oxford ; contained in the printed catalogues of the Bodleian and College Libraries. By F. MADAN. 8vo. 7s. 6d.

The Early Oxford Press. A Bibliography of Printing and Publishing at Oxford, ' 1468 '–1640. With notes, appendices, and illustrations. By F. MADAN. 8vo. 18s.

Bibliography

Cotton's Typographical Gazetteer. First Series. 8vo. 12s. 6d.

Ebert's Bibliographical Dictionary. 4 vols. 8vo. £3 3s. net.

Bishop Stubbs's and Professor Freeman's Books

The Constitutional History of England, in its Origin and Development. By W. STUBBS. Library edition. Three volumes. Demy 8vo. £2 8s. Also in three volumes, crown 8vo, price 12s. each.

Seventeen Lectures on the Study of Mediaeval and Modern History and kindred subjects, 1867–1884. By the same. Third edition, revised and enlarged, 1900. Crown 8vo, half-roan. 8s. 6d.

History of the Norman Conquest of England ; its Causes and Results. By E. A. FREEMAN. Vols. I, II and V (English edition) are out of print.
> Vols. III and IV. £1 1s. each. Vol. VI (Index). 10s. 6d.
> *A few copies of the complete American edition remain.*

A Short History of the Norman Conquest of England. Third edition. By the same. Extra fcap 8vo. 2s. 6d.

The Reign of William Rufus and the Accession of Henry the First. By the same. Two volumes. 8vo. £1 16s.

Companion to English History (Middle Ages). Edited by F. P. BARNARD. With 97 illustrations. Crown 8vo. 8s. 6d. net.

School History of England to the death of Victoria. With maps, plans, and select bibliographies. By O. M. EDWARDS, R. S. RAIT and others. Crown 8vo, 3s. 6d.

Special Periods and Biographies

Life and Times of Alfred the Great, being the Ford Lectures for 1901. By C. PLUMMER. 8vo. 5s. net.

The Domesday Boroughs. By ADOLPHUS BALLARD. 8vo, with four plans. 6s. 6d. net.

Villainage in England. Essays in English Mediaeval History. By P. VINOGRADOFF. 8vo, half-bound. 16s.

The Gild Merchant : a contribution to British municipal history. By C. GROSS. Two volumes. 8vo, quarter-bound, £1 4s.

The Welsh Wars of Edward I ; a contribution to mediaeval military history. By J. E. MORRIS. 8vo. 9s. 6d. net.

The Great Revolt of 1381. By C. OMAN. With two maps. 8vo. 8s. 6d. net.

Lancaster and York. A Century of English History (A.D. 1399–1485). By Sir J. H. RAMSAY. Two volumes. 8vo, with Index, £1 17s. 6d. Index separately, paper covers, 1s. 6d.

Life and Letters of Thomas Cromwell. By R. B. MERRIMAN. In two volumes. [Vol. I, Life and Letters, 1523–1535, etc. Vol. II, Letters, 1536–1540, notes, index, etc.] 8vo. 18s. net.

A History of England, principally in the Seventeenth Century. By L. VON RANKE. Translated under the superintendence of G. W. KITCHIN and C. W. BOASE. Six volumes. 8vo. £3 3s. Index separately, 1s.

Sir Walter Ralegh, a Biography, by W. STEBBING. Post 8vo. 6s. net.

Biographical Memoir of Dr. William Markham, Archbishop of York, by his great-grandson, Sir CLEMENTS MARKHAM, K.C.B. 8vo. 5s. net. With photogravure portrait.

The Life and Works of John Arbuthnot. By G. A. AITKEN. 8vo, cloth extra, with Portrait. 16s.

Life and Letters of Sir Henry Wotton. By L. PEARSALL-SMITH. 8vo. Two volumes. In the Press.

Great Britain and Hanover. By A. W. WARD. Crown 8vo. 5s.

History of the Peninsular War. By C. OMAN. To be completed in six volumes, 8vo, with many maps, plans, and portraits.
Already published : Vol. I. 1807–1809, to Corunna. 14s. net.
Vol. II. 1809–1810, to Talavera. 14s. net.
Vol. III. In the Press.

Frederick York Powell. A Life and a selection from his Letters and Occasional Writings. By OLIVER ELTON. Two volumes. 8vo. With photogravure portraits, facsimiles, etc. 21s. net.

History and Geography of America and the British Colonies

For other Geographical books, see page 58.

History of the New World called America. By E. J. PAYNE.
Vol. I. 8vo. 18s. Bk. I. The Discovery. Bk. II, Part I. Aboriginal America.
Vol. II. 8vo. 14s. Bk. II, Part II. Aboriginal America (concluded).

The Canadian War of 1812. By C. P. LUCAS, C.B. 8vo. With eight maps. 12s. 6d. net.

Historical Geography of the British Colonies. By C. P. LUCAS, C.B.· Crown 8vo.

> **Introduction.** New edition by H. E. EGERTON. 1903. With eight maps. 3s. 6d. In cheaper binding, 2s. 6d.
>
> **Vol. I. The Mediterranean and Eastern Colonies.** With 13 maps. Second edition, revised and brought up to date, by R. E. STUBBS. 1906. 5s.
>
> **Vol. II. The West Indian Colonies.** With twelve maps. Second edition, revised and brought up to date, by C. ATCHLEY, I.S.O. 1905. 7s. 6d.
>
> **Vol. III. West Africa.** Revised to the end of 1899 by H. E. EGERTON. With five maps. 7s. 6d.
>
> **Vol. IV. South and East Africa.** Historical and Geographical. With eleven maps. 9s. 6d.
>
> > Also Part I. Historical. 1898. 6s. 6d. Part II (1903). Geographical. 3s. 6d.
>
> **Vol. V. Canada, Part I.** 1901. 6s.
>
> **Vol. VI. Australasia.** By J. J. Rogers. Immediately.

The History of South Africa to the Jameson Raid. With numerous maps. Crown 8vo. 5s.

History of the Dominion of Canada. By W. P. GRESWELL. Crown 8vo. 7s. 6d.

Geography of the Dominion of Canada and Newfoundland. By the same author. With ten maps. 1891. Crown 8vo. 6s.

Geography of Africa South of the Zambesi. With maps. 1892. By the same author. Crown 8vo. 7s. 6d.

The Claims of the Study of Colonial History upon the attention of the University of Oxford. An inaugural lecture delivered on April 28, 1906, by H. E. EGERTON. 8vo, paper covers, 1s. net.

Historical Atlas. Europe and her Colonies, 27 maps. 35s. net.

Cornewall-Lewis's Essay on the Government of Dependencies. Edited by C. P. LUCAS, C.B. 8vo, quarter-bound, 14s.

History of India

A Brief History of the Indian Peoples. By Sir W. W. Hunter. Revised up to 1903 by W. H. Hutton. Eighty-ninth thousand. 3s. 6d.

Rulers of India : The History of the Indian Empire in a carefully planned succession of Political Biographies. Edited by Sir W. W. Hunter. Crown 8vo. 2s. 6d. each.

Bábar. By S. Lane-Poole.

Akbar. By Colonel Malleson.

Albuquerque. By H. Morse Stephens.

Aurangzíb. By S. Lane-Poole.

Mádhava Ráo Sindhia. By H. G. Keene.

Lord Clive. By Colonel Malleson.

Dupleix. By Colonel Malleson.

Warren Hastings. By Captain L. J. Trotter.

The Marquis of Cornwallis. By W. S. Seton-Karr.

Haidar Alí and Tipú Sultán. By L. B. Bowring.

The Marquis Wellesley, K.G. By W. H. Hutton.

Marquess of Hastings. By Major Ross-of-Bladensburg.

Mountstuart Elphinstone. By J. S. Cotton.

Sir Thomas Munro. By J. Bradshaw.

Earl Amherst. By Anne T. Ritchie and R. Evans.

Lord William Bentinck. By D. C. Boulger.

The Earl of Auckland. By Captain L. J. Trotter.

Viscount Hardinge. By his son, Viscount Hardinge.

Ranjit Singh. By Sir L. Griffin.

The Marquess of Dalhousie. By Sir W. W. Hunter.

John Russell Colvin. By Sir A. Colvin.

Clyde and Strathnairn. By Major-General Sir O. T. Burne.

Earl Canning. By Sir H. S. Cunningham.

Lord Lawrence. By Sir C. Aitchison.

The Earl of Mayo. By Sir W. W. Hunter.

Supplementary volumes.

Asoka. By V. A. Smith. 3s. 6d.

James Thomason. By Sir R. Temple. 3s. 6d.

Sir Henry Lawrence, the Pacificator. By Lieut.-General J. J. McLeod Innes. 3s. 6d.

The Government of India, being a digest of the Statute Law relating thereto; with historical introduction and illustrative documents. By Sir C. P. ILBERT. New edition, 1907. 10s. 6d. net.

The Early History of India from 600 B.C. to the Muhammadan Conquest, including the invasion of Alexander the Great. By V. A. SMITH. 8vo. With maps, plans, and other illustrations. 14s. net.

The English Factories in India, 1618–1621. By W. FOSTER. 8vo. (Published under the patronage of His Majesty's Secretary of State for India in Council.) 12s. 6d. net.

Wellesley's Despatches, Treaties, and other Papers relating to his Government of India. Selection edited by S. J. OWEN. 8vo. £1 4s.

Wellington's Despatches, Treaties, and other Papers relating to India. Selection edited by S. J. OWEN. 8vo. £1 4s.

Hastings and the Rohilla War. By Sir J. STRACHEY. 8vo. 10s. 6d.

European History

Historical Atlas of Modern Europe, from the Decline of the Roman Empire. Containing 90 maps, with letterpress to each map: the maps printed by W. & A. K. JOHNSTON, Ltd., and the whole edited by R. L. POOLE.

> In one volume, imperial 4to, half-persian, £5 15s. 6d. net; or in selected sets—British Empire, etc, at various prices from 30s. to 35s. net each; or in single maps, 1s. 6d. net each. Prospectus on application.

Genealogical Tables illustrative of Modern History. By H. B. GEORGE. Fourth (1904) edition. Oblong 4to, boards. 7s. 6d.

The Life and Times of James the First of Aragon. By F. D. SWIFT. 8vo. 12s. 6d.

A History of France. With maps, plans, and Tables. By G. W. KITCHIN. New edition. In three volumes, crown 8vo, each 10s. 6d. See p. 29.

> Vol. I, to 1453.   Vol. II, 1453-1624.   Vol. III, 1624-1793.

The Principal Speeches of the Statesmen and Orators of the French Revolution, 1789-1795. With introductions, notes, etc. By H. MORSE STEPHENS. Two volumes. Crown 8vo. £1 1s.

Napoleonic Statesmanship: Germany. By H. A. L. FISHER. 8vo, with maps. 12s. 6d. net.

De Tocqueville's L'Ancien Régime et la Révolution. Edited, with introductions and notes, by G. W. HEADLAM. Crown 8vo. 6s.

Documents of the French Revolution, 1789-1791. By L. G. WICKHAM LEGG. Crown 8vo. Two volumes. 12s. net.

Thiers' Moscow Expedition, edited, with introductions and notes, by H. B. GEORGE. Crown 8vo, with 6 maps. 5s.

Geography and Anthropology

Relations of Geography and History. By H. B. George. With two maps. Crown 8vo. Second edition. 4s. 6d.

The Dawn of Modern Geography. By C. R. Beazley. Vol. I (to A.D. 900). Vol. II (A.D. 900–1260). 15s. net each. Vol. III. 20s. net.

Regions of the World. Geographical Memoirs under the general editorship of H. J. Mackinder. Large 8vo. Each volume contains maps and diagrams. 7s. 6d. net per volume.

> Britain and the British Seas. Second edition. By H. J. Mackinder.
>
> Central Europe. By John Partsch.
>
> The Nearer East. By D. G. Hogarth.
>
> North America. By J. Russell.
>
> India. By Sir Thomas Holdich.
>
> The Far East. By Archibald Little.

The Face of the Earth (Das Antlitz der Erde). By Eduard Suess. Translated by Hertha Sollas. Vols. I, II. 25s. net each.

Oxford Geographies. By A. J. Herbertson. Crown 8vo. Vol. I. The Preliminary Geography, with 72 maps and diagrams, 1s. 6d. Vol. II. The Junior Geography, with 166 maps and diagrams, 2s. Vol. III. The Senior Geography. In the press.

Geography for Schools, by A. Hughes. Crown 8vo. 2s. 6d.

The Evolution of Culture, and other Essays, by the late Lieut.-Gen. A. Lane-Fox Pitt-Rivers; edited by J. L. Myres, with an Introduction by H. Balfour. 8vo, with 21 plates, 7s. 6d. net.

Dubois' Hindu Manners, Customs, and Ceremonies. Translated and edited with notes, corrections, and biography, by H. K. Beauchamp. Third edition. Crown 8vo. 6s. net. On India Paper, 7s. 6d. net.

The Melanesians, studies in their Anthropology and Folk-Lore. By R. H. Codrington. 8vo. 16s.

Iceland and the Faroes. By N. Annandale. With twenty-four illustrations and an appendix on the Celtic Pony, by F. H. A. Marshall. Crown 8vo. 4s. 6d. net.

The Masai, their Language and Folk-lore. By A. C. Hollis. With introduction by Sir Charles Eliot. 8vo. With 27 full-page illustrations and a map. 14s. net.

Celtic Folklore: Welsh and Manx. By J. Rhŷs. Two volumes. 8vo. £1 1s.

Studies in the Arthurian Legend. By J. Rhŷs. 8vo. 12s. 6d.

The Mediaeval Stage, from classical times through folk-play and minstrelsy to Elizabethan drama. By E. K. Chambers. With two illustrations. 8vo. £1 5s. net.

PHILOSOPHY
Modern Philosophy

Bacon's Novum Organum, edited, with introduction, notes, etc, by T. Fowler. Second edition. 8vo. 15s.

Novum Organum, edited, with notes, by G. W. Kitchin. 8vo. 9s. 6d.

Bentham's Introduction to the Principles of Morals and Legislation. Crown 8vo. 6s. 6d.

The Works of George Berkeley, formerly Bishop of Cloyne. With prefaces, annotations, appendices, and an account of his Life and Philosophy, by A. C. Fraser. New edition (1901) in crown 8vo. Four volumes. £1 4s. Some copies of the 8vo edition of the *Life* are still on sale, price 16s.

Selections from Berkeley, with introduction and notes, for the use of Students. By the same Editor. Fifth edition. Crown 8vo. 7s. 6d.

The Cambridge Platonists: being selections from the Writings of Benjamin Whichcote, John Smith, and Nathanael Culverwel, with introduction by E. T. Campagnac. Crown 8vo. 6s. 6d. net.

Leibniz's Monadology and other Philosophical Writings, translated, with introduction and notes, by R. Latta. Crown 8vo. 8s. 6d.

Locke's Essay concerning Human Understanding. Collated and annotated with prolegomena, biographical, critical, and historical, by A. C. Fraser. Two volumes. 8vo. £1 12s.

Locke's Conduct of the Understanding. Edited by T. Fowler. Extra fcap 8vo. 2s. 6d.

A Study in the Ethics of Spinoza. By H. H. Joachim. 8vo. 10s. 6d. net.

Hume's Treatise on Human Nature, reprinted from the original edition in three volumes, and edited by L. A. Selby-Bigge. Second edition. Crown 8vo. 6s. net.

Hume's Enquiry concerning the Human Understanding, and an Enquiry concerning the Principles of Morals. Edited by L. A. Selby-Bigge. Crown 8vo. Second edition. 6s. net.

British Moralists, being Selections from writers principally of the eighteenth century. Edited by L. A. Selby-Bigge. Two volumes. Crown 8vo. 12s. net. Uniform with Hume's Treatise and Enquiry, and Berkeley's Works.

Butler's Works, edited by W. E. Gladstone. Two volumes. Medium 8vo, 14s. each, or Crown 8vo, 10s. 6d. (Also, separately—Vol. I (Analogy), 5s. 6d. Vol. II (Sermons) 5s.

Recent Philosophy

The Logic of Hegel, translated from the Encyclopaedia of the Philosophical Sciences, with Prolegomena, by W. WALLACE. Second edition. Two volumes. Crown 8vo. 10s. 6d. each.

Hegel's Philosophy of Mind, translated from Encyclopaedia of Philosophical Sciences, with five introductory essays, by W. WALLACE. Crown 8vo. 10s. 6d.

Lotze's Logic, in Three Books, of Thought, of Investigation, and of Knowledge. Translated by B. BOSANQUET. Second ed. 2 vols. Cr. 8vo. 12s.

Lotze's Metaphysic, in Three Books, Ontology, Cosmology, and Psychology. Translated by B. BOSANQUET. Second ed. 2 vols. Cr. 8vo. 12s.

Bluntschli's Theory of the State. Translated from the sixth German edition. Third edition, 1901. Crown 8vo, half-bound, 8s. 6d.

Green's Prolegomena to Ethics. Edited by A. C. BRADLEY. Fifth edition, 1906. With a Preface by E. CAIRD. Crown 8vo. 7s. 6d.

Types of Ethical Theory, by J. MARTINEAU. Third edition. Two volumes. Crown 8vo. 15s.

A Study of Religion : its Sources and Contents. By the same author. Second edition. Two volumes. Crown 8vo. 15s.

The Principles of Morals. By T. FOWLER and J. M. WILSON. 8vo. 14s. Also, separately—Part I, 3s. 6d. Part II, 10s. 6d.

Logic ; or, The Morphology of Knowledge. By B. BOSANQUET. Two volumes. 8vo. £1 1s.

Lectures and Essays on Natural Theology and Ethics. By W. WALLACE. Edited, with biographical introduction, by E. CAIRD. With portrait. 8vo. 12s. 6d.

Studies in History and Jurisprudence. By Rt. Hon. J. BRYCE. 1901. 2 vols. 8vo. £1 5s. net.

The Theory of Good and Evil. By H. RASHDALL. 8vo. 2 vols. Immediately.

The Herbert Spencer Lecture. Delivered at Oxford, March, 1905, by FREDERIC HARRISON. 8vo, paper covers, 2s. net.

An Introduction to Logic. By H. W. B. JOSEPH. 8vo. 9s. 6d. net.

Essay on Truth. By H. H. JOACHIM. 8vo. 6s. net.

Elementary Logic

The Elements of Deductive Logic. By T. FOWLER. Tenth edition, with a collection of examples. Extra fcap 8vo. 3s. 6d.

The Elements of Inductive Logic. By the same. Sixth edition. Extra fcap 8vo. 6s.   In one volume with Deductive Logic, 7s. 6d.

LAW
Jurisprudence

Bentham's Fragment on Government. Edited by F. C. MONTAGUE. 8vo. 7s. 6d.

Bentham's Introduction to the Principles of Morals and Legislation. Second edition. Crown 8vo. 6s. 6d.

Studies in History and Jurisprudence. By the Right Hon. JAMES BRYCE. 1901. Two volumes. 8vo. £1 5s. net.

The Elements of Jurisprudence. By T. E. HOLLAND. Tenth edition. 1906. 8vo. 10s. 6d.

Elements of Law, considered with reference to Principles of General Jurisprudence. By Sir W. MARKBY, K.C.I.E. Sixth edition revised, 1905. 8vo. 12s. 6d.

Roman Law

Imperatoris Iustiniani Institutionum Libri Quattuor; with introductions, commentary, and translation, by J. B. MOYLE. Two volumes. 8vo. Vol. I (fourth edition, 1903), 16s.; Vol. II, Translation (fourth edition, 1906), 6s.

The Institutes of Justinian, edited as a recension of the Institutes of Gaius. By T. E. HOLLAND. Second edition. Extra fcap 8vo. 5s.

Select Titles from the Digest of Justinian. By T. E. HOLLAND and C. L. SHADWELL. 8vo. 14s.

> Also, sold in parts, in paper covers: Part I. Introductory Titles. 2s. 6d. Part II. Family Law. 1s. Part III. Property Law. 2s. 6d. Part IV. Law of Obligations. No. 1. 3s. 6d. No. 2. 4s. 6d.

Gai Institutionum Iuris Civilis Commentarii Quattuor: with a translation and commentary by the late E. POSTE. Fourth edition. Revised and enlarged, by E. A. WHITTUCK, with an historical introduction by A. H. J. GREENIDGE. 8vo. 16s. net.

Institutes of Roman Law, by R. SOHM. Translated by J. C. LEDLIE: with an introductory essay by E. GRUEBER. Second edition. 1901. 8vo. 18s.

Infamia; its place in Roman Public and Private Law. By A. H. J. GREENIDGE. 8vo. 10s. 6d.

Legal Procedure in Cicero's Time. By A. H. J. GREENIDGE. 8vo. £1 1s.

The Roman Law of Damage to Property: being a commentary on the title of the Digest 'Ad Legem Aquiliam' (ix. 2), with an introduction to the study of the Corpus Iuris Civilis. By E. GRUEBER. 8vo. 10s. 6d.

Contract of Sale in the Civil Law. By J. B. MOYLE. 8vo. 10s. 6d.

The Principles of German Civil Law. By ERNEST J. SCHUSTER. 8vo. 12s. 6d. net.

English Law

Principles of the English Law of Contract, and of Agency in its relation to Contract. By Sir W. R. Anson. Eleventh edition. 1906. 8vo. 10s. 6d.

Law and Custom of the Constitution. By the same. In two parts.

> Part I. Parliament. Third edition. 8vo. 12s. 6d.
>
> Part II. The Crown. Third edition in preparation.

Calendar of Charters and Rolls, containing those preserved in the Bodleian Library. 8vo. £1 11s. 6d.

Introduction to the History of the Law of Real Property. By Sir K. E. Digby. Fifth edition. 8vo. 12s. 6d.

Handbook to the Land-Charters, and other Saxonic Documents. By J. Earle. Crown 8vo. 16s.

Fortescue's Difference between an Absolute and a Limited Monarchy. Text revised and edited, with introduction, etc, by C. Plummer. 8vo, leather back, 12s. 6d.

Legislative Methods and Forms. By Sir C. P. Ilbert, K.C.S.I. 1901. 8vo, leather back, 16s.

Modern Land Law. By E. Jenks. 8vo. 15s.

Essay on Possession in the Common Law. By Sir F. Pollock and Sir R. S. Wright. 8vo. 8s. 6d.

Outline of the Law of Property. By T. Raleigh. 8vo. 7s. 6d.

Villainage in England. By P. Vinogradoff. 8vo, leather back, 16s.

Law in Daily Life. By Rud. von Jhering. Translated with Notes and Additions by H. Goudy. Crown 8vo. 3s. 6d. net.

Cases illustrating the Principles of the Law of Torts, with table of all Cases cited. By F. R. Y. Radcliffe and J. C. Miles. 8vo. 1904. 12s. 6d. net.

Constitutional Documents

Select Charters and other Illustrations of English Constitutional History, from the earliest times to Edward I. Arranged and edited by W. Stubbs. Eighth edition. 1900. Crown 8vo. 8s. 6d.

Constitutional Documents of the Puritan Revolution, selected and edited by S. R. Gardiner. Third edition. Crown 8vo. 10s. 6d.

Select Statutes and other Constitutional Documents, illustrative of the reigns of Elizabeth and James I. Edited by G. W. Prothero. Third edition. Crown 8vo. 10s. 6d.

International Law

International Law. By W. E. Hall. Fifth edition by J. B. Atlay. 1904. 8vo. £1 1s. net.

Treatise on the Foreign Powers and Jurisdiction of the British Crown. By W. E. Hall. 8vo. 10s. 6d.

The European Concert in the Eastern Question, a collection of treaties and other public acts. Edited, with introductions and notes, by T. E. Holland. 8vo. 12s. 6d.

Studies in International Law. By T. E. Holland. 8vo. 10s. 6d.

Gentilis Alberici de Iure Belli Libri Tres edidit T. E. Holland. Small quarto, half-morocco. £1 1s.

The Law of Nations. By Sir T. Twiss. Part I. In time of peace. New edition, revised and enlarged. 8vo. 15s.

Colonial and Indian Law

The Government of India, being a Digest of the Statute Law relating thereto, with historical introduction and illustrative documents. By Sir C. P. Ilbert, K.C.S.I. 8vo, cloth. 10s. 6d. net.

British Rule and Jurisdiction beyond the Seas. By the late Sir H. Jenkyns, K.C.B., with a preface by Sir C. P. Ilbert, and a portrait of the author. 1902. 8vo, leather back, 15s. net.

Cornewall-Lewis's Essay on the Government of Dependencies. Edited by C. P. Lucas, C.B. 8vo, leather back, 14s.

An Introduction to Hindu and Mahommedan Law for the use of students. 1906. By Sir W. Markby, K.C.I.E. 6s. net.

Land-Revenue and Tenure in British India. By B. H. Baden-Powell, C.I.E. With map. Second edition, revised by T. W. Holderness, C.S.I. (1907.) Crown 8vo. 5s. net.

Land-Systems of British India, being a manual of the Land-Tenures, and of the systems of Land-Revenue administration. By the same. Three volumes. 8vo, with map. £3 3s.

Anglo-Indian Codes, by Whitley Stokes. 8vo.
Vol. I. Substantive Law. £1 10s. Vol. II. Adjective Law. £1 15s.
˜pplement, 2s. 6d. 2nd supplement, to 1891, 4s. 6d. In one vol., 6s. 6d.

˜dian **Evidence Act,** with notes by Sir W. Markby, K.C.I.E.
˜. 6d. net (published by Mr. Frowde).

˜ **Droit Ottoman :** un Recueil des Codes, Lois, Règlements,
˜ces et Actes les plus importants du Droit Intérieur, et d'Études
˜t Coutumier de l'Empire Ottoman. Par George Young. Seven
˜Part I (Vols. I–III), cloth, £2 17s. 6d. net ; paper covers,
˜t, published : Part II (Vols. IV–VII), cloth, £1 17s. net, paper
˜6d. net. Parts I and II can be obtained separately, but the
˜Part, bought alone, will be £2 12s. 6d. net in paper covers, or
˜ cloth.

Political Science and Economy

For Bryce's *Studies* and other books of general jurisprudence and political science, see p. 61.

Industrial Organization in the 16th and 17th Centuries. By G. UNWIN. 8vo. 7s. 6d. net.

Relations of the Advanced and Backward Races of Mankind, the Romanes Lecture for 1902. By J. BRYCE. 8vo. 2s. net.

Cornewall-Lewis's Remarks on the Use and Abuse of some Political Terms. New edition, with introduction by T. RALEIGH. Crown 8vo, paper, 3s. 6d. ; cloth, 4s. 6d.

Adam Smith's Wealth of Nations. Edited by J. E. THOROLD ROGERS. Two volumes. 8vo. £1 1s.

Adam Smith's Lectures on Justice, Police, Revenue and Arms. Edited with introduction and notes by E. CANNAN. 8vo. 10s. 6d. net.

Bluntschli's Theory of the State. Translated from the sixth German edition. Third edition. 1901. Crown 8vo, half-bound, 8s. 6d.

Co-operative Production. By B. JONES. With preface by A. H. DYKE-ACLAND. Two volumes. Crown 8vo. 15s.

Elementary Political Economy. By E. CANNAN. Fourth edition. Extra fcap 8vo, 1s.

Elementary Politics. By T. RALEIGH. Sixth edition revised. Extra fcap 8vo, stiff covers, 1s.

A Geometrical Political Economy. Being an elementary Treatise on the method of explaining some Theories of Pure Economic Science by diagrams. By H. CUNYNGHAME, C.B. Cr. 8vo. 2s. 6d. net.

The Elements of Railway Economics. By W. M. ACWORTH. Crown 8vo. Second impression. 2s. net.

Economic Documents

Ricardo's Letters to Malthus (1810–1823). Edited by J. BONAR. 8vo. 7s. 6d.

             Letters to Trower and others (1811–1823). Edited by J. BONAR and J. H. HOLLANDER. 8vo. 7s. 6d.

Lloyd's Prices of Corn in Oxford, 1583–1830. 8vo. 1s.

The History of Agriculture and Prices in En A.D. 1259–1793. By J. E. THOROLD ROGERS.

       Vols. I and II (1259–1400). 8vo. £2 2s.
       Vols. III and IV (1401–1582). 8vo. £2 10s.
       Vols. V and VI (1583–1702). 8vo. £2 10s.
       Vol. VII. In two Parts (1702–1793). 8vo. £2 10s.

First Nine Years of the Bank of England. By 8s. 6d.

THEOLOGY

The Holy Scriptures, Apocrypha, etc

The Bible in English

Reprint of the Authorized Version of 1611. 4to. 1833. £3 3s. net.

The Authorized Version.

Complete lists of Oxford Bibles, Oxford Bibles for Teachers, Oxford Prayer
Books, Church Sets, etc, in all styles and bindings can be obtained from
any bookseller, or from Mr. Henry Frowde, Oxford Warehouse, Amen
Corner, London, E.C.

The Revised Version. See also p. 70.

[The Revised Version is the joint property of the Universities of Oxford
and Cambridge.]

Edition for the Church Desk.

Folio. In buckram, with the Apocrypha, £2 2s. net. Bound in
Grained Cowhide, £2 10s.; with the Apocrypha, £3; in Turkey
Morocco, £4 4s.; with the Apocrypha, £4 16s.

Library editions, in large type (pica). Bound in cloth and greatly reduced
in price.

Royal 8vo, with large margins : with the Apocrypha, 6 vols., from £1 9s. ;
the Apocrypha only, 10s. 6d. ; the other five volumes, 18s. 6d.

Demy 8vo, with the Apocrypha, 6 vols., £1 1s. ; the Apocrypha only,
7s. 6d. ; the other five volumes, 14s.

Single volume editions :

Royal 8vo, on Oxford India Paper, and in large type (pica), in Persian,
£2 12s. 6d.; with the Apocrypha, in Turkey Morocco, £3 19s.

Royal 8vo, small pica type. In cloth, 10s. 6d. ; in leather bindings, from
19s. 6d.

8vo, small pica type. In cloth, 7s. 6d. ; in leather bindings, from 10s. 6d.

8vo, minion type. In cloth, 4s. ; with the Apocrypha, 6s.; the Apocrypha
only, 3s.

16mo, ruby type. In cloth, 2s. 6d ; with the Apocrypha, 4s.; the
Apocrypha only, 2s. ; with the Oxford Helps, in leather, from 7s.

16mo, nonpareil type. In leather, from 3s.

16mo, pearl type. In cloth boards, from 8d. ; with Oxford Helps,
from 2s. 6d.

The Revised Version with marginal references.

8vo, in bourgeois type, from 6s. ; on Oxford India paper, bound in
leather, from 15s.

8vo, in minion type, from 5s.; with the Apocrypha, from 7s. 6d.; with Oxford
Helps, from 11s. ; on Oxford India paper, bound in leather, from 14s.

16mo, in nonpareil type, in leather, from 6s. ; on Oxford India paper,
bound in leather, from 10s. 6d.

The Parallel Bible, containing the Authorized and Revised Versions in
parallel columns. Small quarto, in minion type. On ordinary paper, from
10s. 6d. ; on Oxford India paper, bound in leather, from 16s.

The Two-Version Bible, being the Authorized Version with the
differences of the Revised Version printed in the margins, so that both texts
can be read from the same page. With references and maps. Bourgeois
type. Cloth, 7s. 6d.; leather, from 10s. 6d.; on Oxford India paper—cloth,
10s. 6d.; leather, from 15s. ; interleaved with writing-paper, and bound in
leather, from £1 1s. With the Oxford Helps, leather, from 18s. 6d. Printed
on writing-paper with wide margins for notes, from 10s. 6d. net.

F

Elementary Helps to the Study of the Bible

Oxford Bible for Teachers, containing the texts of the Old and New Testaments, with or without marginal references, and in either the Authorized or Revised Versions, together with the Oxford Helps to the Bible (see below), and 124 full-page plates.

In many styles and bindings. A complete list can be obtained from Mr. Henry Frowde, Amen Corner, London, E.C.

The Oxford Helps to the Study of the Bible, containing Introductions to the several Books, the History and Antiquities of the Jews, the Natural History of Palestine, with copious tables, concordance and indices, and a series of maps. With 124 full-page plates.

8vo, in long primer type—cloth, 5s.; leather, from 6s. 6d.
8vo, in nonpareil type—cloth, 2s. 6d.; leather, 3s. 6d.
16mo, in pearl type—stiff covers, 1s. net; cloth, 1s. 6d.; leather, from 2s.

Bible Illustrations, being 124 full-page plates, forming an appendix to the above. Crown 8vo, cloth, 2s. 6d.

Helps to the Study of the Book of Common Prayer. By W. R. W. STEPHENS. Crown 8vo. Cloth, 2s. 6d. net; also in leather bindings. Printed on Oxford India paper and bound with the Prayer Book, from 11s. 6d.

Dr. Stokoe's Manuals. Crown 8vo

Old Testament History for Schools. By T. H. STOKOE. Part I. (Third edition.) From the Creation to the Settlement in Palestine. Part II. From the Settlement to the Disruption. Part III. From the Disruption to the Return from Captivity. Extra fcap 8vo. 2s. 6d. each, with maps.

Manual of the Four Gospels. With Maps, 3s. 6d. Or, separately, Part I, The Gospel Narrative, 2s.; Part II, The Gospel Teaching, 2s.

Manual of the Acts. 3s.

The Life and Letters of St. Paul. 3s. 6d. Or, separately, Part I, The Life of St. Paul, 2s. Part II, The Letters of St. Paul, 2s.

First Days and Early Letters of the Church. 3s. Or, Part I, First Days of the Church, 1s. 6d. Part II, Early Letters of the Church, 2s.

Graduated Lessons on the Old Testament. By U. Z. RULE, edited by LL. J. M. BEBB. Selected Readings from the O.T. with paraphrases and connecting paragraphs; with notes for teachers and pupils. For use in lower forms, and in elementary and Sunday Schools. The text is that of the R.V., but the book may be used with the A.V. In three volumes. Extra fcap 8vo. 1s. 6d. each in paper covers, or 1s. 9d. each in cloth. Vol. I. Creation to Death of Moses. Vol. II. Conquest of Canaan, Psalms, etc. Vol. III. Israel and Judah, the Captivity, the Prophets.

Notes on the Gospel of St. Luke, for Junior Classes. By Miss E. J. MOORE SMITH. Extra fcap 8vo, stiff covers. 1s. 6d.

A Greek Testament Primer, being an easy grammar and reading-book for the use of students beginning Greek. By E. MILLER. Second edition. Extra fcap 8vo, paper, 2s.; cloth, 3s. 6d.

History of the Bible

List of Editions of the Bible in English, by H. COTTON. Second edition. 8vo. 8s. 6d.

Rhemes and Doway; showing what has been done by Roman Catholics for the diffusion of the Bible in English. By H. COTTON. 8vo. 9s.

The Part of Rheims in the Making of the English Bible, by J. G. CARLETON, containing historical and critical introduction, tables and analyses thereof. 8vo. 9s. 6d. net.

The Holy Bible in the earliest English Versions, by Wycliffe and his followers. Edited by FORSHALL and MADDEN. 4 vols. Royal 4to. 1850. £3 3s.

Wycliffe's Bible, portion edited by W. W. SKEAT. See p. 6.

Studia Biblica et Ecclesiastica. Essays chiefly in Biblical and Patristic criticism, and kindred subjects. 8vo. Cloth.

  Vol. I, 10s. 6d.   Vol. II, 12s. 6d.   Vol. III, 16s.   Vol. IV, 12s. 6d.

  Vol. V, complete, 16s., or, in separate stiff cover parts. Part I, Life of St. Nino, by M. and J. O. WARDROP. 3s. 6d. Part II, Texts from Mount Athos, by K. LAKE. 3s. 6d. Part III, Place of the Peshitto Version in the Apparatus Criticus of the Greek New Testament. 2s. 6d. Part IV, Baptism and Christian Archaeology, by C. F. ROGERS. 4s. 6d.

The Journal of Theological Studies. Edited by J. F. BETHUNE BAKER and F. E. BRIGHTMAN. Published Quarterly, price 3s. 6d. net. Annual subscription 12s. net, post free. Many of the back numbers are still obtainable.

The Old Testament and Apocrypha

The Psalter, or Psalms of David, and certain Canticles, with a translation and exposition in English, by RICHARD ROLLE of Hampole. Edited by H. R. BRAMLEY. With an introduction and glossary. 8vo. £1 1s.

The Parallel Psalter: being the Prayer-Book version of the Psalms and a new version arranged on opposite pages, with an introduction and glossaries by S. R. DRIVER. Second edition. Extra fcap 8vo. 3s. 6d. net.

The Book of Job in the Revised Version. Edited, with introductions and brief annotations, by S. R. DRIVER. Crown 8vo. 2s. 6d. net.

Lectures on the Book of Job. By G. G. BRADLEY. Second edition. Crown 8vo. [Out of print.]

Lectures on Ecclesiastes. By the same. Second edition. Crown 8vo. 5s. 6d.

Astronomy in the Old Testament. By G. SCHIAPARELLI. Authorized translation. Crown 8vo. 3s. 6d. net.

Ecclesiasticus, translated from the original Hebrew by A. E. COWLEY A. NEUBAUER. Crown 8vo. 2s. 6d.

The Place of Ecclesiasticus in Semitic Literature. An essay by D. S. MARGOLIOUTH. Small 4to. 2s. 6d.

The Five Books of Maccabees, with notes and illustrations by H. COTTON. 8vo. 10s. 6d.

The Book of Enoch, translated from Dillmann's Ethiopic text (emended and revised), and edited by R. H. CHARLES. 8vo. 16s.

The Book of the Secrets of Enoch, translated from the Slavonic by W. R. MORFILL, and edited, with introduction, notes, etc, by R. H. CHARLES. 8vo. 7s. 6d.

Deuterographs. Duplicate passages in the Old Testament. Arranged by R. B. GIRDLESTONE. 8vo. 7s. 6d.

History and Song of Deborah (Judges IV and V). By G. A. COOKE. 8vo. Paper covers. 1s. 6d. (Published by Mr. Frowde.)

Libri Psalmorum Versio antiqua Latina, cum Paraphrasi Anglo-Saxonica. Edidit B. THORPE. 8vo. 10s. 6d.

Libri Psalmorum Versio antiqua Gallica e Cod. MS. in Bibl. Bodleiana adservato, una cum Versione Metrica aliisque Monumentis pervetustis. Nunc primum descripsit et edidit F. MICHEL. 8vo. 10s. 6d.

Hebrew and Chaldee

Notes on the Hebrew Text of the Book of Genesis. By G. J. SPURRELL. Second edition. Crown 8vo. 12s. 6d.

Notes on Samuel. By S. R. DRIVER. [Out of print.]

Notes on the Hebrew Text of the Book of Kings. By C. F. BURNEY. 8vo. 14s. net.

A Hebrew and English Lexicon of the Old Testament, with an Appendix containing the Biblical Aramaic, based on the Thesaurus and Lexicon of GESENIUS, by F. BROWN, S. R. DRIVER, and C. A. BRIGGS. Small 4to. 34s. net. The several Parts can be supplied to complete sets.

Gesenius's Hebrew Grammar, as edited and enlarged by E. KAUTZSCH. Translated from the 25th German Edition by G. W. COLLINS. Translation revised and adjusted to the 26th Edition by A. E. COWLEY. 8vo. £1 1s.

A Treatise on the Use of the Tenses in Hebrew. By S. R. DRIVER. Third edition. Crown 8vo. 7s. 6d.

A Commentary on the Book of Proverbs, attributed to ABRAHAM IBN EZRA. Edited from a MS in the Bodleian Library by S. R. DRIVER. Crown 8vo. Paper covers, 3s. 6d.

The Book of Tobit. A Chaldee Text, from a unique MS. in the Bodleian Library; with other Rabbinical texts, English translations, and the Itala. Edited by A. NEUBAUER. Crown 8vo. 6s.

Ecclesiasticus (xxxix. 15—xlix. 11). The Hebrew, with early versions and English translation, etc, edited by A. E. COWLEY and A. NEUBAUER. With 2 facsimiles. 4to. 10s. 6d. net. Translation, see p. 67.

Facsimiles of the Fragments hitherto recovered of the Book of Ecclesiasticus in Hebrew. 60 leaves in Collotype. £1 1s. net. (Published jointly by the Oxford and Cambridge University Presses.)

The Psalms in Hebrew without points. Stiff covers. 2s.

Accentuation of Psalms, Proverbs, and Job. By W. WICKE 8vo. 5s.

Hebrew Prose Accentuation. By the same. 8vo. 10s. 6

Lightfoot's Horae Hebraicae et Talmudicae. A new Edition by R. GANDELL. 4 vols. 8vo. £1 1s.

Greek

Vetus Testamentum ex Versione Septuaginta Interpretum secundum exemplar Vaticanum Romae editum. Accedit potior varietas Codicis Alexandrini. Tomi III. 18mo. 6s. each volume.

A Concordance to the Septuagint and other Greek Versions of the O. T. (including the Apocryphal Books). By the late EDWIN HATCH and H. A. REDPATH. Supplement. By H. A. REDPATH. Fasc. I, containing a Concordance to the proper names occurring in the Septuagint. Fasc. II, containing a Concordance to Ecclesiasticus, other Addenda, and the Hebrew Index to the whole work. Imperial 4to. Cloth in 3 vols. £8 8s. (or Concordance, 2 vols., £6 17s. 6d. Supplement, £2). The several parts are still on sale for the present: Parts I-VI, 21s. each; Supplements I and II, 16s. each.

Origenis Hexaplorum quae supersunt; sive, Veterum Interpretum Graecorum in totum Vetus Testamentum Fragmenta. Edidit F. FIELD. 2 vols. 4to. £5 5s.

Essays in Biblical Greek. By EDWIN HATCH. 8vo. 10s. 6d.

The Book of Wisdom: the Greek Text, the Latin Vulgate, and the Authorized English Version; with an introduction, critical apparatus, and a commentary. By W. J. DEANE. 4to. 12s. 6d.

Coptic

Tattam's Major and Minor Prophets. See p. 83.

The New Testament

Greek and English

The Parallel New Testament, Greek and English; being the Authorized Version, 1611; the Revised Version, 1881; and the Greek Text followed in the Revised Version. 8vo. 12s. 6d.

The New Testament in Greek and English. Edited by E. CARDWELL. 2 vols. 1837. Crown 8vo. 6s.

Greek

The Greek Testament, with the Readings adopted by the Revisers of the Authorized Version—

(1) Pica type. Second edition. Demy 8vo. 10s. 6d. (2) Long Primer type. New edition. With marginal references. Fcap 8vo. 4s. 6d. (3) The same, on writing-paper, with wide margin, 15s. (4) The same, India paper. 6s.

Novum Testamentum Graece. Accedunt parallela S. Scripturae loca, etc. Edidit CAROLUS LLOYD. 18mo. 3s. On writing-paper, with wide margin, 7s. 6d.

Critical Appendices to the above, by W. SANDAY. Extra fcap 8vo. 3s. 6d.

Novum Testamentum Graece (ed. LLOYD), with Sanday's Appendices. Cloth, 6s.; paste grain, 7s. 6d.; morocco, 10s. 6d.

Novum Testamentum Graece juxta Exemplar Millianum. Fcap 8vo. 2s. 6d. On writing-paper, with wide margin, 7s. 6d.

Evangelia Sacra Graece. Fcap 8vo, limp. 1s. 6d.

Novum Testamentum Graece. Antiquissimorum Codicum Textus in ordine parallelo dispositi. Edidit E. H. HANSELL. Tomi III. 8vo. £1 4s.

Athos Fragments of Codex H of the Pauline Epistles. Photographed and deciphered by KIRSOPP LAKE. Full-size collotype facsimiles, large 4to, in an envelope. 21s. net.

Outlines of the Textual Criticism of the New Testament. By C. E. HAMMOND. Sixth edition. Crown 8vo. 4s. 6d.

Horae Synopticae, being contributions to the study of the Synoptic problem. By Sir J. C. HAWKINS, Bart. 8vo. 7s. 6d.

Greswell's Harmonia Evangelica. Fifth edition. 8vo. 9s. 6d.

Diatessaron; sive Historia Jesu Christi ex ipsis Evangelistarum verbe apte dispositis confecta. Edited by J. WHITE. 3s. 6d.

Sacred Sites of the Gospels, with sixty-three full-page illustrations, maps, and plans. By W. SANDAY, with the assistance of PAUL WATERHOUSE. 8vo. 13s. 6d. net.

The Criticism of the Fourth Gospel. Eight Lectures on the Morse Foundation delivered in 1904. By W. SANDAY. 8vo. 7s. 6d. net.

The Logia

Two Lectures on the 'Sayings of Jesus,' delivered at Oxford in 1897, by W. Lock and W. Sanday. 8vo. 1s. 6d. net.

The Oxyrhynchus Logia and the Apocryphal Gospels. By C. Taylor. 8vo, paper covers; 2s. 6d. net.

The Oxyrhynchus Sayings of Jesus, found in 1903; with the Sayings called 'Logia,' found in 1897. By C. Taylor. 8vo, paper covers. 2s. net.

Published by Mr. Frowde for the Egypt Exploration Fund.

ΛΟΓΙΑ ΙΗΣΟΥ, from an early Greek papyrus, discovered and edited with translation and commentary by B. P. Grenfell and A. S. Hunt. 8vo, stiff boards, with two collotypes, 2s. net; with two tone blocks, 6d. net.

New Sayings of Jesus and Fragment of a Lost Gospel. Edited by B. P. Grenfell and A. S. Hunt. With one Plate. 1s. net.

Coptic and Syriac

Novum Testamentum Coptice, ed. D. Wilkins. 1716. 4to. 12s. 6d.

The Coptic Version of the New Testament, in the Northern Dialect, otherwise called Memphitic and Bohairic. With introduction, critical apparatus, and English translation. 8vo. Vols. I and II. The Gospels. £2 2s. net; Vols. III and IV. The Epistles. £2 2s. net.

Tetraeuangelium Sanctum iuxta simplicem Syrorum versionem ad fidem codicum, Massorae, editionum denuo recognitum. Lectionum supellectilem quam conquisiverat P. E. Pusey, auxit, digessit, edidit G. H. Gwilliam. Accedunt capitulorum notatio, concordiarum tabulae, translatio Latina, annotationes. Crown 4to. £2 2s. net.

Collatio Cod. Lewisiani Evangeliorum Syriacorum cum Cod. Curetoniano, auctore A. Bonus. Demy 4to. 8s. 6d. net.

Latin

Nouum Testamentum Domini Nostri Iesu Christi Latine, secundum Editionem Sancti Hieronymi. Ad Codicum Manuscriptorum fidem recensuit I. Wordsworth, Episcopus Sarisburiensis; in operis societatem adsumto H. I. White. 4to. Part I, buckram, £2 12s. 6d. Also separately: Fasc. I, 12s. 6d.; II, 7s. 6d.; III, 12s. 6d.; IV, 10s. 6d.; V, 10s. 6d.; VI, 12s. 6d.; VII, In the Press. A binding case for the first five Fasciculi is issued at 3s.

Old-Latin Biblical Texts : small 4to, stiff covers.

No. I. St. Matthew, from the St. Germain MS (g₁). Edited by J. Wordsworth. 6s.

No. II. Portions of St. Mark and St. Matthew, from the Bobbio MS (k., etc. Edited by J. Wordsworth, W. Sanday, and H. J. White. £1 1s.

No. III. The Four Gospels, from the Munich MS (q), now numbered Lat. 6224. Edited by H. J. White. 12s. 6d.

No. IV. Portions of the Acts, of the Epistle of St. James, and of the First Epistle of St. Peter, from the Bobbio Palimpsest (s), now numbered Cod. 16 in the Imperial Library at Vienna. Edited by H. J. White. 5s.

No. V. In the Press.

The Fathers of the Church and Ecclesiastical History

Editions with Latin Commentaries

Catenae Graecorum Patrum in Novum Testamentum edidit J. A. CRAMER. Tomi VIII. 8vo. £2 8s. net.

Clementis Alexandrini Opera, ex rec. GUIL. DINDORFII. Tomi IV. 8vo. £3 net.

Cyrilli Archiepiscopi Alexandrini in XII Prophetas edidit P. E. PUSEY. Tomi II. 8vo. £2 2s.

In D. Joannis Evangelium. Accedunt Fragmenta Varia. Edidit post Aubertum P. E. PUSEY. Tomi III. 8vo. £2 5s.

Commentarii in Lucae Evangelium quae supersunt Syriace edidit R. PAYNE SMITH. 4to. £1 2s. Translation, 2 vols. 8vo. 14s.

Ephraemi Syri, Rabulae, Balaei aliorumque Opera Selecta. See p. 83.

Eusebii Opera recensuit T. GAISFORD.

Evangelicae Praeparationis Libri XV. Tomi IV. 8vo. £1 10s.
Evangelicae Demonstrationis Libri X. Tomi II. 8vo. 15s.
Contra Hieroclem et Marcellum Libri. 8vo. 7s.
Annotationes Variorum. Tomi II. 8vo. 17s.

Canon Muratorianus. Edited, with notes and facsimile, by S. P. TREGELLES. 4to. 10s. 6d.

Evangeliorum Versio Gothica, cum Interpr. et Annott. E. BENZELII edidit E. LYE. 4to. 12s. 6d.

Evagrii Historia Ecclesiastica, ex rec. H. VALESII. 8vo. 4s.

Fl. Josephi de bello Judaico Libri Septem recensuit E. CARDWELL. Tomi II. 8vo. 17s.

Origenis Philosophumena; sive omnium Haeresium Refutatio e Codice Parisino nunc primum edidit EMMANUEL MILLER. 8vo. 10s.

Patrum Apostolicorum, Clementis Romani, Ignatii, Polycarpi, quae supersunt edidit G. JACOBSON. Tomi II. Fourth edition. 8vo. £1 1s.

Reliquiae Sacrae secundi tertiique saeculi recensuit M. J. ROUTH. Tomi V. Second edition, 1846. 8vo. £1 5s.

Scriptorum Ecclesiasticorum Opuscula recensuit M. J. ROUTH. Tomi II. Third edition, 1858. 8vo. 10s.

Socratis Scholastici Historia Ecclesiastica Gr. et Lat. edidit R. HUSSEY. Tomi III. 1853. 8vo. 15s.

Sozomeni Historia Ecclesiastica edidit R. HUSSEY. Tomi III. 8vo. 15s.

Theodoreti Ecclesiasticae Historiae Libri V rec. T. GAISFORD. 8vo. 7s. 6d.

Graecarum Affectionum Curatio rec. T. GAISFORD. 8vo. 7s. 6d.

Editions with English Commentaries
or Introductions

St. Athanasius. Orations against the Arians. With an account of his Life by W. Bright. Crown 8vo. 9s.

Historical Writings, according to the Benedictine Text. With an introduction by W. Bright. Crown 8vo. 10s. 6d.

St. Augustine. Select Anti-Pelagian Treatises, and the Acts of the Second Council of Orange. With introduction by W. Bright. Crown 8vo. 9s.
[Out of print.]

St. Basil : on the Holy Spirit. Revised text, with notes and introduction, by C. F. H. Johnston. Crown 8vo. 7s. 6d.

Barnabas, Editio Princeps of the Epistle of, by Archbishop Ussher, as printed at Oxford, A.D. 1642. With a dissertation by J. H. Backhouse. Small 4to. 3s. 6d.

Canons of the First Four General Councils of Nicaea, Constantinople, Ephesus, and Chalcedon. With notes by W. Bright. Second edition. Crown 8vo. 7s. 6d.

Eusebius' Ecclesiastical History, according to Burton's text, with introduction by W. Bright. Second edition. Crown 8vo. 8s. 6d.

Eusebii Pamphili Evangelicae Praeparationis Libri XV. Revised text edited, with introduction, notes, English translation, and indices, by E. H. Gifford. 4 vols. [Vols. I, II, text, with critical notes. Vol. III, in two parts, translation. Vol. IV, notes and indices.] 8vo. £5 5s. net. (Vol. III, divided into two parts, containing the translation, £1 5s. net.)

The Bodleian Manuscript of Jerome's Version of the Chronicles of Eusebius, reproduced in collotype, with an introduction by J. K. Fotheringham. 4to, buckram. £2 10s. net.

The Third Book of St. Irenaeus, Bishop of Lyons, against Heresies. With notes and glossary by H. Deane. Crown 8vo. 5s. 6d.

John of Ephesus. See p. 83. Translation, by R. Payne Smith. 8vo. 10s.

Philo : about the Contemplative Life; or, the Fourth Book of the Treatise concerning Virtues. Edited, with a defence of its genuineness, by F. C. Conybeare. With a facsimile. 8vo. 14s.

Socrates' Ecclesiastical History, according to Hussey's Text, with introduction by W. Bright. Second edition. Crown 8vo. 7s. 6d.

Tertulliani Apologeticus adversus Gentes pro Christianis. Edited by T. H. Bindley. Crown 8vo. 6s.

De Praescriptione Haereticorum : ad Martyras : ad Scapulam. Edited by T. H. Bindley. Crown 8vo. 6s.

Works of the English Divines. 8vo

Sixteenth, seventeenth, eighteenth and early nineteenth centuries

Editions of Hooker and Butler

Hooker's Works, with Walton's Life, arranged by JOHN KEBLE. Seventh edition, revised by R. W. CHURCH and F. PAGET. 3 vols. 12s. each. [Vol. II contains the Fifth Book.]

Introduction to Hooker's Ecclesiastical Polity, Book V. By F. PAGET. 7s. 6d.

The Text, as arranged by J. KEBLE. 2 vols. 11s.

The Works of Bishop Butler. By W. E. GLADSTONE. 2 vols. 14s. each. Crown 8vo, Vol. I, Analogy, 5s. 6d. ; Vol. II, Sermons, 5s.

Studies subsidiary to the Works of Bishop Butler. Uniform with the above. 10s. 6d. Crown 8vo, 4s. 6d.

PEARSON'S EXPOSITION OF THE CREED. Revised by E. Burton. Sixth edition. 10s. 6d.
  MINOR THEOLOGICAL WORKS. Edited by E. Churton. 2 vols. 10s.
ENCHIRIDION THEOLOGICUM ANTI-ROMANUM.
  I. JEREMY TAYLOR'S Dissuasive from Popery, and Real Presence. 8s.
  II. BARROW'S Supremacy of the Pope, and Unity of the Church. 7s. 6d.
  III. Tracts by WAKE, PATRICK, STILLINGFLEET, CLAGETT, and others. 11s.
ALLIX'S WORKS. 4 vols. 5s. each.   BENTLEY'S SERMONS. 4s.
BISCOE'S HISTORY OF THE ACTS. 9s. 6d.
BRAGGE'S WORKS. 5 vols. £1 12s. 6d.
BULL'S WORKS, with NELSON'S Life. Ed. by E. Burton. 8 vols. £2 9s.
BURNET'S EXPOSITION OF THE XXXIX ARTICLES. 7s.
BUTLER'S WORKS, 1849. 2 vols. Sermons. 5s. 6d. Analogy. 5s. 6d.
CLERGYMAN'S INSTRUCTOR. Sixth edition. 6s. 6d.
COMBER'S WORKS. 7 vols. £1 11s. 6d.
FELL'S PARAPHRASE ON ST. PAUL'S EPISTLES. 7s.
FLEETWOOD'S WORKS. 3 vols. £1 1s. 6d.
HALL'S WORKS. Edited by P. Wynter. 10 vols. £3 3s.
HAMMOND'S PARAPHRASE ON THE NEW TESTAMENT. 4 vols. 20s.
  PARAPHRASE ON THE PSALMS. 4 vols. 20s.
HORBERY'S WORKS. 2 vols. 8s.   HOOPER'S WORKS. 2 vols. 8s.
JACKSON'S (DR. THOMAS) WORKS. 12 vols. £3 6s.
JEWEL'S WORKS. Edited by R. W. Jelf. 8 vols. £1 10s.
LESLIE'S WORKS. 7 vols. 40s.
LEWIS' (JOHN) LIFE OF WICLIF. 5s. 6d.   LIFE OF PECOCK. 3s. 6d.
LEWIS' (THOMAS) ORIGINES HEBRAICAE. 3 vols. 16s. 6d.
PATRICK'S THEOLOGICAL WORKS. 9 vols. £1 1s.
SANDERSON'S WORKS. Edited by W. Jacobson. 6 vols. £1 10s.
SCOTT'S WORKS. 6 vols. £1 7s.   SMALRIDGE'S SERMONS. 2 vols. 8s.
STILLINGFLEET'S ORIGINES SACRAE. 2 vols. 9s.
  GROUNDS OF PROTESTANT RELIGION. 2 vols. 10s.
STANHOPE'S PARAPHRASE. 2 vols. 10s.   TAVERNER'S POSTILS. 5s. 6d.
WALL'S HISTORY OF INFANT BAPTISM. By H. Cotton. 2 vols. £1 1s.
WATERLAND'S WORKS, with Life by Van Mildert. 6 vols. £2 11s.
  DOCTRINE OF THE EUCHARIST. 3rd ed. Cr. 8vo. 6s. 6d.
WHEATLEY'S ILLUSTRATION OF THE BOOK OF COMMON PRAYER. 5s.

Early Ecclesiastical History

The New Testament in the Apostolic Fathers. By a Committee of the Oxford Society of Historical Theology. 8vo. 6s. net.

The Church's Task under the Empire. With preface, notes, and excursus, by C. BIGG. 8vo. 5s. net.

Bingham's Antiquities of the Christian Church, and other Works. 10 vols. 8vo. £3 3s.

The Church in the Apostolic Age. By W. W. SHIRLEY. Second edition. Fcap 8vo. 3s. 6d.

Harmonia Symbolica: Creeds of the Western Church. By C. HEURTLEY. 8vo. 6s. 6d.

A Critical Dissertation on the Athanasian Creed. By G. D. W. OMMANNEY. 8vo. 16s.

Ecclesiae Occidentalis Monumenta Iuris Antiquissima: Canonum et Conciliorum Graecorum Interpretationes Latinae. Edidit C. H. TURNER. 4to, stiff covers. Fasc. I, pars I, 10s. 6d. ; pars II, 21s.

The Key of Truth: being a Manual of the Paulician Church of Armenia. By F. C. CONYBEARE. 8vo. 15s. net.

Baptism and Christian Archaeology, being an offprint of Studia Biblica, Vol. V. By C. F. ROGERS. 8vo. Cloth, 5s. net.

Ecclesiastical History of Britain, etc
Sources

Adamnani Vita S. Columbae. Edited, with introduction, notes and glossary, by J. T. FOWLER. Crown 8vo, leather back. 8s. 6d. net. With translation, 9s. 6d. net.

Baedae Opera Historica. Edited by C. PLUMMER. Two volumes. Crown 8vo. 21s. net.

Councils and Ecclesiastical Documents relating to Great Britain and Ireland. Edited after Spelman and Wilkins, by A. W. HADDAN and W. STUBBS. Medium 8vo. Vols. I and III, each £1 1s. Vol. II, Part I, 10s. 6d. Vol. II, Part II, 3s. 6d.

Nova Legenda Angliae, as collected by John of Tynemouth and others, and first printed 1516. Re-edited 1902 by C. HORSTMAN. 2 vols. 8vo. £1 16s. net.

Wyclif. A Catalogue of the Works. By W. W. SHIRLEY. 8vo. 3s. 6d. Select English Works. By T. ARNOLD. 3 vols. 8vo. £1 1s. Trialogus. First edited by G. LECHLER. 8vo. 7s.

Cranmer's Works. Collected by H. JENKYNS. 4 vols. 8vo. £1 10s.

Records of the Reformation. The Divorce, 1527–1533. Mostly now for the first time printed. Collected and arranged by N. POCOCK. 2 vols. £1 16s.

Primers put forth in the reign of Henry VIII. 8vo. 5s.

The Reformation of Ecclesiastical Laws, as attempted in the reigns of Henry VIII, Edward VI, and Elizabeth. Edited by E. CARDWELL. 8vo. 6s. 6d.

Conferences on the Book of Common Prayer from 1551 to 1690. Edited by E. CARDWELL. Third edition. 8vo. 7s. 6d.

Documentary Annals of the Reformed Church of England; Injunctions, Declarations, Orders, Articles of Inquiry, etc, from 1546 to 1716. Collected by E. CARDWELL. 2 vols. 8vo. 18s.

Formularies of Faith set forth by the King's authority during Henry VIII's reign. 8vo. 7s.

Homilies appointed to be read in Churches. By J. GRIFFITHS. 8vo. 7s. 6d.

Hamilton's Catechism, 1552. Edited, with introduction and glossary, by T. G. LAW. With a Preface by W. E. GLADSTONE. 8vo. 12s. 6d.

Noelli Catechismus sive prima institutio disciplinaque Pietatis Christianae Latine explicata. Editio nova cura G. JACOBSON. 8vo. 5s. 6d.

Sylloge Confessionum sub tempus Reformandae Ecclesiae edit. Subjic. Catechismus Heidelbergensis et Canones Synodi Dordrecht. 8vo. 8s.

Histories written in the seventeenth (or early eighteenth) and edited in the nineteenth century

Stillingfleet's Origines Britannicae, with LLOYD's Historical Account of Church Government. Edited by T. P. PANTIN. 2 vols. 8vo. 10s.

Inett's Origines Anglicanae (in continuation of Stillingfleet). Edited by J. GRIFFITHS. 1855. 3 vols. 8vo. 15s.

Fuller's Church History of Britain. Edited by J. S. BREWER. 1845. 6 vols. 8vo. £2 12s. 6d. net.

Le Neve's Fasti Ecclesiae Anglicanae. Corrected and continued from 1715 to 1853 by T. D. HARDY. 3 vols. 8vo. £1 10s. net.

Strype's Memorials of Cranmer. 2 vols. 8vo. 11s. Life of Aylmer. 8vo. 5s. 6d. Life of Whitgift. 3 vols. 8vo. 16s. 6d. General Index. 2 vols. 8vo. 11s.

Burnet's History of the Reformation. Revised by N. POCOCK. 7 vols. 8vo. £1 10s.

Prideaux's Connection of Sacred and Profane History. 2 vols. 8vo. 10s. Shuckford's Continuation, 10s.

Gibson's Synodus Anglicana. Edited by E. CARDWELL. 1854. 8vo. 6s.

Recent Works in English Ecclesiastical History

History of the Church of England from the abolition of the Roman Jurisdiction. By W. R. Dixon. 3rd edition. 6 vols. 8vo. 16s. per vol.

Chapters of Early English Church History. By W. Bright. Third edition. With a map. 8vo. 12s.

Registrum Sacrum Anglicanum : an attempt to exhibit the course of Episcopal Succession in England. By W. Stubbs. 2nd ed. 4to. 10s. 6d.

The Elizabethan Clergy and the Settlement of Religion, 1558-1564. By Henry Gee. With illustrative documents and lists. 8vo. 10s. 6d. net.

Liturgiology

Liturgies, Eastern and Western. Vol. I. Eastern Liturgies. Edited, with introductions and appendices, by F. E. Brightman, on the basis of a work by C. E. Hammond. 8vo. £1 1s.

Rituale Armenorum : being the Administration of the Sacraments and the Breviary Rites of the Armenian Church, together with the Greek Rites of Baptism and Epiphany. Edited from the oldest MSS. by F. C. Conybeare ; with the East Syrian Epiphany Rites, translated by A. J. Maclean. 8vo. 21s. net.

Cardwell's Two Books of Common Prayer, set forth by authority in the Reign of Edward VI. Third edition. 8vo. 7s.

Gelasian Sacramentary, Liber Sacramentorum Romanae Ecclesiae. Edited by H. A. Wilson. Medium 8vo. 18s.

Leofric Missal, with some account of the Red Book of Derby, the Missal of Robert of Jumièges, etc. Edited by F. E. Warren. 4to, half-morocco, £1 15s.

Ancient Liturgy of the Church of England, according to the Uses of Sarum, York, Hereford, and Bangor, and the Roman Liturgy arranged in parallel columns, with preface and notes. By W. Maskell. Third edition. 8vo, 15s.

Monumenta Ritualia Ecclesiae Anglicanae : the occasional Offices of the Church of England according to the old Use of Salisbury, the Prymer in English, and other prayers and forms, with dissertations and notes. By the same. Second edition. Three volumes. 8vo. £2 10s.

The Liturgy and Ritual of the Celtic Church. By F. E. Warren. 8vo. 14s.

ORIENTAL LANGUAGES
Sacred Books of the East

Translated by various Scholars, and edited by the late Right Hon. F. MAX MÜLLER. Forty-nine volumes.

An Index Volume (Vol. L) is in preparation.

Sacred Books of India. Brahmanism
Twenty-one volumes

Vedic Hymns, Part I, translated by F. MAX MÜLLER. Part II, translated by H. OLDENBERG. Two volumes (XXXII, XLVI). 18s. 6d. and 14s.

Hymns of the Atharva-veda, translated by M. BLOOMFIELD. One volume (XLII). 21s.

The Satapatha-Brâhmana, translated by JULIUS EGGELING. Five volumes (XII, XXVI, XLI, XLIII), 12s. 6d. each; (XLIV), 18s. 6d.

The Grihya-Sûtras, translated by H. OLDENBERG. Two volumes (XXIX, XXX), each 12s. 6d.

The Upanishads, translated by F. MAX MÜLLER. Two volumes (I, XV Second edition), each 10s. 6d.

The Bhagavadgîtâ, translated by KÂSHINÂTH TRIMBAK TELANG. One volume (VIII), with the Sanatsugâtîya and Anugîtâ. 10s. 6d.

The Vedânta-Sûtras, with Sankara's Commentary, by G. THIBAUT. Two volumes (XXXIV, XXXVIII), each 12s. 6d. The third volume (XLVIII) with Râmânuga's Srîbhâshya. 25s.
Vol. XXXIV—Part I of the Vedânta-Sûtras—is only sold with the other two Parts, viz. Vols. XXXVIII and XLVIII.

The Sacred Laws of the Âryas, translated by G. BÜHLER. Two volumes (II (Second edition) and XIV), each 10s. 6d.

The Institutes of Vishnu, translated by JULIUS JOLLY. One volume (VII). 10s. 6d.

Manu, translated by GEORG BÜHLER. One volume (XXV). 21s.

The Minor Law-books, translated by JULIUS JOLLY. One volume (XXXIII, Nârada, Brihaspati). 10s. 6d.

Jainism and Buddhism. Twelve volumes

The Gaina-Sûtras, translated from Prâkrit by H. JACOBI. Two volumes (XXII, XLV). 10s. 6d. and 12s. 6d.

The Saddharma-pundarîka, translated from Sanskrit by H. KERN. One volume (XXI). 12s. 6d.

Mahâyâna Texts, by E. B. COWELL, F. MAX MÜLLER, and I. TAKAKUSU. One volume (XLIX). From the Sanskrit. 12s. 6d.

The Dhammapada and Sutta-Nipâta, translated by F. Max
Müller and V. Fausböll.
> One volume (X, Second edition). From the Pâli. 10s. 6d.

Buddhist Suttas, translated from the Pâli by T. W. Rhys Davids.
> One volume (XI). 10s. 6d.

Vinaya Texts, translated by T. W. Rhys Davids and H. Oldenberg.
> Three volumes (XIII, XVII, XX). From the Pâli. Each 10s. 6d.
> Vol. XIII—Part I of the Vinaya Texts—will in future only be sold in
> complete sets of the Sacred Books of the East.

The Questions of King Milinda, by T. W. Rhys Davids.
> Two volumes (XXXV, XXXVI). From the Pâli. 10s. 6d. and 12s. 6d.

The Fo-sho-hing-tsan-king, translated by Samuel Beal.
One volume (XIX). From the Chinese translation from the Sanskrit. 10s. 6d.

Sacred Books of the Persians. Zoroastrianism
Eight volumes

The Zend-Avesta Parts I, II, translated by J. Darmesteter. Part III,
translated by L. H. Mills.
> Three volumes (IV (Second edition), XXIII, XXXI). 14s., 10s. 6d., 12s. 6d.

Pahlavi Texts, translated by E. W. West.

> Five volumes (V, XVIII, XXIV, XXXVII, XLVII). 12s. 6d., 12s. 6d.,
> 10s. 6d., 15s., 8s. 6d.

Sacred Books of the Mohammedans
Two volumes

The Qur'ân, translated by E. H. Palmer.
> Two volumes (VI, IX). 21s.

Sacred Books of China. Six volumes

Texts of Confucianism, translated by James Legge.
Four volumes (III, XVI, XXVII, XXVIII). 12s. 6d., 10s. 6d., 12s. 6d., 12s. 6d.

Texts of Tâoism, translated by James Legge.
> Two volumes (XXXIX, XL). Together 21s.

Also published by Mr. Frowde

The Gâtakamâlâ, or Garland of Birth-Stories. By Ârya Sûra. Translated from the Sanskrit by J. S. Speyer. 8vo. 10s. 6d.

The Dialogues of the Buddha. Translated from the Pâli by
T. W. Rhys Davids. 8vo. 10s. 6d.

The Sacred Books as originally numbered

First Series.

I. The Upanishads, i.
II. Laws of the Âryas, i.
III. Confucianism, i.
IV. Zend-Avesta, i.
V. Pahlavi Texts, i.
VI. The Qur'ân, i.
VII. Institutes of Vishnu.
VIII. Bhagavadgîtâ, etc.
IX. The Qur'ân, ii.
X. The Dhammapada.
XI. Buddhist Suttas.
XII. Satapatha-Brâhmana, i.
XIII. Vinaya Texts, i.
XIV. Laws of the Âryas, ii.
XV. The Upanishads, ii.
XVI. Confucianism, ii.
XVII. Vinaya Texts, ii.
XVIII. Pahlavi Texts, ii.
XIX. Fo-sho-hing-tsan-king.
XX. Vinaya Texts, iii.
XXI. Saddharma-pundarîka.
XXII. Gaina-Sûtras, i.
XXIII. Zend-Avesta, ii.
XXIV. Pahlavi Texts, iii.

Second Series.

XXV. Manu.
XXVI. Satapatha-Brâhmana, ii.
XXVII. Confucianism, iii.
XXVIII. Confucianism, iv.
XXIX. Grihya-Sûtras, i.
XXX. Grihya-Sûtras, ii.
XXXI. Zend-Avesta, iii
XXXII. Vedic Hymns, i.
XXXIII. Minor Law-books, i.
XXXIV. Vedânta-Sûtras, i.
XXXV. Questions of King Milinda, i.
XXXVI. Questions of King Milinda, ii.
XXXVII. Pahlavi Texts, iv.
XXXVIII. Vedânta-Sûtras, ii.
XXXIX. Tâoism, i.
XL. Tâoism, ii.
XLI. Satapatha-Brâhmana, iii.
XLII. Atharva-veda.
XLIII. Satapatha-Brâhmana, iv.
XLIV. Satapatha-Brâhmana, v.
XLV. Gaina-Sûtras, ii.
XLVI. Vedic Hymns, ii.
XLVII. Pahlavi Texts, v.
XLVIII. Vedânta-Sûtras, iii.
XLIX. Mahâyâna Texts.

Dictionaries, Grammars, and Editions
Sanskrit

A Sanskrit-English Dictionary, Etymologically and Philologically arranged. By Sir M. MONIER-WILLIAMS. New edition, 1900, greatly enlarged and improved. 4to, cloth, £3 13s. 6d. ; half-morocco, £4 4s.

A Practical Grammar of the Sanskrit Language. By Sir M. MONIER-WILLIAMS. Fourth edition. 8vo, 15s.

Nalopákhyánam. Story of Nala, an episode of the Mahábhárata : Sanskrit Text, with a Vocabulary, etc. By Sir M. MONIER-WILLIAMS. Second edition. 8vo, 15s.

Sakuntalā. A Sanskrit drama, edited by Sir M. MONIER-WILLIAMS. Second edition. 8vo, £1 1s.

Kâtyâyana's Sarvânukramanî of the Rigveda. See p. 23.

The Dharma-Samgraha. See p. 23.

The Mantrapātha, the Prayer Book of the Âpastambins. See p. 23.

The Rig-Veda Samhitâ, with Sâyana's commentary, edited by F. MAX MÜLLER. Second edition, 4 vols. 4to, £8 8s. net. Index, £2 2s. net.

Buddhist Texts from Japan

Va*grakkh*edikâ, by F. Max Müller. 3s. 6d. See p. 23.

Sukhâvatî-Vyûha, by F. Max Müller and B. Nanjio. 7s. 6d. See p. 23.

The Ancient Palm-leaves. 10s. See p. 23.

Bengali, Hindustani, and Pali

Grammar of the Bengali Language; literary and colloquial. By John Beames. Crown 8vo, cloth, 7s. 6d.; cut flush, 6s.

A Burmese Reader. By R. F. St. Andrew St. John. Crown 8vo. 10s. 6d.

A Hindūstānī Grammar. By A. O. Green. In two Parts. Crown 8vo. Part I, 8s. 6d. Part II, 7s. 6d.

Marathi Proverbs, collected and trans. by A. Manwaring. 8vo. 8s. 6d.

The Buddha-*K*arita of A*s*vaghosha (Pali). Edited by E. B. Cowell. 12s. 6d. See p. 23.

Tamil : Dr. Pope's works

I. A Handbook of the Ordinary Dialect of the Tamil Language. Seventh edition. 8vo. 7s. 6d. net.

II. A Key to the Exercises in the Tamil Handbook. With Notes on Analysis. 8vo. 5s. net.

III. A Compendious Tamil-English Dictionary. 8vo. 5s. net.

IV. A Compendious English-Tamil Dictionary. 8vo. 5s. net.
  The above two together. 8s. 6d. net.

V. A Tamil Prose Reader. 8vo. 6s. net.

The First Catechism of Tamil Grammar. With an English Translation by D. S. Herrick. Crown 8vo. 3s.

A Second Catechism of Tamil Grammar. Crown 8vo. 2s. net.

The Nāladiyār, or Four Hundred Quatrains in Tamil. 8vo. 18s. Large Paper, half Roxburgh. £2. Also in paper covers—Part I, Quatrains 1-130, 3s. 6d. Part II, Quatrains 131-320, 4s. 6d. Lexicon only, 6s.

The Tiruvāçagam, or 'Sacred Utterances' of the Tamil Poet, Saint, and Sage Mānikka-vāçagar. The Tamil Text of the Fifty-one Poems, with English translation, introductions, notes, and Tamil Lexicon. Royal 8vo. £1 1s. net.

The 'Sacred' Kurral. 8vo. Cloth, 7s. 6d. ; or in five parts, paper covers, 2s. 6d. each. (Published by Mr. Frowde.)

Zend

The Ancient MS of the Yasna, with its Pahlavi Translation (A.D. 1323), and now in the Bodleian Library : reproduced in facsimile, and edited by L. H. Mills. Half-bound, imperial 4to, £10 10s. net.

G

Hebrew (see also Anecdota, p. 22)

Gesenius's Lexicon and Grammar

A Hebrew Lexicon of the Old Testament, with an appendix containing the Biblical Aramaic, based on the Thesaurus and Lexicon of GESENIUS. By FRANCIS BROWN, S. R. DRIVER, and C. A. BRIGGS. Small 4to. 34s. net. The several parts can still be supplied to complete sets.

Gesenius's Hebrew Grammar, as edited and enlarged by E. KAUTZSCH. Translated from the twenty-fifth German edition by the late G. W. COLLINS, the translation revised and adjusted to the twenty-sixth edition by A. E. COWLEY. 8vo. 21s.

The Book of Hebrew Roots, by Abu 'l-Walîd Marwân ibn Janâh, otherwise called Rabbi Yônâh. Now first edited, with an appendix, by AD. NEUBAUER. 4to. £2 7s. 6d.

Psalms in Hebrew (without points). Crown 8vo. 2s.

Tenses in Hebrew. By S. R. DRIVER. Third edition. Crown 8vo. 7s. 6d.

A Criticism of Systems of Hebrew Metre. An Elementary Treatise. By W. H. COBB. Crown 8vo. 6s. net.

Hebrew Accentuation of Psalms, Proverbs, and Job. By W. WICKES. 8vo. 5s.

Hebrew Prose Accentuation. 8vo. 10s. 6d.

Notes on the Text of the Book of Genesis. By G. J. SPURRELL. Second edition. Crown 8vo. 12s. 6d.

Notes on the Text of the Book of Kings. By C. F. BURNEY. 8vo. 14s. net.

A Textbook of North-Semitic Inscriptions (Moabite, Hebrew, Phoenician, Aramaic, Nabataean, etc.). By G. A. COOKE. 8vo. With fourteen full-page illustrations. 16s. net.

A Commentary on the Book of Proverbs, attributed to Abraham Ibn Ezra; edited from a manuscript in the Bodleian Library by S. R. DRIVER. Crown 8vo, paper covers, 3s. 6d.

A Commentary on Ezra and Nehemiah, by Rabbi Saadiah. Edited by H. J. MATHEWS. 3s. 6d.

Mediaeval Jewish Chronicles and Chronological Notes. Edited by AD. NEUBAUER. Part I, 14s. Part II, 18s. 6d.

Arabic, Coptic, and Ethiopic
(See also Anecdota, p. 22)

A Practical Arabic Grammar, compiled by A. O. GREEN. Crown 8vo.
    Part I. Third edition. Revised and enlarged. 7s. 6d.
    Part II. Third edition. Revised and enlarged. 10s. 6d.

Churches and Monasteries of Egypt; attributed to Abû Sâlih, the Armenian; edited and translated by B. T. A. EVETTS, with notes by A. J. BUTLER. £1 11s. 6d. Translation, with map, buckram, 21s.

The Letters of Abu 'l-ʿAlā of Maʿarrat Al-Nuʿmān, edited from the Leyden Manuscript, with the life of the Author by Al-Dhahabi; and with translation, notes, etc. by D. S. MARGOLIOUTH. 15s.

A Commentary on the Book of Daniel by Japhet Ibn Ali. Edited and translated by D. S. MARGOLIOUTH. £1 1s.

The Coptic Version of the New Testament, in the Northern Dialect. With introduction, critical apparatus, and literal English translation. 4 vols. 8vo. Vols. I and II, The Gospels, £2 2s. net. Vols. III and IV, The Epistles, £2 2s. net.

Novum Testamentum Coptice, cura D. WILKINS. 1716. 12s. 6d.

Libri Prophetarum Majorum, cum Lamentationibus Jeremiae, in dialecto Coptica. Edidit H. TATTAM. Tomi II. 8vo. £1 1s. net.

Libri XII Prophetarum Minorum in Lingua Aegyptiaca vulgo Coptica. Edidit H. TATTAM. 8vo. 15s. net.

The Ethiopic Version of the Hebrew Book of Jubilees. Edited by R. H. CHARLES. 12s. 6d.

The Book of the Bee. Edited by E. A. WALLIS BUDGE. £1 1s.

The Contendings of the Apostles, by E. A. WALLIS BUDGE. Large 8vo. Vol. I. The Ethiopic Text. £1 1s. net. Vol. II. The English translation. £1 5s. net. (Published by Mr. Frowde.)

Syriac

Thesaurus Syriacus : edidit R. PAYNE SMITH. Small folio. Vol. I, containing Fasciculi I–V. £5 5s. Vol. II, completing the work, containing Fasciculi VI–X. £8 8s. The following Fasciculi may also be had separately. Fasc. I–V, £1 1s. each ; IX, £1 5s. ; Fasc. X, Pars I, £1 16s. Pars. II, 15s.

Compendious Syriac Dictionary, founded on the above, edited by Mrs. MARGOLIOUTH. £3 3s. net. Part IV still sold separately, 15s. net.

Dictionary of Vernacular Syriac, as spoken by the Eastern Syrians of Kurdistan, N.W. Persia, and the Plain of Moṣul. By A. J. MACLEAN. Small 4to, £1 5s.

The Book of Kalīlah and Dimnah, by W. WRIGHT. 8vo. £1 1s.

Cyrilli Commentarii in Lucae Evangelium quae supersunt Syriace, e MSS apud Mus. Britan. edidit R. PAYNE SMITH. 4to. £1 2s.

A Translation by the same. 2 vols. 8vo. 14s.

Ephraemi Syri, Rabulae, Balaei, &c. opera selecta primus edidit J. S. OVERBECK. 8vo. £1 1s.

John, Bishop of Ephesus : the third part of his Ecclesiastical History ; in Syriac. First edited by W. CURETON. 4to. £1 12s.

A Translation by R. PAYNE SMITH. 8vo. 10s.

Biblical and Patristic Relics of the Palestinian Syriac Literature, edited by G. H. GWILLIAM, F. C. BURKITT, and J. F. STENNING. 12s. 6d.

The Palestinian Version of the Holy Scriptures : being five fragments in the Bodleian Library. Edited by G. H. GWILLIAM. 6s.

Tetraeuangelium Sanctum. Edited by G. H. GWILLIAM. See p. 71.

Chinese and Japanese

The Chinese Classics : with a translation, critical and exegetical notes, prolegomena, and indexes. By JAMES LEGGE. In eight parts. Royal 8vo.

Vol. I. Confucian Analects, etc. New Edition. £1 10s.

Vol. II. The Works of Mencius. New Edition. £1 16s.

Vol. III. The Shoo-King; or, The Book of Historical Documents. In two parts. £1 10s. each. (Vol. III complete, and Vol. III, Part I, are only sold with the other 4 volumes. Part II may still be bought separately.)

Vol. IV. The She-King; or, The Book of Poetry. In 2 parts. £1 10s. each.

Vol. V. The Ch'un Ts'ew, with the Tso Chuen. In 2 parts. £1 10s. each.

The Nestorian Monument of Hsî-an Fû in Shenhsî, China, relating to the diffusion of Christianity in China in the seventh and eighth centuries. By JAMES LEGGE. 2s. 6d.

Record of Buddhistic Kingdoms; being an Account by the Chinese Monk FÂ-HIEN of his travels in India and Ceylon (A. D. 399–414). Translated and annotated, by JAMES LEGGE. Crown 4to, boards, 10s. 6d.

A Record of the Buddhist Religion as practised in India and the Malay Archipelago (A. D. 671–695). By I-TSING. Translated by J. TAKAKUSU. With a letter from F. MAX MÜLLER. Cr. 4to, with map, 14s. net.

Cantonese Love-Songs. Edited by C. CLEMENTI. Imperial 8vo. Vol. I. Chinese Text. 10s. 6d. net. Vol. II. Translation. 10s. 6d. net.

Catalogue of the Chinese Translation of the Buddhist Tripitaka. Compiled by BUNYIU NANJIO. 4to. £1 12s. 6d.

Handbook of the Chinese Language. Parts I and II. Grammar and Chrestomathy. By J. SUMMERS. 8vo. £1 8s.

Elementary Lessons in Chinese. By A. FOSTER. 8vo, paper covers. 2s. 6d. (published by Mr. Frowde).

Primitive and Mediaeval Japanese Texts. Edited with Introduction, Notes, and Glossaries by F. VICTOR DICKINS, C.B., 2 vols., 8vo, with 11 illustrations. Vol. I, Texts. Vol. II, Translations. 21s. net, or separately, 12s. 6d. net, each volume.

African Languages

English-Swahili Dictionary. By A. C. MADAN. Second edition, Extra fcap 8vo. Half-bound, 7s. 6d. net. Bound with Swahili Grammar. 8s. 6d. net.

Swahili-English Dictionary. By the same author. Extra fcap 8vo. 7s. 6d. net. Bound with Swahili Grammar. 8s. 6d. net.

Swahili (Zanzibar) Grammar. By A. C. MADAN. Ex. fcap 8vo. Paper covers. 1s. net.

Senga Handbook. A short Introduction to the Senga Dialect as spoken on the Lower Luangwa, N. E. Rhodesia. By A.C.MADAN. Fcap 8vo. 2s. 6d. net.

Wisa Handbook. A short introduction to the Wisa Dialect of North-East Rhodesia. By A. C. MADAN. Fcap 8vo, 3s. net.

Grammar of the Bemba Language as spoken in North-East Rhodesia. By Rev. Father SCHOEFFER, edited by J. H. WEST SHEANE. Arranged, with preface, by A. C. MADAN. Fcap 8vo, 2s. 6d. net.

The Masai : language and folk-lore. By A. C. HOLLIS. With introduction by Sir CHARLES ELIOT. 8vo. With 27 full-page illustrations and map. 14s. net.

For books published by Mr. Frowde, see p. 104.

The Melanesian Languages. By R. H. CODRINGTON. 8vo. 18s.

NATURAL SCIENCE AND MATHEMATICS

Botany

Series of Botanical Translations, under the general editorship of Professor I. BAYLEY BALFOUR

Royal 8vo, unless otherwise specified

Schimper's Geography of Plants, authorized English translation by W. R. FISHER, revised by P. GROOM and I. BAYLEY BALFOUR. With maps, collotypes, a portrait of Schimper, and 497 other illustrations. Morocco back, £2 2s. net.

Pfeffer's Physiology of Plants, a treatise upon the Metabolism and Sources of Energy in Plants. Second fully revised Edition, translated and edited by A. J. EWART. Vol. I, Morocco back, £1 6s. net; cloth, £1 3s. net. Vol. II, Morocco back, 16s. net; cloth, 14s. net. Vol. III, completing the work, Morocco back, £1 1s. net; cloth, 18s. net.

Goebel's Organography of Plants, especially of the Archegoniatae and Spermaphyta. Authorized English Edition by I. BAYLEY BALFOUR.
PART I, General Organography. Morocco back, 12s. net; cloth, 10s. net.
PART II, Special Organography. Morocco back, 24s. net; cloth, 21s. net.

Goebel's Outlines of Classification and Special Morphology of Plants. Translated by H. E. F. GARNSEY, and revised by I. BAYLEY BALFOUR. Morocco back, £1 2s. 6d. net; cloth, 20s. net.

Sachs's History of Botany (1530–1860). Translated by H. E. F. GARNSEY, revised by I. BAYLEY BALFOUR. Second impression. Cr. 8vo, cloth, 10s. net.

De Bary's Comparative Anatomy of the Vegetative Organs of the Phanerogams and Ferns. Translated by F. O. BOWER and D. H. SCOTT. Morocco back, £1 4s. net; cloth, £1 1s. net.

De Bary's Comparative Morphology and Biology of Fungi, Mycetozoa and Bacteria. Translated by H. E. F. GARNSEY, revised by I. BAYLEY BALFOUR. Morocco back, £1 4s. net; cloth, £1 1s. net.

De Bary's Lectures on Bacteria. Second edition. Translated by H. E. F. GARNSEY, revised by I. BAYLEY BALFOUR. Crown 8vo, cloth, 5s. net.

Solms-Laubach's Introduction to Fossil Botany. Translated by H. E. F. GARNSEY, revised by I. BAYLEY BALFOUR. Morocco back, 17s. net; cloth, 15s. net.

Fischer's Structure and Functions of Bacteria, translated by A. COPPEN JONES. Cloth, 7s. 6d. net.

Knuth's Handbook of Floral Pollination, based upon Hermann Müller's work, The Fertilization of Flowers by Insects, translated by J. R. AINSWORTH DAVIS. Vol. I, Introduction and Literature. Morocco back, 21s. net; cloth, 17s. net.

On the Physics and Physiology of Protoplasmic Streaming in Plants. By A. J. EWART. With 17 illustrations. 8s. 6d. net.

Index Kewensis; an enumeration of the Genera and Species of Flowering Plants from the time of Linnaeus to the year 1885. Edited by Sir J. D. HOOKER and B. D. JACKSON. 2 vols. 4to, Morocco back, £10 10s. net. Supplement I (1886–1895), can be ordered from Mr. Frowde, price with the Index £12 13s. net ; it is not sold separately. Supplement II (1896–1900), 28s. net. Or Fasc. I, 12s. net ; Fasc. II, 12s. net.

Annals of Botany. Edited by I. BAYLEY BALFOUR, D. H. SCOTT, and W. G. FARLOW ; assisted by other Botanists. Royal 8vo, Morocco back.

Vol. I, Nos. I–IV, pp. 415, and pp. cix, with 18 plates and 6 woodcuts, Sold only as part of a complete set.

Vol. II, Nos. V–VIII, pp. 436, and pp. cxxxviii, with 24 plates and 23 woodcuts. Sold only as part of a complete set.

Vol. III, Nos. IX–XII, pp. 495, and pp. cxviii, with 26 plates and 8 woodcuts. £2 12s. 6d.

Vol. IV, Nos. XIII–XVI, pp. 385, and pp. cxviii, with 22 plates and 13 woodcuts. £2 5s.

Vol. V, Nos. XVII–XX, pp. 526, with 27 plates and 4 woodcuts. £2 10s.

Vol. VI, Nos. XXI–XXIV, pp. 383, with 24 plates and 16 woodcuts. £2 4s.

Vol. VII, Nos. XXV–XXVIII, pp. 532, with 27 plates and 5 woodcuts. £2 10s.

Vol. VIII, Nos. XXIX–XXXII, pp. 470, with 24 plates and 5 woodcuts. £2 10s.

Vol. IX, Nos. XXXIII–XXXVI, pp. 668, with 25 plates and 13 woodcuts. £2 15s.

Vol. X, Nos. XXXVII–XL, pp. 661, with 28 plates and 3 woodcuts. £2 16s.

Vol. XI, Nos. XLI–XLIV, pp. 593, with 25 plates and 12 woodcuts. £2 16s.

Vol. XII, Nos. XLV–XLVIII, pp. 594, with 30 plates, a portrait, and a woodcut. £2 16s.

Vol. XIII, Nos. XLIX–LII, pp. 626, with 29 plates, a portrait, and 9 woodcuts. £2 16s.

Vol. XIV, Nos. LIII–LVI, pp. 736, with 34 plates, 2 portraits, and 14 woodcuts. £2 16s.

Vol. XV, Nos. LVII–LX, with 40 plates and 9 woodcuts. £2 16s.

Vol. XVI, Nos. LXI–LXIV, with 26 plates and 31 woodcuts ; including a Life of Sir WILLIAM HOOKER, with a photogravure portrait. £2 16s.

Vol. XVII, Nos. LXV–LXVIII, with 40 plates and 32 woodcuts. £2 16s.

Vol. XVIII, Nos. LXIX–LXXII, with plates and woodcuts. £2 16s.

Vol. XIX, Nos. LXXIII–LXXVI, with plates and woodcuts. £2 16s.

Vol. XX, Nos. LXXVII–LXXX, with plates and woodcuts. 14s. each.

Index to Vols. I–X of the Annals of Botany (1887–1896).

Prepared by T. G. HILL, under the direction of the Editors. Royal 8vo, paper covers, to subscribers, 5s. ; to non-subscribers, 9s. ; Morocco back, to subscribers, 6s. ; to non-subscribers, 10s. 6d.

Reprints from the Annals of Botany.

A Summary of New Ferns (1874–1890). 5s. net. Synopsis of the Genera and Species of Museae. 1s. 6d. net. New Ferns of 1892–1893. 1s. net. All three by J. G. BAKER. Life of Sir WILLIAM HOOKER, with portrait, 3s. 6d. net.

The Flora of Berkshire ; with short Biographies of the Berkshire Botanists. By G. C. DRUCE. Crown 8vo. 16s. net.

The Herbarium of the University of Oxford. By the same. Crown 8vo. 6d.

The Dillenia Herbaria. An account of the Dillenius Collections in the Herbarium of the University of Oxford. By G. C. DRUCE. Edited with Introduction by S. H. VINES. Crown 8vo. Immediately.

Studies in Forestry. By J. NISBET. Crown 8vo. 6s. net.

The Physical Properties of Soil, by R. WARINGTON. 8vo. 6s.

Biology

Physiological Histology, its method and theory. By G. Mann. 8vo. 15s. net.

Adler's Alternating Generations ; a Biological Study of Oak Galls and Gall Flies. Translated and edited by C. R. Straton. With coloured illustrations of 42 Species. Crown 8vo. 10s. 6d. net.

The Birds of Oxfordshire. By G. V. Aplin. 8vo. 10s. 6d.

The Harlequin Fly : its Structure and Life-History. By L. C. Miall and A. R. Hammond. With one hundred and thirty illustrations. 8vo. 7s. 6d.

Müller's Vocal Organs of the Passeres, translated by F. J. Bell, and edited by A. H. Garrod. With plates. 4to. 7s. 6d.

A Glossary of Greek Birds. By D'Arcy W. Thompson. 8vo. 10s. net.

The Order Oligochaeta, a Monograph, Structural and Systematic. By F. E. Beddard. With illustrations. Demy 4to. £2 2s. net.

Memoirs on the Physiology of Nerve, of Muscle, and of the Electrical Organ. Edited by Sir J. Burdon-Sanderson. Medium 8vo. £1 1s.

Ecker's Anatomy of the Frog. Translated, with Additions, by G. Haslam. Medium 8vo. £1 1s.

Weismann's Essays upon Heredity and kindred Biological Problems. Authorized Translation. Crown 8vo. Vol. I. Edited by E. B. Poulton, S. Schönland, and A. E. Shipley. Second edition. 7s. 6d. Vol. II. Edited by E. B. Poulton and A. E. Shipley. 5s.

Catalogue of Eastern and Australian Lepidoptera Heterocera in the Oxford University Museum. By Colonel C. Swinhoe.

Part I. Sphinges and Bombyces. 8vo, with eight Plates, £1 1s.
Part II. Noctuina, Geometrina and Pyralidina, by Col. C. Swinhoe ; Pterophoridæ and Tineina, by Lord Walsingham and J. H. Durrant. With eight coloured plates containing 218 figures, etc. £2 2s.

The Ancient Races of the Thebaid : an anthropometrical study of the Inhabitants of Upper Egypt from the earliest prehistoric times to the Mohammedan Conquest, based upon examination of over 1,500 crania. By Arthur Thomson and D. Randall-MacIver. Imperial 4to, with 6 collotypes, 6 lithographic charts, and many other illustrations. 42s. net.

The Earliest Inhabitants of Abydos. (A craniological study.) By D. Randall-MacIver. Portfolio. 10s. 6d. net.

Forms of Animal Life, a manual of comparative Anatomy. By G. Rolleston. Second edition. Medium 8vo. £1 16s.

Rolleston's Scientific Papers and Addresses. Arranged and edited by W. Turner. With biographical sketch by E. B. Tylor. 2 vols. 8vo. £1 4s.

Nature and Man. By E. Ray Lankester (being the Romanes Lecture, 1905). 8vo, paper covers. Third impression. 2s. net.

Lectures on the Method of Science. Edited by T. B. Strong. (The Lectures are part of a Course on Scientific Method delivered at the Oxford University Extension Meeting, August, 1905.) 8vo. 7s. 6d. net.

Rivers and Canals, the flow, control and improvement of Rivers, and the design, construction, and development of Canals. By L. F. Vernon-Harcourt. New edition. 2 vols. 8vo. £1 11s. 6d.

Medicine and Hygiene

Criminal Responsibility. By Charles Mercier. 8vo. 7s. 6d. net.

English Medicine in Anglo-Saxon Times : being the Fitz-Patrick Lectures for 1903. By J. F. Payne. 8vo, with twenty-three illustrations. 8s. 6d. net.

Pathological Series in the Oxford Museum. By Sir H. W. Acland. 8vo. 2s. 6d.

The Construction of Healthy Dwellings. By Sir D. Galton. Second edition. 8vo. 10s. 6d.

Healthy Hospitals. By the same, with illustrations. 8vo. 10s. 6d.

A System of Physical Education : Theoretical and Practical. By A. Maclaren. New edition, by W. Maclaren. Crown 8vo. 8s. 6d. net.

Epidemic Influenza, a study in comparative Statistics. By F. A. Dixey. Medium 8vo. 7s. 6d.

Scarlatina, a contribution to the natural history. By D. A. Gresswell. Medium 8vo. 10s. 6d.

Surgical Aspect of Traumatic Insanity. By H. A. Powell. 8vo. 2s. 6d.

Geology

The Face of the Earth (Das Antlitz der Erde). By Eduard Suess. Translated by Hertha B. C. Sollas, under the direction of W. J. Sollas ; with a preface specially written by Professor Suess for the English translation. Royal 8vo. Vol. I, with 4 maps and 53 other illustrations. 25s. net. Vol. II, with 3 maps and 42 other illustrations. 25s. net.

Fossils of the British Islands, Stratigraphically and Zoologically arranged. Part I, Palaeozoic. By R. Etheridge. 4to. £1 10s.

First Lessons in Modern Geology. By A. H. Green, edited by J. F. Blake. With 42 illustrations. Crown 8vo. 3s. 6d.

Geology of Oxford and the Valley of the Thames. By J. Phillips. 8vo. £1 1s.

Vesuvius. By the same. Crown 8vo. 10s. 6d.

Geology, Chemical, Physical, and Stratigraphical. By Sir J. Prestwich. Royal 8vo. Vol. I. Chemical and Physical. £1 5s. Vol. II. Stratigraphical and Physical. With a new geological map of Europe. £1 16s. Geological Map (separately) in case or on roller, 5s.

Astronomy

Astronomy in the Old Testament. By G. Schiaparelli. Authorized English translation, with many corrections and additions by the Author. Crown 8vo. 3s. 6d. net.

A Handbook of Descriptive Astronomy. By G. F. Chambers. Fourth edition.
>   Vol. I. The Sun, Planets, and Comets. 8vo. £1 1s.
>   Vol. II. Instruments and Practical Astronomy. 8vo. £1 1s.
>   Vol. III. The Starry Heavens. 8vo. 14s.

Bradley's Miscellaneous Works and Correspondence. With an account of Harriot's astronomical papers. 4to. 17s.

A Cycle of Celestial Objects, observed, reduced, and discussed by W. H. Smyth ; revised and greatly enlarged by G. F. Chambers. 8vo. 6s. net.

Astronomical Observations made at the University Observatory, Oxford, under the direction of C. Pritchard. Royal 8vo.
>   No. I. On observations of Saturn's Satellites. Paper covers, 3s. 6d. No. II. A Photometric determination of the magnitudes of all Stars visible to the naked eye, from the Pole to ten degrees south of the Equator. 8s. 6d. Nos. III and IV. Researches in Stellar Parallax by the aid of Photography. Part I, 7s. 6d. Part II, 4s. 6d.

Tables for Facilitating Computation of Star-Constants. By H. H. Turner. Second impression. 8vo. 2s. (published by Mr. Frowde).

Chemistry

Mathematical Crystallography. By H. Hilton. 8vo. 14s. net.

Crystallography. A treatise on the Morphology of Crystals. By N. Story-Maskelyne. Crown 8vo. 12s. 6d.

Fock's Introduction to Chemical Crystallography, translated and edited by W. J. Pope; with a preface by N. Story-Maskelyne. Crown 8vo. 5s.

The Molecular Tactics of a Crystal. By Lord Kelvin. With twenty illustrations. 8vo. 3s. 6d.

Elementary Chemistry. Progressive Lessons in Experiment and Theory. By F. R. L. Wilson and G. W. Hedley. 8vo, with many diagrams. Part I. 3s. Part II. 5s.

Class Book of Chemistry. By W. W. Fisher. Fifth edition. Revised and enlarged. Crown 8vo. 4s. 6d.

Exercises in Practical Chemistry. By A. G. Vernon Harcourt and H. G. Madan. Fifth edition. Crown 8vo. 10s. 6d.

Van 't Hoff's Chemistry in Space, translated and edited by J. E. Marsh. Crown 8vo. 4s. 6d.

Original Papers in the Science of Chemistry. A list compiled by V. H. Veley. Third edition. Paper covers, 1s.

Chemistry for Students, with solutions. By A. W. Williamson. Extra fcap 8vo. 8s. 6d.

Tables of Qualitative Analysis. By H. G. Madan. 4to, paper covers. 4s. 6d.

Pure and Applied Mathematics

A Text-Book of Algebra : with Answers. By W. S. Aldis. Crown
8vo. 7s. 6d.

Introduction to the Algebra of Quantics. By E. B. Elliott.
8vo. 15s.

Theory of Continuous Groups. By J. E. Campbell. 8vo. 14s. net.

Treatise on Infinitesimal Calculus. By Bartholomew Price.
  Vol. I.   Differential Calculus.   Out of print.
  Vol. II.   Integral Calculus, Calculus of Variations, etc.   Out of print.
  Vol. III.   Statics, including Attractions; Dynamics of a Material Particle.
  Second edition.   8vo.   5s.
  Vol. IV.   Dynamics of Material Systems.   Second edition.   8vo,   5s.

**The Collected Mathematical Papers of H. J. Stephen
Smith**, late Savilian Professor of Geometry in the University of Oxford.
Edited by J. W. L. Glaisher.   2 vols.   4to.   £3 3s.

**Rigaud's Correspondence of Scientific Men of the Seven-
teenth Century.**   1841.   2 vols.   8vo.   18s. 6d.

Elementary Books

A School Course of Mathematics.   By D. B. Mair.   Crown
8vo.   3s. 6d.

Arithmetic.   With or without answers.   By R. Hargreaves.   Crown 8vo.
4s. 6d.

Lectures on the Logic of Arithmetic.   By M. E. Boole.
Crown 8vo.   8s. ; or interleaved with writing-paper, 3s.

Figures made Easy : a first Arithmetic Book.   By Lewis Hensley.
Crown 8vo.   6d.   Answers, 1s.

The Scholar's Arithmetic.   By the same.   2s. 6d.   Answers, 1s. 6d.

The Scholar's Algebra.   By the same.   Crown 8vo.   2s. 6d.

Elementary Mechanics of Solids and Fluids.   By A. L. Selby.
Crown 8vo.   3s. 6d.

Elementary Plane Trigonometry.   By R. C. J. Nixon.   Crown
8vo.   7s. 6d.

Physics

Hermann von Helmholtz. By Leo Koenigsberger. Translated by Frances A. Welby. With a Preface by Lord Kelvin. Royal 8vo, with 3 portraits. 16s. net.

Modern Views on Matter, being the Romanes Lecture for 1903. By Sir Oliver Lodge. New edition. 1s. net.

Treatise on Electricity and Magnetism. By J. Clerk Maxwell. Third edition. Two vols. 8vo. £1 12s.

Notes on Recent Researches in Electricity and Magnetism. By J. J. Thomson. 8vo. 18s. 6d. [Out of print.]

Maxwell's Elementary Treatise on Electricity. Edited by W. Garnett. 8vo. 7s. 6d.

Introduction to the Mathematical Theory of Electricity and Magnetism. By W. T. A. Emtage. 2nd ed. Crown 8vo. 7s. 6d.

The Measurement of Electrical Resistance. By W. A. Price. 8vo. 6s.

The Mathematical Theory of Electricity and Magnetism. In two volumes. By H. W. Watson and S. H. Burbury. 8vo. 6s. each. Vol. I. Electrostatics. Vol. II. Magnetism and Electrodynamics.

The Application of Generalized Co-ordinates to the Kinetics of a Material System. By the same. 8vo. 2s. 6d.

Lessons on Thermodynamics. By R. E. Baynes. [Out of print.]

Elementary Treatise on Heat, with numerous Woodcuts and Diagrams. By Balfour Stewart. Sixth edition, revised with Additions, by R. E. Baynes. Crown 8vo. 8s. 6d.

Practical Work in General Physics. By W. G. Woollcombe. Crown 8vo. 2s. each part.
> Part I. General Physics. Second Edition, Revised. Part II. Heat. Second Edition, Revised. Part III. Light and Sound. Part IV. Magnetism and Electricity.

The Theory of a Practical Balance. By J. Walker. 8vo. 3s. 6d.

A Treatise on the Kinetic Theory of Gases. By H. W. Watson. Second edition. Crown 8vo. 4s. 6d.

Book-keeping. New and enlarged edition. By Sir R. G. C. Hamilton and J. Ball. Extra fcap 8vo, cloth. 2s.
> Ruled exercise book to the above, 1s. 6d. ; to preliminary course only, 4d.

Acoustics. By W. F. Donkin. Second edition. Crown 8vo. 7s. 6d.

A Treatise on Statics with Applications to Physics. By G. M. Minchin.
> Vol. I. Equilibrium of Coplanar Forces. Fifth edition. 8vo. 10s. 6d.
> Vol. II. Non-Coplanar Forces. Fourth edition. 8vo. 16s.

Hydrostatics and Elementary Hydrokinetics. By the same. Crown 8vo. 10s. 6d.

Geometry

Geometry for Beginners : an easy introduction to Geometry for young learners. By G. M. MINCHIN. Extra fcap 8vo, 1s. 6d.

Elementary Geometry, on the plan recommended by the Mathematical Association.

Experimental and Theoretical Course of Geometry. By A. T. WARREN. With Examination Papers set on the new lines. Crown 8vo. With or without answers. Third edition with additions (1905). 2s.

Elementary Modern Geometry. Part I. Experimental and Theoretical. (Ch. I–IV) Triangles and Parallels. By H. G. WILLIS. Crown 8vo. 1905. 2s.

Euclid Revised, containing the essentials of the Elements of Plane Geometry as given by Euclid in his first six books, edited by R. C. J. NIXON. Third edition. Crown 8vo. 6s.

Sold separately as follows :—Book I, 1s. ; Books I, II, 1s. 6d. ; Books I–IV, 3s. ; Books V, VI, 3s. 6d.

Geometry in Space, containing parts of Euclid's Eleventh and Twelfth Books. By R. C. J. NIXON. Second edition. Crown 8vo. 3s. 6d.

Geometrical Exercises from Nixon's Euclid Revised. With Solutions. By ALEXANDER LARMOR. Crown 8vo. 3s. 6d.

The 'Junior' Euclid. By S. W. FINN. Crown 8vo. Books I and II, 1s. 6d. Books III and IV, 2s.

Pure Geometry, an elementary treatise, with numerous examples. By J. W. RUSSELL. Crown 8vo. New and revised edition (1905). 9s. net.

Analytical Geometry, an elementary treatise by W. J. JOHNSTON. Crown 8vo. 6s.

Notes on Analytical Geometry. By A. CLEMENT JONES. Crown 8vo. 6s. net.

Cremona's Elements of Projective Geometry, translated by C. LEUDESDORF. Second edition. 8vo. 12s. 6d.

Cremona's Graphical Statics, being two treatises on the Graphical Calculus and reciprocal figures in Graphical Statics, translated by T. H. BEARE. 8vo. 8s. 6d.

On the Traversing of Geometrical Figures. By J. COOK WILSON. 8vo. 6s. net. Addendum. 8vo, paper covers. 6d. net.

British Museum Publications

A Complete Catalogue of all the Publications of the British Museum may be
had on application to Mr. FROWDE.

Aristotle on the Constitution of Athens; text, 8vo, third
edition, 10s. 6d. net.   Autotype facsimile, 4to, £2 2s. net

Bacchylides; text, 8vo, 5s.   Autotype facsimile, 4to, £1 1s. net.

Herodas; text, 4to, 7s. 6d.   Autotype facsimile, 4to, 15s.

Catalogue of Greek Papyri; with texts. Vol. I, 4to, £2 2s. net.
Vol. II, £2 10s. net.

The Book of the Dead : Facsimiles of the Papyri of Hunefer, Anhai,
Kerasher, and Netchemet, with supplementary text from the Papyrus of Nu.
With translations, etc. by E. A. WALLIS BUDGE. Folio. £2 10s. net.

Annals of the Kings of Assyria. Cuneiform Texts, with translations, etc. By E. A. WALLIS BUDGE and L. W. KING. 4to. £1 net.

Early Engraving and Engravers in England (1545–1695).
A critical and Historical Essay, by SIDNEY COLVIN, folio, with 41 facsimiles
in photogravure, and 46 illustrations in the Text. £5 5s. net.
With each Facsimile Plate is given a critical description, printed on a separate
interleaf.

Facsimiles of Biblical Manuscripts. With descriptive text by
F. G. KENYON. 4to. Half-bound, 15s. net; cloth, 10s. net.

**Facsimiles of Royal and other Charters in the British
Museum.** Vol. I. William I to Richard I. 4to. £1 10s. net.

Facsimiles from Early Printed Books. 32 plates. Portfolio.
7s. 6d. net.

**Facsimiles in gold and colours of Miniatures, Borders,
and Initials, from Illuminated Manuscripts.** With
descriptive text by G. F. WARNER. Imperial 4to, portfolio. Series II–IV,
each containing 15 plates. £2 10s. net each.

Excavations in Cyprus. Folio. Half-morocco, £2 5s. net; half
cloth, £2 net.

**Catalogue of Early Christian Antiquities and Objects
from the Christian East.** By O. M. DALTON. With 35 plates.
4to. £1 4s. net.

**Antiquities from the City of Benin and from other parts
of West Africa.** By C. H. READ and O. M. DALTON. With 32
collotype plates. Folio. Half-morocco, £1 14s. net; half cloth, £1 5s. net.

THE OXFORD POETS

Crown 8vo, cloth, 3s. 6d.; on Oxford India paper, from 5s.
Each contains a Portrait.

Shakespeare. New large-type edition of the Works, edited by W. J. Craig; with a Portrait and Glossary, pp. viii + 1350. Cloth 3s. 6d., leather from 6s.; illustrated from 4s. 6d. On Oxford India paper, cloth, 7s. 6d., leather from 9s.; illustrated from 8s. 6d.

E. B. Browning. Complete Poetical Works.

R. Browning. Poems, 1833–1863.

Burns. Complete Poetical Works, edited by J. Logie Robertson. With Notes, Glossary, Index of First Lines, and Chronological List.

Byron. Complete Poetical Works.

Chaucer. Complete Works, edited by W. W. Skeat.

Cowper. Complete Poetical Works, edited by H. S. Milford. With Textual Notes, list of Editions, and Chronological Table.

Goldsmith. Complete Poems, edited, with Introduction, Notes, and Appendices by Austin Dobson. With numerous Illustrations.

Hood. Complete Poetical Works, edited by Walter Jerrold.

Ingoldsby Legends. With 25 Illustrations by Cruikshank and others.

Keats. Complete Poetical Works, edited by H. Buxton Forman.

Longfellow. Complete Poetical Works.

Milton. Complete Poetical Works, edited by H. C. Beeching.

Scott. Complete Poetical Works, edited by J. Logie Robertson.

Shelley. Complete Poetical Works, edited, with Textual Notes, by T. Hutchinson.

Tennyson. Poems, including, 'The Princess,' 'In Memoriam,' 'Maud,' 'Idylls of the King,' &c.

Whittier. Complete Poetical Works, edited by W. G. Horder.

Wordsworth. Complete Poetical Works, edited by T. Hutchinson.

OXFORD MINIATURE EDITIONS

Printed on Oxford India paper. (Size, $4\frac{1}{4} \times 2\frac{3}{4}$ inches.) Cloth, gilt top, price 2s. 6d. per volume, with a Portrait.

Shakespeare	Comedies.	E. B. Browning	Aurora Leigh, &c.
	Histories, Poems.		Casa Guidi Windows, &c.
	Tragedies.		
Milton . .	Complete Works.	Longfellow .	Hiawatha, &c.
Burns . .	Complete Works.		Tales, &c.
Tennyson .	Early Poems, &c.		Divine Tragedy, &c.
R. Browning	Early Poems, &c.	Keats . . .	Poetical Works.

Oxford Editions of Standard Authors

Crown 8vo. Bound in cloth, gilt lettered on side and back, 2s. per volume ; or in paste grain, 3s. 6d. New padded binding, gilt edges, gilt design on side, 2s. 6d. net. And in various superior leather bindings.

* The volumes marked with an asterisk may be obtained printed on Oxford India paper from 5s. per volume.

*Boswell's Life of Johnson. Two volumes.

*E. B. Browning. The Complete Poems of ELIZABETH BARRETT BROWNING. 676 pages.

*R. Browning. Poems (1833-1863). 632 pages.

Bunyan. The Pilgrim's Progress. With new illustrations by GEORGE CRUIKSHANK, and a life of John Bunyan. Edited by Canon VENABLES and MABEL PEACOCK. 428 pages.

*Burns. The Complete Poems of ROBERT BURNS. Edited, with notes, glossary, &c., by J. LOGIE ROBERTSON. 656 pages.

*Byron. The Poems of Lord BYRON. Including copyright poems and notes. 936 pages.

*Cowper. Complete Poems. Edited by H. S. MILFORD. 704 pages.

*Goldsmith. The Complete Poetical Works. Edited, with introduction, notes, and appendices, by AUSTIN DOBSON. With numerous illustrations. 316 pages.

Grimm. Popular Stories, by the Brothers Grimm. With Cruikshank's illustrations. 424 pages.

*Hood. The Complete Poetical Works. Edited by WALTER JERROLD, 790 pages.

*Ingoldsby Legends. With 25 illustrations. 584 pages.

Kingsley. Westward Ho ! With 12 illustrations.

Lamb. Tales from Shakespeare. By CHARLES and MARY LAMB. With 16 illustrations. 384 pages.

*Longfellow. The Complete Poems of HENRY WADSWORTH LONGFELLOW. With notes. 888 pages.

*Milton. The Complete Poems of JOHN MILTON. Edited by Canon BEECHING. 572 pages.

*Scott. The Complete Poems. Edited, with introductions and notes, by J. LOGIE ROBERTSON. 980 pages.

Scott. Ivanhoe. With 18 illustrations. 502 pages.

Scott. Old Mortality. With 8 illustrations. 468 pages.

Scott. The Talisman. With 9 illustrations. 484 pages.

*Shakespeare. The Complete Works of WILLIAM SHAKESPEARE. Edited, with glossary, by W. J. CRAIG. 1272 pages.

Sheridan. The Plays. With introduction by JOSEPH KNIGHT, and numerous illustrations.

Oxford Editions of Standard Authors (continued)

*Tennyson. Poems of Lord TENNYSON. Including 'The Princess,' 'In Memoriam,' 'Maud,' 'The Idylls of the King,' &c. 640 pages.

*Whittier. The Complete Poems of JOHN GREENLEAF WHITTIER. Edited, with notes, by W. GARRETT HORDER. 615 pages.

*Wordsworth. The Complete Poems of WILLIAM WORDSWORTH. Edited, with introductions and notes, by T. HUTCHINSON. 1008 pages.

OXFORD LIBRARY OF PROSE AND POETRY

Uniform Volumes, fcap 8vo, cloth, 2s. 6d. net each; lambskin, thin boards, gilt extra, 3s. 6d. net each.

Poems and Extracts chosen by Wordsworth. With introduction by H. LITTLEDALE and preface by J. R. REES. (On Oxford India Paper, 3s. net.)

Wordsworth's Literary Criticism. Edited, with an introduction, by NOWELL C. SMITH. (On Oxford India paper, 3s. net.)

Wordsworth's Guide to the Lakes. Fifth edition (1835). With introduction, notes, and appendices, by E. DE SÉLINCOURT. With map and 8 illustrations. (On Oxford India paper, 3s. net.)

Blake's Lyrical Poems. Text by JOHN SAMPSON. With an introduction by WALTER RALEIGH.

Jowett's Theological Essays. Selected, arranged and edited by L. CAMPBELL.

Trelawny's Recollections of Shelley and Byron. With introduction by E. DOWDEN. Illustrated.

Kinglake's Eothen. With Introduction by D. G. HOGARTH. Illustrated.

Mary Wollstonecraft's Original Stories. With introduction by E. V. LUCAS. With six illustrations by BLAKE.

Palgrave's Treasury of Sacred Song. (On Oxford India Paper, 3s. net.)

Sea Songs and Ballads. Edited by CHRISTOPHER STONE. With an introduction by Admiral Sir CYPRIAN BRIDGE, G.C.B. (On Oxford India paper, 3s. net.)

Cobbett's Grammar of the English Language. With an introduction by H. L. STEPHEN.

Selections from The Rambler. Edited, with introduction, by W. HALE WHITE.

Cobbett's Advice to Young Men, and (incidentally) to Young Women in the Middle and Higher Ranks of Life.

Scripture and Truth. Dissertations by the late BENJAMIN JOWETT. With Introduction by LEWIS CAMPBELL.